THE NEW SOVEREIGN

The New Sovereignty

Compliance with International Regulatory Agreements

ABRAM CHAYES

ANTONIA HANDLER CHAYES

Harvard University Press
Cambridge, Massachusetts
London, England

Second printing, 1998

First Harvard University Press paperback edition, 1998

Library of Congress Cataloging-in-Publication Data

Chayes, Abram, 1922–
The new sovereignty : compliance with international regulatory
agreements / Abram Chayes, Antonia Handler Chayes.
p.   cm.
Includes bibliographical references and index.
ISBN 0-674-61782-7 (cloth)
ISBN 0-674-61783-5 (pbk.)
1. Treaties.   2. Compliance.   3. Sovereignty.
I. Chayes, Antonia Handler, 1929–   . II. Title.
JX4165.C43   1995
341.3′7—dc20
95-21960

To each other

Contents

Preface

We did not start out to write this book. We started out to teach together. The only area in which we both had professional qualifications was arms control—Abe, starting in 1963 as Legal Adviser to the State Department, was involved in the Limited Test Ban Treaty, and Toni, as Undersecretary of the Air Force in the Carter administration, was involved in the MX missile deployment. Our course, "Law, Doctrine, and Politics in Nuclear Weapons Management," which we taught for more than a decade, increasingly focused on the question of why, in an environment of inveterate ideological confrontation, mutual suspicion, and hostility, the two superpowers continuously sought to negotiate arms control agreements—and substantially complied with the obligations they assumed.

This question seemed to grow somewhat less urgent with the end of the cold war and the dissolution of the Soviet Union. So we began to ask ourselves whether some of the things we had learned would be applicable to the problem of treaty compliance in general. In particular, we had been impressed with the work of a little-known body, the Standing Consultative Commission (scc), established by the SALT agreements to "consider questions concerning compliance with the obligations assumed and related situations which may be considered ambiguous." It is perhaps not surprising that, as lawyers, we assumed that the question of compliance with legal obligations would have something to do with the institutions for the settlement of disputes about their interpretation and application. The scc was interesting because, although it had no adjudicative or enforcement authority and was little more than a negotiating forum, it was the instrument through which some important issues between the treaty parties were resolved, even when, as in the early Reagan years, the confrontation between them was at its height.

So our course became "Dispute Settlement under International Agreements." It did not take us long to realize that "dispute settlement," at least in the form that lawyers traditionally conceive it or even in the broader sense that has come to be known in the United States as alternative dispute resolution, or ADR, was only a small part of the compliance problem. We began to see that a treaty regime in operation is a hugely complex interactive process that engages not only states and their official representatives but also, increasingly, international organizations and their staffs, nongovernmental organizations, scientists, business managers, academics, and other nonstate actors, and that it penetrates deeply into domestic politics. This book is an attempt at mapping that process. We try to look across the wide range of international regulation to find insights and elements that transcend differences in subject matter, specificity, and importance to the states that are involved or affected.

Both of us are lawyers by profession. We are students, observers, and sometime practitioners of international relations by avocation. We are not number crunchers, and little in this book betrays a strong bent for quantitative or correlational methods. Although we claim no expertise in economics, rational choice theory, game theory, or jurisprudence, we have tried to use such insights as we have been able to glean from these pursuits. We knew from our work in arms control that there was much to be learned from cognate disciplines—international relations, game theory, security studies, and the like. So in our broader enterprise, as well, we looked for help to these bodies of knowledge outside our own field. In particular, we found much to sustain us in the emerging work on regime theory and, more generally, in work by the new institutionalists in international relations and elsewhere— although they tended to be discomfited by our insistence that most of what they were talking about was really international law. We do not pretend to an exhaustive mastery of the literature of these disciplines, but we have referred to the authors and works that have stimulated us and helped advance our thinking.

Our basic methodological sympathy lies with what Oran Young calls "causal analysis"—the use of detailed studies of cases to illuminate the sources of actor behavior—but we have surely not pursued it with the rigor he would insist on (see Oran R. Young and Marc A. Levy, *The Effectiveness of International Regimes,* forthcoming). Our method is primarily descriptive, with prescriptive overtones. Essentially we have made use of existing secondary material on the treaties and regimes that are the principal subjects of the book. For some, there is considerable scholarly analysis. For others, we have had to rely mainly on official materials or press accounts. Except for occasional interviews and interaction with officials, we do not base our analysis on original empirical investigations that we have conducted.

Our underlying notion is that it is important to understand what states, international organizations, officials, and other actors actually do when they are trying to implement regulatory treaties. That process occupies vast amounts of time and energy of many people—often competent and dedicated people—in the United States and abroad. The first step to criticism and improvement is to understand what they are doing and what they think they are doing. That is not at all obvious, either from the scholarly literature or from journalistic or personal accounts. It has to be pieced together and inferred from sympathetic observation of a considerable range of experience and practice.

We have tried to provide a persuasive account of these activities—what Ronald Dworkin might call an interpretation of the practice in its best light (see Ronald Dworkin, *Law's Empire*, Harvard University Press, 1986). We think our analysis and conclusions are controversial enough that scholars will test their validity—and value—in the context of specific treaty regimes that they choose to study firsthand.

An earlier version of this book's first chapter appeared in *International Organizations*, and the argument is presented in condensed form in the chapters "Regime Architecture: Elements and Principles," in *Global Engagement: Cooperation and Security in the 21st Century*, edited by Janne E. Nolan (Washington, D.C.: Brookings Institution, 1994), and "Managing Compliance: A Cooperative Perspective," in *National Compliance with International Environmental Accords*, edited by Harold Jacobson and Edith Brown Weiss (Social Science Research Council, forthcoming).

Portions of the book in various stages were presented, discussed, and criticized at numerous academic seminars, conferences, and meetings at Harvard and elsewhere. All of those critiques contributed greatly to the final work. A special role was played by Robert Keohane and the group of remarkable graduate students he gathered around him in the years this book was being written—among them, Ronald Mitchell, Marc Levy, Edward Parson, and Beth deSombre. The Program on Negotiations at the Harvard Law School gave us a home when we began to turn our attention to the broad problems of international dispute settlement, and ever since, we have been codirectors of the Project on International Compliance and Dispute Resolution.

The major funding for the book was provided by the Pew Charitable Trusts. The basic research plan was developed under a planning grant from the Carnegie Corporation of New York. "Regime Architecture: Elements and Principles" received financial assistance from the cooperative security project of the Carnegie Corporation, and "Managing Compliance" from the Social Science Research Council.

Since the book is so much an outgrowth of our teaching, it is only fitting that most of the shoe-leather research was performed by our students. There is one, Jan Martinez, of whom it can be truly said that without her the book would not have been written. She started as a member of the class and gradually assumed the role of straw boss and dear friend. Others who made substantial contributions include Daly Bryk, Sean Coté, Melissa Crow, Amy Deen, David Huntington, Rima Hartzenbach, Michael Rinzler, and Manley Williams. But all of them—whether they were associated with the project only briefly or longer, whether their research eventually turned up in these pages or turned out to be a dead end, whether we have appropriated their ideas, mangled them, or rejected them—have been part of the enormously exciting intellectual ferment that these past years have been for us, and to all of them we are grateful. They are: Kathleen Campbell, Eric Dolin, Monica Eppinger, Ellen Goodman, Cathy Hampton, Karen Hunter, Karl Irving, Frederic Jacobs, David Laws, Matthew Lorin, Sharmini Mahendran, Linda Netsch, Carol Reardon, Lisa Roberts, Christopher Rossomondo, Alan Schwarts, Greg Shapiro, Alex Tselos, Lily Vakili, Anthony Winden, and Michael Woods.

The age of computers means we can omit the usual thanks to devoted secretaries for typing the manuscript. Nevertheless, we are deeply indebted to Marilyn Byrne, Abe's devoted secretary, for countless services and for bearing with us through the long gestation period of this book.

THE NEW SOVEREIGNTY

Note

The names of treaties are almost as elaborately embellished as chapter headings in picaresque novels. To avoid cluttering up the text with inessential verbiage, treaties referred to or canvassed in this book are listed in the appendix by their official name, with a full citation and a popular name or acronym where applicable. Almost all references to treaties in the text use acronyms or popular names and, where necessary, an indication of the relevant provision, without further citation.

1

A Theory of Compliance

In an increasingly complex and interdependent world, the negotiation, adoption, and implementation of international agreements are major elements of the foreign policy activity of every state. In earlier times, the principal function of treaties was to record bilateral (or sometimes regional) political settlements and arrangements. But in recent decades, the main focus of treaty practice has moved to multilateral regulatory agreements addressing complex economic, political, and social problems that require cooperative action among states over time. Chief among the areas of concern are trade, monetary policy, resource management, security, environmental degradation, and human rights.

Scholarship on international regimes teaches that these cooperative efforts take place within a dense and complex web of norms, rules, and practices. What is less clear from the work on regimes is that at the center there is almost always a formal treaty—sometimes more than one—that gives the regime its basic architecture. These treaties are the concern of this book.[1]

The agreements vary widely in scope, number of parties, and degree of specificity, as well as in subject matter. Some are little more than statements of principle or agreements to agree. Others contain detailed prescriptions for behavior in a defined field. Still others may be umbrella agreements for consensus building in preparation for more specific regulation later. Often they create international organizations to oversee the enterprise.

The focus on treaties does not imply that they are the only source of international legal or normative obligation. International lawyers have long recognized an unwritten "customary" or "general" international law comprising, indeed, some of the most fundamental principles of the system. The

International Court of Justice has held that a state is bound by its unilateral statement intended to convey that it was accepting a firm obligation.[2] A wide variety of instruments, declarations, joint statements, and expressions, loosely categorized as "soft law," are accepted and enforced as constraints by processes that differ little from those applicable to formal legal undertakings. And, as regime theorists constantly point out, the formal pronouncements are enshrouded in a maze of informal and tacit customs and practices that orient behavior and flesh out the scope of the obligations. But what they are less willing to acknowledge is that, in complex regulatory regimes, the armature on which the whole is constructed is commonly an act of formal law-making—a treaty.[3]

If treaties are at the center of the cooperative regimes by which states and their citizens seek to regulate major common problems, there must be some means of assuring that the parties perform their obligations at an acceptable level. To provide this assurance, political leaders, academics, journalists, and ordinary citizens frequently seek treaties with "teeth"—that is, coercive enforcement measures. In part this reflects an easy but incorrect analogy to domestic legal systems, where the application of the coercive power of the state is thought to play an essential role in enforcing legal rules. Our first proposition is that, as a practical matter, coercive economic—let alone military—measures to sanction violations cannot be utilized for the routine enforcement of treaties in today's international system, or in any that is likely to emerge in the foreseeable future. The effort to devise and incorporate such sanctions in treaties is largely a waste of time.

The deficiencies of sanctions for treaty enforcement are related to their costs and legitimacy. The costs of military sanctions are measured in lives, a price contemporary publics seem disinclined to pay except for the most urgent objectives, clearly related to primary national interests. The costs of economic sanctions are also high, not only for the state against which they are directed, where sanctions fall mainly on the weakest and most vulnerable, but also for the sanctioning states. When economic sanctions are used, they tend to be leaky. Results are slow and not particularly conducive to changing behavior. The most important cost, however, is less obvious. It is the serious political investment required to mobilize and maintain a concerted military or economic effort over time in a system without any recognized or acknowledged hierarchically superior authority.

Because the political cost is high, efforts to impose sanctions will be intermittent and ad hoc, responding not to the need for reliable enforcement of treaty obligations, but to political exigencies in the sanctioning states. There is nothing inherently wrong with these characteristics. But an effort that is necessarily ad hoc cannot be systematic and evenhanded. Like cases are not treated alike. Such an effort to ensure compliance with treaty obligations is fatally deficient in legitimacy. Moreover, to have a chance of being effective, military and, especially, economic sanctions must have the support and participation of the most powerful states. In practice, active support if not direction by the United States is decisive for the success of any important sanctioning action. It is evident that the United States neither could nor would nor should play such a universal policing role for ordinary treaty obligations. In any event, a system in which only the weak can be made to comply with their undertakings will not achieve the legitimacy needed for reliable enforcement of treaty obligations. We return to the question of legitimacy in Chapter 5.

As against this "enforcement model" of compliance, this book presents an alternative "managerial model," relying primarily on a cooperative, problem-solving approach instead of a coercive one.[4] It is less easy to give a succinct and satisfying description of this alternative to sanctions, and much of this book is devoted to the attempt.

The Propensity to Comply

We start with a somewhat novel conception of compliance and the compliance problem. The position of mainstream realist international-relations theory goes back to Machiavelli: "[A] prudent ruler cannot keep his word, nor should he, where such fidelity would damage him, and when the reasons that made him promise are no longer relevant."[5] This rational-actor conception of compliance may be useful for theory or model building, but no calculus can supply rigorous, nontautological support for the proposition that states observe treaty obligations—or any particular treaty obligation—only when it is in their interest to do so.

By contrast, foreign policy practitioners operate on the assumption of a general propensity of states to comply with international obligations. Foreign ministers, diplomats, and government leaders devote enormous time and energy to preparing, drafting, negotiating, and monitoring treaty obligations. It is not conceivable that they could do so except on the assumption that entering into a treaty commitment ought to and does limit their own freedom of action, and in the expectation that the other parties to the agreement will feel similarly constrained. The meticulous attention devoted to fashioning treaty provisions no doubt reflects the desire to limit the state's own commitment as well as to secure the performance of others. But either way, the enterprise makes sense only if the participants accept (presumably on the basis of experience) that as a general rule, states acknowledge an obligation to comply with the agreements they have signed. For these officials, dealing with the occasional egregious violator is a distinct problem, but it is not the central issue of treaty compliance.

We identify three sorts of considerations that lend plausibility to the assumption of a propensity to comply: efficiency, interests, and norms. Of course these factors, singly or in combination, will not lead to compliance in every case or even in any particular case. But they support the assumption of a general propensity for states to comply with their treaty obligations, and they will lead to a better understanding of the real problems of noncompliance and how they can be addressed.

Efficiency

Decisions are not a free good. Governmental resources for policy analysis and decision making are costly and in short supply. Individuals and organizations seek to conserve these resources for the most urgent and pressing matters.[6] In these circumstances, standard economic analysis argues against the continuous recalculation of costs and benefits in the absence of convincing evidence that circumstances have changed since the original decision. The alternative to recalculation is to follow the established treaty rule. Compliance saves transaction costs. In a different formulation, students of bureaucracy tell us that bureaucratic organizations operate according to routines and standard operating procedures, often specified by authoritative rules and regulations.[7] The adoption of a treaty, like the enactment of any other law, establishes an authoritative rule system. Compliance is the normal organizational presumption. A heavy burden of persuasion rests on the proponent of deviation.

Interests

A treaty is a consensual instrument. It has no force unless the state has agreed to it. It is therefore a fair assumption that the parties' interests were served by entering into the treaty in the first place. Accordingly, the process by which international agreements are formulated and concluded is designed to ensure that the final result will represent, to some degree, an accommodation of the interests of the negotiating states.[8] Modern treaty making, like legislation in a democratic polity, can be seen as a creative enterprise through which the parties not only weigh the benefits and burdens of commitment but also explore, redefine, and sometimes discover their interests. It is at its best a learning process in which not only national positions but also conceptions of national interest evolve and change.[9]

This process goes on within each state and at the international level. In a state with a well-developed bureaucracy, the elaboration of national positions in preparation for treaty negotiations requires extensive interagency vetting in what amounts to a sustained internal negotiation. For example, Philip Trimble's roll of the groups normally involved in arms control negotiations includes the National Security staff, the Departments of State and Defense, the Arms Control and Disarmament Agency, the Joint Chiefs of Staff, the Central Intelligence Agency, and sometimes the Department of Energy or the National Aeronautic and Space Administration (NASA).[10] These organizations themselves are not unitary actors. Numerous subordinate units of the major departments have quasi-independent positions at the table. Much of the extensive literature on U.S.-Soviet arms control negotiations is devoted to analysis of the Byzantine complexity of these internal interactions.[11]

The same process may be seen in every major U.S. international negotiation. For example, at the end of what Ambassador Richard Benedick calls "the interagency minuet" in preparation for the Montreal Protocol to the Vienna Convention for the Protection of the Ozone Layer, the final U.S. position "was drafted by the State Department and was formally cleared by the Departments of Commerce and Energy, The Council on Environmental Quality, EPA, NASA, NOAA, OMB, USTR, and the Domestic Policy Council (representing all other interested agencies)."[12] In addition to this formidable alphabet soup, White House units, like the Office of Science and Technology Policy, the Office of Policy Development, and the Council of Economic Advisors, also got into the act.

In the United States in recent years, the increasing involvement of Congress and, with it, nongovernmental organizations and the broader public has introduced a new range of interests that must ultimately be reflected in the national position.[13] Similar developments seem to be occurring in other democratic countries. Robert Putnam has described the process as a two-level game, in which the negotiations with the foreign parties must eventuate in a treaty that is acceptable to interested domestic constituencies.[14]

For contemporary regulatory treaties, the internal analysis, negotiation, and calculation of benefits, burdens, and impacts are repeated at the international level. In anticipation of negotiations, the issues are reviewed in international forums long before formal negotiation begins. The negotiating process itself characteristically involves an intergovernmental debate that often lasts years, not only among national governments but also among international bureaucracies and nongovernmental organizations as well. The most notable case is the United Nations Conference on the Law of the Sea (UNCLOS III), which lasted for more than ten years and spawned innumerable committees, subcommittees, and working groups, only to be torpedoed by the United States, which, having sponsored the negotiations in the first place, refused to sign the agreement.[15] Bilateral arms control negotiations between the United States and the Soviet Union were similarly extended, although only the two superpowers were directly involved. Environmental negotiations on ozone and global warming have followed very much the UNCLOS III pattern. The first conference on stratospheric ozone was convoked by the United Nations Environment Program (UNEP) in 1977, eight years before the adoption of the Vienna Convention.[16] The formal beginning of the climate-change negotiations in February 1991 was preceded by two years of work in the Intergovernmental Panel on Climate Change, convened by the World Meteorological Organization (WMO) and UNEP to consider scientific, technological, and policy response questions.[17]

Especially in democracies, but to a certain extent elsewhere as well, this negotiating activity is open to some form of public scrutiny, triggering repeated rounds of national bureaucratic and political review and revision of tentative accommodations among affected interests. The two-level game gives some assurance that the treaty as finally signed and presented for ratification is based on considered and well-developed conceptions of national interest that have themselves been informed and shaped to some extent by the preparatory and negotiating process.

Yet treaty making is not purely consensual. Negotiations are heavily affected by the structure of an international system in which some states are much more powerful than others. It is no secret that the United States got its way most of the time in the negotiations over the post–World War II economic structure.[18] In the case of the law of the sea, after holding out for more than a decade, the United States was able to secure substantial revisions of the convention even after it had entered into force, on the basis of which, in 1994, it announced its intention to adhere.[19] And almost single-handedly, the United States was able to keep a firm commitment to reduction of carbon dioxide emissions out of the Framework Convention on Climate Change in Rio in 1992.

At the same time, a multilateral negotiating forum provides opportunities for weaker states to form coalitions and organize blocking positions. In

UNCLOS III, the caucus of "land-locked and geographically disadvantaged states," which included such unlikely colleagues as Hungary, Switzerland, Austria, Uganda, Nepal, and Bolivia, had a crucial strategic position. The Association of Small Island States, chaired by the republic of Vanuatu, played a similar role in the global climate negotiations.

Thus, like domestic legislation, the international treaty-making process leaves a good deal of room for accommodating divergent interests. In such a setting, not even the strongest state will be able to achieve all of its objectives, and some participants may have to settle for much less. The treaty is necessarily in some measure a compromise, "a bargain that [has] been made."[20] From the point of view of the particular interests of any state, the outcome may fall short of the ideal. But if the agreement is well designed—sensible, comprehensible, and with a practical eye to probable patterns of conduct and interaction—compliance problems and enforcement issues are likely to be manageable. If issues of noncompliance and enforcement are endemic, the real problem is likely to be that the negotiating process did not succeed in incorporating a broad enough range of the parties' interests, rather than willful disobedience.[21]

It is true that a state's incentives at the treaty negotiating stage may be different from those it faces at the stage of performance.[22] Parties on the giving end of the compromise, especially, might have reason to seek to escape the obligations they have undertaken. But the very act of making commitments entrenched in an international agreement changes the calculus at the compliance stage, if only because it generates expectations of compliance in others that must enter into the equation. Although states may know they can violate their treaty obligations if circumstances or their calculations go radically awry, they do not negotiate agreements with the idea that they can break them whenever the commitment becomes "inconvenient."

In any case, the treaty that comes into force does not remain static and unchanging. Treaties that last must be able to adapt to inevitable changes in the economic, technological, social, and political setting. Adjustment may be accomplished by formal amendment, or by the less cumbersome "non-amendment amendment" devices devised by modern treaty lawyers. The simplest method is to vest the power to "interpret" the agreement in some organ established by the treaty. The U.S. Constitution, after all, has kept up with the times not primarily by the amending process but through the Supreme Court's interpretation of its broad clauses. These adaptation processes are more fully discussed in Chapter 9.

Norms

Treaties are acknowledged to be legally binding on the states that ratify them.[23] In common experience, people—whether as a result of socialization or otherwise—accept that they are obligated to obey the law.[24] The existence of legal obligation, for most actors in most situations, translates into a presumption of compliance, in the absence of strong countervailing circumstances. So it is with states. It is often said that the fundamental norm[25] of international law is *pacta sunt servanda*—treaties are to be obeyed.[26] In the United States and many other countries, they become a part of the law of the land.[27] Thus, a provision contained in an agreement to which a state has formally assented entails a legal obligation to obey and is presumptively a guide to action.

It seems almost superfluous to adduce evidence or authority for a proposition that is so deeply ingrained in common understanding and so often reflected in the speech of national leaders. Yet the realist argument that national actions are governed entirely by a calculation of interests is essentially a denial of the operation of normative obligation in international affairs. This position has held the field for some time in mainstream international relations theory (as have closely related postulates in other positivist social science disciplines).[28] Nevertheless, it is increasingly being challenged by a growing body of empirical study and academic analysis.

Such scholars as Elinor Ostrom[29] and Robert Ellickson[30] show how relatively small communities in contained circumstances generate and secure compliance with norms, even without the intervention of a supervening sovereign authority. Others, like Frederick Schauer[31] and Friedrich Kratochwil,[32] analyze how norms operate in decision-making processes: The norm is itself a "reason for action" and thus becomes an independent basis for conforming behavior. Norms help define the methods and terms of the continuing international discourse in which states seek to justify their actions.

Jon Elster, often regarded as one of the most powerful scholars of the "rational actor" school, says, "I have come to believe that social norms provide an important kind of motivation for action that is irreducible to rationality or indeed to any other form of optimizing mechanism."[33] As applied to treaty obligations, this proposition seems almost self-evident. An example: in the absence of the Anti–Ballistic Missile (ABM) Treaty, the Soviets would have been legally free to build an ABM system. If they had exercised this freedom, it would surely have posed serious military and political issues for U.S. analysts, diplomats, and intelligence officers. In due course the United States would have responded, either with its own ABM system or some other suitable military or political move. The same act, the construction of a Soviet ABM system, would be qualitatively different, however, if it were done in violation of the specific undertaking of the ABM Treaty. Transgression of such a fundamental engagement would trigger not a limited response but an anxious and hostile reaction across the board, jeopardizing the possibility of cooperative relations between the parties for a long time to come. Outrage when solemn commitments are treated as "scraps of paper" is rooted in U.S. history.[34] It is unlikely that this kind of reaction is unique to the United States.

Even in the stark, high politics of the Cuban missile crisis, State Department lawyers argued that the United States could not lawfully react unilaterally, since the Soviet emplacement of missiles in Cuba did not amount to an "armed attack" sufficient to trigger the right of self-defense under Article 51 of the UN Charter. It followed that use of force in response to the missiles would be lawful only if approved by the Organization of American States (OAS). Though it would be foolish to contend that this legal position determined President Kennedy's decision, there is little doubt that the asserted need for advance OAS authorization for any use of force contributed to the mosaic of argumentation that led to the decision to respond initially by means of the quarantine rather than with an air strike. Robert Kennedy said later, "It was the vote of the Organization of American States that gave a legal basis for the quarantine . . . and changed our position from that of an outlaw acting in violation of international law into a country acting in accordance with twenty allies legally protecting their position."[35]

The Sources of Noncompliance

If a state's decision whether or not to conform to a treaty is the result of a calculation of costs and benefits, as the realists assert, the implication is that noncompliance is a premeditated and deliberate violation of a treaty obligation. Clearly some of the most worrisome cases of noncompliance take that form: Iraq's invasion of Kuwait, and North Korea's refusal to permit International Atomic Energy Agency (IAEA) inspection in accordance with its obligation under the Nuclear Non-Proliferation Treaty (NPT), for example. On occasion a state may enter into a treaty to appease a domestic or international constituency, with little intention of carrying it out. This may have been the case when the Soviet Union and some other totalitarian states signed the international human rights covenants—although in the event, the undertakings did not prove to have been as empty as had been supposed (see

Chapter 11). A passing familiarity with foreign affairs, however, suggests that such cases are the exception rather than the rule. Only infrequently does a treaty violation fall into the category of a willful flouting of legal obligation.[36]

Yet enough questions remain about noncompliance and incomplete compliance with significant treaty obligations to warrant analysis of the methods by which international systems can bring deviant behavior into conformity with treaty norms. The analysis must begin with a diagnosis of the reasons for observed noncompliance. If the violations are not deliberate, what explains this behavior? We identify three circumstances, infrequently recognized in discussions of compliance, that in our view often lie at the root of much of the behavior that may seem to violate treaty requirements: (1) ambiguity and indeterminacy of treaty language, (2) limitations on the capacity of parties to carry out their undertakings, and (3) the temporal dimension of the social, economic, and political changes contemplated by regulatory treaties.

In one sense, these factors might be considered "causes" of noncompliance. But from a lawyer's perspective, they might be thought of as defenses—matters put forth to excuse, justify, or extenuate a prima facie case of breach (subject, like all other issues of compliance, to the overriding obligation of good faith in the performance of treaty obligations).[37] If the plea is accepted, the conduct is not a violation, strictly speaking. Of course, in the international sphere, these charges and defenses are rarely made or determined in a judicial tribunal, but diplomatic practice in other forums can be understood in terms of the same basic structure. Still a third perspective—the one that animates this book—is that of regime management. Where and how can resources and energy be most effectively committed to improve compliance with treaty obligations?

Ambiguity

Treaties, like other formal statements of legal rules, frequently do not provide determinate answers to specific disputed questions.[38] Language is unable to capture meaning with precision. Drafters do not foresee many of the possible applications, let alone their contextual settings. Issues actually foreseen often cannot be resolved at the time of treaty negotiation and are swept under the rug with a formula that can mean what each party wants it to. Economic, technological, and scientific conditions change, to say nothing of political circumstances. All these inescapable incidents of the effort to formulate rules to govern future conduct can produce a zone of ambiguity within which it is difficult to say with precision what is permitted and what forbidden.

Of course treaty language, like other legal language, comes in varying degrees of specificity.[39] The broader and more general the language, the wider the ambit of permissible interpretations to which it gives rise. Yet precision is not always a virtue, and frequently there are reasons for choosing a more general formulation of the obligation. The political consensus may not support more precision. Or, as with certain provisions of the U.S. Constitution, it may be wiser to indicate a general direction, to try to inform a process, rather than seeking to foresee in detail the circumstances in which the words will be brought to bear. If there is a degree of trust in those who are to apply the rules, a broader standard may be more effective in realizing the general policy behind the law than a series of detailed regulations. The North Atlantic Treaty has proved remarkably durable, though its language is remarkably general: "In order more effectively to achieve the objectives of this Treaty, the Parties, separately and jointly, by means of continuous and effective self-help and mutual aid, will maintain and develop their individual and collective capacity to resist armed attack."[40] In the arms control field, the United States has opted for increasingly detailed agreements, on the ground that they reduce interpretative leeway. The 1963 Limited Test Ban Treaty (LTBT), the first bilateral arms control agreement between the United States and the Soviet Union, consisted of five articles covering two or three pages. The Strategic Arms Reduction Treaty (START) signed in 1989 is the size of a telephone book.[41] Nor is increasing detail confined to the security area. The original General Agreement on Tariffs and Trade (GATT) was made up of thirty-five sections in as many pages. In 1994, the Uruguay Round produced a new agreement for world trade that is three or four times as long, with numerous subsidiary agreements and annexes.

Yet detail also has its difficulties. It invites the maxim, *expressio unius est exclusio alterius* (to express one thing is to exclude the other). As in the U.S. Internal Revenue Code, precision generates loopholes, necessitating a procedure for continuous revision and authoritative interpretation. The corpus of the law may become so complex and unwieldy as to be understandable to (and manipulable by) only a small coterie of experts. The complexities of the rule system may give rise to shortcuts in practice that reduce inefficiencies when things are going well but may lead to friction when the political atmosphere darkens.

In short, more often than not there will be a considerable range within which parties may reasonably adopt differing positions as to the meaning of the relevant treaty language. In domestic legal systems, courts or other authoritative institutions are empowered to resolve such disputes about meaning as between parties in a particular case. The international legal system can provide tribunals to settle such questions if the parties consent, but compulsory means of authoritative dispute resolution—by adjudication or otherwise—are not highly regarded at the international level.[42] Moreover, the issue of interpretation may not arise in the context of an adversary two-party dispute but as a more general question of debate among the parties. In 1965, the parties to the International Coffee Agreement disagreed sharply about whether the organization had power to set quotas selectively for different types of coffee or was limited to establishing a global quota to be divided among the exporters according to a preestablished formula. The issue was put to an advisory legal panel, which decided against the selective quota authority, but ultimately the Coffee Council voted to interpret the treaty as authorizing the action.[43] In all such cases, it remains open to a party, in the absence of bad faith, to maintain its position and try to convince the others. In fact this kind of discourse among the parties, often in the hearing of a wider audience, is an important way of clarifying the meaning of the rules, much like the discourse of courts in common law countries.

In many such controversies, a consensus may exist or emerge among knowledgeable professionals about the legal rights and wrongs.[44] In many others, however, the issue will remain contestable. Although one party may charge another with violation and deploy legions of international lawyers in its support, a detached observer cannot readily conclude that there is non-compliance, at least in the absence of "bad faith." The long list of alleged violations of arms control treaties with which the Soviets were annually charged were, with the exception of the Krasnoyarsk radar, contestable in this sense.[45]

It is, of course, by no means unheard of that states, like other legal actors, take advantage of the indeterminacy of treaty language to justify indulging their preferred course of action. Indeed a state may consciously seek to discover the limits of its obligation by testing its treaty partners' responses. There was speculation that the pattern of Soviet deployment of Pechora-type radars prior to the construction of their phased-array radar at Krasnoyarsk was an attempt to test the limits of the deployment prohibitions in the ABM Treaty. The Pechora sites were located up to 400 kilometers from the border, arguably "on the periphery of the national territory," as required by the treaty—but also arguably not.[46] The failure of the United States to react was thought by some to have contributed to the decision to site Krasnoyarsk even further from the nearest border—some 700 kilometers.

Justice Oliver Wendell Holmes said, "The very meaning of a line in the law is that you intentionally may come as close to it as you can if you do not pass it."[47] Nevertheless, deliberate testing of the kind just described might in ordinary circumstances be thought to be inconsistent with good faith observation of the treaty obligation. On the other hand, in the early years of SALT I, the United States played a similar game by erecting opaque environmental shelters over missile silos during modification work, despite the treaty undertaking "not to use deliberate concealment measures which impede verification by national technical means."[48] In the context of the long cold-war confrontation between the United States and the Soviet Union, a certain amount of such probing, despite the dangers, was inherent in the relationship and seems to have been within the expectations of the parties.[49]

Another way to operate in the zone of ambiguity is to design the desired activity to comply with the letter of the obligation, leaving questions about the spirit for another day. The GATT prohibits parties from imposing quotas on imports. When Japanese exports of steel to the United States generated pressure from domestic producers that the Nixon administration could no longer withstand, U.S. trade lawyers invented the "voluntary restraint agreement" (VRA), under which private Japanese producers agreed to limit their U.S. sales.[50] The United States imposed no official quota, but the Japanese producers might well have anticipated some such action had they not "volunteered." Did the arrangement violate the GATT obligation?

Limitations on Capacity

According to classical international law, legal rights and obligations run between states. A treaty is an agreement among states[51] and an undertaking by them as to their future conduct. The object of the agreement is to affect state behavior. This simple relationship between agreement and relevant behavior continues to exist for many treaties. The Limited Test Ban Treaty prohibiting nuclear testing in the atmosphere, in outer space, and under water is such a treaty. Only states conduct nuclear weapons tests, so only state behavior is implicated in the undertaking. The state, simply by governing its own actions, determines whether it will comply with the undertaking or not. Moreover there is no doubt about the state's capacity to do what it has undertaken. Every state, no matter how primitive its structure or limited its resources, can refrain from conducting nuclear tests in the atmosphere.

Even if only state behavior is at stake, the issue of capacity may arise when the treaty involves an affirmative obligation. In the 1980s it may have been a fair assumption that the Soviet Union had the capacity to carry out its undertaking to destroy certain nuclear weapons as required by the Intermediate Nuclear Forces (INF) and START agreements. In the 1990s, that assumption was threatened by the deterioration of the Russian political and military structure and the emergence of a congeries of successor states in place of the Soviet Union, many of which may not have the technical knowledge or material resources to do the job.[52]

The problem is even more acute in contemporary regulatory treaties. Such treaties are formally among states, and the obligations are cast as state obligations—for example, to reduce sulfur dioxide (SO_2) emissions by 30 percent against a certain baseline. The real object of the treaty, however, is not to affect state behavior but to regulate the activities of individuals and private entities that produce SO_2—generating power, smelting, and the like. The state may be "in compliance" when it has formally enacted implementing legislation, and despite the vagaries of legislative and domestic politics, it is appropriate to hold it accountable for its failure to do so. But the ultimate impact on private behavior depends on a complex series of further steps. It will normally require detailed administrative regulations and vigorous enforcement efforts. In essence, the state will have to establish and enforce a full-blown domestic regime designed to secure the necessary reduction in emissions. Quite apart from political will, the construction of such a regulatory apparatus is not a simple or mechanical task. It entails choices and requires scientific and technical judgment, bureaucratic capacity, and fiscal resources. Not the least of these limited resources are places on crowded government agendas and priority lists. Even developed Western states have not been able to construct such systems with the confidence that they will achieve the desired objective.[53]

The deficit in domestic regulatory capacity is not limited to environmental agreements. Much of the work of the International Labor Organization (ILO) has, from the beginning, been devoted to improving its members' domestic labor legislation and enforcement. The NPT is supported by a side agreement among nuclear-capable states not to export sensitive technology to non–nuclear weapons states, an agreement implemented by national export control regulations. However, the UN/IAEA inspections in Iraq revealed that the Iraqi nuclear weapons program was able to draw on suppliers in the United States and West Germany, among others, where the governmental will and ability to control such exports are presumably at their highest.

In developing countries, the characteristic situation is a severe dearth of the requisite scientific, technical, bureaucratic, and financial wherewithal to build effective domestic enforcement systems. Four years after the Montreal Protocol was signed, only about half of the member states had fully complied with the requirement of the treaty that they report annual chlorofluorocarbon (CFC) consumption.[54] The Conference of the Parties established an Ad Hoc Group of Experts on Reporting, which quickly saw that the great majority of the nonreporting states were developing countries that for the most part were simply unable to comply without technical assistance from the treaty organization.[55]

The Montreal Protocol is the first treaty under which the parties have undertaken to provide significant financial assistance to defray the incremental costs of compliance for developing countries.[56] The same issue, on a much larger scale, figured in the negotiations on the biodiversity and global climate change conventions concluded at the 1992 United Nations Conference on Environment and Development (UNCED), and the final instruments contain provisions similar to those in the Montreal Protocol.[57] Indeed, in these instruments, the obligations of the developing countries are explicitly conditioned on provision of financial resources by developed countries. The last word has surely not been spoken in these forums, and the problem is not confined to environmental agreements.

The Temporal Dimension

The regulatory treaties that are our major concern are, characteristically, legal instruments of a regime for managing a major international problem area over time. Significant changes in social or economic systems mandated by regulatory treaties take time. Thus, a cross section at any particular moment may give a misleading picture of the state of compliance.

Treaty drafters often recognize at the negotiating stage that there will be a considerable time lag after the treaty is concluded before some or all of the parties can bring themselves into compliance. Thus modern treaties, from the International Monetary Fund Agreement in 1945[58] to the Montreal Protocol in 1987,[59] have provided for transitional arrangements and made allowances for special circumstances. But whether the treaty provides for it or not, a period of transition is always necessary.[60]

Similarly, if the regime is to persist over time, adaptation to changing conditions and underlying circumstances will require a shifting mix of regulatory instruments to which state and individual behavior cannot instantaneously respond. Often the original treaty is only the first in a series of agreements addressed to the issue area. For example, the START agreement to reduce nuclear arsenals contemplates a process extending over seven years, by which time it is expected that new and further reductions will have been mandated.[61]

Activists in all fields lament that treaty negotiation tends to settle on a least common denominator. But the drive for universality (or universal membership in the particular geographical or issue area of concern) may necessitate accommodation to the response capability of states with limited financial, technical, or bureaucratic resources. A common solution is to start with a low obligational ante, and then to increase the level of regulation as experience with the regime grows. The convention-protocol strategy adopted in a number of contemporary environmental regimes—though it is unwieldy and may be sluggish in response—exemplifies this conception.[62]

The Vienna Convention for the Protection of the Ozone Layer, signed in 1985, contained no substantive obligations. It required only that the parties, "in accordance with the means at their disposal and their capabilities," cooperate in research and information exchange and in harmonizing domestic policies on activities likely to have an adverse effect on the ozone layer.[63] Two years later, as scientific consensus jelled on the destructive effect of CFCs on the ozone layer, the Montreal Protocol was negotiated, providing for a 50 percent reduction from 1986 levels of CFC consumption by the year 2000.[64] By June 1990, the parties agreed to a complete phaseout by 2000 and to regulate a number of other ozone-destroying chemical compounds.[65] At Copenhagen two years later, the phaseout date for most of the controlled substances was advanced to January 1, 1996.[66] A similar sequence marks the Convention on Long-Range Transboundary Air Pollution (LRTAP), beginning with a general agreement to cooperate signed in 1979, followed by a protocol imposing limits on SO_2 emissions in 1985, and by another in 1988 on nitrogen dioxide (NO_2).[67] The Framework Convention on Climate Change has started, like the others, with a general undertaking for cooperation and no quantitative obligations.

The pattern has a long pedigree, extending back to the ILO, the first of the modern international regulatory agencies, whose members agreed in 1921 only to "bring the recommendation[s] or draft convention[s] [prepared by the Organization] before the authority or authorities within whose competence the matter lies, for the enactment of legislation or other action."[68] The ILO then became the forum for drafting and propagating a series of specific conventions and recommendations on the rights of labor and conditions of employment, for adoption by the parties.

The effort to protect human rights by international agreement may be seen as an extreme case of the time lag between undertaking and performance. Human rights norms, despite their almost universal acceptance, are slow to establish themselves in places where they may clash with local customs, culture, and systems of government. Although the major human rights conventions have been widely ratified, compliance leaves much to be desired. It is apparent that some states have adhered to the conventions without any serious intention of abiding by them. It is also true that even parties committed to the treaties had different expectations about compliance than they did with most other regulatory treaties. Indeed the Helsinki Final Act, which contained important human rights provisions applicable to the Soviet Union and Eastern Europe, is by its terms not legally binding.[69]

Yet it is a mistake to call these treaties merely "aspirational" or "hortatory." To be sure, they embody ideals of the international system but, like other regulatory treaties, they were designed to initiate a process that over time, perhaps a long time, would bring behavior into greater congruence with those ideals. These expectations have not been wholly disappointed. The vast amount of public and private effort devoted to enforcing these agreements—not always in vain—evinces their obligational content. Moreover, the legitimating authority of these instruments was an important catalyst of the revolutions of the 1980s against authoritarian regimes in Latin America and Eastern Europe, and it continues to spark demands for democratic politics elsewhere in the world. We return to this subject in Chapter 11.

Levels of Compliance

Compliance is not an on-off phenomenon. For a straightforward prohibitory norm like a highway speed limit, it is in principle a simple matter to determine whether any particular driver is in compliance. Yet there is a considerable zone within which behavior is accepted as adequately conforming. Most communities and law enforcement organizations in the United States, at least, seem to be perfectly comfortable with a situation in which the average speed on interstate highways is perhaps ten miles above the limit. The problem for the system is not how to induce all drivers to obey the speed limit, but how to contain deviance within acceptable levels.[70] And, so it is for international treaty obligations.

The Standard of Acceptable Compliance

An "acceptable level of compliance" is not an invariant standard. It changes over time with the capacities of the parties and the urgency of the problem. It may depend on the type of treaty, the context, the exact behavior involved. The matter is further complicated because, for many legal norms, as we have noted, questions of compliance are often contestable and call for complex, subtle, and frequently subjective evaluation.

It would seem, for example, that the acceptable level of compliance would vary with the significance and cost of the reliance parties place on the others' performance.[71] Flouting a cease-fire under a peace agreement or refusing to allow inspection of nuclear reactors under the NPT would be expected to evoke very different responses from a failure to meet the reporting requirements of an environmental treaty. On this basis, treaties implicating national security would demand strict compliance, because the stakes are so high, and to some extent this prediction is borne out by experience. Yet even in this area, some departures seem to be tolerable.

The U.S. emphasis during the cold war on the importance of verification of arms control agreements seems to confirm the insistence on a strict compliance standard.[72] However, at least since the Reagan administration, annual presidential reports to Congress, mandated by the Arms Control and Disarmament Act, have listed a long series of alleged Soviet violations without igniting any serious move to withdraw from the applicable treaties.[73]

One of these violations, already mentioned, was the phased-array radar constructed at Krasnoyarsk in Siberia. It was widely regarded as a deliberate and egregious breach of the ABM Treaty. As we noted earlier, Article VI of the treaty requires that early-warning radars be sited "along the periphery of [the] national territory and oriented outward." Krasnoyarsk was 700 kilometers from the Mongolian border and pointed northeast over Siberia. The issue was repeatedly thrashed out between the two governments over a period of years, sometimes at the highest levels. The United States linked future arms control progress to the satisfactory resolution of the controversy. The Soviets at first maintained that the installation was a space-tracking radar and thus not subject to the prohibition, but ultimately they acknowledged the breach and agreed to eliminate the offending installation. Nevertheless, throughout this entire period the ABM Treaty regime continued in full force and effect. The basic treaty bargain—that neither side would deploy ABM systems—remained intact, and the U.S. administration never seriously pursued the option of withdrawal or abrogation.[74] Even in connection with its cherished Strategic Defense Initiative (SDI), the Reagan administration preferred to attempt to "reinterpret" the treaty rather than accept the more serious political costs of abrogation.

In the last analysis, the catalogue of asserted "violations" presented no threat to the U.S. security interests that the treaties were designed to safeguard, so the level of Soviet compliance was "acceptable." American political and military leaders remained willing to tolerate nonperformance at the margin as the price of continuing constraint on any meaningful Soviet attempts to shift the strategic balance.

In the case of the NPT, indications of deviant behavior by parties have been severely dealt with. In the 1970s, U.S. pressures resulted in the termination of programs to construct reprocessing facilities in South Korea and Taiwan.[75] In the 1990s, a menu of even more stringent pressures was mounted against North Korea. Ultimately North Korea signed an IAEA safeguards agreement and submitted to an initial inspection, but it balked at accepting a "special inspection" of two suspicious facilities, and later at permitting the IAEA to observe the refueling of its research reactor.[76] After public threats of economic sanctions (and even some calls for military action) by the United States, a visit to Pyongyang by former President Jimmy Carter resulted in the renewal of active negotiations. The two countries reached a comprehensive agreement, under which North Korea would give up its weapons program in return for two nuclear power reactors of a type less susceptible to plutonium diversion, plus other economic assistance and political gestures. The implementation of this agreement predictably ran into snags, but as of mid-1995, the process was still under way.[77] Moreover, although more than 130 states are parties to the NPT, the treaty is not universal,[78] and some nonparties have acquired or are seeking nuclear weapons capability. Despite these important deviations and holdouts, compliance with the NPT by the parties remains high. In fact in recent years, prominent nonparties—including France and China among the nuclear weapons states, and Brazil, Argentina, and South Africa among the non nuclear weapon states have either adhered to the treaty or announced that they will comply with its norms.[79] Even the recalcitrant nonparties, like Israel and India, have not openly tested or acknowledged the possession of nuclear weapons. The level of compliance has been acceptable enough to enable the NPT and the nonproliferation regime built around it to survive

If national security regimes have not collapsed in the face of significant perceived violation, it should be no surprise that economic and environmental treaties can tolerate a good deal of noncompliance. Such regimes are in fact relatively forgiving of violations that can be plausibly justified by extenuating circumstances in the foreign or domestic life of the offending state, provided the action does not threaten the survival of the regime. As we have noted, a considerable amount of deviance from strict treaty norms may be anticipated and allowed for from the beginning, whether in the form of transitional periods, special exemptions, or limited substantive obligations, or by the informal expectations of the parties. The propensity to comply means that most states will continue to carry out their treaty obligations even in the face of such deviant behavior. In other words, the free rider problem has been overestimated. Defections will not necessarily unravel the treaty if the level of compliance is acceptable.

Determining What Is Acceptable

How is the acceptable level of compliance to be determined in any particular instance? Economists have a straightforward answer: invest additional resources in enforcement (or other measures to induce compliance) up to the point where the value of the incremental benefit from an additional unit of compliance exactly equals the cost of the last unit of additional enforcement.[80] Unfortunately, the usefulness of this approach is limited by the impossibility of quantifying or even approximating, let alone monetizing, any of the relevant factors in the equation. There are no markets in international enforcement and compliance.

In such circumstances, as Charles Lindblom has said, the process by which preferences are aggregated is necessarily a political one.[81] It follows that the choice of whether to intensify (or slacken) the international enforcement effort is a political decision. It implicates all the same interests, pro and con, that were involved in the initial formulation of the treaty norm, as modified by intervening changes of circumstances. Although the balance will take account of the expectations of compliance that the parties entertained at that time, it is by no means rare, in international as in domestic politics, to find that what the lawmaker has given in the form of substantive regulation is taken away in the implementation. The problem referred to earlier, of changing interests over the life of the treaty, can be handled by changes in the acceptable level of compliance rather than by defection. What is acceptable in terms of compliance will reflect the perspectives and interests of the participants in an ongoing political process, rather than some external, scientifically or market-validated standard.

More commonly, the level of acceptable compliance rises over the life of the treaty. If the treaty establishes a formal organization, that body may serve as a focus for mobilizing the political impetus for a higher level of compliance. A strong secretariat itself can sometimes exert compliance pressure, as in the IMF or ILO (see Chapter 12). Within the organization, states committed to a level of compliance higher than that acceptable to the generality of the parties may seek to ratchet up the standard. The Netherlands seems often to play the role of leader in European environmental affairs, both in the North and Baltic Sea regimes and in LRTAP.[82] Similarly, the United States may be a leader for improving compliance with the NPT, where its position is far stronger than that of its allies.

Since the international system is flat rather than hierarchical, a state willing to commit enforcement resources may be able to short-circuit cumbersome organizational procedures and pursue improved levels of compliance on its own. Trade sanctions imposed by the United States under Section 301 of the Tariff Act or under the Marine Mammal Protection Act[83] can be thought of as reflecting a unilateral U.S. political decision that existing levels of compliance with the GATT or the whaling convention were not acceptable, and that it would pay the costs of additional enforcement.[84] In such cases, however, gains in compliance with substantive obligations must be weighed against the losses attendant on departure from the procedural norms mandating multilateral dispute settlement.[85]

Finally, a characteristic activity for nongovernmental organizations (NGOs), especially in the fields of the environment and human rights, is campaigning to improve a level of compliance that the states concerned regard as perfectly acceptable and would just as soon leave alone. Increasingly, these organizations have direct access to the political process both within the treaty organization and in the societies of which they are a part. Their technical, organizational, and lobbying skills are an independent resource for enhanced compliance at both levels of the two-level game (see Chapter 11).

It seems plausible that treaty regimes are subject to a kind of critical-mass phenomenon, so that once defection reaches a certain level, or in the face of a particularly egregious violation by a major player, the regime might collapse.[86] Either the character of a particular violation or the identity of the violator may pose a threat to the regime that evokes a higher demand for compliance. States committed to the regime may sense that a tipping point is close, and that an enhanced compliance effort will be necessary to preserve the regime.

The Convention on International Trade in Endangered Species (CITES), for example, ordinarily displays a good deal of tolerance for noncompliance. But the alarming and widely publicized decline in the elephant population in East African habitats in the 1980s galvanized the treaty regime. The parties first made the decision to list the elephant in Appendix I of the treaty, with the effect of banning all commercial trade in ivory. The treaty permits any party to enter a reservation to such an action, in which case the reserving party is not bound by it.[87] Nevertheless the United States and a group of European countries, strongly urged on by their domestic environmental constituencies, insisted on universal adherence to the ban. Washington hinted at trade sanctions. It was freely suggested that Japan's offer to host the next meeting of the Conference of Parties, which was accepted on the last day of the 1989 conference, after Japan changed its position and announced that it would comply with the ivory ban, would have been rejected if Japan had entered a reservation.[88] The head of the Japanese Environment Agency explained that the Japanese move was made "to avoid isolation in the international community."[89] Although from the realist perspective only a relatively peripheral national interest was involved, a reservation—permitted under the treaty—threatened the collapse of the regime. A concerted and energetic defense resulted.

The New Sovereignty and the Management of Compliance

If we are correct that the principal source of noncompliance is not willful disobedience but the lack of capability or clarity or priority, then coercive enforcement is as misguided as it is costly. A more sophisticated strategy directly addressing these deficiencies is needed to deal with the large bulk of compliance problems. Elements of such a strategy can be discerned in the characteristic activities of regulatory regimes, although they are not always employed with a full consciousness of their implications, and they are seldom integrated into a unified and coherent whole.

At the simplest level, participating in the regime, attending meetings, responding to requests, and meeting deadlines may lead to a realignment of domestic priorities and agendas, setting policies in motion that will operate to improve performance over time. But an array of more pointed activities can reinforce this general effect.

Ensuring Transparency

Transparency—the generation and dissemination of information about the requirements of the regime and the parties' performance under it—is an almost universal element of management strategy. Transparency influences strategic interaction among parties to the treaty in the direction of compliance:

- It facilitates coordination converging on the treaty norms among actors making independent decisions.
- It provides reassurance to actors, whose compliance with the norms is contingent on similar action by other participants, that they are not being taken advantage of.
- It exercises deterrence against actors contemplating noncompliance.

In pure coordination problems, the parties have a common interest in achieving a common objective, and the potential for relative gains is small.

The treaty, by establishing the rules, avoids the transaction costs of ad hoc coordination. Most international regulatory problems, however, are not pure coordination problems. The parties have incentives to compete as well as to cooperate. They need reassurance that the others are complying, if the cooperative incentives are to prevail. Elinor Ostrom's study, *Governing the Commons,* shows that in successfully managed common pool resources, the members pursue a "contingent strategy." They will follow the rules so long as most others similarly situated follow them also.[90] Transparency is the key to reassurance, and thus to compliance.[91]

For the principal cold war arms control agreements, unilateral verification with national technical means of verification (NTM), authorized and facilitated by the treaties themselves, provided the needed level of transparency. In contemporary regulatory agreements, the same function is fulfilled by a combination of reporting, monitoring, and verification under the aegis of the regime.

The first step toward transparency is the development of data on the performance of the parties as to the principal treaty norms and on the general situations of concern to the regime. Self-reporting is the method of choice in most regimes. In fact, the incidence of reporting requirements is so high that they seem to be included almost pro forma in many agreements, with little concern about whether they will be taken seriously. The record of compliance with reporting requirements varies. It is excellent in the ILO, fair to poor in many environmental treaties, and seriously deficient in human rights treaties. Here as elsewhere, the level of compliance depends on what the parties as a group are prepared to live with. Experience shows that performance can be substantially improved by technical and financial assistance to build capacity, by clarifying and simplifying the requirements, and by giving greater emphasis and attention to the reporting function (see Chapter 7).

Verification, both to check the reliability of reported baseline data and to ensure compliance, was the most hotly contested issue in cold war arms control agreements, and U.S. insistence on stringent verification standards was a major limitation on the scope and number of arms control agreements. Although some aspects of the cold war paradigm have continuing value, especially in nonproliferation regimes, much of its elaboration and thoroughness reflects the extreme caution and low financial constraints of an earlier era.

Short of formal and costly verification systems, external checks are often available against which the reliability of national reports can be tested. Other states and nongovernmental scientific and interest groups make their own measurements of atmospheric conditions, ozone depletion, species populations, or, in the area of human rights, the condition of prisoners, minorities, and others who may face harsh treatment. National governments, business groups, and private organizations generate and publish a wide range of economic data for a variety of purposes. Nongovernmental organizations are playing an increasing role in providing information to treaty managers. These sources are generally sufficient to provide the necessary reassurance, if in fact the items or goals are measurable. Compliance problems that are exposed by verification and monitoring are then addressed in other phases of the process. These matters are discussed in Chapter 8.

Dispute Settlement

Where ambiguity or vagueness in treaty language creates compliance problems, the traditional prescription is dispute settlement machinery. Despite the fixation of international lawyers on the virtues of binding adjudication (preferably in the International Court of Justice, but if not, then by a specialized tribunal or arbitral panel), most treaty regimes turn to a variety of relatively informal mediative processes if the disputants are unable to resolve the issues among themselves. Authoritative interpretation of controverted provisions, either by the plenary body of the regime, the secretariat, or a designated interpretative organ, is common, perhaps surprisingly so. It is less contentious than conventional dispute resolution procedures, and in many cases it has a preventive or anticipatory value. On the whole, it has not seemed to matter whether the dispute settlement procedure is legally required or the decision is legally binding, so long as the outcome is treated as authoritative.

Although formal international adjudication, like its domestic counterpart, is costly, contentious, cumbersome, and slow, there is a recent disposition on the part of some regimes to revert to compulsory and more binding forms of dispute settlement. The most important instance is the GATT, which, after almost two decades of incremental tinkering, adopted a new procedure in the Uruguay Round that is to all intents and purposes binding adjudication.[92] Compulsory adjudication for some issues is also stipulated in the Canadian-U.S. Free Trade Agreement and in the North American Free Trade Agreement (NAFTA).[93] Likewise, although the dispute settlement chapter of the Law of the Sea Convention presents a menu of choices, if the parties fail to agree on an alternative, they must accept binding arbitration.[94]

A possible middle ground found in some recent agreements is compulsory conciliation resulting in a nonbinding recommendation from the conciliators on the issues in dispute.[95] This ensures that the regime will be able to address the entire range of disputes. The reported views of the conciliators are likely to carry considerable weight both with the parties in general and with the disputants. Yet the niceties of sovereignty are observed, and the parties are not forced to accept the decision (see Chapter 9).

Capacity Building

Deficits of technical and bureaucratic capability and financial resources have received increasing attention in the context of the difficulties of domestic enforcement of measures adopted in compliance with recent international environmental obligations. The current jargon is "capacity building," but technical assistance has been a major function of many treaty organizations for many years. In practice this aid has inevitably carried a certain tacit conditionality, but the Montreal Protocol, for perhaps the first time, expressly provides for technical assistance as an affirmative device for enabling countries to comply with both the reporting and the control requirements of the treaty.[96] In establishing priorities for the use of financial resources contributed under the Framework Convention on Climate Change (FCCC), the Conference of the Parties decided that "in the initial period emphasis should be placed on enabling activities undertaken by the developing country Parties such as planning, endogenous capacity building including institutional strengthening, training, research and education, that will facilitate implementation, in accordance with the Convention, of effective response measures."[97]

The Uses of Persuasion

These disparate elements—transparency, dispute settlement, capacity building—all of which are to be found in some regimes, can be considered to be parts of a management strategy. They merge into a broader process of "jawboning"—the effort to *persuade* the miscreant to change its ways—that is the characteristic method by which international regimes seek to induce compliance. It is remarkable that lawyers and international relations scholars, whose everyday stock-in-trade is persuasion—including persuasion of decision makers—should pay so little attention and, by implication, attach so little significance to the role of argument, exposition, and persuasion in influencing state behavior. Our experience as well as our research indicates that, on the contrary, the fundamental instrument for maintaining compliance with treaties at an acceptable level is an iterative process of discourse among the parties, the treaty organization, and the wider public.

We propose that this process is usefully viewed as management, rather than enforcement. As in other managerial situations, the dominant atmosphere is one of actors engaged in a cooperative venture, in which performance that seems for some reason unsatisfactory represents a problem to be solved by mutual consultation and analysis, rather than an offense to be punished. States are under the practical necessity to give reasons and justifications for suspect conduct. These are reviewed and critiqued not only in formal dispute settlement processes but also in a variety of other venues, public and private, formal and informal, where they are addressed and evaluated. In the process, the circumstances advanced in mitigation or excuse of nonperformance are systematically addressed. Those that seem to have substance are dealt with; those that do not are exposed. Often the upshot is agreement on a narrower and more concrete definition of the required performance, adapted to the circumstances of the case. At all stages, the putative offender is given every opportunity to conform. Persuasion and argument are the principal engines of this process, but if a party persistently fails to respond, the possibility of diffuse manifestations of disapproval or pressures from other actors in the regime is present in the background.

In its most advanced form, this justificatory discourse is expressly recognized as a principal method of inducing compliance. The treaty itself or practices that have grown up under it require each member to report systematically and periodically on policies and programs relevant to the achievement of regime norms and objectives. After analysis by the secretariat (and sometimes by concerned nongovernmental organizations), these reports are reviewed and assessed at a general meeting of the members, where the reporting state presents and defends its report. The discussion and debate culminates in agreement on ever more narrowly specified undertakings and targets to be achieved by the reporting state in the next reporting periods (see Chapter 10).

The process works because modern states are bound in a tightly woven fabric of international agreements, organizations, and institutions that shape their relations with each other and penetrate deeply into their internal economics and politics. The integrity and reliability of this system are of overriding importance for most states, most of the time. These considerations in turn reflect profound changes in the international system within which states must act and decide.

Traditionally, sovereignty has signified the complete autonomy of the state to act as it chooses, without legal limitation by any superior entity. The state realized and expressed its sovereignty through independent action to achieve its goals. If sovereignty in such terms ever existed outside books on international law and international relations, however, it no longer has any real world meaning.[98] The largest and most powerful states can sometimes get their way through sheer exertion of will, but even they cannot achieve their principal purposes—security, economic well-being, and a decent level of amenity for their citizens—without the help and cooperation of many other participants in the system, including entities that are not states at all. Smaller and poorer states are almost entirely dependent on the international economic and political system for nearly everything they need to maintain themselves as functioning societies.

That the contemporary international system is interdependent and increasingly so is not news. Our argument goes further. It is that, for all but a few self-isolated nations, sovereignty no longer consists in the freedom of states to act independently, in their perceived self-interest, but in membership in reasonably good standing in the regimes that make up the substance of international life. To be a player, the state must submit to the pressures that international regulations impose. Its behavior in any single episode is likely to affect future relationships not only within the particular regime involved but in many others as well, and perhaps its position within the international system as a whole.[99] When nations enter into an international agreement, therefore, they tend to alter their mutual expectations and actions over time in accordance with its terms. The need to be an accepted member in this complex web of international arrangements is itself the critical factor in ensuring acceptable compliance with regulatory agreements. Robert Putnam, in *Making Democracy Work*, traces the difference between low levels of effective cooperation in regional governments in southern Italy and the much higher levels in the north to the existence of a similarly thick network of associations, on the domestic plane, in the northern regions. As in the international arena, "The sanction for violating [the norms and expectations generated by this network] is not penal, but exclusion from the network of solidarity and cooperation."[100]

Sovereignty, in the end, is status—the vindication of the state's existence as a member of the international system. In today's setting, the only way most states can realize and express their sovereignty is through participation in the various regimes that regulate and order the international system. Isolation from the pervasive and rich international context means that the state's potential for economic growth and political influence will not be realized. Connection to the rest of the world and the political ability to be an actor within it are more important than any tangible benefits in explaining compliance with international regulatory agreements.

The need to be a member in good standing of the international system ensures that most compliance problems will yield to the management process we describe. If they do not, the offending state is left with a stark choice, between conforming to the rule as defined and applied in the particular circumstances and openly flouting a concrete and precisely specified undertaking endorsed by the other members of the regime. This turns out to be a very uncomfortable position even for a powerful state to find itself in. The Krasnoyarsk story represents an example of this process in action. Not even the so-called hermit state of North Korea has been completely able to resist this kind of escalating pressure. Indeed an important consequence of the process is the winnowing out of reasonably justifiable or unintended failures to fulfill commitments—those that might be consistent with a good faith compliance standard—and the identification and isolation of the few cases of egregious and willful violation. This in turn becomes part of the mobilization of consensus for harsher sanctions in the rare cases in which they may be necessary.

Inducing compliance through these interacting processes of justification, discourse, and persuasion is less dramatic than using coercive sanctions, but it is the way operational regimes in the real world go about it, for the most part. The remainder of this book is designed to show, first, the limited scope for the enforcement model in today's international system, and second, how the management model functions in practice and how it can be made more effective.

I

Sanctions

Preoccupation with sanctions as a method of treaty enforcement continues to be disproportionate to either the frequency of their use or their effectiveness when used. The focus of public attention is on the use of military force and economic sanctions in urgent situations of cross-border or civil conflict. However, the record of success is not encouraging, ranging from some accomplishments in Korea and Iraq, to the ambiguities of Rhodesia (now Zimbabwe) and South Africa, to the more recent frustrations of the former Yugoslavia, Somalia, and Haiti. Although the results are at best inconclusive, the absence of alternatives (or perhaps imagination) leads to continued consideration of sanctions in the hope of accomplishing a quick and decisive end to high-profile, egregious violations of international norms affecting security and human life. At a minimum, it is hoped that the threat of sanctions will heighten the response to diplomatic pressures.

But the demand for sanctions is not confined to cases of "threat to the peace, breach of the peace and acts of aggression," in the language of Chapter VII of the UN Charter. This book covers a broad range of international agreements that regulate the behavior of states, and of parties within states, and in these, too, the desire for positive enforcement powers remains strong. Although it is obvious that military sanctions would not be appropriate for the vast body of regulatory agreements, proponents of regulation in a wide range of subject areas, from endangered species to nuclear proliferation, demand treaties with "teeth"—by which they mean some form of coercive enforcement. Other kinds of pressures, which are often termed "diplomatic" but which can be quite unpleasant, can be and are mobilized to change state behavior to bring it into compliance with treaty obligations. We discuss this process at great length in Part Two. But we do not regard such pressures as "sanctions," properly so called, and we do not think the public has them in mind when it calls for treaties with teeth.

Part One examines the major categories of such sanctions in some detail and in the contexts in which they have been applied:

- *Treaty-based sanctions*—military or economic action authorized by the treaty instrument to punish violations of the norms established by it (Chapter 2);
- *Membership sanctions*—expulsion or suspension of rights and privileges of a party to the treaty (Chapter 3); and
- *Unilateral sanctions*—coercive action not expressly authorized by the treaty but applied unilaterally or by several states in concert to bring a party into compliance (Chapter 4).

Only the UN Charter and its Western Hemisphere analog, the Charter of the Organization of American States (OAS), authorize the imposition of military or economic sanctions, and then only in cases of threats to international peace and security. Although a number of treaties authorize the parties to impose restrictions or other measures affecting trade in certain situations, for the most part these are not, properly speaking, provisions for sanctions. For example, in almost all the circumstances in which the GATT authorizes withdrawal of trade concessions or imposition of restrictions, the underlying theory is compensatory, not punitive: the complaining party is to be given the benefit of its bargain.[1] Indeed, in many cases, there is no need to show that the harm complained of is due to violation of a GATT obligation. The GATT Contracting Parties may authorize true retaliatory sanctions if they "consider that the circumstances are serious enough to justify such action,"[2] but this authority has been used just once in the history of the GATT, in 1951, in favor of the Netherlands against the United States.[3] The distinction is considered at greater length in Chapter 4, in the context of unilateral trade measures that are truly sanctions.

In some treaties, the very purpose is to eliminate or regulate a particular type of trade. The restriction is not imposed as a penalty for violation or noncompliance—it is the essence of the regulation. Thus the Convention for the Suppression of the Slave Trade prohibits trade in slaves—whether by parties or nonparties, compliers or violators. The Convention on Trade in Narcotic Drugs is similar, although with exceptions. The Convention on International Trade in Endangered Species prohibits trade for commercial purposes in "species threatened with extinction," and limits trade in species "that may become so in the absence of strict regulation."[4] The Basel Convention prohibits the export of wastes to another country without notice to that country and its written consent. The Chemical Weapons Convention likewise is a comprehensive regulation of trade in potentially dangerous chemicals, but the only recourse provided in case a party violates the treaty is a reference to the UN Security Council. None of these trade regulations falls in the category of sanctions.

Finally, treaty restrictions on trade in the regulated goods with *nonparties* are also not true examples of sanctions. In many of these, the object is to penalize free riders, rather than to enforce the obligations of parties. For example, CITES permits trade with nonparties if accompanied by documentation comparable to that required by the treaty for shipments between parties.[5] Another provision of this sort is Article 4 of the Montreal Protocol, which bans imports of controlled substances from nonparties unless the exporting country is certified by a meeting of the parties to be in full compliance with the treaty limits on CFC consumption.[6] In fact, the real objective was to protect the existing export markets of the signers. In commodity agreements, the object of the restrictions is to preserve the market for members of the agreement. The restrictions do not address the question of what to do about a party that has violated its export quota.

Perhaps a misperception of the nature of these treaty-based trade restrictions underlies the clarion call for trade sanctions to enforce treaty obligations. More likely, the ongoing pressure for treaties with teeth reflects an easy but incorrect analogy to domestic legal systems, where formal sanctions imposed by the coercive power of the state are thought to play an essential role in enforcing compliance with legal rules.[7] Public discussion of existing and proposed treaties is often conducted in terms of what we have elsewhere called the criminal law or law enforcement model of treaty implementation.[8] The Kellogg-Briand Pact, in which the parties agreed to outlaw war as an instrument of national policy but provided no enforcement procedures, is cited as the very exemplar of utopian—and useless—international lawmaking. Even informed participants and observers of international affairs are not immune to the enforcement model. The idea of some kind of effective sanctioning capability seems to be a central feature of recurring calls for a new world order.

The false analogy to the domestic legal system feeds and feeds on the endless tautological debate about whether "international law" is law at all. The difficulty of providing for sanctions ex ante and of marshaling them even when authorized is cited as evidence that it is not. The argument, rooted in

John Austin's *Lectures on Jurisprudence,* is that there can be no law without enforcement power.[9] Only governments have enforcement power, and whatever the existing international order may be, it is not a government. Since international agreements are therefore by definition unenforceable, they are not law. The issue is further confused by the frequent characterization of the international system as "anarchic." The term is not meant necessarily to signify a Hobbesian state of war of all against all. It is widely accepted that the international order does maintain rules of behavior generally accepted and obeyed by the members.[10] But unlike a domestic society, where the state is conceived as wielding sovereign authority over persons and actions within its jurisdiction, in an anarchic system, by definition, there is no international superior with legal authority to compel members to act in accordance with the norms and rules of the system.

An example of the persistence of academic belief in the importance of coercive sanctions is a recent paper provoked by earlier drafts of this book.[11] The authors argue that although what they call "no-fault compliance" may be sufficient to account for the generally satisfactory existing levels of treaty observance, it will not suffice if really "deep" international cooperation is required, as they expect it to be when the world addresses the increasingly complex problems of interdependence. In such cases, they believe the gains to be made by departing from treaty norms will be much higher, and only the threat or application of significant material sanctions will be sufficient to outweigh them.

Despite these theoretical debates, the teaching of experience, reviewed at length in the next three chapters, is quite uniform as to the limits and potential of sanctions in international law. As noted, except for the UN and OAS Charters, the international system is very leery of treaty-based military and economic sanctions. Although many regulatory treaties contain membership sanctions that limit or deny privileges of membership for failure to comply with the provisions of the treaty, they are only rarely invoked, and almost invariably in support of broad foreign policy aims rather than simply for the enforcement of international legal obligations. Anthropologists, sociologists, and now lawyers know that all societies use informal or nonlegal sanctions to secure compliance with legal as well as other social rules. Here, too, however, the experience in the international arena is that unilateral sanctions in the more coercive form of military or economic penalties are but infrequently and sporadically deployed to redress violations of treaty obligations, and are not very effective when they are.

In sum, sanctioning authority is rarely granted by treaty, rarely used when granted, and likely to be ineffective when used. This record has to be disappointing for those who think the key to compliance with international agreements is treaties with teeth. Even when power disparities between the sanctioner and the target are very great and commonality of interest among potential sanctioners seems high, effective mobilization of sanctions to influence state behavior has been rare.

We argue that this record is not the result of accidental or random factors. The use of sanctions entails high costs to the sanctioner—military, economic, and political—and can raise serious problems of legitimacy. These systemic features of international life place severe limits, both practical and normative, on the range of circumstances in which coercive sanctions can be a viable policy instrument. The remainder of Part One examines the relatively small universe of cases in which sanctions have actually been employed, in order to elucidate the nature of the inherent cost and legitimacy limitations of the enforcement model, and to pave the way for the discussion in Part Two of the management model, the actual mechanism by which compliance with international agreements is induced in regulatory regimes.

2

Treaty-Based Military and Economic Sanctions

Although the UN Charter and the OAS Charter—the only two treaties that formally authorize and establish regularized procedures for the imposition of economic or military sanctions—created a legal norm prohibiting the use of force except in self-defense, the primary objective of the granted powers was not law enforcement but collective defense. Only in situations threatening international peace and security could the power to use military or economic coercion be activated. Even so, the great powers demanded the further safeguard of the veto in the UN Security Council, and the United States has the de facto power to prevent action in the OAS.

The use of these extraordinary powers has been correspondingly rare—occurring less than half a dozen times in the period bounded by the Korean War and the Gulf War and perhaps as many since then. We will review all of those cases in this chapter, not to add yet another analysis of their effectiveness in achieving their objective of international peace and security, but to see what the prospects may be for adapting them to the more routine tasks of enforcing ordinary treaty obligations.

Both of the charters are the product of the immediate aftermath of World War II, and they share the common conceptions of that period. Like generals fighting the last war, the drafters of the UN Charter had the failure of the League of Nations firmly in mind.[1] The fatal defect of the League, according to the common diagnosis, was its lack of power to enforce its decisions. Its inability to impose effective sanctions on Italy for invading Ethiopia, and on Japan for its war against China, in effect marked the end of the League as a functioning system. These episodes were taken as proof of the futility of a League of Nations that could not compel its members to act against states that had been condemned for breach of the peace.[2]

Chapter VII of the UN Charter was designed to cure this defect.[3] Under its provisions, once the Security Council had "determined the existence of a threat to the peace, breach of the peace or act of aggression," it could impose economic and diplomatic sanctions as spelled out in Article 41, and if these measures should prove inadequate, could "take such action by air, sea, or land forces as may be necessary to maintain or restore international peace and security."[4] Actions under Chapter VII could take the form of "decisions," which UN members "agree to accept and carry out" under Article 25.

The OAS Charter recapitulates the approach of the UN Charter on a regional plane. Historically the chief perpetrator of intervention in the Western Hemisphere had been the United States. The charter was designed to ensure that the United States would forswear any right of unilateral intervention, and that "no state or group of states" would intervene in the internal affairs of an American state except as a result of OAS decision. Response to intervention was to be the collective responsibility of the organization. Like the UN Security Council, the OAS could order economic and diplomatic sanctions and authorize the use of force against an offender in a case of "aggression . . . extra-continental or intra-continental conflict, or . . . any other fact or situation that might endanger the peace of America."[5]

The handful of cases in which these unique enforcement powers have been invoked in the half century since they were granted illustrate the difficulties inherent in building consensus for economic and military sanctions. The costs—sometimes in lives, inevitably in money—are high, as are the demands on domestic and international political capital. Though small in number, the cases can be grouped for discussion according to some distinct characteristics.

1. The authorization of military force in response to large-scale military action that comfortably fits the definition of a threat to international peace and security. These actions were essentially organized, operated, and, for the most part, manned by the United States. (Korea, Cuba, Iraq)
2. Economic sanctions promoted by newly independent African states as part of the process of ending colonialism and racial oppression in Africa. (South Africa, Rhodesia)
3. Use or threat of sanctions as one of an array of instruments to manage and contain ongoing international crises in the period since the Gulf War. Each of these spawned a variety of Chapter VII actions with mixed great-power sponsorship, as part of a larger international effort

including negotiation and humanitarian initiatives. (Iraq in the aftermath of the Gulf War, the former Yugoslavia, Somalia, Haiti)

Each of these groups will be discussed in turn.[6]

Military Enforcement Action

In the long period from the end of World War II to the breakup of the Soviet Union, the UN Security Council invoked its military powers under Chapter VII only twice, once in Korea, at the beginning of this period, and again in the Gulf War, just at the end. In the same period, the OAS authorized the use of force once, in response to the Soviet emplacement of nuclear missiles in Cuba.

North Korea

Korea was a pre–World War II Japanese colony. At the end of the war, the Soviets accepted Japan's surrender to the north of the 38th parallel of latitude and the United States to the south, splitting the country into North and South Korea. It was contemplated that Korea would be reunited under UN auspices, and although Soviet troops stayed on in the north, by June 1949 almost all remaining U.S. forces had been withdrawn, leaving only a military assistance and training detachment of about five hundred men.[7] In early 1950, Secretary of State Dean Acheson made a celebrated speech implying that South Korea was outside the U.S. defense perimeter in the Far East, but affirming the overall U.S. security interest in the area.[8] On June 25, 1950, North Korean troops thrust across the 38th parallel. In four days they were in Seoul. South Korean and local U.S. forces, reinforced by troops from Japan, were driven back to a narrow perimeter around the southern port of Pusan before the lines were finally stabilized.

With the cold war at its height, the invasion of South Korea was seen in Washington as a challenge to the whole U.S. position in the western Pacific. On the very day of the invasion, the United States called for a meeting of the UN Security Council, which passed Resolution 82, determining that "the armed attack on the Republic of Korea by forces from North Korea . . . constitutes a breach of the peace" and demanding immediate cessation of hostilities and the withdrawal of North Korean forces to the 38th parallel.[9] The resolution escaped a veto only because the Soviet representative was boycotting the Security Council in protest against its refusal to seat the People's Republic of China.[10] Two days later, as North Korean troops continued down the peninsula, the council passed a second resolution recommending "that the Members of the United Nations furnish such assistance to the Republic of Korea as may be necessary to repel the armed attack and to restore international peace and security in the area."[11] Within the week, a third resolution established a "unified command under the United States" for forces operating in South Korea, requested that the United States designate the commander, and authorized the use of the UN flag.[12]

The resolutions were passed to the tune of cold war rhetoric in the UN and in the U.S. Congress and press. The Korean war dominated U.S. and international politics for three years, until the newly elected President Eisenhower concluded a truce on July 27, 1953, with the forces on both sides substantially in the same positions in which they had been at the beginning. Apart from South Korea itself, whose entire military was engaged, the United States bore most of the costs of the military operations, and took most of the losses. Eighteen other nations contributed small contingents. U.S. willingness to assume leadership was anchored in cold war concerns during a period in which no cost seemed too great in the effort to prevent the spread of communism. The legitimating mantle of the UN had been made possible only by the fluke of the Soviet representative's absence, and the situation was not replicated as long as the cold war continued. Domestically, the early enthusiasm for U.S. intervention waned as the war dragged on and casualties mounted. "Truman's war" was a central issue in the 1952 presidential campaign. There is little doubt that Eisenhower's campaign promise to "go to Korea" to end the war contributed to the electoral outcome.[13]

Cuba

The drama of the 1962 Cuban missile crisis has often been recounted, analyzed, and reenacted.[14] At the time, the discovery of offensive nuclear missiles in Cuba resolved an acrimonious debate in Washington about suspicious events that had been taking place on the island over the previous months. With congressional elections scheduled for November, the exchanges had inevitably assumed a partisan cast. Republican critics of the Kennedy administration maintained that the Soviets were emplacing offensive missiles on the island. Many called for a naval blockade of Cuba or an even stronger response. Administration spokesmen insisted that the installations were advanced air defense systems and required no U.S. action. President Kennedy, making this point in an early September press conference, warned that "were it to be otherwise, the gravest issues would arise."[15]

Photographs taken by U-2 planes and shown to the president on October

16 revealed sites in Cuba for nuclear-armed medium-range ballistic missiles (MRBMS) and intermediate-range ballistic missiles (IRBMS).[16] President Kennedy immediately convened a specially selected group of his advisors, which became known as the Executive Committee of the National Security Council (EXCOM). They deliberated in secret for a week on the appropriate course of action. There was agreement from the outset (except briefly from Secretary of Defense Robert McNamara) that the United States had to make some kind of forceful response, although there was sharp division about the form it should take. The EXCOM quickly winnowed the possibilities down to two: an air strike against the missile installations (probably to be followed by invasion) and a naval blockade (a "quarantine").

Within this framework, the main legal question was whether the Soviet action could be characterized as "an armed attack" within the meaning of Article 51 of the UN Charter, which would have permitted a unilateral use of force by the United States in the exercise of its right of self-defense. If not, as the State Department lawyers argued, the action would require collective authorization by an international organization.[17] The element of surprise necessary for an air strike would have precluded advance international authorization. Thus the legal as well as the political argument favored the choice of the quarantine.

The OAS was the only available forum that could act in the circumstances, although its power to order enforcement action without Security Council authorization under Article 53 was not free from doubt. Resort to the Security Council was precluded, because, unlike the case of Korea, the Soviet representative was in attendance and would certainly veto any enforcement action. Although the crisis continued to dominate the Security Council agenda, it was unable to take any action. The OAS, however, passed an authorizing resolution in record time, drafted by the United States and introduced by Secretary of State Dean Rusk.[18]

With cold war concerns heightened by a nearby and apparently imminent nuclear threat to the Western Hemisphere, the United States was able to mobilize a coalition within the hemisphere. The felt urgency of the situation was more than enough to overcome financial constraints, even if an air strike had been the chosen route. Eleven Latin American nations contributed either vessels, troops, or facilities to the operation of the quarantine.[19] NATO was asked only for verbal support, and both the political leaders and the public in NATO countries were cautious about offering much more.

The quarantine lasted for six harrowing days. It was ended by an exchange of letters in which Chairman Khrushchev agreed to withdraw the missiles under UN supervision, and President Kennedy promised that the United States would not invade Cuba. It is now widely believed that the United States also gave tacit assurances that it would withdraw comparable NATO IRBMS stationed in Turkey.[20]

The crisis was considered a brilliant coup for U.S. diplomacy, but there were political costs. The willingness of the OAS to do Washington's bidding started a weakening of that organization as a potential collective security instrument. In the 1980s the United States had to resort to unilateral action to deal with recurring problems in the region—Grenada, Panama, Nicaragua, El Salvador.

Iraq

Iraq invaded Kuwait on August 2, 1990, and established complete control over the country within twenty-four hours. As it had in the Korea case, the UN Security Council reacted on the same day, with Resolution 660 determining that "there exists a breach of international peace and security as regards the Iraqi invasion of Kuwait" it condemned the invasion and called for Iraq to withdraw immediately from Kuwait.[21] Four days later, again at the instance of the United States, the Security Council, "acting under Chapter VII of the Charter," imposed a comprehensive economic embargo on trade and financial dealings with Iraq to secure compliance with the withdrawal demanded in the earlier resolution.[22]

At the same time, news stories reported that Iraqi troops were massing on the Saudi Arabian border. Secretary of Defense Richard Cheney visited Riyadh and returned with a Saudi invitation for the United States to send ground troops. On August 9, President Bush announced that U.S. forces were being deployed to Saudi Arabia at its request, "to take up defensive positions . . . to assist the Saudi Arabian Government in defense of its homeland."[23] Large U.S. naval contingents were already in the Gulf, and troops and planes were quickly deployed by air. Although the contemplated initial deployment was only 50,000, the *New York Times* characterized the president's tone as "that of a leader preparing his country for war."[24]

Over the next months, the forces deployed in Saudi Arabia and the Persian Gulf expanded both in the number of troops and of contributing nations. The initial U.S. deployment was enlarged to 250,000 troops, and thirty-seven other countries ultimately contributed forces.[25] Unlike in the Korean operation, the Security Council did not authorize a UN command. As a practical matter the United States was in charge, but it led by coordination with the military leaders of the other principal contingents.

In early November, the combined forces were doubled, to 500,000, to give the coalition "an offensive option."[26] The United States and the United Kingdom claimed legal authority under Article 51 to act in collective self-defense of Kuwait at its request, and argued that no further Security Council action was required to authorize use of military force against Iraq itself.[27] Nevertheless, to meet political concerns of other members of the coalition and to remove any legal doubt, President Bush decided to seek Security Council endorsement. Extended negotiations in the Security Council produced Resolution 678, which established a grace period until January 15, 1991, for compliance with the earlier Security Council mandates. Thereafter, the resolution "authorize[d] member states . . . to use all necessary means to uphold and implement the Security Council Resolution 660 . . . and to restore peace and security in the area."[28]

The grace period quickly became a deadline. The Soviet Union, anxious to cooperate with the United States in the new post–cold war setting but apprehensive about the consequences for its former ally, Iraq, strove in vain to negotiate an Iraqi withdrawal from Kuwait. Within twenty-four hours after the grace period ended, the offensive against Iraq began. After five weeks of bombardment from the air, the coalition launched a ground attack. Four days later, on February 28, 1991, with the Iraqi army routed, President Bush announced that "all United States and coalition forces will suspend offensive combat operations."[29]

Some Comparisons

The Indispensable Role of the United States. The military action and political aftermath in Korea, Cuba, and Iraq were extraordinarily complex episodes spanning the cold war period. Each generated wide-ranging repercussions, both short and long term. In each case, the rhetoric of international law and law enforcement was a major theme of the debates in the UN Security Council and the OAS. Yet it is evident that the outstanding common feature in all three episodes was the central and indispensable role of the United States, responding to a sudden disruption of the status quo that it perceived as an unacceptable threat to its vital interests. In each case, the United States took the initiative to bring the matter to the international forum and to shape and organize the institutional response. It marshaled the evidence and arguments (and sometimes twisted arms) to convince other parties that its perception of an unacceptable threat to peace and security was correct.

The United States also dominated the military action in all three cases. It provided the overwhelming bulk of the military muscle in terms of manpower and materials. Although other coalition members contributed troops and equipment, except in the case of the Gulf War, these were mainly symbolic gestures. All three operations were under U.S. command—by express authorization of the Security Council in the Korea case, and de facto in Cuba and the Gulf. The United States did the strategic and tactical planning; major political-military decisions were made in Washington.

Finally, the United States decided when to end the operations. In Korea there were extended truce negotiations, and other countries, particularly some of the developing countries in the UN General Assembly, played a role in putting pressure on the United States to come to terms.[30] The final decision to conclude the truce, however, was President Eisenhower's. As to Cuba, an exchange of letters between Khrushchev and Kennedy ended the crisis without consultation with the OAS on either the timing or the terms of the exchange.[31] In Iraq, four days after the commencement of ground operations, and with the Iraqi army in full retreat, President Bush announced that the U.S. coalition forces were suspending offensive operations. By happenstance, British foreign secretary Douglas Hurd was in Washington at the time and attended the White House meeting. But that was the extent of the consultation with coalition partners.[32]

The Problem of Legitimacy. The American people have not always understood that even when the United States has the military or economic power to act alone, the effectiveness of its actions might be undermined if it did not seek and achieve a degree of international consensus to give its actions legitimacy. Even though the initiative and the organizing force of the United States were central in all three cases, the international organizations were more than merely a facade for unilateral U.S. policy. They were the forum for mobilizing the necessary political support. In fact, there is some doubt whether the United States could have put together an effective response without their participation, most clearly against Iraq, where cooperation of countries in the area and logistical and financial support were essential. That participation, in turn, would have been impossible if U.S. allies and also neutral nations had not shared, at least to some degree, the U.S. perception of the gravity of the situation.

The United States gave up some freedom of action in return for this organizational support. In Korea, it did not cross the 38th parallel until it had secured General Assembly authorization.[33] In the case of Cuba, U.S. officials weighed the risks of a reference to the OAS. Robert Kennedy said that if the OAS turned down the resolution, "the U.S. position would be untenable."[34] In Iraq, questions about the extent of the authority granted by the Security Council, arising in connection with the naval blockade and the use of force against Iraq, were resolved by new explicit resolutions rather than by unilateral decisions.[35] To secure the support of other Security Council members, the United States had to make concessions. As a prime example, it appears that the United States favored authorization for the immediate use of force in Resolution 678, but acceded to a grace period until January 15 under pressure from other Security Council members.[36] The country's leaders and the American public display considerable impatience at such constraints on national decision making. Still, the UN Security Council and the OAS in these cases served primarily to help legitimize U.S. policy and to mobilize other members in support of it.[37] They exercised little control over objectives or operations.

Costs. At the outset of the UN era, an observer remarked with somewhat rueful surprise: "The Korean War . . . has shown us that an international enforcement action is, for all practical purposes, a war."[38] Ground forces under the UN flag in Korea ranged from half a million in 1951 to nearly a million in 1953, mostly from the United States and South Korea. Total UN casualties were more than 500,000 with 94,000 killed, more than 33,000 from the United States. Chinese and North Korean casualties are estimated at more than 1.5 million, including prisoners of war.[39]

The other international military operations have been much less bloody. The Cuban quarantine ended without a military engagement, and the only U.S. casualty was one U-2 pilot. In Iraq, although the troop deployments matched those in Korea, the coalition's dead numbered less than six hundred, about half from the United States.[40] But in each case the specter of much higher potential losses had shadowed the planning and decision making. In democratic countries, at least in recent years, tolerance for casualties on international missions that do not directly threaten the nation's security seems to be extremely low.

Even if military losses can be kept within acceptable bounds, the financial burden of international enforcement actions is high. The cost of the Korean war was $265 billion in 1991 dollars.[41] There is no official cost figure for the six days of naval quarantine and air and ground alerts in Cuba; the bill for the Gulf War came to $61 billion, although most of it was paid by countries other than the United States.[42] These are large sums in a time of universal budgetary stringency, when the UN has difficulty collecting assessments even for existing peacekeeping activities, much less new ones.

Political costs are the hardest to measure. Success, especially if achieved with low casualties, may bring net gains in both foreign and domestic political accounts. Nevertheless, maintaining the coalition that is necessary to legitimize the operation requires that the interests and needs of the other members be taken into account, with burdens and costs to the coalition leader, as we have noted.[43] All three cases reveal the characteristic American tendency to rally round a presidential show of strength, but this surge is not necessarily long-lived. Although the Cuban missile crisis remains part of the Kennedy legend, in Korea, initial public support eroded, and this hurt President Truman. Iraq gave an immense boost to President Bush and was credited by many with helping to dispel the defeatist legacy of Vietnam. But as the aftermath of the Gulf War grew messy and its consequences inconclusive, presidential popularity waned, and caution about putting the American military "in harm's way" reasserted itself.

The spur of the cold war was sufficient to induce the United States to assume the high costs of collective action and the burdens of mobilizing a legitimizing coalition. With the disappearance of this overriding motivation, even situations that raise serious problems of international political and military stability have not been enough to overcome these hurdles, as the discussions below of Bosnia, Somalia, and Haiti illustrate.

Economic Sanctions in Africa

The cases of South Africa and Rhodesia (modern Zimbabwe) are the only ones in which a group of smaller states was able to force the imposition of UN sanctions against the opposition of the United States and the West.

There has been lively discussion over many years about the effectiveness of the economic sanctions on South Africa. The criteria for success have been elusive and often not fully articulated by the contestants. There seems to be agreement that the cumulative impact of all the sanctions, particularly from the mid-1980s, made some contribution to the process that brought about the end of apartheid and the transition to multiracial democracy.[44] But it was a thirty-year process. The years immediately before Nelson Mandela's release from prison are considered to have been a time of both financial squeeze and painful isolation from the world for the white citizens of South Africa. But the sanctions imposed collectively under the UN Charter were only a small part of the sanctions picture, and perhaps their most important effect was to help legitimate boycotts by public and private groups not only in the economic sphere, but also in sports, entertainment, and science. The United States enacted the Comprehensive Anti-Apartheid Act in 1986, over President Reagan's veto.[45] Major U.S. multinational corporations faced shareholder pressure to disinvest in South Africa, and if they did not, many state and local laws prohibited government contracts with them. The international banking community, following the lead of Chase Manhattan's refusal to roll over its loans, demonstrated a loss of confidence in the South African economy, and the curtailed access to capital cut back economic growth drastically. On top of all this was the gradual exclusion of South Africa from most major international organizations (discussed in Chapter 3). There is no doubt that these actions, fanned by repeated General Assembly condemnations, are to be credited with a negative impact on South African economy and morale.

In Rhodesia, mounting pressures apart from UN sanctions—guerrilla warfare within the country, beginning in 1972; the 1974 coup in Portugal, which resulted in the independence of Mozambique; and the withdrawal of South African police forces in 1975—were what chiefly brought the Ian Smith regime to accept a new constitution providing for transition to a black majority government in December 1979.[46] At best, it can be argued that the Chapter VII sanctions made some contribution to an extended and varied program of pressures that ultimately isolated the white community and achieved results. As in South Africa, a principal function of the UN sanctions was to express the solidarity of the world with the local opposition.

In the 1960s, with the admission of large numbers of ex-colonial countries, particularly from Africa, the character of the UN began to change. The new nations had their own objectives and agendas. A high priority was the speedy termination of the last vestiges of colonialism and of official racism in Africa. On this issue, as on others, the Soviets and their allies generally ranged themselves on the side of the Africans.

The West, although sympathetic with African aspirations, resisted forceful action. The reasons for this were many. The colonial powers—England, Belgium, France, Portugal—were members of the Western alliance, and the United States needed their loyalty for the essential theaters of the cold war. Though South Africa was not formally a member of the alliance, in the early 1960s it was closely linked to Great Britain by Commonwealth bonds. European settlers, the ruling political and economic elements, had continuing ties to the metropolitan countries and were the ones who stood to lose in any major alteration of the status quo. Minority rule in Rhodesia and apartheid in South Africa intersected with developments in race relations of great political sensitivity in the West, particularly in the United States. And to a significant extent, the Western states really believed that these matters were "essentially within the domestic jurisdiction" and thus could not be the object of UN intervention, at least in the absence of a genuine threat to international peace and security.[47]

The weight of the new members' numbers was first felt in the General Assembly. As early as 1962, the assembly passed resolutions calling for an economic embargo against South Africa[48] and declaring the situation in Rhodesia a threat to the peace and security of Africa.[49] But effective action could be taken only in the Security Council, and there the record is one of resistance by the Western states, including the use of the veto, against increasing pressure for action mobilized by African states in the General Assembly and among Western publics.

The Security Council first condemned South Africa's racial policies and called for an end to apartheid after the Sharpeville incident in April 1960. Even then, the United Kingdom and France abstained.[50] The United States, in voting for the resolution, emphasized its opposition to any sanctions.[51] In August 1963, France and the United Kingdom abstained again on a Security Council call for a voluntary arms embargo,[52] and the United States specifically stated that the situation was not appropriate for action under Chapter VII.[53] Not until 1976, after the Soweto riots in which hundreds of blacks were killed, did the council act under Chapter VII, and then it was only to impose an arms embargo.[54] By that time, however, South Africa had developed an extensive arms manufacturing industry of its own. Security Council sanctions never went any further than that. As late as 1985, when the South African government declared a state of emergency, the United States and the United Kingdom vetoed mandatory economic sanctions, although they abstained in order to permit a resolution to pass calling for voluntary sanctions covering new investment, nuclear energy assistance, computers for police use, and trade in Krugerrands.[55]

Rhodesia, in 1960, was still nominally a British colony, although ruled by a white settler government. British policy was to bring it to full independence by the same path as other African states, arriving at a new multiracial state,[56] but the Rhodesian government would have none of that. On November 11, 1965, it issued a Unilateral Declaration of Independence (UDI), and Britain, responding to African ex-colonies with whom the future of the British Commonwealth now rested, took the matter to the Security Council.[57] The council condemned the UDI and called on states not to recognize the white settler regime.[58] A second resolution, pointedly refraining from invoking Chapter VII powers, called on states to "do their utmost in order to break all economic relations with Southern Rhodesia, including an embargo on oil and petroleum products."[59] Even so, France abstained on the ground that the situation was within the domestic jurisdiction of Great Britain.

The African states again turned to the Commonwealth. At a Commonwealth meeting in September 1966, Prime Minister Harold Wilson agreed that, if Rhodesia did not end its "rebellion" by the end of the year, he would sponsor a Security Council resolution calling for mandatory economic sanctions.[60] When the deadline expired, he carried out his commitment. The Security Council, acting under Chapter VII, determined that the situation in Southern Rhodesia constituted a threat to international peace and security, and imposed selective economic sanctions.[61] African and other developing countries continued to press for further action, and the Council finally adopted substantially comprehensive economic sanctions in May 1968.[62]

Nearly all members of the United Nations complied with the sanctions resolutions in the sense that they issued a decree or order prohibiting the importation and exportation of the products covered. Domestic enforcement, however, was weak, and neither South Africa nor Portugal (then still in control of Mozambique) accepted the resolution, thus punching gaping holes in the sanctions regime.[63] The United States itself flouted the sanctions in 1971 when Congress passed the Byrd Amendment, in effect requiring the secretary of commerce to license imports of chrome ore from Rhodesia.[64]

In the cases of South Africa and Rhodesia, like the those previously discussed, the proponents of enforcement action were motivated by strongly perceived national interest. There is no doubt that the primary goal was to complete the liberation of the continent from a centuries-old yoke of repression, but more conventional security interests also played a role. South Africa was already deploying covert forces against the "front line" African states, and its military power would have been much strengthened by an alliance with a white-ruled Rhodesia.[65] From the viewpoint of the African states, therefore, the elimination of the remaining white governments on the continent was a matter of primary national security interest. In the absence of military resources, one of their few available alternatives was UN economic sanctions. With no superpower initiative, however, the newly decolonized members of the UN had to generate consensus by a slow accumulation of pressure on the Western states. The Security Council moved at an agonizingly slow pace from Chapter VI to Chapter VII—that is, from recommendations to mandatory decisions. It took three years in the Rhodesian case to mandate more or less comprehensive sanctions, an objective that was never reached against South Africa.

The legal basis for Chapter VII action was shaky. A state's treatment of its own citizens was then beginning to emerge as an important international concern, based on the human rights provisions of the UN Charter[66] and the 1948 Universal Declaration of Human Rights. But it had not yet matured into a universally acknowledged legal norm. The Covenants on Civil and Political Rights and on Economic and Social Rights were not opened for signature until 1965, and the development by which their principal provisions were incorporated into customary international law was still in the future. Indeed the African sanctions cases made an important contribution to that development.[67] It was not easy to bring colonialism and racism within the rubric of threats to international peace and security, the Charter predicate for enforcement action. The issue was hotly debated in the Rhodesia case. Dean Acheson, in a letter to the *Washington Post*, gave a curmudgeonly summary of the argument: "Since Rhodesia, by doing what it has always done and with which the United Nations cannot constitutionally interfere, incites the less law-abiding members to violate their solemn obligation not to use force or the threat of force in their international relations, Rhodesia becomes a threat to the peace and must be coerced . . . 'Who's loony now?' "[68]

Nevertheless, the African states did succeed in inducing the Security Council to take action in both cases. One of the important legacies of that success, with large implications for the post–cold war period, was that direct military aggression was no longer the sole trigger for the exercise of the Security Council's power to impose collective sanctions under Chapter VII. The first expansion of the original concept of a threat to international peace and security occurred in these cases. The development of international consensus by the cumulative effort of smaller, less powerful nations, over initial great-power resistance, was a significant achievement. But the difficulty and length of the process and the many other factors that contributed to the results underscore how far from ordinary treaty enforcement these economic instruments are.

Chapter VII Sanctions after the Gulf War

There was never much of a hope that conflict throughout the world would diminish with the end of the cold war. True, the Gulf War fed the expectation that the new cooperative relationship between Russia and the United States would turn the Security Council into a more powerful and focused instrument for the exercise of enforcement powers, as the UN founders had intended. The two countries cooperated in the liquidation of ongoing proxy wars in Angola, Cambodia, Central America, and elsewhere, securing agreement by the parties to a UN presence for a variety of peacekeeping tasks.

But once the lid of superpower constraint was removed, smoldering issues reignited into conflicts that have proven bloody, complex, subtle, and intractable. These have not involved the projection of power across boundaries. Although most have been marked by fighting—including sizable armed engagements, often as a result of the disintegration of state authority—there has been no military action that could plausibly be termed an immediate threat to international peace and security. In most of the conflicts, there have been international ramifications, but the main issues have been "internal," played out within the territory of a state or former state. At first they looked much like many other chronic problems that received the fitful attention of the UN and other international political actors during the cold war—Kashmir, Tibet, West Irian, and the Sahel, to name a few—but that had been kept at the margins of international attention by the preoccupation with the superpower rivalry.

At the beginning of the 1990s, some combination of mostly internal violence, political collapse, natural disaster, violations of human rights, proximity, and media attention pushed a number of these problems onto the Security Council's agenda. We will discuss four cases here: Iraq after the Gulf War, Yugoslavia, Somalia, and Haiti. In each, the Security Council took unprecedented responsibility for situations whose humane appeal may have outrun any strategy for resolving them. Despite the U.S.-Russian rapprochement, the familiar problems of the need for consensus for military and economic sanctions and the difficulty of achieving it have remained critical. Indeed they have intensified, because there is no unified conception of the importance of these issues or of whether and how to intervene. The debate is played out in an "n-party game," not only among states and within alliances but also in internal domestic negotiations taking place in all major capitals. Awareness of cost and risk is heightened by the greater uncertainty that intervention will produce a successful outcome. Because these cases do not seem to present life-or-death consequences for the international system, they seem closer to violations of regulatory treaties than to major transborder aggressions or the racial brutalities of apartheid. While it is important to learn how UN processes can be made to function better and faster, for the purposes of this book it should be evident that they are unlikely to offer a route to simple or routine enforcement of even established norms.

The Changing Legal Basis for Chapter VII Action

The traditional law governing the exercise of the Security Council's powers was relatively straightforward. Under the prevailing view of the Charter, the Security Council has broad authority to take action with respect to situations affecting international peace and security under Chapter VI, *with the consent or acquiescence of the parties concerned.* The International Court of Justice held that even the deployment of UN forces is valid under Chapter VI, provided that the state on whose territory they are to operate consents.[69] Only under Chapter VII, however, can the council take decisions that bind member states *without their consent.*

The post–cold war pattern of Security Council action conforms to this legal framework, at least formally. The UN forces known as UNPROFOR I in Yugoslavia and UNOSOM I in Somalia were deployed pursuant to a cease-fire or other agreement subscribed to by all the parties to the controversy. Thus they could be said to be operating by consent, and Chapter VII action was not required.[70] When, in both Bosnia and Somalia, it became impossible to secure consent—either because the authorities were unwilling to grant it or because there were no constituted authorities—the Security Council resorted to its mandatory powers. The forces designated UNPROFOR II and UNOSOM II are Chapter VII forces. The enforcement of the no-fly zone over Bosnia, discussed below, was separately authorized under Chapter VII, as was the effort to capture General Mohammed Farah Aidid in Mogadishu, since these operations were conducted without the consent of those targeted. Only in Iraq, where the situation was strongly colored by the original Security Council response to the invasion of Kuwait and by the scope and circumstances of the cease-fire, were the United States and its close allies prepared to resort to force without specific Security Council authorization, and then only on a strictly limited basis.

Economic measures, if they were to operate with binding force on all members of the United Nations, also had to be adopted under Chapter VII. In accord with this requirement, the arms embargoes in all four cases and the general economic sanctions against Yugoslavia, Iraq, and Haiti were all imposed by resolutions under Chapter VII. The UN oil cutoff against Haiti overrode the asserted treaty obligations of the Europeans under the Lomé Convention where the OAS resolution could not, because members are obligated to comply with Chapter VII decisions, and obligations under the UN Charter supersede all others.[71] The use of force to enforce these boycotts both against Iraq and against the former Yugoslavia, since it was not consensual, was authorized by a separate Chapter VII resolution.

What has changed markedly in this period is the conception of "a threat to the peace, breach of the peace or act of aggression" on which, according to Article 39, the exercise of enforcement power is predicated. The first expansionary move came, as we noted, in the African cases, where the Western powers eventually accepted mandatory economic sanctions even though there was no international military conflict. In the case of Yugoslavia, when the first Chapter VII resolution imposed the arms embargo, the independence of the constituent republics had not yet been recognized, so the situation was still technically one of civil war. The resolution expresses concern at "the consequences for the countries of the region, in particular in the border areas of neighboring countries."[72] Subsequent resolutions simply reiterated this determination with little attention to the international ramifications of the hostilities.[73] In Somalia, the linkage to international peace and security in its original meaning was still more remote. The first resolution notes the consequences of the deteriorating situation and the loss of human life "on the stability and peace of the region,"[74] but the subsequent determinations of a threat to international peace and security are unsupported by any references to the international situation. The Security Council's effort to contain the precedential effect by emphasizing "the unique character" of the situation failed when it resorted to the same formula to authorize sanctions against Haiti.[75]

The UN framers and their immediate successors held a common-speech conception of a threat to international peace and security as a situation in which significant interstate hostilities are in train or at least imminent. By mid-1993, the words had become little more than a necessary incantation to transmute a Security Council resolution into a formally binding obligation. Where in 1945, action under Chapter VII was regarded as the Jovian thunderbolt of the international system, fifty years later it seemed to be only one among many instruments at the disposal of the Security Council. It was simply a specialized tool, to be called on when agreement could not be negotiated for a particular action and there was the political will to impose it. In the immediate post–cold war period, these developments were welcomed as evidence that the Security Council would be able to address new crises as they arose. Since then it has become evident that the mere recitation of the legal formula—"threat to international peace and security"—is not enough by itself to mobilize support for enforcement action in either domestic or international forums.

The Implementation of the Cease-Fire in Iraq

To enforce its will in the aftermath of the Gulf War, the Security Council had unusual advantages. Iraq had been defeated in a war waged under UN auspices, and international economic sanctions were already in place. At the same time, however, Saddam Hussein was stubbornly determined to resist, and although the Security Council consensus was strong, it was not unshakable. Hussein was able to exploit members' increasing concern over the hardships being imposed on the civilian population. What followed was a struggle of wits and wills between the UN and Saddam Hussein.[76]

Resolution 687, the cease-fire resolution adopted on April 3, 1991, provided for the elimination of Iraq's nuclear, chemical, and biological weapons and ballistic missiles, and for the destruction of the facilities for their manufacture.[77] Thomas Pickering, the U.S. Ambassador to the UN, said that the provisions for the inspection and monitoring of the destruction of Iraq's weapons and manufacturing facilities were "the strongest, most extensive verification procedures and the most effective enforcement provisions in the history of arms control."[78] The economic sanctions imposed at the time of the invasion were to remain in place, subject to periodic review in light of Iraq's compliance with the other terms of Resolution 687. It was a harsh peace imposed on a vanquished country.

In accordance with the resolution, a UN Special Commission (UNSCOM) was created to perform the inspection and elimination of Iraq's weapons of mass destruction—with the assistance of the International Atomic Energy Agency (IAEA) for nuclear weapons. From the outset, Hussein sought to obstruct UNSCOM, challenging its authority by a variety of means, including twice detaining inspection teams during the performance of their duties. One team spent forty-eight hours in a parking lot, surrounded, while their fate and that of the incriminating documents they had discovered was debated in New York. Yet in each confrontation, Hussein blinked. Despite the many efforts to thwart the UN, it now seems probable that any significant Iraqi capacity in nuclear, chemical, and biological weapons and in ballistic missiles will be eliminated, as required by the Security Council resolutions.[79]

A second major issue was Iraqi treatment of the Kurdish minority in the north of the country and the Shiites, another dissident group, in the south. After the end of the fighting, Saddam Hussein regrouped the remains of his army for a savage campaign to repress revolts that had broken out among these groups. A large proportion of the Kurdish population fled northward toward their kinsmen, across the Turkish and Iranian borders. An estimated

750,000 crossed into Iran and 250,000 into Turkey,[80] but those two countries were not prepared to admit all who clamored to get in. The Kurds—many of them women and children—were trapped, in winter, in the mountainous border regions, some in makeshift camps but many clinging to the bare mountain passes. The images shown on television could not be ignored in New York or in Western capitals.

The Kurdish question was a good deal more troublesome for the Security Council than the cease-fire was. United Nations members, in particular China and the Soviet Union, were sensitive about interfering with a country's treatment of its own population, which seemed close to the core of the traditional concept of "domestic jurisdiction," in which, according to Article 2(7) of the Charter, the UN is not to interfere. Accordingly, the Security Council's response was more circumspect than it was on issues like weapons of mass destruction or reparations. Resolution 688, adopted two days after the cease-fire, limited itself to condemning the repression of the Kurds, demanding that it be stopped immediately, and insisting that Iraq allow immediate access by international humanitarian organizations.[81]

Citing this resolution as their authority, U.S., British, and French forces moved into northern Iraq to protect refugee camps that had been established by the International Red Cross and other private agencies and to persuade the refugees to come down from the mountains.[82] The show of force was enough to induce Iraq to agree to the establishment of humanitarian centers (UNHUCS) staffed by UN personnel, and ultimately led to a Memorandum of Understanding providing for the deployment of a United Nations Guard Contingent of 500 troops,[83] at which point the coalition forces withdrew from the Kurdish areas.

Later, presumably acting under the terms of the cease-fire agreement, the allies established no-fly zones in both northern and southern Iraq, monitored by U.S. and other NATO-member planes flying from Turkish and seaborne bases. Under this cover, and by dint of fitful negotiations with Baghdad, the Kurds were able to maintain a semi-autonomous area to the north of the 36th parallel.[84]

The Security Council had two principal cards to play in the two intertwined games of compliance with weapons reductions and refugee protection. The first was economic sanctions.[85] True, the Iraqi regime was able to survive the sanctions and even to rebuild a good deal of the infrastructure that had been destroyed in the war. But the sanctions imposed severe hardship, particularly on the poorer parts of the population, a fact that Hussein exploited for the international TV audience while doing little to mitigate it.

More important from Hussein's perspective, the sanctions severely limited the reconstitution of Iraq's military power. Iraq thus had strong incentives to want the sanctions lifted. The basic UN position was that an affirmative act of the Security Council, subject to the veto, was required to bring them to an end. Although there was some sentiment in the council for modifying the sanctions, particularly in light of reports of the hardships on Iraqi children, the United States, Britain, and France were able to insist that nothing short of full compliance with the cease-fire terms would warrant relief. Periodic reviews by the Sanctions Committee ended with a brief report by the council president that "there was no agreement in the Security Council that the necessary conditions existed for a modification of the sanctions."[86]

The second card was the implicit threat of military action in case of persistent refusal by Iraq to cooperate with UNSCOM, or of other egregious violations of the cease-fire resolution. Although the matter was not much discussed, the United States acted on the premise that the existing resolutions authorized military action to enforce them. Vague threats, often unattributed, issued from Washington in response to cases of Iraqi intransigence. Until close to the end of the Bush administration, this minuet repeatedly induced Iraq to stand down.

In the last months of President Bush's tenure, a complex intermixture of disputes came to a head simultaneously. The Iraqi army undertook a repressive campaign against the Shiites in the southern marshes; Iraq tried to force the UN inspection teams to travel to Baghdad on the Jordanian airline from Amman rather than in their own aircraft; Iraqi troops moved south of the newly demarcated border, claiming to be removing installations in accordance with UN instructions; and Iraqi radar locked on to U.S. planes patrolling the southern no-fly zone, and later attacked U.S. planes with anti-aircraft fire. The tried-and-true pattern of threats from New York and Washington failed to achieve results. Without further UN authorization, U.S. planes bombed the offending radar sites and several industrial targets inside Iraq. Despite misgivings in the Western press and protest from Islamic countries, Iraq's intransigence melted away—only to reappear early in the Clinton administration, when a U.S. aircraft on patrol returned the fire of an anti-aircraft battery.

As the verification phase of the UNSCOM effort continued, Iraq again refused to comply with UNSCOM inspection procedures. After considerable arm wrestling, the Clinton administration ordered the most impressive military action against Iraq since the end of the Gulf War—a cruise missile raid on the Iraqi intelligence headquarters in Baghdad (purportedly in punishment for Iraqi complicity in an attempt to assassinate former president Bush). Despite loud Iraqi protests, at that point Rolfe Eckeus, the head of UNSCOM, visited Iraq and worked out a mutually satisfactory agreement.[87] In mid-1995, UNSCOM announced that Iraq had substantially complied with the inspection requirements of the cease-fire resolution, and the terms of the continuing monitoring arrangements were under negotiation. Economic sanctions continued in force, although France joined Russia and China in efforts to modify them.[88]

Participants in the UN Special Committee unanimously acknowledge that the continuing economic sanctions, backed up periodically by military threats or limited actions, were indispensable to realizing the agreed goal of gaining access to Iraq's nuclear, chemical, and biological weapons programs and preventing Iraq from reestablishing itself as the major military power in the region. But the sanctions were not as effective as the Security Council had hoped. Although they took a heavy economic toll, they worked slowly, and the main impact was on the poor and the weak, which tested the will of the Security Council almost as much as that of Iraq. They had to be backed up by swifter and more decisive, if limited, military action. Even so, they did not prevent continued resistance to UNSCOM, the suppression of the Shiites in the south, or the harassment of the Kurds in the north. And they did not shake the regime of Saddam Hussein. Maintaining the coalition was also an increasing problem. Britain remained firm, but Russia and China, joined by France in early 1995, displayed growing skepticism about further intervention, and the U.S. air attacks, though largely symbolic, put a serious strain on the Security Council's cohesion.

The Former Yugoslavia

The savagery of the violence in the former Yugoslavia, the "ethnic cleansing" with its echoes of genocide, the systematic violation of the rights of non-combatants, and the urgent humanitarian needs in the context of the dissolution of the state have put unprecedented pressures on all of the regional and international organizations operating in the area. The Bosnian war especially has put the UN to its severest test to date. The organization has responded with a wide range of measures, but a resolution to the conflict has remained elusive. The chief lesson, in the context of this book, is the difficulty of assembling and maintaining a coalition capable of and willing to apply forceful economic and military sanctions when the costs and risks of intervention are high, the results are uncertain, and the impetus of American or other great-power leadership is lacking.

As the cold war came to an end, so did Yugoslavia. Until Marshal Tito's death in 1980, it had existed as a federation of six republics: Serbia, Croatia, Slovenia, Bosnia-Herzegovina, Macedonia, and Montenegro. Thereafter the republics persisted as a loose federation, held together in large part by the cold war. The external pressures evaporated with the collapse of the Soviet empire in Eastern Europe and later of the Soviet Union itself, and long-suppressed nationalisms erupted in the constituent republics of Yugoslavia. The conflicts soon turned into wars of ferocious savagery: looting, burning, rape, wanton attacks on civilian populations. By mid-1993, it was said that 150,000 to 200,000 people had been killed, most of them civilians. The UN high commissioner for refugees (UNHCR) estimated that there were three million refugees within the borders of Yugoslavia.[89] Half a million flooded into Germany. No side, apparently, had a monopoly on barbarism, but it is generally acknowledged that most of the atrocities were the work of the Serbian faction.

In broad outline, the Serbians, who were the dominant group in what soon became the former Yugoslavia, sought to control directly or through local militias the areas of substantial Serbian population in Croatia and Bosnia, while those states struggled to vindicate their independence.

Trouble began when Croatia declared independence on June 25, 1991.[90] Croatians are Roman Catholic and Central European in cultural orientation. But Croatia abuts Serbia on the east, and more than 12 percent of its people are Serbs. The Croatian Serbs took up arms and, with the backing of the federal army stationed in Croatia, occupied almost a third of the country during July and August. The efforts of regional organizations—primarily the European Community and the Conference on Security and Co operation in Europe (CSCE), but with warning noises from NATO and the Western European Union (WEU) proved unable to end the fighting. At first the UN resisted involvement in what was initially characterized as "low-intensity regional conflicts."[91] But in late September, at the urging of France and Austria, the Security Council invoked Chapter VII to impose "a general and complete embargo on all deliveries of weapons and military equipment to Yugoslavia."[92] The arms embargo did not reduce the tensions, and it has been argued that its main effect was, later, to cripple the efforts of the Bosnian government to defend the country against the rebel Serbs.

In November Cyrus Vance, as the UN secretary general's personal envoy, negotiated a cease-fire between Croatia and the Serbian faction with an agreement for a UN peacekeeping force. The Security Council, acting under Chapter VI on "the request of the Government of Yugoslavia for a peacekeeping operation," authorized the establishment of a UN Protective Force (UNPROFOR I) of 10,000 to 12,000 troops.[93] In the field, UNPROFOR I operated under very restrictive rules of engagement. Although it was authorized to use weapons in self-defense, it was reluctant to confront, thus setting a restrictive precedent for future operations. Ultimately the cease-fire ripened into an agreement for the complete withdrawal of the Yugoslav army from Croatia, the establishment of a demilitarized zone, and the removal of heavy weapons from neighboring areas of Croatia and Montenegro. The UN force was charged with monitoring the agreed arrangements.[94] The fighting in Croatia began to wind down, but the Serbs maintained substantially independent jurisdiction in their area of Krajina. There were subsequent outbreaks in which the heavy weapons reappeared, but on the whole the situation held until mid-1995, when Croatia, after demanding a withdrawal of UNPROFOR troops, renewed the war and drove the Serbs from the Krajina.

Earlier, in January 1992, under strong pressure from Germany, the EC had voted to recognize Croatia (along with Slovenia).[95] The United States followed suit in April, and the UN admitted the two states, together with Bosnia, on May 22, 1992.[96] At the time, and in retrospect, many considered the EC action a critical blunder in the effort to contain the conflict. It made it inevitable that Bosnia, too, would declare independence, which it did in February 1992, after a plebiscite boycotted by the Serbian third of the population. The Serbian response there was even more violent than in Croatia.

Bosnia, with its mixed population of Serbs, Croats, and Muslims, lies squarely between Croatia to the north and Serbia to the east, and it shares a long border with Serbia. After its declaration of independence, local Serbian militias, with help and support from regular Serbian forces, took up arms against the government. Bosnian Croats fought sometimes on one side, sometimes on the other, ultimately joining in a confederation with the Muslims. The cruelty and brutality of the Yugoslav wars seemed to reach a climax in Bosnia.

In a constantly deteriorating situation, with none of the major powers willing to make a significant military commitment, the Security Council responded with a stream of resolutions that were more palliative than decisive. The most important was a full-scale economic embargo of "the Federal Republic of Yugoslavia (Serbia and Montenegro)" imposed on May 30, 1992, covering imports, exports, financial transactions, air communications, scientific and technical cooperation, and sporting events.[97] Six months later, when it was apparent that the embargo was being widely violated, the council called on states to use all necessary measures "to halt all inward and outward shipping in order to inspect" for embargoed items.[98] The NATO alliance deployed warships in the Adriatic to carry out this mandate.[99]

As the fighting continued, large quantities of public and private humanitarian aid were dispatched, much of it destined for Bosnian Muslim towns under siege by Serbian militias. In August the Security Council authorized "all measures necessary to facilitate . . . the delivery of humanitarian assistance."[100] France, Britain, Spain, and Canada ultimately contributed a total of 7,500 troops to a new UNPROFOR II to implement this resolution. However, although UNPROFOR II was created under Chapter VII, there was no change in the earlier rules of engagement. Serbian irregulars repeatedly held up aid convoys; the vice president of Bosnia was assassinated while under French protection; by May 1995 the peacekeeping force had suffered 1,242 casualties, including 162 deaths.[101] There were many acts of courage and even heroism on the part of UN forces. The UN commander, General Morillon, personally stayed at risk in the Muslim town of Srebrenica until the Serbian siege was lifted. But unlike UNSCOM in Iraq, UNPROFOR was never able to master the situation.

In October 1992, again under the rubric of ensuring the delivery of humanitarian aid, the Security Council proclaimed a "ban on military flights in the air space of Bosnia and Herzegovina,"[102] and the following March, in the face of "blatant violations," it authorized "all necessary measures . . . to ensure compliance with the ban."[103] Russia, however, insisted that the authorization be limited to air-to-air combat and hot pursuit. Strikes at Serbian airfields from which the flights originated were precluded.[104] In February 1994 there was a further escalation when the Security Council authorized NATO to use air strikes to enforce the lifting of the siege of Sarajevo, which it had declared a UN safe haven. With a nudge from the Russians, the Bosnian Serbs withdrew their heavy weapons without testing the threat, although some time later NATO F-16s shot down four Serbian aircraft within minutes of their violating the no-fly zone. The Serbian advance continued, however, with new ethnic cleansing in Prejidor and Banja Luka and an assault on another UN safe haven at Gorazde. In April the Serbs agreed to lift the siege, and after a first-ever NATO bombing raid against Serb ground positions, partially withdrew. The same inconclusive pattern was repeated around Bihac in early 1995, with NATO planes bombing airfields in the Serbian-held portion of Croatia. Each of these actions fueled the ongoing debate among the Western allies about the appropriateness and adequacy of forceful measures. Russia grew increasingly restive and gradually moved toward its traditional position as patron of the Serbs. The prospects remained dim for unanimity among the permanent members of the Security Council in support of coercive action. In mid-1994 the major powers presented yet another map, which gave the Bosnian Serbs 49 percent of the territory and a Croatian-Muslim confederation 51 percent. Again there were dire predictions of what would befall any parties that rejected the proposal, but the Serbs did so without immediate consequences. The U.S. Congress passed legislation mandating a unilateral end to the arms embargo if the Serbs were still holding out by November 15. Although the United States ended its participation in the enforcement of the embargo in the Adriatic, the deadline passed without further action. The other major powers continued to oppose such action, and Britain and France threatened to withdraw their troops if it were taken.[105] In 1995 the U.S. Congress, under threat of veto, voted to halt the Bosnia embargo.

It is too early for a full evaluation of the role of sanctions in the international effort to deal with the collapse of Yugoslavia. The final curtain may not fall for a generation. While the economic embargo had a severe impact on the Serbian economy, it did not dissuade the Bosnian Serbs from continuing their acts of violence, nor did it encourage them to honor the numerous cease-fires or bring them to accept settlements proffered by mediators. It also failed to oust the leadership in either Bosnia or Belgrade, although in late 1994 President Slobodan Milosevic agreed to close the border between Serbia and Serb-controlled Bosnia in exchange for some easing of the sanctions. The arms embargo, in fact, tilted the advantage toward the Serbs, who had the equipment of former Yugoslav armed forces, and only by violating it could the Muslims redress the balance somewhat.[106]

Some argue that the Serbs might have been influenced by more energetic but still limited enforcement action. Whenever military intervention seemed imminent, they appeared at the bargaining table, apparently ready to accede to the latest UN demands. But when the threat receded, they reneged. Again and again the council expressly authorized the use of force in support of its own directives—to enforce the embargo, to ensure the delivery of humanitarian aid, to enforce the no-fly zone, and to protect UN-established safe havens. Yet hardly a shot was fired, even to defend UN troops and installations against direct attack. In fact the French and British troops in UNPROFOR became quasi-hostages. Their vulnerability was cited to discourage more forceful action on the few occasions when that seemed like a possibility.

It is hard to resist the temptation to cynicism. Thomas Weiss's conclusion, in a review of the UN operation in the former Yugoslavia, is that "the United Nations provided a convenient means for governments to appear to be doing something without really doing anything substantial to thwart aggression, genocide, and forced movement of people."[107] But the plain fact is that although the Security Council characterized the situation as a threat to international peace and security, none of the powers was prepared to underwrite military intervention on a scale large enough to be potentially decisive. With no direct U.S. interest and in the face of dubious practical and political prospects for success, the United States did not take the initiative to organize a major military effort, as it had in Korea and Kuwait. Nor did the Europeans, whose interests seemed more directly engaged. Meanwhile, the Chinese and Russian positions began to diverge from those of the Western states. Moral outrage and the "CNN factor" were not enough to sustain an effective coalition for coercive military action.

Somalia

Somalia was one of the unlikely theaters of the cold war. Whichever side the country was on, it received massive military assistance from its superpower patron. When the patrons lost interest, the region was awash in weapons and refugees. The dictator, General Siad Barre, bereft of his outside backing, was deposed by an alliance of clans that historically had provided the basic structure of Somali society. Then the clans turned on each other. Drought and famine worsened, and Somalia collapsed into anarchy. The statistics of suffering mounted. According to Red Cross estimates, 95 percent of Somalis were malnourished, 70 percent severely so. In September 1992, 1.5 million faced imminent starvation, and by November 300,000 had died.[108] More than 300,000 refugees had fled the country. More than two million more—altogether, a third of the population—were homeless within it. Public international assistance was ineffectual, and private efforts were inadequate.[109]

In January 1992 the Security Council passed its standard arms embargo resolution under Chapter VII.[110] It was like banning the exportation of coals to Newcastle. In April the council established a UN operation in Somalia (UNOSOM)[111] with a security force of 3,500 troops to supervise a precarious UN-brokered cease-fire among the clans and warlords. Thereafter Somalia receded again to the back burner. Gangs of armed youths looted, preyed on the aid organizations, and prevented the delivery of food to distribution centers. Only 500 of the projected 3,500-person security force, a Pakistani unit, were deployed, and they were essentially confined to their barracks at the airport. The situation continued to deteriorate.[112]

At length, in late November, President Bush offered the UN up to 30,000 U.S. troops for the purpose of ensuring the delivery of humanitarian assistance. As *The Economist* said, it was an "offer that should not be refused."[113]

On December 3, 1992, the Security Council, acting under Chapter VII, welcomed the U.S. offer (though without naming the country), and authorized the use of all necessary means "to establish a secure environment for humanitarian relief operations in Somalia."[114] Five days later the first contingents of U.S. troops arrived in Mogadishu. They moved cautiously at first, avoiding conflict with the wild and armed teenagers that constituted the bulk of the local militias and slowly fanning out into the countryside. There were casualties on both sides. But over time it seemed that, the "secure environment" was being established. A reconciliation conference in Addis Ababa among the major factions made some progress.

A crucial shift came at the end of March 1993, when the United States handed off to UNOSOM II, a force of 18,000 constituted under Chapter VII, with a mission extending beyond feeding Somalia's hungry to "peace enforcement."[115] To ensure the disarmament of the guerrilla gangs, UNOSOM II was to operate under more aggressive rules of engagement, and it was not long before those rules were tested. On June 5, twenty-three Pakistani troops on patrol were killed in what the UN said was a deliberate ambush organized by General Mohammed Farah Aidid, the leader of the largest Somali armed faction. In the fire fight, an additional fifty-four Pakistanis and three Americans were wounded, and at least fifteen Somalis were killed. It was the largest loss taken by the UN in a single incident since 1961 in the Congo. The UN responded quickly and forcefully. The Security Council, with the full support of the United States and the secretary general, passed a resolution calling for the arrest and prosecution of those responsible, and U.S. forces still in the country led a three-day aerial and ground attack on Aidid's headquarters.[116] Admiral Jonathan Howe, the chief of the UN operation, issued an arrest warrant for Aidid, backed by a $25,000 reward. The fighting in Mogadishu intensified, for the first time with open disagreements among senior UN military officers about the conduct of the operation.

The United States sent reinforcements in the form of AC-130 helicopter gunships and 400 Army Rangers, elite special-operations infantry, to intensify the hunt for Aidid and the pacification of the city. In a search-and-destroy mission on October 3, the Rangers were ambushed, leaving eighteen Americans dead and seventy-eight wounded.[117] A roar of congressional and public protest led to a panicky response by the administration. The search for Aidid was called off amid acrimonious exchanges with Boutros-Ghali, and it was announced that U.S. troops would be withdrawn from Somalia willy-nilly, before March 1994.[118] Thereafter a lightly armed UNOSOM presided over an increasingly uneasy truce until, in March 1995, the UN forces finally left, without any real settlement in sight. United States Marines were sent in to provide a rear guard for the UN withdrawal.

In Somalia, the obstacles to sanctions seen in the cases were magnified. The legal basis for Chapter VII action—a threat to international peace and security—was even more attenuated than in the Balkans. The state apparatus of Somalia had collapsed, and the UN had to deal with a welter of clan leaders and guerrilla warlords. The mission was ill-defined, and from the beginning there were sharp differences between Washington and the UN about its scope. The United States was uneasy about putting its forces under UN command (even though the commander on the ground was a retired American admiral). There was never a "grand coalition," as there was in the Gulf. Command and control arrangements were confused and to some extent improvised. The Italian contingent was redeployed to the countryside after a public squabble between the national commander and UN headquarters over strategy and tactics. The rationale for intervention became murky, and whatever common purpose there had been quickly faded before the exigencies of urban guerrilla warfare in Mogadishu.

Haiti

With a per capita income of $360, an illiteracy rate estimated at 60 to 90 percent, a ravaged and eroded land, and an unbroken history of brutal dictatorship, Haiti can claim to be the poorest and most miserable of Western Hemisphere states. Occupation by the U.S. Marines from 1915 to 1934 gave way to three decades of dictatorial rule by "Papa Doc" Duvalier and his son Jean-Claude. In 1986, with the help of the United States, Duvalier was eased out. A period of political turbulence followed, and then, in February 1990, Haiti held the first free election in its history, monitored by the OAS and the UN in combination. The winner was Jean-Bertrande Aristide, a populist priest, who, to everyone's astonishment, won an absolute majority of more than 67 percent of the vote. He remained in office just seven months. In September he was deposed by a military coup, assertedly to forestall an islandwide uprising against the tiny military and economic oligarchy. Aristide fled to the United States.

Invoking an emergency procedure that had recently been put in place for just such eventualities, the OAS met promptly and voted "to urge Member states to proceed immediately to freeze the assets of the Haitian State and to impose a trade embargo on Haiti, except for humanitarian aid."[119] The embargo never seemed to get off the ground. It was only recommendatory and in any event did not affect European countries. The Europeans contended that they were prevented by the Lomé Convention—a trade agreement between the EC and numerous developing countries, including Haiti—from cutting off ordinary trade with Haiti.[120] They continued to supply oil as well as other products. Latin American and African traders also breached the embargo. More important, the Bush administration, despite strong words in the OAS from Secretary of State Baker,[121] did not fully implement the sanctions, exempting U.S. owners of assembly plants on the island and declining to deny visas to or freeze the personal assets of the coup supporters. According to one observer, "The poor, who overwhelmingly supported Aristide, have suffered the most . . . In contrast, the embargo has merely inconvenienced the well-to-do, who largely approved the coup."[122] The UN dispatched a small human-rights observer mission to join OAS monitors on the island.

The new Clinton administration, anxious to blunt criticism of its continued refusal to admit Haitian refugees despite a campaign promise, stepped up the pace of negotiations. After the Haitian military again repudiated several tentative agreements, the United States turned to the UN. On June 16, 1993, the Security Council ordered a worldwide ban on oil shipments to Haiti, an arms embargo, and the freezing of Haitian assets abroad.[123] Brazil, with the support of other Latin American states, was able to defeat a U.S. proposal for naval enforcement of the oil cutoff. A pattern began of hopeful negotiations soon repudiated by the Haitian military. Gangs of armed thugs, with the tacit support of the police and military, roamed the streets of Port-au-Prince attacking known supporters of the democratic government. They were emboldened by the events in Mogadishu and openly taunted UN human rights observers. The mayor of Port-au-Prince was assassinated in full view of UN officials. When the United States tried to land a small party of U.S. and Canadian troops who were to train the police and military in preparation for the scheduled return of Aristide, the troops were driven off by a gang on the dock. The United States beat a humiliating retreat. From time to time, sanctions were tightened to take care of newly discovered loopholes. One after another, the deadlines for Aristide's return passed. Desultory negotiations continued, but with small prospect that they would realize UN and U.S. goals. In July 1994, in a gesture of defiance, the military government expelled all UN and OAS human rights monitors. The Security Council authorized a U.S. military intervention in July, but it was not until September that the United States decided to mount an invasion. Then, with the planes of the invasion force in the air, a last-minute mediatory effort by former president Jimmy Carter, Senator Sam Nunn, and General Colin Powell produced an agreement that the military junta would not oppose the landing or the subsequent return of President Aristide, and would leave the island shortly thereafter. The invasion scenario was converted in midcareer to a peaceful landing. This time the agreement was implemented with only minor hitches. United States troops handed off to a UN peacekeeping force with a large U.S. component in the spring of 1995,[124] and the United States supported the June 1995 Haitian national elections with financial aid and observers.

The Limits of Treaty-Based Sanctions

We recognized at the outset that the UN and OAS have the power to impose military and economic sanctions not for law enforcement purposes but in the service of collective security. It is therefore inappropriate to measure the fifty-year record against law enforcement criteria. In Korea and Kuwait the basic norm against aggressive war was flouted, but many of the episodes did not involve violations of rules of international law accepted as such at the time. And there was no pretense of a need to treat like cases alike. Neither the Security Council nor the OAS acts like a body obligated to deal systematically even with instances of aggressive use of force within its jurisdiction, let alone with violations of fundamental human rights. Any attempt to do so would soon overwhelm the political and fiscal resources of the organization.

Nevertheless, these fifty years of experience have much to teach about the possibilities of using treaty-based military or economic sanctions for treaty enforcement purposes. We draw five broad lessons.

1. *Treaty-based sanctions can be imposed only as a consequence of independent national decisions of the parties.* It seems almost necessarily true that so long as national contingents carry out international enforcement actions, decisions to commit will be taken by national governments sensitive to domestic political forces. So long as the costs of economic sanctions must ultimately be borne by states, votes to impose them and choices to abide by them will reflect a broad range of state interests and pressures, only one of which—and by no means the strongest—will be concern for enforcement of the relevant international legal rules. The foundations of international enforcement action are essentially voluntary.

Neither the UN Security Council nor the OAS has organized or deployed its own "police force." The UN Charter originally contemplated that the Security Council should be able, if it so decided, to order troops into combat under its own command and direction. Article 43 provided that states should make advance agreements with the Security Council, undertaking to make available designated troop units and facilities for this purpose. But these provisions have never been implemented. The OAS Charter grants no power to compel the use of force.[125] In every case involving the use of force to date, therefore, the organization's action was not a direction but rather an authorization to members to take arms against the offender. The question of whether or not to respond was left to the individual decisions of the member states. The ability to sustain the force in the field depended on the continued willingness of member states to supply troops and funds.

The weaknesses of voluntarism have operational effects as well. Each UN force is a separate entity that has to be newly created from the ground up. Each force is established under its own name, as if to emphasize the lack of connection among them. The units reflect different military traditions and doctrines and have no experience of working together. Although there is obviously some accumulation of experience at UN headquarters, arrangements must be worked out for each new force, covering the scope of the mission, command and control, rules of engagement, logistics, communications, status of forces, and many other operational matters. In a major operation made up of contingents from a number of powerful states, the adoption and implementation of such arrangements is a continuous source of friction and misunderstanding among the participants and between them and the UN Secretariat.

All this recalls the insight of collective action theorists that the organization of sanctions is itself a collective action problem. The familiar obstacles to cooperative action, free riders and holdouts, operate equally against the establishment and maintenance of a sanctions regime. On this analysis, it is no easier to get the parties to comply with sanctions than with the substantive treaty norm itself.[126]

2. *The broad consensus necessary for the legitimacy of sanctions is extraordinarily difficult to assemble and maintain.* At a minimum, since action under the treaty must be taken by vote in a treaty organ, a political coalition will have to be assembled. Beyond that, for effective sanctioning action, certainly in the economic sphere, widespread cooperation will be necessary. But consensus is necessary for a more fundamental reason. Broad support is a safeguard to ensure that the action is not simply the imposition of the will of the stronger. It establishes the legitimacy of the enterprise.

In Korea, Cuba, and Kuwait, where the egregious character of the aggression alarmed and offended a broad spectrum of states and could be seen as an immediate threat to their vital security interests, it was possible to mobilize broad agreement for action. Even then, however, the depth and durability of the consensus left something to be desired. Although the United States was able to muster a General Assembly majority in support of General Mac-Arthur's decision to recross the 38th parallel, the action was widely criticized and fostered a deepening divergence of aims and policies between the United States and much of the developing world, led by India. Few states stood staunchly with the United States in the endgame. In the Cuba case, Brazil and Mexico abstained on the critical paragraph of the quarantine resolution, because they thought it was a blank check for further military action. And although NATO leaders provided gratifying expressions of support, they had little stomach for an invasion if, as many believed, it should prove necessary to force the withdrawal of the Soviet missiles. In the Gulf, Russian commitment was less than wholehearted, and it is not clear how the coalition, to say nothing of U.S. public opinion, would have withstood an extended war. In the aftermath, Arab states and others have increasingly pressed for relieving Iraq of the burden of economic sanctions.

For economic sanctions against South Africa and Rhodesia, in the absence of Western initiative and a perceived security threat, it took years, even decades, to achieve nominal consensus in the Security Council. And although the Security Council was willing to characterize the situations in Bosnia, Somalia, and Haiti as a threat to international peace and security, the overriding fact in the travails of the UN since Kuwait has been the inability of the members—in the face of widespread violence, repudiation of agreements, wanton violations of human rights, and horrific suffering—to achieve a consensus for coercive military action.

In short consensus, though necessary, is maddeningly elusive.

3. *Economic sanctions may be easier to adopt than military action, but it is harder to make them effective.* In the first place, economic measures are excruciatingly slow to operate. The end of apartheid in South Africa took place three decades after the beginning of the sanctions campaign. Iraq seems to be a classic case for an effective economic boycott—dependence on imports for major consumption and industrial needs, few and remote land borders, a single major export that can be easily monitored. Yet although there is no doubt that the embargo contributed to the success of UNSCOM, Saddam Hussein remains in place four years later, and his repression of the Kurds and the Shiites has continued unabated. Serbia, too, has suffered from the economic sanctions against it, but the war has gone on for two years since they were imposed. And the Haitian military showed extended resilience to economic measures, although, again, the island seemed a classic target for sanctions.

In military enforcement action, if a few powerful states are prepared to shoulder the burden, effective force may perhaps be brought to bear without universal participation, at least against a smaller state. But for economic sanctions, the holdout problem is severe. Even if the major trading partners of the target state are prepared to cut their ties, leakages elsewhere can defeat the regime. The defection of Portugal and South Africa undermined the sanctions on Rhodesia. Romania's relatively open border thwarted the embargo of Serbia and Montenegro. The absence of the Europeans made a mockery of OAS sanctions against Haiti.

Even in nominally complying countries, possibilities and incentives for evasion are great.[127] The Bush administration provided U.S. businesses with generous exemptions from the economic embargo against Haiti. Congress insisted on buying embargoed chrome from Rhodesia. The resistance of European customers prevented a cutoff of Libyan oil exports. Moreover, the burden of economic sanctions often falls most heavily on countries less able to bear them. Jordan has sustained trade losses in the billions of dollars as a result of the sanctions against Iraq, and the frontline African states had to bear the brunt of the sanctions effort against South Africa. Article 50 of the UN Charter provides that states "with special economic problems arising from the carrying out of [enforcement] measures shall have the right to consult the Security Council with regard to the solution of those problems." But the consultations have rarely proved productive.

Finally, as we have said, the costs to the target state of comprehensive economic sanctions are invariably paid by the poorest and most vulnerable, those least likely to have been responsible for the offensive conduct. This in turn feeds pressures for relaxation of the sanctions.

4. *As a practical matter, under present conditions, the active participation and even leadership of the United States is a necessary requirement for treaty-based sanctions.* In Korea, Cuba, and the Gulf, the necessary if not quite sufficient condition for military enforcement action was the leadership and unwavering commitment of the United States. It was the only state that could project decisive military power in the amounts and over the distances required. Its commitment was overwhelming, and its political will was evident. Where the United States has been unwilling to make such a commitment, authorization for coercive sanctions has not been forthcoming. Although the French intervention in Rwanda was not formally a Chapter VII action, it had many of the characteristics of the successful U.S. operations: a strong commitment by a capable military power, pursuing basic national interests within its sphere of influence.[128]

Again, the requirement of committed U.S. participation is even stronger for economic sanctions. Although it may be that relative U.S. economic power is declining, its markets and financial facilities are still the largest in the world. There is no prospect of a successful economic embargo if access to them remains open. Even technical exceptions to U.S. economic controls, as was the case for a considerable period in Haiti, can decisively prejudice the effect of the cooperative effort.

True, the newly freed African colonies were able ultimately to force the Security Council to endorse economic sanctions over the opposition of the United States and its allies. But the sanctions against South Africa were limited in scope, and those against Rhodesia were undermined in practice by the defection of major powers, including the United States. The principal impact was symbolic.

5. *Sanctions are a one-way street.* What is true of the United States applies in some degree to other major powers. If sanctions, particularly economic sanctions, are to be effective, the major powers must be involved to some extent. Thus sanctions are mostly imposed by bigger states against smaller ones, richer against poorer. This follows both from the voting rules in the Security Council, where the major powers can protect themselves with the veto, and from the practicalities of the distribution of military and economic power. The professions of equality before the law in domestic legal systems must be accepted with some qualifications; nevertheless, wealthy and influential criminals do sometimes go to jail. In the international context, however, it is unlikely that the United States would ever face sanctions for its invasion of Panama, or Great Britain for its violations of human rights in Northern Ireland—much less for smaller treaty violations. For the exigency of a threat to international peace and security, the UN and the OAS had no alternative to vesting enforcement authority in the great powers. Nevertheless it seems equally unlikely that the generality of states will be prepared to establish one-way sanctioning authority, necessarily dominated by the powerful few, to enforce ordinary treaty obligations.

We derive these lessons from situations in which the UN Security Council was called upon to deal with threats to the peace, however broadly defined. But the lessons are not confined to such situations. They are inherent characteristics of the international system. If anything, they have even greater impact when the high stakes and the unifying and galvanizing features of a threat to the peace are absent. Coercive sanctions are more infeasible for everyday treaty enforcement than as a response to crisis. Treaties with teeth are a will-o'-the-wisp.

3

Membership Sanctions

Unlike enforcement action under the UN and OAS Charters, membership sanctions are explicitly designed to police compliance of states with the obligations of membership in an international organization. Thus there is textual warrant for using them for treaty enforcement purposes. In addition, they can be imposed by a simple vote (though usually by a special majority), and they are a good deal less onerous than military action or an economic embargo, both for the target and the sanctioners. As Professor Louis Sohn points out, "The concept of expulsion prove[s] in practice to be an elastic one . . . A member state may be excluded from some, but not all activities of an organization; it may be invited to withdraw, . . . [V]arious steps unpleasant to a member state may be taken to make clear to it that it is no longer welcome."[1]

For these reasons, it might be supposed that membership sanctions would be an attractive and frequently used method of enforcing treaty obligations, less severe but still meaningful, given the increasing prominence of international organizations in international affairs. Yet a review of the experience with treaty provisions for expulsion or suspension from membership reveals a picture much like that of the military and economic sanctions discussed in Chapter 2. Even this milder, more flexible form of punishment is infrequently employed. When membership sanctions are invoked, it is generally as a political response to issues arising primarily outside the organization, rather than as a method of enforcing compliance with the norms of the basic treaty. They have been used to isolate nations and exclude them from the international community, as in the case of South Africa. But the risk of politicizing the international organization has been high in such cases, and the diversion from the work of the regime palpable. Even as the "new sovereignty" raises the costs to a nation of expulsion, the need to include all relevant states for the regime to function limits the utility of membership sanctions. In addition, the potential adverse impact on the ability of the regime to function, reducing benefits for all members, creates a special inhibition against the use of membership sanctions. Likewise there are few instances of withdrawal by nations in order to "sanction" the regime, or even to sound a battle cry in a broader political game. This parallel experience also suggests the strong pull toward regime maintenance and inclusiveness.

The United Nations Charter provides for both expulsion and suspension.[2] No nation has ever been expelled. Article 5 provides that "a Member of the United Nations against which preventive or enforcement action has been taken by the Security Council may be suspended from the rights and privileges of membership." However, it was not invoked against South Africa, Iraq, Yugoslavia, or Haiti when they were targets of Chapter VII sanctions.[3] A number of treaties have similar provisions for expulsion or suspension.[4] They are seen most often in the charters of UN agencies, but even there, often they were added by amendment as in the controversy over expulsion of South Africa, discussed below. The treaty members have applied them, or sought to apply them, in only a handful of cases.

During the cold war, membership sanctions were part of the arsenal of negative diplomacy. Membership issues became one more battleground on which the superpowers contended for power and influence. Although the diplomatic message may have been clear, the controversies over membership did not appreciably change the political behavior of either bloc and certainly did not serve to enhance compliance with the applicable treaties. Moreover, disputes about membership necessarily imposed costs in terms of regime performance, exacerbating the dampening effect of the superpower rivalry on the development of any form of international cooperation. Though there was much diplomatic sound and fury, membership sanctions turned out to be a relatively ineffective weapon of the cold war.

Outside the cold war context, the growing international concern about the human devastation caused by South African apartheid was the major impetus for the application of membership sanctions in UN organizations. As with economic sanctions, the initiative came from the newly independent African states, as part of their general effort to isolate South Africa from the international community. Again the United States and its allies objected, citing the importance of universal membership if the organizations were to perform their intended functions, and the technical rather than political character of the organizations.[5] The political importance of the remaining colonial powers (especially Portugal) to the Western alliance was a powerful but unstated consideration. Again, in the end the Western states were forced to acquiesce.

In many of these cases, South Africa technically withdrew, but these were anticipatory withdrawals, under such pressure and attack that for all practical purposes they can be considered expulsions. Later in this chapter we will briefly discuss the major cases in which nations used withdrawal to express their displeasure with a treaty regime or as a broader instrument of international politics, because these cases shed light on the difficulty involved in imposing any kind of membership sanction.[6]

As with enforcement action, although the membership sanction cases are few, they can usefully be sorted into groupings for comparison. First, as a unique case, we consider the decade-long effort to exclude South Africa from the UN system; next, the use of membership sanctions as a weapon in the cold war; and finally, a group of cases in which withdrawal has been used in an effort to influence regime performance.

Membership Sanctions against South Africa: The Making of a Pariah

The gradual isolation of South Africa from the UN and its agencies went hand in hand with the drive for economic sanctions described in Chapter 2. Both reflected the increasingly harsh international condemnation of apartheid. Both began with the March 1960 Sharpeville massacre, in which sixty-seven unarmed blacks in a protest march were killed by the South African police. The establishment of the Organization of African Unity (OAU) in 1963[7] gave cohesion and direction to the African bloc in the UN. In October 1963 the movement gained fresh impetus when South Africa banned the African National Congress (ANC) and the Pan-Africa Freedom Movement of East and Central Africa Committee (PAC) and launched a series of treason trials against African leaders, leading ultimately to the imprisonment of Nelson Mandela and other leaders of the ANC. These events helped to put and keep the human rights and political dimensions of apartheid high on the UN agenda.

The overriding objective of the African states, assisted by the already organized Asian-African caucus, was to end apartheid and white rule in South Africa. The method was to be mandatory economic sanctions combined with ostracism in UN agencies and, finally, expulsion from the UN itself. In the early 1960s, the campaign moved forward on all three fronts simultaneously. As noted in Chapter 2, the drive for economic sanctions achieved only limited success. Not until the Soweto uprising in 1976 did the Security Council exercise Article 41 authority, and then it was only to impose an arms embargo.[8] By that time the application of membership sanctions was well advanced.

The attempt to unseat South Africa at the UN itself, where the claims of universality were strongest, was initially beaten back by Western states.[9] But beginning in 1963, membership sanctions were imposed on South Africa in an impressive and growing list of specialized agencies: the International Labor Organization (ILO), the International Telecommunication Union (ITU), the World Health Organization (WHO), the Food and Agriculture Organization (FAO), the UN Economic and Social Council (ECOSOC), the UN Educational, Scientific, and Cultural Organization (UNESCO), the UN Economic Commission for Africa (ECA), the United Postal Union (UPU), the International Civil Aviation Organization (ICAO), the International Atomic Energy Agency (IAEA), and the World Meteorological Organization (WMO).

Among these organizations were the oldest and most "technical" of the UN specialized agencies and thus presumably the most insulated from political controversy. Yet the arguments (made mostly by Western states) for universality and the exclusion of political matters not relevant to the function of the organization were regularly overridden. Likewise rejected was the contention that it would be better to keep South Africa within the fold, to maintain pressure in as many forums as possible for change in its policies. The African states turned these arguments upside down with mass walkouts and implicit threats of their own withdrawal. These actions were combined with skillful parliamentary maneuver in a coordinated campaign that generated irresistible pressure within the organizations. Often the effect was strong enough to make South Africa withdraw preemptively in the face of a clear prospect of expulsion. One way or another, the cumulative impact was dramatic.

The ILO. The tone of the membership battles for many of the UN agencies was set by this most established international organization, with its history going back to 1921. In 1961 the General International Labor Conference had passed a resolution condemning "the racial policies of the Government of the Republic of South Africa" as "inconsistent with the aims and purposes of the Organization."[10] Since there was no provision in the ILO charter for expulsion of a member, the resolution "advised" South Africa to withdraw until it reformed. South Africa rejected the action as "devoid of any constitutional basis."[11]

In 1963 Joseph L. Johnson, Nigeria's minister of labor, was president of the ILO General Conference. When a move to prevent the South African delegate from speaking failed, Johnson resigned as chairman, and thirty-two African states walked out of the session.[12] As a result, the question of a charter amendment to provide for expulsion was placed on the agenda for the 1964 conference.[13] At that point, South Africa withdrew, citing "hostile acts" of the ILO, including the refusal to seat some of its worker delegates, its exclusion from a number of committees, "interference in its domestic affairs," and the preparation of the expulsion amendment itself.[14]

The ITU. The ITU was the arena for an almost identical imbroglio. In 1964, the African Conference of the organization met in Geneva because no African state would give a visa to the South African delegate. The conference promptly voted to expel the South African representative. He refused to leave, and the African states walked out of the conference. Western delegations followed, and then the secretariat.[15] The next year, South Africa was excluded from the Plenipotentiary Conference, which also voted not to invite it to any African regional meetings.[16] South Africa left the conference, and though it continued to adhere to ITU conventions, it also continued to be excluded from conferences and regional activities.[17]

The WHO. Like the ITU, the WHO transferred its 1963 African regional conference, from Dakar to Geneva, when the government of Senegal refused to give visas to the South African delegation.[18] African countries boycotted the Geneva meeting.[19] At the World Health Assembly in 1964, they were successful in pushing through a resolution suspending South Africa's voting privileges, whereupon South Africa withdrew.[20] In his annual report, the director general bemoaned this "hazardous incursion into the non-medical areas," and warned of "the perils of playing at politics, for which we have neither the training nor aptitude nor experience."[21] Nevertheless, the following year the assembly adopted an amendment to the WHO constitution providing for expulsion of a member that "deliberately practic[es] a policy of racial discrimination."[22] In 1966 South Africa refused to pay its assessed contribution, and the organization ended all services to it.[23]

The FAO. The FAO's 1963 conference rejected a proposal for a constitutional amendment to permit exclusion of a member from the organization.[24] The African states had to settle for a resolution that the FAO would not invite South Africa "to participate in any capacity in FAO conferences, meetings, training centers, or other activities in the African region."[25] The action was made more pointed by the organization's refusal to reassign South Africa to any other region. South Africa then notified the director general that it was withdrawing from the organization.[26]

UNESCO. As early as 1955, South Africa had withdrawn from UNESCO to protest its "interference in South Africa's racial problems" through its publications. At that time, the organization denied the accusation and appealed to South Africa to reconsider its decision.[27] But in 1963, UNESCO refused to invite South Africa to its International Conference on Education, and in 1968 it decided to withhold all assistance from the governments of South Africa, Portugal, and Rhodesia, and not to invite them to participate in its activities.[28]

The ECA. The first expulsion resolution in the Economic Commission for Africa came in 1962 and was beaten back by Western states in the UN Economic and Social Council, which controlled the membership in the regional UN economic commissions.[29] The next year, the ECA resolved that "all African states members of the Commission [should] take into consideration the policies of South Africa when granting visas or entry permits for the purpose of enabling [representatives] to participate in the conferences or meetings of the Commission or of the specialized agencies."[30] South Africa then "decided not to attend any ECA conferences in the future nor to participate in the other activities of the Commission while the hostile attitude of the African States toward South Africa persists."[31] Nevertheless, the African states continued to press for formal expulsion, and in 1963, ECOSOC capitulated and excluded South Africa from participation in the work of the ECA until "conditions for constructive cooperation have been restored by a change in its racial policy."[32]

UPU, ICAO, and IAEA. These three agencies posed special problems, since the considerations favoring universal membership in them are especially strong. In 1964, in response to threats by Kenya, Tanzania, and Uganda to boycott the African regional organization of UPU, the UPU Congress passed a resolution expelling South Africa from the organization, despite the absence of any provision for expulsion in its charter. The South African delegate refused to leave the session until expressly told to do so by the president.[33] Thereafter South Africa did not attend UPU congresses and other meetings, although it remained a party to the international postal conventions.[34] In 1979 the congress formally expelled it.[35]

The International Civil Aviation Organization, in which African states held only six out of twenty-five seats on the council, refused to recognize UN General Assembly Resolution 1761 calling on states to deny landing rights to

South African airlines.[36] The 1965 ICAO General Conference rejected a proposed amendment to the charter to permit expulsion of South Africa.[37] Not until 1971 was South Africa excluded from regional and local conferences of the organization.[38] In 1974, after falling two years in arrears in its assessed contributions, South Africa lost its voting rights.[39]

The IAEA was the most problematic of all for membership sanctions, because it imposed constraints on the development of nuclear weapons. It is an example of how an obvious dilemma can act as an important restraint on the use of membership sanctions: if a member is excluded from a regulatory regime, it faces international embarrassment but is free to act without legal constraint in that field, to the detriment of other parties. But if not, it remains in good standing while continuing to flout the regime. The Africans themselves, in this case, were concerned to retain whatever limitations membership might impose on South Africa's nuclear programs. Nevertheless, in 1964 South Africa was not permitted to represent the African region on the agency's Board of Governors.[40] The IAEA finally removed the South African member from the Board of Governors in 1977, and in 1979 South Africa was barred from participation in the agency's General Conference.[41]

The WMO. In an echo of the hectic days of the 1960s, the WMO fell into line when in 1975 it "suspended [South Africa] from exercising its rights and enjoying its privileges as a Member of the World Meteorological Organization until it renounces its policy of racial discrimination and abides by the UN (Security Council) Resolution regarding Namibia."[42]

In 1974, the credentials committee of the UN General Assembly rejected South Africa's credentials, "and for the first time in UN history, a member state was suspended from participation in the General Assembly session."[43] South Africa was for most purposes no longer a participant in the United Nations system. It was banished from the General Assembly and the major specialized agencies. It was excluded from the public forums of international diplomacy. Social sanctions on a multilateral level were effectively complete.

There can be no confident estimate of the impact these sanctions had over a thirty-year period. Cumulatively, they certainly went a long way toward the goal of making South Africa a pariah state. In the eyes of some observers, this isolation helped to create a climate for political change, leading in 1991 to the multiparty negotiations, to a period of transition, and to elections in 1994.[44] Others feel it slowed change by permitting Afrikaaners to consolidate political power, strengthen their economic hold, and further entrench apartheid.[45] In any case, membership sanctions in the UN were only one piece of the mosaic. To some extent, the efforts diverted energies from the main business of the organizations, generating dissatisfaction among some secretariats and Western members. Since the developing countries are the principal clientele of the agencies, however, the objectors had no choice but to accede to their demands.

In terms of actually achieving the expulsion of a state from the organization, the efforts of the African states against South Africa represent the most successful use of membership sanctions on record. The experience, however, is not one from which generalizations can be easily made. It reflects the almost universal condemnation of apartheid, which is not likely to be repeated often. More to the point here, whatever success they had in achieving political objectives in South Africa, the sanctions were not directed toward enhancing compliance with treaty obligations.

Withdrawals and Membership Sanctions as Cold War Weapons

The Chinese Representation Issue

In the early years of the cold war, the Soviet Union used withdrawal as a weapon in its campaign to expel Nationalist China from the UN and to replace it with the representatives of the People's Republic of China (PRC) in the UN itself and in its specialized agencies. Although this case involves withdrawal rather than expulsion, like the others discussed in this section, it demonstrates an effort to manipulate organizational membership as an aspect of the broader pattern of cold war behavior rather than out of concern for the regime in which the drama was played out. Perhaps the most significant move in this campaign, and from the Soviet point of view, the most disastrous one, was the USSR's boycott of the Security Council in January 1950 in protest over the refusal to seat the PRC.[46] As noted in Chapter 2, the consequence was that the Soviet representative was absent when the Korean War broke out and so was unable to veto the Security Council action in response to the North Korean invasion.

A carefully orchestrated series of Soviet walkouts, both from integral UN organs and from specialized agencies, paralleled the Security Council boycott.[47] In the UN itself, representatives of the Soviet Union, Czechoslovakia, or Poland, or a combination of the three, withdrew from meetings of the UN Economic Commission for Asia and the Far East (ECAFE), the Trusteeship Council, the Economic and Social Council (including a number of its subsidiary bodies), and the International Law Commission, after decisions on Chinese credentials.[48] The Soviet representative also withdrew from the UN

Atomic Energy Commission, which was then considering plans for general nuclear disarmament.[49] The commission decided that it could not proceed, because the USSR was crucial to the performance of its mission, whereupon the General Assembly dissolved the commission in 1952. All the other UN organs, however, went ahead with their agendas in the absence of the Eastern bloc countries, just as the Security Council had done.[50] For the period from 1950 to 1952, the only subsidiary entity of the UN in which the USSR sat was the Economic Commission for Europe (ECE).

The campaign in the specialized agencies was more ragged. Quite apart from the Chinese representation issue, the Soviet Union was at first deeply ambivalent and even hostile toward the work of these bodies, on both practical political and ideological grounds.[51] At length, in 1947 and 1948, the Soviet bloc, including Albania, Bulgaria, Hungary, and Romania (not yet members of the UN)[52] joined WHO, UPU, ITU and WMO.[53] These were the most technical and least political of the specialized agencies, and presumably direct benefits were expected from them.[54] The Soviet Union itself did not join any of the other, more political agencies in the early years of the UN, but Czechoslovakia, Hungary, and Poland became members of ILO, UNESCO and FAO, mostly in 1947.[55] As to the economic institutions, although the Soviet Union had participated in the Bretton Woods negotiations and was assigned a quota in both the International Monetary Fund (IMF) and the International Bank for Reconstruction and Development, it did not ratify either of the constitutive agreements. Czechoslovakia and Poland, however, were charter members in 1947, and Czechoslovakia was an original member of the GATT. Thus stood the situation when Mao Tse-tung proclaimed the People's Republic of China on September 21, 1949, and the issue of Chinese representation in the UN began to heat up.

Soviet bloc withdrawals from WHO actually began before the campaign to seat the PRC and seem to have been triggered originally by the Soviet perception that the expected benefits had not materialized and the agency was being politicized. Beginning with the Soviet Union in February 1949, all nine Eastern bloc members severed their connections with WHO. In a letter to the director general, the deputy minister of public health of the USSR complained, "Tasks connected with the international measures for the prevention and control of diseases and with the spread of medical science achievements are not being accomplished by the Organization satisfactorily. At the same time, maintenance of the Organization's swollen administrative machinery involves expenses which are too heavy for Member States to bear."[56]

Over the next two years, the other eight members of the Soviet bloc sent substantially identical letters. Although the withdrawals were not formally linked to the PRC representation problem, Romania, Albania, Czechoslovakia, Hungary, and Poland did not deliver their letters until after the PRC's bid had been turned down in the UN and in some of the other specialized agencies.[57] In May 1950, when the issue of Chinese representation had been joined in earnest, Polish, Hungarian, and Czechoslovak delegates withdrew from the meeting of the General Conference of UNESCO after the Nationalist Chinese representative was seated.[58] A month later, the same countries walked out of the General International Labour Conference under similar circumstances.[59] The UNESCO walkouts ripened into formal withdrawals, with the charge that "UNESCO is becoming one of the instruments of the cold war" and a blast at the biased membership practices of the organization and its support of "the American war policy" in Korea.[60] The same three countries also withdrew from the FAO.[61] Along the way, Poland quit the World Bank and the IMF, charging that both bodies were controlled by the United States.

By the end of 1952, participation by Soviet bloc states in the specialized agencies had virtually ceased. Although the agencies refused to be diverted from their programs and activities, they were not unconcerned at the departures.[62] The World Health Organization did not recognize the withdrawals and treated the Eastern European nations that had withdrawn as temporarily inactive members, continuing to send meeting notices and other documentation; UNESCO continued to carry them on its membership rolls. When, within a year or two of Stalin's death, the wayward states began to return to the fold, some organizations made special arrangements to reduce the burden of the contributions that had accumulated in the interim.

The most serious reaction to the withdrawals came from the Bretton Woods institutions. They not only accepted the Polish resignation with a rather curt rejection of its charges, but soon afterward expelled Czechoslovakia, which, as the only surviving communist member of these institutions, had continued to carry the battle on Chinese representation. In November 1953, the IMF declared Czechoslovakia ineligible to use its resources because of an unauthorized change in its par value.[63] And in 1954, Czechoslovakia was expelled from the fund on the ground that it had failed to fulfill its obligations to provide economic and financial information.[64]

The Soviet withdrawal campaign of the early 1950s backfired, and the political costs to the Warsaw Pact countries were substantial. The issue became a major battleground of the early cold war, with the United States pulling out all the stops in a relentless and successful effort to defend the position of Nationalist China.[65] The result was a significant victory for the United States, at least in the short term. Although all the organizations thought universal membership was theoretically desirable, with the one exception of the UN Atomic Energy Commission, the practical work of the agencies, though disrupted, did continue. When it became apparent that the campaign would not succeed in its ostensible objective of seating the PRC, the USSR and its allies came sheepishly back to the agencies, with diminished status and influence that persisted for some time. The PRC did not arrive at the UN for another two decades.

The political costs of resistance were not trivial for the United States either. Politicization itself reduced the effectiveness of the agencies. The alarums and excursions in the battle over the seating of "Red China" diverted time and energy from the primary business of the subsidiary UN institutions and specialized agencies, all of which other members (even some who supported the United States) resented in varying degrees. When the United States sought to resist the application of membership sanctions to South Africa and, later still, to Israel, on the grounds that such actions would "politicize" the agencies, the proponents were not slow to recall who had cast the first stone.

Soviet Voting Rights in the UN General Assembly

A decade later, it was the United States that fell into a trap of its own making. The most spectacular membership sanctions episode of the cold war—and the most spectacular failure—was the U.S. effort from 1962 to 1965 to deprive the Soviet Union of its voting rights in the UN General Assembly. It highlights not only the difficulty of mounting such an effort, but also the disappointing results and the unintended consequences that can ensue.

By the beginning of the 1960s, the United Nations was almost $100 million in debt, largely as a result of expenses in connection with the peacekeeping operations in the Middle East (UNEF) and the Congo (UNOC).[66] The Soviet Union asserted that these operations were illegal under the Charter and refused to pay its share of the expenses as apportioned by the General Assembly. Article 19 of the Charter provides that "a Member of the United Nations . . . shall have no vote in the General Assembly" if it is more than two years in arrears in the payment of its financial contributions to the organization. The Kennedy administration embarked on a program to deal with the UN deficit, the primary feature of which was a bond issue to be subscribed in large part by the United States. To induce Congress to approve the program, the administration pledged to enforce Article 19 against the Soviet Union.

At the instigation of the United States, the General Assembly requested an advisory opinion from the World Court on whether the USSR was obligated to pay its share of the costs of the peacekeeping operations.[67] The court upheld the validity of the two peacekeeping actions and thus the assembly's assessment of the costs to the members.[68] In 1964, the Soviet arrearages passed the two-year mark. The United States, with the support of some reluctant allies, girded for the battle to suspend the USSR's voting rights.[69]

Even at that time, the United States could not be sure of the two-thirds majority in the General Assembly that is required on a measure like suspending the voting rights of a member.[70] So the United States took the position that because Article 19 says the delinquent "shall have no vote," the suspension of voting rights was automatic and occurred without the necessity of any further action by the General Assembly. It bolstered its position by citing some practice of UN specialized agencies with charter provisions comparable to Article 19, but the record was by no means unambiguous.[71]

There followed an extraordinary spectacle. Neither side was willing to push the issue to the final point of confrontation. It was not altogether clear which one would win if it came to a vote, and whichever won, it was thought that the consequences for the organization of rebuffing either of the two superpowers on an issue of this magnitude would be potentially disastrous. So for two years the General Assembly conducted its business without voting on any issue. It acted on all matters by consensus, announced by its president after consultation with the members.[72] This arrangement was obviously not very satisfactory, since nothing very important, not to say controversial, could be acted on under this procedure. In fact, the most significant issue decided was the annual UN budget.

At length, in the waning moments of the nineteenth session in early 1965, the Albanian delegate succeeded in forcing a vote on the validity of the consensus procedure. The assembly voted to approve the procedure, but it was at best a Pyrrhic victory. The United States took what comfort it could from maintaining that the vote had been "only" a procedural one, but there was no denying that the General Assembly, including the Soviet Union, had voted.[73] At the next session of the assembly, in Ambassador Arthur Goldberg's first appearance as U.S. representative, the United States withdrew its objection and the ordinary procedure was resumed, with the USSR voting. Ambassador Goldberg warned, however, that if the Article 19 membership sanction did not apply to the Soviet Union, the United States reserved the right to take the position that it was also inapplicable to U.S. arrearages (what was sauce for the goose....)[74] And so it did in the 1980s, when it was in arrears.

The debacle could hardly have been more complete. The United States was humiliated. Not only did the Soviet arrearages remain unpaid, but a sanction enshrined in the Charter and designed for the express purpose of enforcing this particular obligation had also been ignored. Article 19 has since become a dead letter. Moreover, until 1973 when UNEF II was deployed in the Middle East, by tacit agreement all UN peacekeeping operations were financed by voluntary contributions instead of assessments by the General Assembly.[75]

In the 1980s, UN arrearages again became a major problem, threatening the ability of the organization to carry out its functions. The United States was the most serious offender. The 1965 experience only underscored the obvious: it is not possible to threaten credibly the application of Article 19, at least against a major power. But even sensible dialogue on sterner management efforts to ensure full payment in the future seems to be cast in shadow by the UN voting rights caper.

Cuba and the Organization of American States

As might be expected, the United States deployed membership sanctions as part of its long confrontation with Cuba. Although it managed to secure the "exclusion of Cuba from participation in" the Organization of American States, the episode fell considerably short of a complete success.

The OAS Charter contains no provision for expulsion, "exclusion from participation," or indeed any other membership sanction. Nevertheless, in April 1961, the Inter-American Defense Board, an OAS organ, excluded Cuba from participating in joint defense planning on the grounds that an "evident military alliance exists between Cuba and the Soviet bloc."[76] In January 1962, ten months before the missile crisis, the United States moved to oust Cuba from the inter-American system altogether. At the Punta del Este meeting of OAS foreign ministers, it proposed a resolution "that adherence by any member of the Organization of American States to Marxism-Leninism is incompatible with the Inter-American system" and "that this incompatibility excludes the present Government of Cuba from participation in the Inter-American system."[77]

Mexico, among others, maintained that "exclusion is not juridically possible" under the charter. To meet this objection, the resolution recited that by adhering to the principles of Marxist-Leninist ideology, "the present government of Cuba has voluntarily placed itself outside the Inter-American system." Cuba had not been expelled, the argument ran. It had taken itself out of the organization by its own actions. The resolution passed with fourteen affirmative votes, barely enough for the requisite two-thirds majority.

Argentina, Bolivia, Brazil, Chile, Ecuador, and Mexico were unmoved by the U.S. argument and abstained. Cuba voted against the resolution[78] and subsequently challenged it in the UN Security Council, to no avail.[79] As of 1995, Cuba is still not participating in the work of the OAS.[80]

It was not a simple or costless matter for the United States to mount its effort to exclude Cuba from the OAS, even at the height of the cold war and in "its own backyard." Most of the most important countries in the hemisphere refused to support the United States, publicly revealing significant resistance to U.S. hemispheric leadership, and grumbling continues in the OAS at the breach in hemispheric solidarity resulting from Cuba's absence. Nor have the consequences been very satisfactory. The exclusion of Cuba from the OAS did not weaken the Cuban political system during the ensuing quarter century. It only reinforced Cuba's dependence on the Soviet Union and its loyalty as a Soviet ally. The difficulties in creating consensus for expulsion even where ideology and hegemony were at their strongest are instructive for a world in which clear lines are harder to draw and power is diffused.

Sanctions and Withdrawals Related to Performance

We have been able to find very few instances in which membership sanctions were used wholly—or even primarily—to penalize a failure to comply with the obligations of a regime. Even in the case of the former Yugoslavia, which has flouted Security Council resolutions and is widely accused of complicity in genocide, the organizational reaction has been guarded. The UN treated the issue as one of state succession. The Security Council "considered" that "the State formerly known as the Socialist Federal Republic of Yugoslavia has ceased to exist" and that the new Yugoslavia "cannot continue automatically the [UN] membership" of the old. The council therefore recommended to the General Assembly that it decide that the new Yugoslavia "should apply for membership in the United Nations and shall not participate in the work of the General Assembly."[81] On September 22, 1992, the General Assembly endorsed the council's recommendations.[82] Nevertheless, the old Yugoslav flag and nameplate remained in their accustomed places at the United Nations. The UN legal advisor characterized the situation as follows: "The resolution neither terminates nor suspends Yugoslavia's membership in the Organization . . . The resolution does not take away the right of Yugoslavia to participate in the work of the organs other than Assembly bodies."[83] At its Helsinki summit in July, the Conference on Security and Co-operation in

Europe also limited its action to "suspending" Yugoslavia's membership after accusing Yugoslavia of aggression in Bosnia and Croatia. The meeting ended with a statement entered into the record blaming "the authorities in Belgrade," the Yugoslav federal and Serbian capital, for the "violence and aggression" in Bosnia and Croatia.[84]

Membership issues involving other Eastern European countries have arisen in the Council of Europe, an organization constituted by Western European states soon after World War II as the guardian of democracy and human rights in Europe. Although it confers no tangible benefits, such as the security guarantees that NATO offers or the economic benefits of the European Union, membership in the council itself has been of importance, because it is considered to be an imprimatur of good standing in the European democratic community. The council asserts the power to suspend or expel members that violate democratic and human rights norms. But although it has condemned many of its members for violation of human rights, during the cold war period, the Committee of Ministers invoked the council's suspension mechanism only once—against the "colonels' regime" in Greece. Military rule in Turkey in the early 1980s did not evoke a similar response, despite repeated requests for such action from the Parliamentary Assembly. In the post–cold war period, with Eastern European states clamoring for admission, the Parliamentary Assembly adopted a relatively liberal admission policy, but declared that "honouring these commitments [to democracy and human rights] is a condition of the full participation of the parliamentary delegations of new member states." The implication is that failure to do so would be met by some kind of membership sanction, but it remains to be seen whether the practice will be any more severe than in the past.[85]

In the late 1970s and the 1980s, the United States was the prime actor in highly publicized withdrawals from three international organizations, the ILO, the IAEA, and UNESCO. In these three cases, the causes of the action were diverse and complex, and all are related to the growing U.S. disenchantment with the UN and the UN system, as Western dominance began to give way before the growing numbers of newly independent states. In each instance, the United States had a well-defined grievance against the performance of the organization, but a common thread was the need for a political response to attempts by the new majority of developing states to use the agencies as instruments in the campaign to ostracize and isolate Israel. The United States used withdrawal and the ensuing cutoff of major financial support to retaliate against what it regarded as objectionable conduct of the majority. In the ILO and IAEA, the United States acted with real hesitation and regret. Withdrawal was followed by something of a scramble on both sides to get back together, and in fact, the United States returned to full participation within a short time. By contrast, as of late 1995 the U.S. absence from UNESCO continues.[86]

The U.S. withdrawal in each case had an impact on the policies and behavior of the organization, primarily because of the massive reductions in budgetary contributions, an emphasis available only to the United States, by far the largest contributor to all three agencies. When it left the ILO in 1974 after the adoption of a resolution condemning Israel for human rights violations and granting the Palestine Liberation Organization (PLO) observer status, the organization's budget was reduced by 21.6 percent, leading to the discharge of 230 employees. President Carter expressed the desire of the United States "to return whenever the ILO is again true to its proper principles and procedures." For a two-year period, the ILO took no further actions against Israel, and at the same time it adopted a report critical of Czechoslovakia on the issue of discrimination, a cold war issue that had previously led to American dissatisfaction with ILO policies. This was apparently enough for the United States to rejoin the ILO, which it did in February 1980 after an absence of a little over two years.

The break with the IAEA came in the aftermath of the 1981 Israeli bombing attack on the Osirak reactor in Iraq. The United States voted for strong condemnation of the bombing in the UN Security Council, but it opposed the IAEA's move to suspend Israel. The IAEA resolution failed, but a challenge to the credentials of the Israeli delegation to the conference succeeded after contentious debate and an apparently erroneous ruling on voting procedure.[87] Although the United States had been the moving force in the creation of the IAEA and the organization has been a keystone of U.S. nonproliferation policy, it walked out of the conference and suspended financial contributions and participation in the activities of the agency. It did not formally withdraw but instead announced that it would "reassess" its overall policy toward the IAEA. Maneuvers began immediately on both sides for the resumption of full U.S. participation, which occurred when the IAEA certified (as required by the appropriations act) that Israel was legally permitted to participate fully in the organization's activities.

The U.S. withdrawal from UNESCO at the end of 1984 seems to have been based primarily on the ideological orientation of the Reagan administration toward the policies, attitudes, leadership, and agenda of the organization. The roots of the opposition, however, can be traced back to 1974, when the UNESCO General Conference condemned Israeli archeological work in the Old City of Jerusalem and criticized its education policy in the occupied territories. As in the other cases, the organization made significant changes in response to the U.S. withdrawal. However, UNESCO, which made the most fundamental reforms, was the only agency that failed to achieve reconciliation with the United States.

Because of its size and influence, the United States has obvious power to impose severe penalties on a regime by withdrawing or threatening to withdraw, but in some cases, smaller nations can also threaten the regime. The checkered life of the International Whaling Commission (IWC), which will be further explored in several chapters,[88] is an important example.

High whaling quotas in the 1950s and 1960s led to serious depletion of major whale stocks, and environmentalists began to push for a moratorium on all further commercial whaling. After a membership campaign in the decade of the 1970s, spearheaded by major environmental organizations,[89] the necessary three-fourths majority in the IWC was achieved and a moratorium was voted in 1982, to take effect after a three-year phase-in period and to last until at least 1990.[90] Norway and Japan exercised their opt-out rights with respect to the moratorium. Iceland did not, but it continued to take a significant number of minke whales (the most plentiful species)[91] under the rubric of scientific research, which is exempt from regulation under the International Convention for the Regulation of Whaling (ICRW). But under pressure from the United States, all three limited their whaling for the remainder of the decade.[92]

In 1991 the three whaling countries put forward a plan for resuming commercial whaling with worldwide management of stocks. The IWC rejected the proposal even though it was supported by the organization's Scientific Committee. At that point Iceland became convinced that the conservationist majority, acting on a moral and ethical imperative Iceland did not share, was bent on the permanent elimination of commercial whaling.[93] On December 28, 1991, Iceland's cabinet decided unanimously to withdraw from the IWC, and the following June, at the annual meeting in Glasgow, it carried out the threat. Norway followed with a decision to resume commercial whaling in disregard of the IWC moratorium, and Japan then announced that it "would not wait indefinitely" for the ban to be lifted. The three countries, together with other whaling nations, met to consider the formation of a North Atlantic Marine Mammal Commission as an alternative to the IWC.[94] These developments have left the fate of the IWC and the international whaling regime in considerable doubt.[95]

Although the ability of diplomats to patch up seemingly irreconcilable quarrels is formidable, the Icelandic withdrawal has posed a real threat to the existence of the IWC as functioning regulatory body. The organization faces a painful choice between abandoning its moratorium policy to keep Iceland and perhaps others within the fold, or releasing them altogether from regulatory obligations.[96]

Conclusion

In the context of membership sanctions, the problems of cost, political motivation, and legitimacy appear in a somewhat different guise than they do with UN military and economic measures. As Professor Robert Keohane persuasively contends, international organizations perform valuable, even essential services for their members, and the members have a strong interest in maintaining the integrity and performance of the organizations.[97] According to Keohane, often this in itself is enough to account for organizational durability. It should be no surprise, therefore, that suspension, expulsion, and withdrawal have been used only in extraordinary circumstances. If a major power or grouping of powers were to withdraw or be expelled from a treaty regime, the result would likely be a serious dilution of its effectiveness. Where universality is important to the organizational mission, as in the whaling case and perhaps increasingly in environmental agreements, the departure of a few lesser members—even one—could have an important impact on regime function that will ultimately be felt by the remaining members. The World Health Organization as well as other agencies went to some lengths to induce the Eastern bloc countries to remain as members and, when that failed, to facilitate the prodigals' return. The very effort to impose sanctions, even when it is successful, turns into a major issue, disrupts the work of the organization and generates dissatisfaction and resentment among supporters as well as opponents of the action. In other words, as with military and economic sanctions, the political costs of membership sanctions are high.

For the most part, membership sanctions have been motivated by high politics that transcend the issues of the treaty regime itself. The UN voting rights case was a major cold war event, even though it was a case—the only case—in which the sanction was invoked to secure the very performance for which it was designed—payment of assessed UN contributions. Not only did it fail to achieve that end, but the attempt also effectively destroyed the sanction itself.

In the U.S. withdrawal cases, regime performance was an important element, but the overriding issue remained fidelity to Israel, an important ally.

Only in Iceland's withdrawal from the IWC can the central issue plausibly be characterized as a question of treaty compliance. What was really at stake there was a political dispute about the content of the basic bargain among the parties. Iceland contended that a treaty originally designed to make possible "the orderly development of the whaling industry"[98] had been improperly converted into a regime designed to prevent the killing of whales.

As the outcome of the UN voting rights case indicates, membership sanctions, like others, cannot generally be levied against a major power. As members of organizations, the major powers have all their usual advantages, one of which is that it is not prudent to offend them. In addition, their situation is such that expulsion may seriously impair if not destroy the sanctioning regime. Universal membership within an agency's sphere of action is an attested organizational goal, and inclusion of all the major players is essential to the functioning of the regime. It is serious that potential nuclear powers have not adhered to the Non-Proliferation Treaty; it would be significantly worse if they were out of the IAEA. That became an important constraint on expelling South Africa. Likewise, the permanent absence of important whaling states from the IWC would mean its end as a functioning organization. It would be perverse—cutting off your nose to spite your face—to expel a member with that kind of strategic position.

The obverse is also true. Withdrawal can be effective only when it can plausibly be said to threaten regime collapse. Even concerted Soviet bloc action on the China representation issue could not pose such a threat, and it failed to secure action against Nationalist China. The UN organizations, with their headquarters and principal financial support in the West and their principal clientele in the Southern Hemisphere, were inconvenienced by the East's departures but not seriously at risk. Similarly, the United States was not able to turn the General Assembly voting rights question into an issue of UN survival, and despite the expenditure of enormous capital, it lost ignominiously. The U.S. walkouts from the specialized agencies, entailing large reductions in financial support, did not stop them in their tracks—though their activities inevitably shrank—and the accommodations to U.S. views made in order to heal the breach were largely cosmetic.

The African states, by contrast, as the major clients of the specialized agencies, could, by walking out, mount a plausible threat to the agencies' existence, and they were successful in forcing membership sanctions against South Africa. What will happen after Iceland's withdrawal from the IWC remains to be seen. If the withdrawal continues, one long-time observer predicts that "the IWC may turn into a 'club' of countries with no whaling interests or traditions."[99]—and, it might be added, with little influence on the actual practice of whaling. The upshot is that only major players (though not only major powers) can participate in the membership sanctions game, and this in turn undermines the legitimacy of membership sanctions as a treaty enforcement tool.

Overall, the experience with membership sanctions tends to confirm the hypothesis underlying the new sovereignty. Membership and participation in the major international organizations is an important, perhaps critical index of the statehood of states. That would lead readily to the prediction that there would be few withdrawals, as there are. What is more difficult to explain is the almost complete absence of expulsions and suspensions. There is really only one major instance in the fifty-year period—the expulsion of South Africa from the UN organizations—and only one other important, if failed, attempt—the Soviet voting rights case. It would seem that if membership is such a desideratum, its denial or qualification would be a potent sanction. Perhaps the answer is that it is too potent to be usable. Expulsion, like banishment in other societies, has to be reserved for conduct that negates the most fundamental and deeply felt community norms—conduct that in itself rejects the notion of membership in a community.

4

Unilateral Sanctions

Treaty-based sanctions do not exhaust the possibilities for coercive action to induce treaty compliance. States have many other ways of expressing displeasure and imposing pains and penalties on members of the system. They run the gamut from the use of force (overt, covert, or surrogate), through interruption of economic or diplomatic relations (complete or partial) and the withholding of courtesies or amenities (such as state visits), to verbal expressions of disapproval (more or less public). The ordinary experience of diplomatic life teaches a state and its leaders to expect embarrassment, political isolation, and subtler forms of shaming, shunning, and loss of status if it acts against strongly held views of others. Pressures and disapproval of these kinds are the stock-in-trade of political and diplomatic intercourse among states.[1]

For the purposes of this chapter, we focus on actions at the coercive end of this range.[2] We are not concerned here with such sanctions as general instruments of foreign policy. They are useful if not essential tools for these purposes, and in addition to seeking to change the behavior of the target country, they may serve a variety of other functions, foreign and domestic, whether to send a signal, to demonstrate resolve, to make a statement, or to respond to demands of domestic constituencies. No observer of foreign affairs would contend that they would or should be forsworn by foreign ministries for these purposes.

The question we address here is different: How useful are unilateral sanctions, or how useful could they be, in enforcing treaty obligations? Traditional international legal doctrine seems to confirm their utility. The right of retaliation is built into the law of treaties.[3] A material breach entitles the aggrieved party to terminate or suspend the treaty. But the practice of states seems at odds with any notion of easy recourse to "self-help" enforcement.[4] Unilateral military coercion is of course forbidden under Article 2(4) of the UN Charter. With that, a great deal of pre-1945 learning on forceful reprisals became obsolete. Although militarily capable states in pursuit of political ends do not always abide by the Charter prohibition, it would seem to preclude unilateral resort to force as an instrument of treaty enforcement. Thus the concern of this chapter is the unilateral interruption of trade and other economic interchange by a state in response to violation of its treaty rights by another.

The chapter is divided into four parts. We deal first with the empirical evidence for the efficacy of sanctions and second with the more speculative matter of their impact on regime maintenance. Most of the episodes discussed are U.S. actions. The third part assesses the theoretical arguments for retaliation in cases of violation. And the fourth, in a more normative vein, considers the question of legitimacy. On the record, it cannot be said that unilateral economic sanctions imposed by the United States have been uniformly ineffective in inducing other countries to fulfill treaty obligations. In some issue areas they have worked at least moderately well in a fair proportion of cases. The symmetry of reciprocal action gives it instinctive appeal. But we argue that, although the United States and some other economically powerful states will no doubt continue to deploy economic sanctions in a variety of situations including response to treaty violation, they cannot be an effective strategy for *the regime* in seeking to improve compliance. Although there is theoretical support for such a course in the work of Robert Axelrod and his followers, the conditions they stipulate for success are not likely to hold in the realm of international politics. In the end, we argue, the risks to the integrity of the regime are serious enough and the inherent compromise of legitimacy severe enough to counsel against a reliance on unilateral sanctions as a central strategy for treaty compliance.

The United States is not the only practitioner of economic sanctions, but it has certainly been the most significant one in the years since World War II. Because of its economic importance and the size of its market, it is peculiarly well situated to make sanctions stick. There is a significant body of academic and policy literature to draw on. Our empirical base, therefore, is U.S. economic sanctions, particularly in areas in which they have been mandated by Congress in retaliation for behavior that the United States regards as detrimental to important treaty-based regimes.

This effort has been increasingly prominent on the congressional foreign policy docket in recent years. The geometric growth of economic interdependence and the dominant U.S. position in the international economy has bound the nations of the world to the United States by a varied and complex mesh of economic ties—private trade, investment, financial services, and public military and economic assistance. Congress has provided authority for the manipulation of nearly all of these economic relationships to forward U.S. policy objectives.[5] Despite GATT prohibitions on discriminatory trade restrictions,[6] the United States refuses to permit a developing country to qualify for the Generalized System of Preferences unless it satisfies a wide range of conditions, ranging from eschewing terrorism and expropriation to cooperating with U.S. drug enforcement programs.[7] Foreign assistance, too, is conditioned by law on the recipient's willingness to cooperate with numerous U.S. foreign policy objectives, on the sensible ground that there is no reason to help those who are frustrating strongly held U.S. purposes. Power to administer these prohibitions and to waive them if the requirements of foreign policy seem to call for it is ordinarily vested in the president, as the person responsible for conducting U.S. foreign policy. Such cases conform to the general pattern of the use of economic pressure as a discretionary policy instrument.

Sometimes, however, Congress has sought to reverse this pattern and require the president to impose restrictions on trade, assistance, or other economic ties with foreign countries that violate particular international norms or obligations. In other words, Congress seeks to use unilateral economic sanctions systematically to enforce treaty or regime obligations. We concentrate on these areas because for the purposes of our inquiry they are in the nature of controlled experiments. As such, they provide unique insight into both the possibilities and the difficulties involved in unilateral enforcement. We consider five such areas:

1. *Section 301 of the Trade Agreement Act of 1974,* requiring the president to retaliate against countries that violate their GATT obligations to the United States and giving the affected private party the right to initiate proceedings before the U.S. International Trade Commission (ITC) to challenge a trade practice of a foreign country.[8] "Super-301," enacted in 1988, required the U.S. trade representative (USTR) to publish a target list of egregious offenders as priority countries for corrective action under Section 301. The USTR must seek to eliminate such barriers by negotiation, but if no progress is made after twelve months, the section mandates retaliatory action.[9]

2. *The Packwood-Magnuson Amendment to the Fishery Conservation and Management Act,* calling for mandatory sanctions against countries conducting "fishing operations . . . which diminish the effectiveness of an international fisheries program," in the form of a reduction of at least 50 percent in their fishery allocation in waters under U.S. jurisdiction. Packwood-Magnuson strengthened the earlier Pelly Amendment to the Fisherman's Protection Act, which gave the president discretionary authority to prohibit imports of fish from such countries.[10]

3. *Human rights provisions in foreign assistance legislation* barring economic or military assistance to any government that engages in "a consistent pattern of gross violations of fundamental human rights."[11] During the Carter administration, Congress sought to control U.S. votes in the international financial institutions according to the same principles it had applied to bilateral foreign aid. The legislative effort was successful in the case of the World Bank,[12] but on the IMF, the executive branch was able to fend off the amendment.[13] All of these provisions contained an exception for projects directed to satisfying "basic human needs" (or, in the military assistance legislation, for "extraordinary circumstances.)"

4. *The Nuclear Non-Proliferation Act of 1978*[14] *and related legislation* mandating the termination of assistance to countries involved in unauthorized transfers of nuclear materials or technology.[15] Each of these permitted the president to waive the sanction if he found that termination of assistance "would be seriously detrimental to the achievement of United States non-proliferation objectives, or would otherwise jeopardize the common defense and security." Originally Congress could override these waivers by a concurrent resolution passed by a majority in each house,[16] but in 1983 the Supreme Court held in *Immigration and Naturalization Service v. Chadha* that all provisions for congressional veto of presidential action were unconstitutional (there were more than two hundred of them). Thereafter the president's waiver of these aid cutoffs was final and not subject to any congressional review.[17]

5. *The Hickenlooper amendment,* requiring that "the President shall suspend assistance to the government of any country [that] . . . (1) has nationalized or expropriated or seized ownership or control of property owned by any United States citizen . . . (2) . . . [and] fails within a reasonable time . . . to take appropriate steps . . . to discharge its obligations under international law towards such citizen."[18]

Efficacy

Summarizing the extensive literature on economic sanctions, Sidney Weintraub concludes that, in terms of changing the behavior of the target country, "most theorists insist that economic coercion is rarely successful."[19] The most comprehensive recent overview of the entire experience with economic sanctions in this century is G. C. Hufbauer, J. J. Schott, and K. A. Elliott, *Economic Sanctions Reconsidered,* first published in 1983 and revised and supplemented in 1990, covering 116 separate cases from 1914 to 1990 and including the actions of other countries as well as the United States.[20] The authors, who seem to have begun their study with a modest predilection for rehabilitating sanctions,[21] wind up skeptics. By their count, the use of sanctions was "successful" in only 34 percent of the cases in the sample, and in the most recent half (after 1973), the figure had fallen to about 25 percent.[22] According to the authors, the outlook for the future is not much brighter. They argue that the declining predominance of the United States, the diffusion of economic power, the diversification of trade and financial patterns and the shrinking of foreign military and economic assistance budgets portend declining economic leverage for the United States, smaller prospects for success, and thus a more limited use of unilateral economic sanctions for political purposes.[23]

Hufbauer, Schott, and Elliott were examining the use of sanctions for general foreign policy objectives, not treaty enforcement. Indeed their definition of foreign policy objectives excludes "the normal range of economic objectives sought in banking, commercial and tax negotiations between sovereign states."[24] (Thus, they do not consider U.S. unilateral trade sanctions related to GATT violations and the whaling regime). It is no surprise, then, that violation of a treaty obligation by a target state did not figure prominently in more than a handful of the cases considered in the study.[25] However, their explanations of why economic sanctions are only of limited efficacy would seem to apply equally to the uses of sanctions for treaty enforcement, where, if anything, the interests at stake seem less urgent and the potential benefits are unlikely to loom large. Do their conclusions hold in the five areas of congressionally mandated treaty enforcement we have identified?

Section 301

Two major studies of Section 301 have produced somewhat divergent conclusions as to effectiveness. In all, some eighty-eight actions were initiated under the section between January 1975, when it came into force, and June 1991.[26] According to Professor Alan O. Sykes, Section 301 action was "successful" in more than 70 percent of the cases, measured by whether "the target country acceded to US demands either in whole or in part by modifying or abandoning the challenged practice."[27] The results of the second study, by Thomas O. Bayard and Kimberly A. Elliott, are less favorable. It finds that "U.S. negotiating objectives were at least partially achieved 54 percent of the time overall."[28] The discrepancy reflects the more demanding criterion of success adopted by Bayard and Elliott:

> In our view, and in contrast to some other observers, conclusion of an agreement is not sufficient to call an outcome a negotiating success. If a case recurs, because the agreement was too loosely written, was not implemented to U.S. satisfaction, or was circumvented in some other way, it is classified as a failure . . . [W]e have also designated as failures other cases in which agreements were reached if it appears that they did not lead to improved market access . . . Agreements to monitor, discuss, or negotiate in other fora that result in no change in the targeted policy or practice also are considered failures.[29]

By our count, the majority of these actions (fifty-four) were directed at violations of GATT obligations, but a substantial number (thirty four) addressed other U.S. trade grievances. The success rate does not seem to vary between the groups. According to Bayard and Elliott, "Unexpectedly, GATT does not appear to add much leverage: the success rate for cases in which GATT panels were convened (55 percent) was not significantly different from that for cases in which either no GATT panel was appointed or GATT rules were not applicable (53 percent)."[30] But in the relatively few Section 301 cases that were pursued to the end in a GATT panel and resulted in a decision for the United States, the other party changed its policy.[31]

Both of the studies agree that in the vast majority of successful cases, simply filing the Section 301 action was sufficient to elicit a positive response. A more explicit threat of sanctions by the president was made in only sixteen of the successful cases. Perhaps the most spectacular of these was the oilseed case begun by a Section 301 petition in 1987. At the end of 1992, after the EC had refused for four years to comply with a panel decision holding its subsidies illegal, the United States announced that it would impose a 200 percent tariff increase on $350 million of EC agricultural products as a first installment of retaliation. The issue was resolved with concessions on both sides in the context of an overall resolution of outstanding agricultural issues in the Uruguay Round negotiations.[32] Sanctions were actually imposed only nine times in the first sixteen years of Section 301.

These analyses seem to provide important support for the efficacy of retaliatory trade sanctions as a mode of enforcing trade obligations. But it appears that the threat of sanctions may be more potent than the actuality. There is a significant difference between a *threat* strategy and a *retaliation* strategy. When sanctions are threatened, "the outcome is still a negotiated one, with the U.S. negotiators trying to get as much liberalization as they can, and foreign negotiators trying to give up as little as possible."[33] What is a satisfactory negotiated outcome remains ultimately up to USTR, who is responsible to the president. Instead of a punishment for a violation, the threat is a forceful move in a continuing bargaining process.[34] That is rather different from what would be implied by an enforcement strategy, and perhaps from what Congress intended. But as we will suggest, its consequences for the integrity of the regime are the same.

Whaling

The whaling cases present a similar pattern of effective use of the threat of sanctions with few actual applications. In 1974, Japan and the Soviet Union, which had opted out of International Whaling Commission decisions to limit the taking of certain species of whales (as permitted by the International Convention to Regulate Whaling), were certified under the Pelly Amendment. In response they agreed to "strengthened conservation measures."[35] In 1978 Chile, Peru, and South Korea, nonmembers of the IWC, were certified, and they promptly joined. But in none of these cases did the president exercise his discretionary authority to impose sanctions.

Between 1978 and 1982 the United States raised the possibility of Pelly or Packwood-Magnuson certification with four countries. In response, Korea and Chile, which had opted out of various IWC restrictions, withdrew their objections and decided to abide by the established quotas. Spain, a new member of the IWC, promised to require its whalers to comply with the quotas. Taiwan, a nonmember, terminated its whaling operations.[36]

In 1981 the IWC ushered in a new era of tight control of whaling by establishing a zero quota on sperm whales, and a year later it adopted a moratorium on commercial whaling, to begin in 1986 and extending at least through 1990.[37] Japan opted out of both decisions, and Japanese boats continued to hunt sperm whales in disregard of the IWC ban. Again the United States warned of a possible certification. The two countries negotiated a settlement whereby Japan agreed to end commercial whaling by 1988 and the United States agreed not to certify Japan under the amendments. Environmental groups challenged the action in court on the ground that the secretary of commerce was required by the statute to certify any state that failed to observe IWC whaling quotas. The Supreme Court upheld the refusal of the Office of the Secretary of Commerce to certify even though Japan had taken whales in excess of quota. The secretary, it said, had discretion to determine that if Japan kept its bargain for the future, its activities would not "diminish the effectiveness" of the ICRW.[38]

Only two countries were actually certified after the enactment of the Packwood-Magnuson requirement of automatic sanctions: the USSR in 1985 and Norway in 1986. Both had opted out of the moratorium. The impact of the mandatory cancellation of fishing allowances was insignificant in both cases, however, since the Soviet Union had only a minimal allocation and Norway had no allocation at all.[39] The president did not impose the discretionary trade sanctions under the Pelly Amendment in either case. Nevertheless, the Soviet Union ceased commercial whaling in 1987 and Norway agreed to do so a year later, although it subsequently resumed whaling without sanction.

During this period Korea and Iceland were warned of the possibility of certification when they continued to issue permits to whalers under the ICRW provision permitting the taking of whales for scientific research.[40] Korea decided to drop its program after failing to secure the advisory approval of the IWC Scientific Committee, and Iceland substantially reduced the number of whales it proposed to take. The acting secretary of commerce maintained that "the effectiveness of the IWC is better served by keeping Iceland fully involved in the IWC process rather than by risking alienation of Iceland by certifying it for continuing its research program."[41] No doubt it was only a coincidence that during the course of the discussions, Iceland indicated that it might have to reassess its position on the NATO base at Keflavik.[42]

At the end of the 1980s, the U.S. sanctions policy could boast a remarkable record. In the period from 1974 to 1988, certification under the Pelly and Packwood-Magnuson Amendments was carried out or was threatened a total of fourteen times. In every case, a significant change in the whaling activities or declaratory policies of the target state resulted. "Thus, the USA managed what the IWC had no means to accomplish: halt commercial whaling." It became "the self-appointed 'policeman' of the IWC."[43]

In practice, however, the executive branch was willing to settle for promises of future good behavior, not all of which were fulfilled.[44] Despite the moratorium, none of the whaling states has actually terminated its whaling enterprises. Since 1986, Japan, Norway, and Iceland have continued to take whales under the "scientific research" exception to the ICRW.

As in the Section 301 cases, the president was able to exploit his residual discretion to mount a threat strategy in an attempt to influence the future behavior of the targets. The distinction was the basis for Justice Thurgood Marshall's dissent in the *American Cetacean Society* case. "The regulation of future conduct," he argued, "is irrelevant to the certification scheme, which affects future violations only by punishing past ones."[45]

Human Rights

The Nixon and Ford administrations, under the tutelage of Henry Kissinger, were avowed practitioners of realpolitik, and it is hardly surprising that they opposed and evaded congressional instructions to deploy U.S. economic power in support of human rights. President Carter, however, entered the White House with a well-publicized commitment to human rights as a key element of his foreign policy.[46] A new State Department Bureau of Human Rights entered the bureaucratic fray, and foreign assistance decisions were contested within the State Department. But the administration's response to attempted legislative direction was not so different from its predecessors'. Its policy was "never to determine formally, even in a classified decision, that a particular government was engaged in gross abuse."[47] Military assistance was terminated for only eight countries, all in Latin America.[48]

The Carter administration was no less ready to exploit the "basic human needs" exception for multilateral aid than Nixon and Ford had been. According to one contemporary study, as of the end of June 1978, the United States had abstained or voted no on thirty-five proposed loan projects in the multilateral development banks (MDB) and had supported twenty-five others under the basic human needs exception.[49] In any case, since the United States did not wield a veto in those institutions, it could not make the congressional policy effective without a very large investment of political capital to secure the cooperation of other members of the financial institutions. This it was unwilling to do.[50] The upshot was that "overall, the United States never succeeded in blocking any MDB loan on human rights grounds, except for a few in the Fund for Special Operations of the Inter-American Development Bank, where the United States had veto power."[51] The congressional effort to mandate human rights sanctions ended with the advent of the Reagan administration.

There is little doubt that congressional insistence played an important part in elevating the priority accorded to human rights issues by U.S. policy makers, although, as noted in Chapter 11, Congress itself was responding to the pressures of an aroused and articulate constituency. There is also a basis for thinking that these legislative actions helped legitimate the broader human rights movement of the 1970s and 1980s, which in turn contributed to the demise of dictatorships in Latin America and ultimately in Eastern Europe. Whether the sanctions had much to do with this development, except as a convenient vehicle for expressing outrage, is more dubious. For the United States, the net economic effect of the aid cutoffs was a small budgetary saving. The economic impact on the targets was equally insignificant.

Nonproliferation

As in the human rights area, congressional action on nuclear nonproliferation was as much a reflection as a cause of an increasing public concern that was also felt in the executive branch. It, too, was plagued by mixed motives and competing political considerations. The continuation of assistance to Pakistan, Israel, and Iraq, for example, despite their well-known nuclear weapons programs, predictably led to accusations of a double standard, feeding the resentment among non–nuclear weapon states of the built-in discriminatory character of the nonproliferation regime. The vagaries of the response to Pakistan's nuclear program are illustrative. President Carter suspended military assistance to Pakistan in 1977 and again in 1979, but with the Soviet invasion of Afghanistan in December 1979, nonproliferation considerations were swept aside, and Congress, by express legislation, enacted a $3.5 billion five-year military assistance package.[52] The Pakistani nuclear program continued to rankle, however. On two separate occasions, Pakistani agents were discovered seeking to export nuclear weapons components from the United States in violation of export control laws, and other intelligence was increasingly ominous.[53] When the special legislation for Pakistan ran out, Congress passed the country-specific Pressler Amendment, requiring a cutoff of foreign assistance unless the president certified annually "that Pakistan does not possess a nuclear explosive device."[54] Presidents Reagan and Bush dutifully made this certification, as no doubt they were expected to do, every year until 1990, when the Afghan war ended. At that point the certifications ended too.

Expropriation

The Hickenlooper Amendment was applied only once in 1963, against Sri Lanka (then Ceylon) for taking over the storage and distribution networks of an American oil company on the island.[55] The expropriation was not reversed.

Measured by immediate, short-term results, then, the five different fields in which Congress has tried to impose mandatory sanctions for violation of regime norms display a wide variance, ranging from an almost 100 percent success rate for whaling to the fair to middling record of Section 301 to almost no effect in the areas of human rights, nonproliferation, and expropriation. (Accounting for this variance seems like an ideal subject for doctoral dissertations.) The raw figures must be discounted to reflect how significant the target response really was, but they should also be enhanced by some amount for deterrent effect and for the gains with domestic (and perhaps foreign) constituencies from the appearance of resolute action.[56]

There are costs to be offset against these benefits. The most obvious are the economic costs to the sanctioning state. Hufbauer, Schott, and Elliott's "seventh commandment" on sanctions is, "*If You Need to Ask the Price, You Can't Afford the Yacht.*"[57] Surprisingly, then, they point out that the gross economic costs of sanctions to the United States as a percentage of GNP were in most cases negligible, amounting ordinarily to less than 1 percent.[58] In some cases, such as the denial of financial assistance, the budgetary impact can even be positive.[59] The costs of Section 301 in terms of U.S. trade forgone were also minimal. As noted, sanctions were actually imposed in only nine cases, and there has been only one counterretaliation—by the EC in a case involving citrus imports.[60] At the same time, sanctions often result in substantial trade diversion and important losses for specific sectors of the economy, translating into significant domestic political pressures on the administration in power.[61] Trade losses to the United States from all economic sanctions in place during 1987 came to almost $7 billion, most of it because of long-standing restrictions on trade with Eastern European countries.

The net value of these economic benefits and costs, if it were the only factor in the equation, would be evaluated differently by different observers and in different contexts. At a minimum it might suggest that the conventional tendency to deprecate the value of unilateral economic sanctions, and particularly the threat of sanctions, is overdone. A final appraisal cannot be based simply on the balance of economic costs and benefits to the sanctioning state, however. It must also consider the impact of unilateral sanctions on the regime itself.

Consequences of Unilateral Sanctions for Regime Maintenance

If the threat or use of unilateral sanctions, whether as a penalty or a bargaining counter, is successful in requiring other states to live up to their treaty obligations, it should be counted as a gain not only for the sanctioning state, the United States in the usual case, but also for the regime. However, resorting to "self-help," or taking the law into one's own hands, can operate to undermine and weaken the cooperative effort. There is considerable evidence that diplomats appreciate the risks of unilateral sanctions in terms of regime maintenance. In the U.S.-Soviet arms control relationship, the dangers were great enough to preclude retaliation altogether. In the GATT context, it is clear that the risks were real and became a major issue in the Uruguay Round. In the other settings we have examined, the evidence is more circumstantial and warrants further development and analysis, but it suggests the validity of Robert Keohane's insight that there is a significant tension between specific reciprocity and the preservation of a multilateral treaty regime.[62]

Bilateral Arms Control

Robert Axelrod, in *The Evolution of Cooperation,* gives pointed advice for ensuring Soviet compliance with arms control treaties: in case of violation, retaliate promptly and unambiguously. "The Soviet Union has occasionally taken steps which appear to be designed to probe the limits of its [arms control] agreements with the United States. The sooner the United States detects and responds to these Soviet probes, the better. Waiting for them to accumulate only risks the need for a response so large as to evoke yet more trouble."[63]

This advice went unheeded by U.S. arms control policy makers. At one point well on in the Reagan administration, Assistant Secretary of Defense Richard Perle urged such a policy. In a memorandum entitled "Response to Soviet Violations Policy (RSVP)," he argued that the administration should adopt a systematic tit-for-tat strategy, retaliating in kind to every Soviet violation.[64] It is not clear how seriously the proposal was considered in the White House, but in any event, it did not carry the day. Over the many repeated plays of the strategic arms control game between the nuclear superpowers, and despite the prevailing attitude of hostility to the Soviet Union, not once did the United States retaliate directly against any of the numerous asserted Soviet violations. What accounts for this persistent refusal to adopt a strategy of retaliation?

Most of the asserted violations were contestable, both as to factual predicate and as to the meaning of the applicable treaty norm.[65] The question whether the SS-25 was or was not a "new missile" within the meaning of SALT II or whether the Soviets were or were not improperly encrypting telemetry on missile tests turned on debatable technical assessments and analysis. Some of the accusations were challenged within the U.S. government itself, and more widely by academics and defense analysts.[66] Moreover, even when the violation was clear-cut, as in the case of the Krasnoyarsk radar, it was difficult to design an appropriate retaliatory response. The United States had no need for a mirror image of the Soviet radar. Nor was it easy to identify another treaty obligation the suspension of which would be useful to the United States or disagreeable to the Soviets and would not risk bringing down the whole treaty.

The most important consideration, however, was that the issue of responding to technical violations of the arms control agreements could not be disentangled from the overall course of arms control negotiations or the broader aspects of relations with the Soviet Union. The United States, even under the Reagan administration, was unwilling to take the risk that narrowly focused retaliatory action would be used as a ground—or even a pretext—for terminating the treaty or for some other destabilizing response. Arguments for retaliation necessarily gave way to the broad consensus of the U.S. security community that preservation of the SALT treaty regime was in the U.S. national interest.[67]

It is instructive that when the Reagan administration determined to develop a space-based ABM system arguably prohibited by the treaty, it did not justify its action as retaliation for previous Soviet violations. Instead it advanced a novel and much disputed interpretation of the treaty under which the Strategic Defense Initiative (SDI) policy was permissible, an approach that had serious political liabilities, domestic and international.[68] Even then, the administration could not generate broad support for what might have been seen not as retaliation but as defection. Congress imposed limitations to ensure that the operational as opposed to the declared U.S. policy remained well within the treaty limits as traditionally conceived.[69]

Section 301

The GATT was founded on the underlying procedural norm of multilateral action, both in arriving at trade agreements and in administering them. The central lesson the drafters took from interwar history was that unilateral action on trade questions and disputes led ultimately to the collapse of the international trading system.[70] One important expression of this norm was the GATT dispute settlement procedure. When the United States invoked Section 301, therefore, trading partners in Europe and elsewhere argued that "by threatening to take unilateral action, the United States was violating an underlying principle of GATT."[71] Academic commentary has also, for the most part, been disapproving.[72]

Section 301 tried to accommodate these criticisms by requiring that when the unfair practice charged is the violation of a GATT obligation, USTR must resort to GATT dispute settlement procedures before sanctions may be imposed. However, until the conclusion of the Uruguay Round, the GATT dispute settlement system operated by consensus, meaning that the member changed could delay or even veto the approval of a panel ruling.[73] Section 301 therefore imposes an eighteen-month deadline.[74] If GATT procedures have not produced a settlement by then, the president is to move on his own. The deadline has never been strictly invoked in practice, but in the eyes of most GATT members the threat of extralegal self-help hanging over GATT dispute settlement in itself compromised the validity of Section 301.[75]

The Section 301 cases not involving GATT violations obviously make no pretense of enforcing legal obligations.[76] In these cases, the United States makes a unilateral determination that another state's practice, though not forbidden by any agreement, is nevertheless unfair or unduly burdensome. If the other party is a GATT member, a U.S. restriction against its trade is itself a violation of the agreement. And again, the decision process is unilateral. Thus, it is doubly a departure from multilateral norms.[77]

Resentment and resistance by GATT treaty partners mounted during the 1980s.[78] Finally, in the late stages of the Uruguay Round negotiations, they secured the adoption of a little noticed provision that in effect outlaws Section 301. Article 23 of the disputes settlement understanding is entitled "Strengthening of the Multilateral System." It requires a member seeking redress for wrongful trade practices to "have recourse to, and abide by, the rules and procedures of this Understanding." In addition, it prohibits a party from making a determination that a violation has occurred, except through the panel procedures; it requires the use of the new World Trade Organization (WTO) procedures to determine the amount of allowable retaliation; and it bars retaliation without WTO permission.[79] The actions prohibited by Article 23 are, of course, the very actions that are mandated by Section 301. The United States maintains that there is no inconsistency between the two provisions, but only on the basis that the new WTO dispute settlement provisions will necessarily result in decisions made within the eighteen-month time limit established by Section 301. Either way, it would mark the end of two decades of U.S. "aggressive unilateralism."[80]

Other Congressionally Mandated Sanctions

The U.S. sanctions policy also contributed to a deep crisis in the whaling regime in the early 1990s. The apparent U.S. successes of the 1980s proved evanescent. At the 1992 IWC meeting, the Scientific Committee, after a major review of the situation, recommended a revised management procedure that would have permitted some commercial whaling, especially for minke whales, of which, in its view, stocks were large and increasing. The antiwhaling group, led by the United States, was successful in getting the report sent back to the Scientific Committee for further study, and the effect was to extend the moratorium for another year. All the prime targets of U.S. sanctions responded in outrage. As discussed in Chapter 3, Iceland, undeterred by Pelly or Packwood-Magnuson, promptly carried out its threat to withdraw from the ICRW. Norway reactivated its 1982 opt-out from the ban and sent six ships to sea through ranks of protesting environmentalists. Both Russia and Japan indicated that they might resume whaling in the near future. Iceland called a meeting of the dissidents to consider the formation of a new North Atlantic whaling regime. Norway was certified in 1992 and again in 1993, but as of mid-1995, no sanctions had been imposed on any of them.[81]

As will be discussed in Chapter 5, the crisis in the IWC is one of fundamental policy and philosophy and cannot be attributed solely to U.S. sanctions. It is rooted in a clash between two irreconcilable conceptions of the basic purpose of the organization. One maintains that whales are a resource like any other and can properly be exploited on a sustainable basis. The other believes that it is wrong to kill whales. The minority, the remaining whaling countries, challenges the legitimacy of the majority's imposing its view on such a fundamental matter by vote. As a result, the continued existence of the whaling regime is at risk, with some possibility that unregulated whaling might occur for the first time since 1960. If U.S. sanctions did not create the crisis, there is little doubt that they fed the sense of grievance that has led the minority to take drastic action. The depth of this feeling is revealed in the Norwegian foreign minister's remark, "It would be intolerable if a small country were to be pressured into submission by big countries who only wish to pay environmental penance in currency of negligible value to them."[82]

In the other three areas, the evidence of tension between unilateral sanctions and regime maintenance is not so pronounced. But it is often said that the exercise, by successive presidents, of the discretionary authority they fought so hard to defend contributed to an air of cynicism and opportunism about U.S. policy on human rights and nuclear proliferation that reflected not only on the policy but also on the integrity of the regime itself.[83]

The balance between the compliance gains of unilateral sanctions and the costs of fraying regime norms will depend to a large extent on the weight attached to these two values. That rests mainly in the eye of the balancer. From a national perspective, what counts is the net value of the costs and benefits to the United States. But for one whose concern is to maximize treaty compliance over the long term, the health of the regime should weigh more heavily in the balance.

What about Tit for Tat?

An evaluation of unilateral sanctions would be incomplete without considering the powerful contemporary theoretical work that seems to support their use.[84] Robert Axelrod's pathbreaking book, *The Evolution of Cooperation,* and its many subsequent commentators have examined iterated "prisoners' dilemma" games in which the incentive structure of each individual game is such that each "rational" prisoner is driven not to cooperate with the other, although cooperation would be more beneficial to both than independent actions in which both "defect." Axelrod found that in these sequential bargaining situations, a tit-for-tat strategy was the most successful.[85] In this strategy, one player begins with a cooperative move, and thereafter responds in kind to each action of the other. If the first cooperative move is reciprocated, the original player will continue cooperating until the partner defects. Then, swift punishment follows. Good is to be returned for good, bad for bad. Presumably, the defector will learn the error of his ways and return to the path of cooperation.[86]

Axelrod's analysis seems to have obvious applications in the field of international relations, as he himself noted, along with Keohane and many others. One arena in which it intuitively seems appropriate is treaty compliance. In that setting, as was seen in the arms control case, Axelrod's prescription is to sanction or punish noncompliance.

But as that case also shows, the theoretical model does not migrate easily to the realm of ordinary diplomatic interchange. Under Axelrod's theory, each player must be able not only to see the other's moves, but also to interpret them accurately as either cooperation, defection, or retaliation for a previous defection.[87] The requirement has two corollaries. The first is consistency. If moves are random, there is no way of telling whether they are responses to the previous move or not. The second is proportionality. The response must be, in Keohane's words, "of roughly equivalent value" to the original action. Otherwise it cannot be confidently characterized as a retaliation.

In the U.S.-Soviet strategic relationship, the noise level was high, and the necessary clarity was missing. Uncertainty about the real meaning of the Soviet Union's actions and about how it would respond to "retaliatory" moves of the United States haunted the arms control dialogue. So it is in international relations more generally. Clarity about the nature and quality of state conduct is not a prominent feature of the world of diplomacy. Much of the daily work of foreign offices is devoted to interpreting the actions of other states in an effort to decide just what significance to attribute to them.

The whaling and trade cases most nearly satisfy the conditions of clarity and proportionality. In Section 301 proceedings, the petition must specify the trade restrictions against which it is directed. In the whaling cases, the secretary of the interior identifies the objectionable practice in the certificate. The statutory measure of retaliation also meets the criterion of proportionality: the trade retaliation must be in "an amount that is equivalent in value to the burden being imposed by [the target] country on U.S. commerce."[88] The whaling sanctions are related to fisheries interests, for example. The higher success rates in these areas can perhaps be accounted for on this basis.

Nevertheless, consistency and predictability were clearly lacking in the application of these and other congressionally mandated sanctions. In terms of achieving the congressional objective of automatic retaliation for proscribed conduct, the efforts were failures. The president, after all, executes the policy, and it is impossible to tie his hands completely. In the Section 301 cases, as noted, the executive decides what kind of response by the target is sufficient. It is also the president who determines whether an expropriating country is taking "appropriate steps . . . to discharge its obligations under international law."[89] It is he who decides whether conduct by a foreign government amounts to "a consistent pattern of gross violations of internationally recognized human rights."[90] And he will necessarily exercise his discretion with an eye to interests other than treaty compliance. "The confused signals sent by administrations that were forced to implement legislatively mandated sanctions may have led other countries to believe, often correctly, that the sanctions would not be sustained."[91] If clarity and proportionality would account, under Axelrod's theory, for the success of some of the sanctioning policies, inconsistency may be the reason that, for most, success was modest after all.

A further problem with retaliatory action relates to "the shadow of the future," which is of crucial importance in Axelrod's analysis.[92] The knowledge that the relationship will endure and provide many future opportunities for retaliation dampens the incentive of the prisoners' dilemma player to defect and pocket the short-run gains. "The good thing about international relations," Axelrod writes, "is that the major powers can be quite certain they will be interacting with each other year after year. Their relationship may not always be mutually rewarding, but it is durable. Therefore, next year's inter-action should cast a large shadow on this year's choices, and cooperation has a good chance to evolve eventually."[93]

Axelrod's argument stresses the potential loss of future benefits to an actor contemplating *defection*. But the actor considering *retaliation* must also think of the possible future costs. It may be dangerous to prejudice the possibility of support from the violator at some point in the future when it may be needed. Moreover, in bilateral relationships like arms control and trade, the risk of setting off "a long echo of alternating retaliations"[94] will often dwarf the consequences of overlooking what are arguably relatively minor or "tech-nical" violations.

From the perspective of other GATT members, a unilateral U.S. action against a Section 301 target is a "defection." If the other GATT members were to follow Axelrod's strategic injunction to retaliate, it would precipitate the very kind of escalatory spiral that was successfully avoided in the arms control area. Unless checked, it would presage the end of the multilateral trading system. In practice, the targets of Section 301 have not resorted to counterretaliation, despite some dire predictions.[95] Risk aversion may account for the low incidence of uncontrolled escalation, but if so, it also reduces the potential of retaliation as a disciplinary measure for treaty vio-lations.

Finally, the Axelrod analysis—and specific reciprocity generally—focuses on bilateral interactions. In contemporary conditions of interdependence, however, regulatory treaties and sanctions episodes are not strictly bipolar. Even the most powerful states subsist in a lattice of relationships and issue areas in which everything seems ultimately to be linked in some way to everything else. In this environment, retaliation is a cruder and therefore less useful tool than it seems to be in game theory.

Every bilateral exchange gives rise to consequences outside the particular deal—analogous to the "externalities" that, in economics, must be included in a full accounting of profit and loss. As we have said, retaliation under Section 301, even though accepted as such by the target, may be seen as defection by third-party GATT members. Tit for tat against the Soviet Union may alarm the allies. Trade sanctions against China's human rights violations raise worries in Japan and may prejudice Chinese participation in nonpro-liferation or environmental regimes or affect the status of Hong Kong. Moves interact across issue areas as well as within them. Actions in the trade area have side effects in the environmental field, and vice versa. A prominent example is the U.S. ban on the importation of Mexican tuna because the method of fishing resulted in dolphin kills that were excessive by U.S. environmental standards.[96] A GATT panel found the restriction to be in conflict with U.S. obligations under the agreement, to the consternation of the environmental community and the cheers of free traders. The clash has precipitated a much broader reexamination of the interaction between trade and environmental regulation, the outcome of which is unpredictable.

Systemwide consequences of unilateral actions are inevitable, given the interdependence, extensive as well as intensive, of contemporary international life. The conflict between Congress and the president over whether sanctions should be automatic can be interpreted as a difference about the weight to be given to these broader consequences. Congress, for obvious institutional reasons, focuses on the direct costs and benefits in the bilateral relationship, like a player in Axelrod's game. The executive is more sensitive to the other potential consequences and, when he resists mandatory action, by inference judges that the collateral costs of an automatic sanctions policy might be too high.[97]

The Evolution of Cooperation is an enormously stimulating and insightful theoretical work. The economy and simplicity of the thesis give it great persuasive power. But the transfer of these theoretical concepts to the forums of international relations where decisions about sanctions and compliance are made is not as direct as may at first appear. Crucial conditions for the validity of the analysis are seriously compromised in the real-world environment, where the moves lack clarity and predictability, and the costs and benefits cannot be confined to the bilateral transaction or even the parties to it. Accordingly, the prescriptive power of the analysis must be discounted.

Legitimacy

Not only is the theoretical support for retaliation weaker than it at first appears, but in addition, normative considerations tell strongly against the use of sanctions. The enforcement model implies that inducing compliance with treaty obligations is an exercise in law enforcement. It is fair, then, to test unilateral sanctions by the standards that are applied to other law enforcement activities. The most fundamental of these standards are that like cases should be treated alike, that the crucial determinations should be made by basically fair procedures, and that all actors should be equal before the system. Unilateral sanctions are defective on all three counts.

So long as sanctions decisions are made by national leaders and commit national resources, the legal issue can be only one among many considerations on which the decision is based. Congress, in mandating sanctions, has to accept an area of presidential discretion, no matter how little the legislators trust it. In general, both branches are in agreement on the overall objectives set out in the legislation, but implementation is in the hands of an executive pursuing a complicated array of sometimes divergent foreign policies and interests. In the day-to-day conduct of foreign affairs, the legislative policies have to be balanced against other interests. Thus, for the president, in the concrete circumstances of particular cases, nonproliferation had to give way to the support of the Afghan rebels, human rights to the independence of the international financial institutions, the whales to the NATO base at Keflavik. In exercising his sanctioning authority, the president did not, and indeed cannot, treat like cases alike.

The decision to impose unilateral sanctions is made by the sanctioning government. Therefore both the existence of a violation and the appropriate punishment are determined by the "plaintiff." Under Section 301, the "defendant" has an opportunity to be heard, but as a matter of grace, not of right. For the other congressionally mandated sanctions there is not even that. To be judge in one's own cause is the paradigmatic offense against due process of law. The bona fides of the sanctioner are never an adequate safeguard. The United States imposed unilateral sanctions against Nicaragua for conduct that was later vindicated by two neutral tribunals, the World Court and the GATT.[98]

In *Coercive Cooperation*, Lisa Martin concludes that sanctions are most effective when the sanctioning party gets others to join in the effort.[99] Inducing others to join not only strengthens the economic impact of the sanctions but also may be dictated by the needs of legitimacy. Not unlike authorization from an international organization, the participation of other states might operate as a voucher for the fairness of the decision and a counter to the charge of unilateralism. But if, as is usually true, the states that can be induced to cooperate are mostly bound to the sanctioner by ties of political alliance, the legitimating effect would be small.

Finally, unilateral sanctions entail a disparity of power between sanctioner and target. It is not too much to say that unilateral and even concerted sanctions are essentially a monopoly of the great powers. In more than 80 percent of the cases considered by Hufbauer, Schott, and Elliott, the United States, Great Britain, or the USSR was a sanctioner. In almost two-thirds, the United States was the sanctioning party either alone or in concert with others. Moreover, it seems obvious that sanctions will be more successful and thus more frequently used against economically vulnerable and politically weak countries.[100] Hufbauer, Schott, and Elliott's third commandment is *"The Weakest Goes to the Wall,"* and they find that "senders' economies are almost always much bigger than their targets'."[101]

Where such a power differential is not present, either the incidence or the effectiveness of sanctions seems to decline. In the context of U.S.-Soviet arms control agreements, equality of power between the parties, far from nurturing a tit-for-tat strategy, tended to inhibit it. In the trade area, Bayard and Elliott report that half of the Section 301 cases targeted the EC, Japan, and Canada, the three largest U.S. trading partners. More than one-fourth were brought against the EC alone.[102] The success rate against the EC and Canada is below the overall average—40 percent for the EC, as opposed to 54 percent.[103] Japan seems to be an exception. The comparable figure is 75 percent. Perhaps the excursion can be explained by that country's greater political dependence on the United States, despite its economic power.[104]

The consistent use of threats or sanctions by a big state against smaller ones is apt to seem less like disinterested enforcement of common norms and more like the exertion of power in the interest of the stronger. The sense of grievance is intensified when, as is so frequently the case, the coercion runs from North to South. That unilateral sanctions can be imposed only by major industrialized powers renders their legitimacy as a device for treaty enforcement deeply suspect.

In the broadest sense, the experience reviewed in this chapter suggests a fundamental tension between the conception of sanctions as a foreign policy instrument and as a strategy to enforce legal obligations. Political motivations sit uneasily with the predictability and evenhandedness associated with application of the law. When the foreign policy objectives of the sanctioning state—usually the United States—happen to coincide with treaty norms, economic sanctions may be used and sometimes used effectively to enforce compliance or to punish violations. But the United States neither can nor should be "the enforcer" for the world—in regulatory treaties any more than in the security area. That is not an effective *system* for the enforcement of any particular treaty, much less for the complex network of treaties that establishes much of the framework for state and individual action in today's world. A more cooperative and participatory process is needed—and that is the subject of the rest of this book.

II

Toward a Strategy for Managing Compliance

If coercive sanctions are not a viable instrument for achieving treaty compliance, what are the alternatives? In Part Two we identify the elements of a management strategy for improving compliance by examining the practice and activities of states and international organizations that are grappling with that problem. This strategy has not yet been articulated and conceptualized as a coherent whole. Indeed, the notion that compliance can be actively managed with a comprehensive strategy is not widely understood. Like *le bourgeois gentilhomme*, who did not realize he was speaking prose, states and treaty organizations do what comes naturally without bothering much about linkages between individual instruments or theoretical implications. Not every element we discuss can be found in every treaty regime. In particular, with a few important exceptions, such as the International Monetary Fund, parties have been unwilling to commit the bureaucratic and financial resources that would be necessary for the developed forms of issue management found in domestic government agencies and private corporations. Nevertheless, there is enough commonality across regimes that it is possible to identify the outlines of the actual process that keeps treaty compliance at acceptable levels, and to try to make some sense of it.

For the most part, compliance strategies seek to remove obstacles, clarify issues, and convince parties to change their behavior. The dominant approach is cooperative rather than adversarial. Instances of apparent noncompliance are treated as problems to be solved, rather as than wrongs to be punished. In general, the method is verbal, interactive, and consensual. In some cases—again the IMF is a salient example—the regime may have benefits it can withhold. In the background more generally there is the threat of various manifestations of disapproval: exposure, shaming, and diffuse impacts on the reputation and international relationships of a resisting party. In the conditions of the new sovereignty, a state's willful and persistent refusal to comply can mushroom into a situation in which its overall status in the international system is threatened.

The foundation of compliance strategy is the normative framework provided by the treaty. The strategy builds on the parties' general sense of obligation to comply with a legally binding prescription in the absence of strong countervailing considerations, bolstered by the requirement of justifying departures from treaty norms that is both a practical and a legal requirement in the international system. Much of the compliance process consists of a kind of discourse among states, international organizations, and, to some extent interested publics, elaborating the meaning of these norms and specifying the performance required in particular circumstances. The norms themselves are coordination points by which the parties can harmonize their actions, and the discourse helps to give the reassurance about the performance of others that is necessary if parties are to remain in compliance.

The treaty norms provide the leverage for a series of measures and activities that separately and in intricate combination press toward compliance. Although we present them sequentially, in practice there is more or less continuous interaction among all the stages of the process.

Analytically, the first stage is the development of data about the situation under regulation and the activities of the parties with respect to it. This is accomplished through reporting requirements, which are found in various forms in almost all regulatory treaties. Reported information, especially if it bears directly on compliance, may be subjected to a variety of informal cross-checks or more formal verification procedures.

More active management begins with the identification of behavior that raises significant compliance questions. Initially, the response is exploratory and seeks to clarify the exact nature of the behavior and the surrounding facts and circumstances. If concern persists, the next step may be diagnosis of the sources of the apparently deviant behavior, in the hope of identifying an obstacle that can be removed or a problem that can be solved. The issue of the party's capacity to carry out its obligations is examined and addressed, perhaps by some form of technical assistance or other resources if available. Frequently there is a real or asserted difference between parties about the meaning of the norm or the performance required in the particular circumstances. Mechanisms to settle such disputes are an essential part of a management strategy, though formal adjudication or other binding procedures are rare. In some contemporary regimes a more powerful, proactive management tool is emerging in the form of a regular systematic review and assessment of party performance and future plans, conducted by the conference of the parties, usually with the technical assistance of the secretariat.

In the end, the interactive process for dealing with compliance may disclose the need to modify the norms themselves, by interpretation, by other adaptive procedures authorized in the treaty, or by amendment.

Although the treaty parties play an active role, ideally the management strategy should be implemented with the support of a strong and effective international organization. States have developed a deep skepticism about international bureaucracies, however, in part because they have the defects of other bureaucracies, and in part because, like other bureaucracies, they generate a degree of autonomy that impinges on the states' freedom of action. The deficiencies of public organizations are supplied in part by the growth in importance and influence of nongovernmental organizations. Their programs parallel the strategy outlined above at many points. They develop information in the field of their concern, help check and verify party reports, and analyze and critique the performance of treaty parties in a public analogue to review and assessment that is often harsher than a diplomatic forum can accommodate. In the end, they contribute greatly to the exposure and shaming of persistent offenders and often organize dissenting elements in the domestic political arena.

Although it may seem mild in comparison with military force or economic embargo, the management strategy surveyed in these chapters disposes of powerful instruments for enhancing compliance and improving the capacity of regime members to carry out their obligations. The claim here is not that all these instruments are found in all or even most international treaty regimes. On the contrary, what we see is fragmentary evidence of the emergence of a variety of tools, the effectiveness of which depends heavily on the skill and strategic imagination with which they are used by the leaders of the regime. Still less do we claim that this process results in universal compliance. What enforcement procedure does? Nevertheless, by piecing together the disparate elements found in the practice of many regimes, we can begin to form a picture of a process of treaty implementation that is theoretically sound and practically effective.

5

Norms

The role of norms in treaty compliance seems at first glance to be a fairly straightforward matter. The treaty text embodies the authorized version of the relevant norms, describing the required (or prohibited) conduct. The state's behavior must then be matched with these externally imposed requirements. We know, however, that the mere existence of a treaty does not ensure automatic compliance by parties that have assented to it. Although much compliant behavior can be explained by the state's adherence to the agreement, the norms of the treaty have to be understood and accepted in their application to concrete situations for them to have the power to induce obedience. This chapter describes the complex process of interaction among states by which norms are interpreted and elaborated in the course of application and enforcement.

Because of the great importance attached to consent in an international legal system that still regards itself as arbitrating among sovereign and independent states, a key feature of this process is the participation of the state whose conduct is challenged. The essence of the international legal process is a dialectic that, by emphasizing assent at every stage, operates to generate pressure for compliance.

This chapter is not meant to be a predictive exercise. Still less does it seek to provide empirical support for the idea that state behavior conforms to applicable norms all or most of the time. (It seems clear that neither that proposition nor its opposite can be established by quantitative or analytic methods). The object, rather, is to provide a schematic description of the mechanisms by which international treaty norms weight the decision process of states in the direction of compliance.

What Are Norms?

We use "norms" in a generic sense to include a broad class of generalized prescriptive statements—principles, standards, rules, and so on—both procedural and substantive.[1] The term includes statements that are reduced to writing or some other authoritative formulation as well as informal, tacit, or background norms. We do not attempt to distinguish in any systematic way among these categories, and in practice they all interact in complex ways.[2] Although the foregoing list is in order of decreasing generality, it is not hierarchically ordered, in the sense that the more general statement does not always trump the more specific or vice versa. A directive that is specific and pointed enough can override a more general principle. In the United States, the general principle of compliance with treaties gives way if the intention of Congress to violate one is expressed clearly enough.[3] And there is no teleological implication by which "principles" are progressively refined into more precise "standards" and ultimately into more or less determinate "rules." The classical method of the common law was the reverse: principles were to be induced from a long succession of more concrete applications, as Anglo-American common law claimed to derive a unifying tort principle of "no liability without fault" from analysis of a series of apparently disconnected rules governing particular classes of situations.[4] International law contains many similar examples. Much of the work of the International Law Commission consists in the reduction of general principles of customary international law to concrete and determinate form in treaties. *Pacta sunt servanda* (treaties must be observed) becomes Article 26 of the Vienna Convention on the Law of Treaties. Just as easily, a specific "rule" repeated in numerous treaties, like the prohibition against torture, can generate a norm or principle of customary international law.[5] Our usage does not differ much from that of international regime theorists, who define regimes as "sets of implicit or explicit principles, norms, rules, and decision-making procedures around which actors' expectations converge in a given area of international relations"[6] without much concern with precise distinctions among them.

What brings all of these different kinds of statements into a single generic category is that they are *prescriptions for action in situations of choice,* carrying a sense of obligation, a sense that they *ought* to be followed.[7] Norms in this sense are not predictive. Since they are prescriptions for action in situations of choice, the actor may or may not choose to obey them. Unlike a scientific or predictive rule, a norm is not falsified by counterexamples.[8] Thus, departure from a norm, even frequent or persistent departure, does not necessarily invalidate it. That there have been many instances since 1945 of the use of force in violation of Article 2(4) of the UN Charter, or that many people drive in excess of the speed limit, does not disprove the continuing existence, validity, or even operational effect of the norm. Nevertheless actors, in general, do comply with prescriptions to which they are subject. For present purposes it is not necessary to identify the causes of this phenomenon. Utility, stasis, internalization, social pressure, moral compulsion, and fear of punishment doubtless all contribute.

A thought experiment will test this proposition about the tendency to comply with norms. Assume you are a new arrival in a community. You are told that a rule prescribes the wearing of black on Sunday. It is Sunday. You know nothing else about the situation. You are required to make an even money bet on the whether the next person who approaches will be wearing black. How do you bet?

Of course the probability that the next person will be wearing black is not nearly as high as the probability, for example, that everyone will drive on the prescribed side of the road. The next person to approach may be a stranger to the community and not know the rule, may be opposed to it on principle, may have no black clothes, may not give a damn. Countless other factors, unknown to the observer, will bear on his action. But if you have no other knowledge and are forced to bet, you will bet on compliance. The result holds, even though you know nothing about the system, if any, for enforcing the rule. Nor does it matter whether you yourself subscribe to the rule, or would obey it in the test situation. If you understand the concept of rules and rule following, the rational bet in the circumstances would be that the next person will be wearing black, whereas in the absence of the norm, it would be the other way. A somewhat weaker but still significant formulation is that the probability of a particular action's being taken is higher in the presence of a norm prescribing that action, other things being equal, than in its absence.

"The famous problem of order . . . cannot be solved without a common normative system," said Talcott Parsons.[9] It sometimes seems as though the main objective of rational choice theory, which has bulked so large in contemporary international relations analysis, has been to disprove that dictum. Yet even the most dedicated among those theorists are beginning to acknowledge that they have set themselves an impossible task. Although Robert Axelrod's carefully structured games have provided much insight, the complex patterns of cooperation in modern society cannot be generated by computers interacting randomly in a state of nature.[10] The basic problem is that, on the assumptions of rational choice theory, most of the interesting situations generate not one determinate solution but a number of possible equilibriums, and the theory cannot within its own terms predict which among them will be chosen.[11] The choice is not a product of simple, self-regarding value maximization, but of decisions made in a social and institutional context.

Analytically it is common to distinguish between coordination norms, operating almost automatically in situations where the interests of all participants coincide, and norms involved in mixed motive situations, where the actors have incentives to defect as well as to cooperate. In the first case, exemplified by the rules of the road, the norm is more like an indicator rather than a prescription. It identifies the convention that solves the coordination problem. Strictly speaking, there is no issue of compliance. All participants readily conform because they have no incentive to do otherwise.[12] In the second case, by definition the rational incentive structure does not necessarily dictate cooperation. Something more is needed, and that something is often a norm that prescribes cooperative behavior. Since pure coordination problems are very rare in international affairs, most international norms raise questions of compliance rather than conformity (see Chapter 6).

Thomas Schelling recognized the context dependence of these problems in his classic work, *The Strategy of Conflict*:

> The fundamental psychic and intellectual process is that of participating in the creation of traditions; and the ingredients out of which traditions can be created, or the materials in which potential traditions can be perceived and jointly recognized, are not at all coincident with the mathematical contents of the game ... [They include] historical and literary precedent, legal and moral casuistry, mathematics and aesthetics, as well as familiar analogues from other walks of life.[13]

A significant component of the contextual materials that guide and shape decisions consists of legal and social norms. Norms are therefore crucial to achieving cooperative action in general, and the conclusion applies with special force in the area of international relations.

Legal Norms

Our concern is compliance with treaties—"agreement[s] concluded between states in written form and governed by international law."[14] The treaty establishes a system of norms designed to govern the conduct of states in the area of concern. The norms established by treaties are *legal* norms, at least in that they embody rules acknowledged in principle to be legally binding on states that ratify them. Indeed, treaties are the most unproblematic source of international law. The rule that "every treaty in force is binding on the parties to it and must be performed in good faith," codified in Article 26 of the Vienna Convention on the Law of Treaties, has long been recognized as a fundamental background norm of international law. As Stanley Hoffman says, "there can be no social order without *pacta sunt servanda.*"[15]

What does it mean to say that a norm is legally binding? Law is a well-nigh universal feature of human societies, but it resolutely eludes satisfactory definition. All attempts to define "law"—let alone "international law"—on the basis of one or a few factors have been abject failures. We can note some characteristic attributes, however. In contrast to other kinds of norms, legal norms have a relatively high degree of formality. They are often authoritatively stated in formal instruments (like treaties). Nevertheless, the possibility of informal or unwritten legal norms is not precluded, and many of the most important (like *pacta sunt servanda*) take that form. The norm system is operated by professionals (usually lawyers or bureaucrats), who use recognized techniques and practices that specify the arguments and evidence that count as probative or persuasive or relevant.[16] The production of legal norms is linked to the apparatus of government, and compliance often involves public coercive action. But in the last analysis, law, domestic or international, like any other basic cultural manifestation, has an enormously complex derivation that stubbornly resists specification.[17]

One attribute of almost all legal norms is that they carry an obligation of obedience. Of course the obligation is not felt with uniform intensity by all persons at all times and places and as to all legal norms. The laws against murder presumably generate a weightier sense of obligation than the speed limit. The tax code is perhaps somewhere in between. Some laws, like most of those governing private sexual behavior in the United States, have even lapsed into desuetude.[18] But in general, legal norms are at least presumptively "accepted as a guide to conduct and a basis for criticism, including self-criticism."[19] Actors subject to a legal system for the most part acknowledge an obligation to obey its norms—an obligation that goes beyond the fear of penalties that may be imposed for violation.[20] Again, it is unnecessary here to explore the source of legal obligation—whether pure utilitarian calculation, social conditioning, threat of punishment, or belief in God. Contemporary academic discussion tends to emphasize the importance of tradition, expectations generated by social interaction, and the belief, grounded in historical and cultural experience, that social life would be impossible without some kind of obligation to follow prescriptions of the general types here involved.[21] Whatever the basis, "legal systems [and] legal rules . . . confront particular individuals as external and frequently coercive. Indeed, their externality is a social fact, reflected in pressure to conform."[22]

If it is accepted that individuals acknowledge some kind of general obligation to comply with legal norms, it does not necessarily follow that collective bodies like states do. Stanley Hoffman's remarks about the relevance of individual morality to state behavior are suggestive:

> For a person, "self-transcendence" is both possible and sometimes even expected, or rewarded; whereas groups in general are expected to behave selfishly; they are there literally to promote the interests of the members. If they did something else they would betray the interests of the group. Not only is selfish behavior accepted but one also expects of groups that they will sometimes behave in a way that would be immoral if it were indulged in by individuals.[23]

But states act by and on behalf of human beings, and as Hoffman also says, "considerations of good and evil, right or wrong are therefore both inevitable and legitimate."[24] It is true that when individuals act in an official capacity they are supposed to represent not their personal interests and concerns, but those of the collectivity. Weber, in a loftier version of Machiavelli, argued that statesmen are bound by an "ethics of responsibility" to safeguard the national interest at the expense of their personal moral imperatives.[25] But to quote Hoffman again, "to say that he must have an ethics of responsibility does not tell you at all *how* the statesman will calculate the consequences. It depends entirely on the nature of his ends and on his views of his constituency."[26]

Recent analysis of the principal agent problem, to say nothing of the traditional law of fiduciary obligations, proceeds from the premise that persons like officials, who act in a representative capacity, will have the motivation and opportunity to indulge their own propensities and interests rather than those of the principal.[27] The focus of attention has been the conflict between the interests of the organization and the *selfish* interests of the agent, a divergence that appears in public organizations as well as private corporations, as the prevalence of political corruption testifies. But if officials cannot wholly divest themselves of their individual human characteristics, it is equally possible that their defections should reflect their individual responses to normative requirements, like obedience to the law. If princes could readily discard ordinary morality when they ascended the throne, Machiavelli would not have had to instruct them in the necessity of doing so. Nevertheless, it is not very comforting to rest the case for states' obligation of obedience to law on this inversion of the principal-agent problem.

It may be more straightforward to accept the practice of states, and of the diplomats, international lawyers, political theorists, journalists, and others who think about them professionally. States (though they must speak through human agents) characteristically talk as though they regard themselves to be bound by applicable legal norms, as do other collective bodies, such as corporations. Domestic and international laws treat states (as well as certain other kinds of collective bodies) as "artificial persons" with legal rights and obligations, some of them judicially enforceable. And students of state behavior, whether in the academy, the press, or public life, assume that states respond to interests, incentives, and penalties in much the same way that individuals do.[28] It is no more difficult to explain that states as such feel a general obligation to follow legal norms than to explain why they respond to "self-interest."

How Legal Norms Work

How do legal rules operate to regulate conduct? It is often assumed that this is a simple causal phenomenon: the rule is the cause of which the conduct is the effect.[29] In Chapter 1, we argued that economic efficiencies and organizational imperatives tend to induce compliance in just this causal sense. But this is far from the only possible explanation. In this section we examine three closely related and more complicated processes by which the development and elaboration of norms operate to influence state behavior. The first is the role of justification in international life. The second is the enormous complexity and interdependence of contemporary international affairs. And the third is the increasing importance of international organizations. The central proposition is that the interpretation, elaboration, application, and, ultimately, enforcement of international rules is accomplished through a process of (mostly verbal) interchange among the interested parties.

Justification and Discourse

A crucial element in the process by which international norms operate to control conduct, is that, as a matter of international practice, questionable action must be explained and justified—sometimes in advance, but almost without exception after the fact. "Accountability . . . is a critical rule- and norm-enforcement mechanism ... The fact that people are ultimately accountable for their decisions is an implicit or explicit constraint on virtually everything they do. Failure to behave in ways for which one can construct acceptable accounts leads to varying degrees of censure—depending of course on the gravity of the offense and the norms of the organizations."[30]

It is also crucial that international relations are conducted in large part through diplomatic conversation—explanation and justification, persuasion and dissuasion, approval and condemnation. These efforts make up the ordinary business of foreign ministries as they seek to generate support for policy positions or to elicit cooperative action, even when no question of impropriety arises.[31] In this discourse, the role of legal norms is large. It is almost always an adequate explanation for an action, at least prima facie, that it follows the legal rule. It is almost always a good argument for an action that it conforms to the applicable legal norms, and against, that it departs from them. The argument may not persuade, but there is no doubt where the burden of proof lies. It is almost always a ground for disapproval that an action violates the norms. It may be true, as Hans Morgenthau said, that states can always find a legal argument to justify their position.[32] But the range of possibilities is not infinite, and within some limits good legal arguments can generally be distinguished from bad.[33] It was not too difficult, for example, to discredit the "new interpretation" of the Anti–Ballistic Missile Treaty that the Reagan administration trotted out in support of its Strategic Defense Initiative.[34]

In theory, the sovereign state is entitled to pursue its course in silence, without regard to the reactions of others. As a practical matter, however, this expedient is not open in contemporary international society. In the conditions we have called the new sovereignty, there are too many audiences, foreign and domestic, too many relationships present and potential, too many linkages to other issues to be ignored. When a state's conduct is challenged as inconsistent with a legal norm or otherwise questionable, the state, almost of necessity, must respond—it must try to show that the facts are not as they seem to be; or that the rule, properly interpreted, does not cover the conduct in question; or that some other matter excuses nonperformance. This justificatory effort, as Friedrich Kratochwil says of legal reasoning in general, is neither a logical nor an empirical demonstration, but "an effort to gain assent to value judgments on reasoned rather than idiosyncratic grounds."[35] It is an effort at persuasion.

As an exercise in persuasion, justification is addressed to others. It is designed to secure their approval and agreement, or at least their assent or acquiescence. Thus even if, as the realists assert, the state's decisions are made on the basis of its "subjective" interests, reasons adduced in explanation or justification cannot be merely self-regarding but must have an "objective" appeal to the interlocutor. It is not enough to say "I like it" or "it suits my interests." "When Bill promises Jane to look after her terrier . . . in her absence, he has an obligation. It can be overridden only by exceptional circumstances. Bill's serious injury may serve as an excuse, as might the sickness of Bill's mother . . . His claim that he changed his mind will simply not do."[36]

Legal norms are not the only available grounds for justification, but the alternatives have characteristic problems. Arguments invoking the other parties' interests and broadly utilitarian appeals face the familiar difficulties of divining subjective preferences and aggregating utilities. In economic transactions, these issues are supposed to be mediated by money payment in the market, but there is no legal tender in international affairs. "Purely utilitarian ethics simply cannot cope with the complexity and the shortcomings of the calculations statesmen must make."[37]

Alternatively, justification of questioned conduct often relies on broadly accepted background principles rooted in practical experience and common sense: rough fairness, the status quo, precedent, custom.[38] In bargaining situations, there is a similar quest for objective criteria or principles to justify the position taken, where reliance on personal interest would entail the costs and inefficiencies of "positional bargaining" and a contest of wills between the negotiators.[39] In most situations, however, there will be more than one plausible objective criterion, and none of them will be neutral.[40]

Where the questioned conduct is in an area governed by treaty, the choice of governing principle is simplified. The parties have agreed in advance to the standards by which the conduct is to be judged: the text not only identifies the relevant norms but also provides an authoritative formulation for them. Even so, there is no linear, determinate path that dictates the application of the norm to specific conduct. "A case in course of decision must undergo *interpretation* and *analysis* by which its raw empirical representations are rendered into standardized versions, cast into categories corresponding to the vocabulary—necessarily categorical—of the external norm."[41]

To begin with, it is far from uncommon for treaties to contain competing norms. The UN Charter, for example, proclaims the sanctity of self-determination of peoples and the inviolability of the territorial integrity of states.[42] The collision of these two principles has been a prominent feature of debates over the fate of the former Yugoslavia and the former Soviet Union after the cold war, to say nothing of decolonization three decades earlier. Likewise, the General Agreement on Tariffs and Trade, which is said to be founded on the principles of nondiscrimination and most-favored-nation treatment, contains provisions for common markets, whose members are permitted to discriminate against nonmembers in trade matters.[43] In such cases, the problem may be determining which principle governs, rather than how to apply it to the facts. The answer is not a matter of syllogistic logic.

Even when there is agreement on the applicable norm, "events are always ambiguous."[44] For the most "objective" rules—like a speed limit, where, in principle, it seems possible to determine whether a particular actor was within the rule—there may be problems both with interpreting the norm and appraising the conduct.[45] First, there is a zone of indifference around the stated limit: Is a driver going 50.1 miles per hour in a 50-mph zone in violation? 51 mph? The boundaries of the zone are determined by a subjective sense of what matters and perhaps by the accuracy and availability of monitoring technology. Even in such apparently bright line regulations, the true limit shades off. And it may vary also with occasions and circumstances. Moreover, an appraisal of the disputed conduct can be made only on the basis of the available evidence, which may range from the rough estimates of a witness to the imperfect accuracy of radar. The resulting judgment never attains the assurance of the "in principle" determination.[46]

In some areas, like drug control and arms control, the slogan "zero tolerance" has been invoked to avoid these problems. But as Thomas Franck remarks, "A rule without exculpation, while seeming to court legitimacy by its apparent simplistic clarity, may actually appear illegitimate by producing results that appear so extraordinarily unjust, cavalier, unfair, even absurd, as to undermine the rule's ability to exert a strong pull to compliance."[47] The Limited Test Ban Treaty, for example, prohibits any nuclear explosion that "causes radioactive debris to be present outside the territorial limits of the State" conducting the explosion.[48] When is radioactive debris from an explosion "present" outside the boundaries of the originating state? The United States maintained that, like the tree falling in the forest, it was present only when it could be detected. In practice, however, even this standard proved too strict. Neither side's underground tests were always completely contained. "Venting" occurred, and when it did, detectable radiation often drifted beyond the boundaries of the testing state. The parties exchanged diplomatic notes about these incidents and tacitly agreed to disregard them.[49]

Unlike the zero tolerance rule or the paradigm of the speed limit, however, treaty requirements are commonly phrased in general language that must be interpreted to be applied in concrete cases:

- What is "national treatment" of imported goods?[50] Does an import fee on finished chemicals designed to offset a domestic excise tax on feed stocks qualify?[51]
- What kind of state behavior will "assure orderly exchange arrangements and promote a stable system of exchange rates"?[52] Does it require "cold shower" fiscal and monetary policies? What constitutes "manipulating exchange rates . . . to gain an unfair competitive advantage over other members"?
- Does placing environmental shelters over missile silos during construction work in cold weather constitute "deliberate concealment measures which impede verification by national technical means"?[53]
- When is whaling engaged in "for purposes of scientific research"?[54]

Such examples can be multiplied almost indefinitely.

This problem is not unique to international treaties. It is characteristic of all legal norms. "The notion that law is an interpretative practice, in which legal materials must be given meaning by purposive agents" has become a truism in modern legal thought.[55] "Rule following does not involve blind habit . . . but argumentation."[56]

In the U.S. legal system, the judiciary is a major player in this interpretative process. But, as Ronald Dworkin puts it, "though judges may have the last word, their word is not for that reason the best word."[57] The case may be decided, but even in the domestic system, the dialogue remains open.[58] In the international system, which does not have the benefit of much judicial assistance, the norms are interpreted, elaborated, shaped, reformulated, and applied in large part in the course of debate about the justification for contested action.[59] The discourse is not confined to the meaning of the norm, but extends to the acceptable grounds or excuse for nonperformance,[60] in accordance with the principle that treaties are "to be performed in good faith." Much will turn on the subjective intention of the actor or the fine grain of the factual context, which ties the dialogue closely to the specific situation. Detailed analysis and appraisal of the facts will be a central element. Indeed, as noted in Chapter 1, the formal structure of the discourse may be compared to that of a lawsuit, in which the claims and defenses of the parties are stated serially, exchanges of "pleadings" and pretrial procedures narrow and refine the issues, and the resulting framework limits both the scope of the argument and the range of relevant proof.

The discursive elaboration and application of treaty norms is the heart of the compliance process. The dynamic of justification is the search for a common understanding of the significance of the norm in the specific situation presented. The participants seek, almost in Socratic fashion, to persuade each other of the validity of the successive steps in the dialectic. In the course of this debate, the performance required of a party in a particular case is progressively defined and specified. Since the party has participated in each stage of the argument, the pressures to conform to the final judgment are great. "The process by which egoists learn to cooperate is at the same time a process of reconstructing their interests in terms of shared commitments to social norms."[61]

Interdependence and Complexity

Contemporary developments in the field of international relations impose new demands for complex cooperative activity among states and other international actors, extending over time. It is increasingly clear that no single country—or small group of countries—no matter how powerful, can consistently achieve its objectives through unilateral action or ad hoc coalition. It is this condition that we call the new sovereignty. First, as Joseph Nye and Robert Keohane pointed out two decades ago, the number, velocity, types, and complexity of international and transnational interactions are increasing exponentially.[62] Second, the international community itself has expanded decisively, not only in the number of states, which has tripled since 1950, but also in the increased diversity of the histories and cultures of the newer members in comparison with the small group of relatively homogeneous Western states that made up the "community of civilized nations" at the end of the nineteenth century.[63] Third, the environment and human rights "third wave" issues that do not yield so readily to the calculus of power and interest, in contrast to first and second wave preoccupation with physical and economic security—have increasingly shouldered their way onto the international agenda. And fourth, since World War II the jurisdiction and agendas of international organizations have encompassed a rapidly increasing arc of the international horizon.

Two common threads link these developments: they require very high levels of coordination and cooperation among complex activities, and they seriously limit the possibility of meeting that demand through informal, customary, or ad hoc responses. Robert C. Clark argues that parallel developments on the domestic scene have created a demand for the "potentially enormous" contribution of law and lawyers in "stabilizing expectations and reducing the transaction costs of later misunderstandings, conflicts and dispute resolution."[64] In the same way, these developments on the international level operate to engender a demand for regulatory norms and to create a "compliance prone" environment. The traditional attributes of effective foreign policy in the security area—flexibility, energy, secrecy—tend to give way before the growing importance for the new sovereignty of predictability, reliability, and stability of expectations. These requirements are intensified by the enmeshment of foreign policy in the internal political, legal, and economic life of the state.[65] As in the domestic setting, one important dimension of the response to these new demands is better-developed legal and regulatory arrangements. It is certainly true that these arrangements create opportunities for exploitation and strategic behavior in pursuit of immediate self-interest. But the need to operate in a multifaceted, interacting, and interdependent international environment with relatively diffuse power tends to lengthen the time horizon of states and lead them to take account of longer-term consequences. Compliance with the norms governing this environment becomes not so much a curb on the will or preferences of the state as a condition for realizing the full range of its objectives.

The Role of Organizations in International Legal Discourse

Since justification is a pervasive requirement of international relations, discourse about the meaning and application of international legal norms takes place in all the many channels for the conduct of foreign affairs—diplomatic correspondence, meetings of leaders, press statements, speeches, and policy pronouncements of all kinds, as well as in public debate, the media, and academic writing. Contemporary international life, however, is marked by what David Kennedy calls "the move to institutions."[66] With increasing frequency and over a broadening range of international business since World War II, international organizations have become a central instrument for management of international affairs and in particular for actualizing international legal norms.[67]

There is, of course, no one-to-one correlation of treaty to regime to organization.[68] Nevertheless, "a constitutional framework is essential to advanced collective arrangements, given of course levels of scale and complexity which preclude purely 'informal' arrangements."[69] In the early European regulatory treaties of the nineteenth century, which dealt with telephone and telegraph, intellectual property, postal services, and the like, it was customary to establish a "bureau" to administer the affairs of the treaty in the intervals between meetings of the parties.[70] Modern regulatory treaties, particularly the multilateral ones, commonly either establish an organization to carry out their provisions or vest responsibility for implementation in an existing body.[71]

The presence of a formal organization with responsibility for administering a treaty changes the compliance situation in important ways, a subject to which we return in Chapter 12.[72] For present purposes, the important consideration is that international organizations "are a focused and intensified arena of public justification."[73] As such, they intensify the legal content of the discourse and heighten the importance of legal norms.

An international organization is a creature of law. It is typically established by a constitutive treaty that identifies and limits the powers of the organization and its subparts, specifying the range of matters over which each can act. It prescribes the terms and conditions of membership. It lays out the procedures and decision rules that each of the organs must follow to take legally effective action. And it defines the formal relations, hierarchical and otherwise, among the constituent parts.[74] In consequence, organizational decision making necessarily has a heavily legal component. Much of the debate and discussion seems to go not to the merits of a proposed action but to matters of interpretation, jurisdiction, and procedural regularity. These issues should not be dismissed as procedural technicalities, however. Since compliance with substantive norms depends in significant degree on their perceived validity and legitimacy, the functioning of these institutional rules can be crucial for the compliance problem.

For example, as was seen in Chapter 2, Article 39 of the UN Charter says that the Security Council must "determine the existence of a threat to the peace, breach of the peace or act of aggression" in order to impose economic sanctions or authorize the use of military force against a country. The determination could be construed simply as a procedural precondition to enforcement action. On this reading, if the necessary eleven votes (including the concurrence of the five permanent members) could be aggregated, the Council would be empowered to make the orders. But the requirement of a Security Council finding is generally read to incorporate substantive limits on the council's powers: it cannot act unless the situation is "really" a "threat to the peace, breach of the peace or act of aggression." In the politics of assembling the necessary votes in the council (and persuading domestic publics of the members), the question of the substantive limits on the Council's authority is often a key factor. Thus, Western states were able to resist the imposition of economic sanctions against Rhodesia for more than a year on the ground that, no matter how heinous the policy of the minority white government was, it did not constitute any threat to its neighbors and therefore could not provide the predicate for Security Council enforcement action. As was also discussed, in the debates over Libya, Somalia, and Bosnia, members agonized over the power of the Security Council to act under Chapter VII in situations presenting little if any threat to international peace, and the issue increased the leverage of those opposing more forceful action.

The legalistic emphasis does not stop with interpreting the basic charter of the organization. It cascades down through an increasingly complex network of resolutions, decisions, and policy statements, all of which are framed in language—much of it normative—that must be expounded and applied to concrete situations. Inevitably the same questions recur: Does the resolution authorize the proposed actions? Has the agency properly interpreted and applied the relevant norms? In this way, an international organization becomes in large part an arena of discourse about the norms within its area of competence. Anyone who doesn't believe that international law is a discursive practice should be sentenced to spend some time reading the proceedings of the UN or its agencies.[75]

This legalistic quality of international organizational activity is sometimes ridiculed as overblown rhetoric, but closer analysis reveals important ways in which it tends to promote compliance with the regulatory norms of the regime.

First, the seemingly endless discussion of the scope and meaning of norms in the formal proceedings of the organization enhances their authoritative character. It becomes harder for a party to reject the normative command after treating it seriously and at length in debate within the organization.

Second, in the course of debates in the various bodies of the organization, the content of the substantive norms becomes more transparent. They are elaborated and given more concrete and specific form so that parties can more readily adapt their conduct. International legal pronouncements, like their domestic counterparts, are often cast in broad, general terms, and even where there has been an effort at precision, further elaboration is frequently necessary. In common law countries, judicial decisions perform this function; in the civil law, it is carried out by the writings of scholars and publicists. It is a large part of the work of private lawyers and bureaucrats everywhere. International organizations carry a good deal of this burden in the international system.

Third, in applying the norms to a case of asserted noncompliance, the organization defines and specifies the performance required in the particular case if the delinquent party is to remain in good standing. Compliance issues are worked through organizational procedures, usually resulting in some kind of recommendation or a resolution calling on the defaulting party to take or refrain from some specific action. The effect is to make it much easier to observe and verify the actions of the defaulting party and much harder for that party to disguise nonperformance behind a legalistic smoke screen.

The Legitimacy of Norms

We introduced the importance of legitimacy in our discussion of coercive sanctions in Part One. In the context of norms, this element is even more central, because the claim of the norm to obedience is based in significant part on its legitimacy. The notion of the legitimacy of a norm (or norm system or regime) invokes characteristics broadly related to "fairness" that enhance the prospects for compliance. For the pure realist, legitimacy is an empty set, because only calculations of interest (including the prospect of sanctions) enter into the compliance decision. But if, as we have argued, a discursive process of explanation, justification, and persuasion is a central attribute of international affairs, then fairness considerations can hardly fail to play a major role in that process, whether in relation to the origins of the norm, its meaning and application, or its content. Legitimacy, then, depends on the extent to which the norm (1) emanates from a fair and accepted procedure, (2) is applied equally and without invidious discrimination, and (3) does not offend minimum substantive standards of fairness and equity. These are admittedly nebulous criteria, and they are admittedly aspirational. No existing legal system fully meets them. As Thomas Franck says, "legitimacy is a matter of degree."[76]

Not surprisingly, since this conception of legitimacy is put forward by two American lawyers, it carries more than faint echoes of the core U.S. consti tutional principles of due process and equal protection of the laws. Yet we think it is not simply a projection of parochial preconceptions. In practice, members of a treaty regime do in fact assess its norms and procedures against something like these standards (as well as calculating costs and benefits).[77] Pure hegemony, as we argued in Part One, comes out poorly by these standards. The hegemon may induce obedience through the exercise of coercive power, but it is exceedingly costly to rule solely by fear or favor. Norms offer one way to reduce those costs, and so they are prominent even in hegemonic systems.[78] But the norm structure will have this effect only if it is to some extent truly normative, and not just a disguise for willful command. Thus even the hegemon will have to accept some attributes of legitimacy to make the norm system work.[79] For example, the post–World War II trade regime embodied in the GATT is said to have been a hegemonic regime, imposed by the United States. To make the system function effectively, however, the United States regularly had to accept decisions that went against its position.[80]

Fair and Accepted Procedures

In classical international law, the source of obligations was the consent of the state to be bound. It was thought fair to hold a state to what it had agreed to do. Moreover, the idea of consent as the basis for the legitimacy of international obligations resonated with the Western contractarian tradition, from Hobbes to Rawls, espousing consent as the basis for the legitimacy of domestic governmental institutions. As in contract law, however, a simple reliance on formal consent is inadequate to ensure legitimacy. Bargains reflect power as well as the pull of fairness. Leviathan himself was a creature of contract.[81] Although modern international law, as codified in the Vienna Convention, holds that a treaty is void if "procured by the threat or use of force" in violation of the UN Charter, forms of duress falling short of that do not affect the formal validity of the agreement.[82]

Legitimacy accrues with tradition, precedent, and acquiescence, as the treaty persists over time. Acceptance ex post is assimilated to consent ex ante, and treaty norms tend to gain strength and legitimacy with time.

In modern times, the sovereign is no longer a unitary actor who can bind the domain by his own will. Power in modern states is recognized as being distributed along formal and informal networks, and legitimacy is compromised unless consent to international commitments is elicited through internal procedures, formal or informal.[83] Even among dictators, few can convincingly claim "*l'état, c'est moi.*" In democratic states, the onetime ideal of "open covenants openly arrived at" is rapidly becoming a political imperative. Yalta, the Molotov-Ribbentrop Agreement, the Maastricht Treaty—all in their separate ways illustrate the consequences for legitimacy and ultimately for efficacy when international agreements are made in disregard of the domestic dimension of consent.[84]

On the international plane also, the simple extrapolation from formal consent to legitimacy is open to question. In the first place, as we have said, *pacta sunt servanda*—the rule that the state is bound by its consent—is not itself a consensually grounded norm. But even if the state may be said to have consented to the text of the treaty, that doesn't carry very far if the meaning of the text depends significantly on the relatively open process of norm elaboration and application described earlier in this chapter. Moreover, modern treaties often provide procedures for modifying the substantive obligations by agreement among the parties, without a formal amendment or the conclusion of a new treaty.[85] It may be argued that these processes of interpretation and supplementary norm creation are legitimated by the consent of the state in adhering to the treaty in the first place. But as the story of the International Whaling Commission shows, such imputed consent is less persuasive as a legitimator of outcomes if the procedures turn out to be unfair in operation.

A truly open-ended dialectical process of norm interpretation and application, one that persists until a resolution is freely accepted by the parties, would meet the test of legitimacy, at least if it actually produced results.[86] International consultations and negotiations frequently have this character. The Standing Consultative Commission (scc) was established under the SALT I agreements between states of relatively equal power and interest. In its early years it was able to resolve a number of serious issues on a basis legitimated by mutual satisfaction. This ideal is not easy to sustain, however, especially between adversaries on basic security issues. The Reagan administration came to believe that the Soviets were stonewalling in the scc to avoid dealing with U.S. objections, and the legitimacy as well as the usefulness of the commission was soon dissipated (see Chapter 9).

On the issue of legitimacy, too, the presence of an international organization makes a difference: interpretations, rules changes, and even compliance decisions are made by vote, rather than by the individual assent of the affected state. The charters of almost all the international organizations established since the immediate postwar years adopt the rule of one country, one vote—although often, as in the case of the General Assembly, a special majority is required for "important" or substantive questions. Majority rule means that decisions can be imposed on the minority without its consent. In practice, however, international organizations seek to preserve the consensual principle despite the formal voting rules.[87] First, almost all treaty provisions granting organizational authority to alter obligations permit a member to opt out of a decision taken over its objection.[88] Second, with increasing frequency international organizations, as a matter of practice, proceed by consensus and avoid formal votes. The GATT, for example, acts by consensus, although the agreement provides that each party should have one vote and that the organization should make decisions in most cases by a simple majority.[89] In a number of modern treaties, the voting article itself provides for decision by consensus if at all possible, and it may mandate a cooling off period or other procedures before a formal vote, if consensus is not achieved.[90]

The tension between the appearance and the reality of consent reemerges in the operation of consensus voting and opting out. As discussed in Chapter 11, when the Convention on International Trade in Endangered Species decided to ban the ivory trade, Japan, among other states, came under enormous pressure not to exercise its treaty rights to opt out. An implicit threat to reject Kyoto as the venue for the next meeting of the General Conference induced Japan to accept the ban. The southern African states of Zimbabwe, Botswana, and South Africa had effective elephant conservation programs, unlike Kenya and governments in other East African habitats where elephant populations were declining precipitously, and the southern states did formally opt out of the CITES decision. However, under pressure from the majority, they agreed not to exercise their right to trade in ivory, pending a review of the situation at the next CITES meeting. The 1992 conference, after hearing the arguments of the southern African states, persisted in its decision, and the dissenters finally abandoned their effort.[91] However acceptable such pressures may be as a means of inducing compliance with accepted treaty obligations, their deployment against states that have exercised their right to opt out is hard to square with the consensual basis of the legitimacy of international obligations.

The issue now coming to a head in the IWC can be seen as a essentially an issue of legitimacy. The supporters of the moratorium on whale hunting argue that the ban is essential to the preservation of endangered whale species. But there is little doubt that, for some, it reflects a new conception of the purpose of the organization, a purpose that is itself the product of a new "deep environmentalist" approach that regards commercial whale hunting as morally unacceptable. The whaling states believe that the new majority is seeking to impose its moral position on them and end whaling altogether, rather than to manage whale stocks on a sustained-yield basis for commercial exploitation, in accord with the original intention of the International Convention for the Regulation of Whaling. Neither insistence on majority rule nor a continuing holdout by the minority will sustain the legitimacy of the organization[92] (see the discussion in Chapters 3, 4, and 11).

As with the opt-out right, the pressures for going along with the consensus are heavy. Thus, although consensus voting seems tantamount to a rule of unanimity,[93] it can itself become a vehicle for silencing the minority. The most dramatic breakout from a consensus procedure came on the issue of Soviet voting rights in the UN General Assembly, described in Chapter 3.

During the impasse, the business of the General Assembly was conducted by consensus throughout the 1965 and 1966 sessions. Before the adjournment of the 1966 session, however, the Albanian representative, in the face of almost universal opposition of the membership, insisted on a formal vote on whether to continue the consensus procedure. The vote was overwhelmingly in favor of the procedure, but the Soviet vote was counted. The sanction of Article 19 withdrawing the vote from a delinquent member was nullified permanently, and the consensus on consensus was broken.[94] But only a state with as little to lose as Albania was able to muster the courage to challenge it.

The veto implicit in consensus voting can itself become a source of abuse and unfairness. The GATT council's practice of acting by consensus in effect permitted a losing party to block the adoption of a panel decision that went against it. Resentment of the use of this power—particularly by the United States and the EC—to delay adoption of adverse panel decisions for lengthy periods ultimately led to the Uruguay Round reforms, embodied now in the World Trade Organization Charter. Panel reports are now to be adopted automatically, *unless there is a consensus against them* (see Chapter 9).

These examples show that formal and mechanical arrangements for ensuring consent may be flawed in practice. Nevertheless, the principle of actual consent remains pretty close to the surface in most functioning international regimes, and a variety of expedients have been developed to deal with inherent abuses.

Equal Application without Invidious Discrimination

The essence of law is often said to be to treat like cases alike. The difficulty lies in deciding which cases are alike.[95] Much of the process of norm interpretation and application described above is devoted to this question.

Problems of equality and discrimination also appear in the context of decision rules, voting arrangements, and membership criteria of international organizations. Weighted voting schemes, as in the Security Council and in the IMF and World Bank, were favored by the United States in the immediate post–World War II era. It was able to get its way partly because there was arguably a rational basis for a weighted distribution and partly because of its overwhelming power. Since then, the international system has elevated "the sovereign equality of states" to a supreme principle, and weighted voting no longer seems acceptable in new agreements.[96] Even the old bastions of the practice are under pressure. It is widely acknowledged that the present organization of the Security Council cannot survive indefinitely in its present form. Meanwhile, for many years neither the United Kingdom nor France has cast a veto in the Security Council without the United States. The World Bank and the IMF characteristically act by consensus, and the 1970s and 1980s have seen a determined and to a large extent successful effort by developing countries to secure membership on the dominant policy committees.[97]

Some major treaties have built-in discriminatory provisions. Perhaps the most significant is the Nuclear Non-Proliferation Treaty, which divides its members into two classes: the five states that already possessed nuclear weapons when the treaty went into force and are permitted to keep them; and the remainder—some one hundred thirty states—that undertake not to acquire nuclear weapons. The NPT included a quid pro quo for this sharp differentiation. The non–nuclear weapon states were ensured the right of access to nuclear technology for peaceful purposes, and the weapon states agreed to move forward on nuclear disarmament. Neither of these trade-offs have proved satisfactory, however. Advanced states have joined in an informal Nuclear Suppliers Group (NSG) to enforce the ban on weapons proliferation by imposing export controls on sensitive materials and equipment. The safeguards arrangements have been seen by the non–nuclear weapon states as an additional source of discrimination. And until the end of the cold war, almost twenty-five years after the NPT was adopted, the superpowers had made little progress on nuclear arms control. Although the NPT is in many ways an extremely successful international agreement, the basic discrimination between weapon and non-weapon states has cast a shadow on its legitimacy that has plagued it throughout its history and has at times even seemed to threaten its survival.[98] By contrast, the Chemical Weapons Convention, after a shaky moment when President Bush proposed that the United States and the USSR should be permitted to retain some chemical weapons during a transitional period, has adopted the opposite approach and imposes a universal ban on the production, possession, or use of chemical weapons.

Not all treaties are universal in scope or object. Most deal with bilateral or regional issues or matters of concern to a limited number of states. In some cases, like the European Community, membership restrictions may reflect the capacity of states to carry out burdensome treaty obligations or, as in the many Nordic agreements, may reflect a close-knit culture, history, and outlook. In such cases, there may be no "invidious discrimination" in limiting participation in the treaty according to relevant criteria. Even in such cases, however, as is shown by the unfolding experience with the expansion of the European Community, applicants for membership are in a strong position to insist that entrance requirements should be reasonable and administered on a nondiscriminatory basis.

Limited-membership clubs must be prepared to defend exclusionary policies on principled grounds. In 1959, twelve countries, all of which maintained major scientific programs in the Antarctic and seven of which had territorial claims in the continent, concluded the Antarctic Treaty. In it they agreed to stabilize territorial claims (without recognizing the validity of any), demilitarize the continent, and cooperate in scientific research in the area. Although other states were free to adhere to the treaty, the power of decision was confined to "consultative parties," including the original members and any other qualified party with a major scientific commitment in the area.[99] In recent years, the broader international community has been increasingly concerned in the fate of Antarctica, and it is growing harder for the original parties to maintain their policy-making monopoly. On some issues where broader participation has seemed essential, like the conservation of marine living resources, the treaty parties have sponsored separate conventions with more general participation in policy-making.[100] In the Antarctic Treaty itself, the inner sanctum of consultative parties is under growing pressure for broader participation that would include developing countries as members.[101]

The principle of "sovereign equality of states" speaks to formal equality, but in the daily conduct of treaty relations, formal equality carries only so far. It cannot erase the manifold differences in power, economic position, or cultural and political orientation among states. Power differentials count, and poorer states often lack the resources to participate effectively in treaty activities. At the same time, the demands of legitimacy make it increasingly difficult for treaty regimes to resist the claims of equality, and there is little reason to suppose that broader participation does not translate to some extent into policy outcomes.

Minimum Substantive Standards of Fairness and Equity

Whether some minimum of substantive fairness is an essential element of a legal system is the issue that has divided positivists from natural lawyers for two centuries.[102] We do not propose to settle it here. Even the strictest positivists agree that a legal system is subject to criticism from the standpoint of ethics or equity. Indeed, they say, the very point of separating "law" from substantive morality is to enable criticism of the law from the perspective of morals or fairness or equity.[103]

Thomas Franck's *The Power of Legitimacy among States,* the most recent effort at a systematic examination of legitimacy in the international legal system, advances a strictly procedural conception of legitimacy.[104] Nevertheless, he agrees that the "justice" or "fairness" of a rule also exerts "a pull towards compliance." For our purposes, it is not important whether justice and fairness are necessary elements of a legitimate legal system (so that a system of rules utterly lacking in these qualities could not be called a legal system),[105] or whether the deficiency of justice or fairness is simply a basis for fundamental criticism of a system acknowledged to be a legal system. In either case, the question of the legitimacy of a rule or system cannot be kept wholly distinct from the fairness of its substantive content. And the same applies to international legal norms. As Oran Young says, "While it is important to recognize that there are no objective standards of equity which can be applied to human affairs, it is also worth noting that identifiable community standards regarding equity do exist in specific social settings. And there is much to be said for the proposition that satisfying these standards is a necessary condition for international regime formation."[106] If empirical support is needed for that proposition, the Versailles Treaty stands as a harrowing example.

Conclusion

This chapter has discussed the nature of international legal norms—in particular, treaty norms—and their power to promote compliant behavior. Even the rational choice literature now accepts that norms do have such power, but for the most part, it continues to analyze the operation of norms in linear causal terms, either as affecting costs and benefits of action or as providing opportunities for strategic behavior. Treaty norms have a certain authority stemming from the mere fact that they have been promulgated by an accepted and acknowledged treaty-making procedure. Fundamentally, however, normative power derives from a much more complicated dialogic process of interpretation and application, extending over time. It is closely linked to the pervasive demand of the international legal and political systems, that states and other international actors be prepared to justify their actions when challenged. The new sovereignty puts the normative force of the treaty rules at the heart of the compliance process.

6

Transparency, Norms, and Strategic Interaction

In this chapter we examine the question of how transparency—the availability of and access to information—operates to enhance compliance with treaty norms. In the context of international regulation, we mean by transparency the availability and accessibility of knowledge and information about (1) the meaning of norms, rules, and procedures established by the treaty and practice of the regime, and (2) the policies and activities of parties to the treaty and of any central organs of the regime as to matters relevant to treaty compliance and regime efficacy.

Economics, game theory, and related disciplines have turned increasing attention to how the availability of information affects decision processes and the prospects for solving collective action problems.[1] These analysts focus on the problem of "cooperation,"[2] which is not the same thing as compliance with treaty obligations, but the structure of the compliance problem is similar enough that their insights can be fruitfully applied to it. Their work suggests three important ways in which transparency, as defined above, may operate to promote treaty compliance:

- It facilitates *coordination* converging on the treaty norm among independent actors.
- It provides *reassurance* that they are not being taken advantage of when their compliance with the norms is contingent on similar action by other (or enough other) participants in the regime.
- It exercises *deterrence* against actors contemplating noncompliance.

For these reasons, we argue that, in general, increased transparency sets up a powerful dynamic for compliance with treaties. The three effects will be treated separately here for purposes of analysis, but in practice transparency may operate simultaneously in all three dimensions.

This chapter discusses strategic interaction among regime participants, mediated only by the treaty norms and the available information about the behavior of others. Often independent "rational" responses of the parties are sufficient to produce satisfactory compliance.[3] But where such strategic interaction is insufficient by itself to avoid or correct unacceptable defection, further action within the regime will be needed to deal with suspect behavior. The essential power of transparency in such cases is that deviations from prescribed conduct can be observed and the actor called to account. We discuss this process further in Chapters 10, 11, and 12.

Coordination

In "pure" coordination problems, the parties have a common interest in achieving a common objective, and the potential for relative gains as between parties is small.[4] It has been said that such situations are "not interesting," because if the aims of the parties are completely in harmony, there is no difficulty in achieving cooperative action.[5] That view is belied by the experience of domestic legal systems, where much of the enterprise consists in designing "facilitative" rules and institutions to make it easier for actors to coordinate independent activities. A good deal of the law of contract can be seen in this light.

In some cases, international institutions, simply by providing information, can assist coordination even without a related norm framework.[6] The system of national reporting on infectious diseases established under the World Health Organization, for example, enables members to adjust their own policies to the current epidemiological threat.[7] Similarly, during the long period before the Law of the Sea Convention was in force and the International Seabed Authority came into being, a group of industrial states agreed to notify each other of any national permits each issued for seabed mineral exploration.[8] The notice allows states issuing new permits to take care that the area covered does not overlap licenses issued by other parties, thus avoiding contested claims between the licensees of different states. Many of the numerous notification provisions in treaties perform the same kind of coordination function.

Very often, however, rules are helpful or even necessary for solving coordination problems.[9] In the absence of an applicable rule of the road, drivers would try to coordinate their actions so that they could operate swiftly and safely. When two drivers approached each other going in opposite directions, each would seek to drive on one side of the road leaving the opposite side for the other. However, even though the pressures for coordination are strong and there are no countervailing incentives, there would be many accidents, because drivers would not at the outset decide uniformly to drive on the right or the left or might not understand the signals of the oncoming driver or would be inattentive, or for any of a number of other reasons.

The rule of the road avoids the "transaction costs" involved in ad hoc coordination. In a situation where the incentives for cooperative action are strong, little more may be needed than transparency of the rule system itself to induce compliance. If drivers are aware that the rule is to drive on the right (or, in England, the left), they will comply. Sometimes the exact performance that the norm requires may not be obvious. A white line down the center of the road specifies the expected performance: it tells the driver what it means to drive on the right. Again, the driver, almost automatically, will stay to the right of the line.[10] Rules and specifications achieve prominence as coordination points, in the sense first proposed by Thomas Schelling in *The Strategy of Conflict*.[11]

On the international plane, treaties dealing with coordination problems take a bewildering variety of forms. Following are some illustrative examples.

International transport and communication. As would be expected, agreements on "rules of the road" elicit high compliance with a minimum of effort by publicizing the rules to the relevant constituencies and setting up decision procedures when necessary, to specify the expected performance. The actors may not care which of a number of possible rules is adopted, but they are very much concerned that there should be a single rule to govern the activity. Thus, operational and safety rules promulgated by the International Civil Aviation Organization are readily accepted by the parties. Indeed, as a practical matter, compliance is a condition of access to the international air transport system.[12] The Universal Postal Union, one of the oldest international treaty regimes,[13] has operated reliably through wars, hot and cold, for more than a century. The long-distance telephone lines to Beijing remained open during the quarter of a century in which the United States refused to recognize the People's Republic of China, under procedures developed by the International Telecommunication Union.[14] Likewise, throughout the cold war confrontation between the United States and Cuba, U.S. callers had direct-dial service to Havana. When, in 1993, the United States tried to freeze Cuba's portion of the proceeds, the calls were smoothly rerouted through Canada.[15]

Communications satellites. The ITU system for allocation of orbital slots for communications satellites displays a somewhat greater level of complexity.[16] The International Telecommunications Convention prohibits "harmful interference" between transmissions of members.[17] The geostationary orbit, 22,000 miles above the earth, is the optimal location for communications satellites, but each must be deployed at a distance from the next, sufficient to avoid mutual interference. The ITU has further specified the required performance by dividing the geostationary orbit into "slots" occupying an arc of the orbit large enough that transmissions from a satellite in one slot will not interfere with those of its neighbor. Before a satellite is placed in orbit, the flag state is required to record the slot to be occupied in a registry established by the ITU. At any given time, the registry provides a comprehensive picture of the places still available. New operators select slots that the registry shows to be open, so as not to have their transmissions interfered with, and they comply with the registration requirement so that still later arrivals will not interfere with them. The registration system permits coordinated use of the spectrum resource (so long as the parties are satisfied with a first come first served rule).[18] Communications satellite operators are not unlike drivers in the road traffic example. They might have been able to coordinate their activities to avoid harmful interference even in the absence of the ITU Convention and regulations. It is not unlikely, however, that they would have failed, or that the solution they reached would have entailed higher transaction costs or been more contentious than the ITU regime.

Acid rain. The intra-European controversy over acid rain in the 1970s and early 1980s is an illustration of treaty-induced coordination in the conduct of research and scientific investigation that led ultimately to coordinated policy responses. In the beginning, only Norway and Sweden contended that emissions of sulfur dioxide (SO_2) from foreign industrial installations were causing extensive damage to forests and lakes. All other European states, particularly the United Kingdom and Germany, rejected this diagnosis. The Convention on Long-Range Transboundary Air Pollution (LRTAP), concluded in 1979, at first required only that the parties periodically report on their levels of SO_2 emissions, without setting quantitative limits on permissible emissions. A year earlier, the Organization for Economic Co-operation and Development had organized a network of atmospheric scientists in governments, the academy, and industry—known as the European Monitoring and Evaluation Program (EMEP)—to collect and evaluate data on air pollution in Europe.[19] National reports submitted under LRTAP were available to EMEP, which embarked on an elaborate evaluative process, developing uniform collection and reporting protocols, collating time-series data on emissions, and integrating the results with other relevant knowledge about the pathways and impact of the emissions. The studies ultimately produced a uniform reporting system and a scientific consensus on the destructive effects of acid rain on European forests. Sweden and Norway from the beginning had favored a protocol calling for a 30 percent reduction of emissions against an agreed baseline, but it was not until 1985, more than five years after the agreement was concluded, that the LRTAP members adopted a protocol setting a firm requirement of 30 percent reductions by 1993. Many European states had already taken national action with the aim of reaching that limit.[20]

Coordination was a two-stage process: the original transparency norm requiring national reporting provided the basis for coordinating national scientific efforts. According to Marc A. Levy, "Coordination of national research programs can be considered the bedrock of all LRTAP's activity. One reason coordination is important is that it insures comparability of results across Europe. Without standardization of data collection, measurement, and analysis procedures, even those countries with active interests in acidification would be unable to pool their results."[21] The coordinated research led in turn to coordinated policy responses at the national level and finally to a uniform international substantive norm.[22] Without LRTAP, many if not most of the European countries would have published national statistics on SO_2 emissions, and no doubt some would have reduced emissions independently, but the credible, integrated database that precipitated common scientific judgment and coordinated government action would not have emerged—or at least not so soon.

The Mediterranean Sea. A similar two-stage development occurred under the umbrella of the Barcelona Convention for the Protection of the Mediterranean Sea, signed in February 1976.[23] The convention provided for cooperation among the parties in monitoring and in scientific and technological work, again without imposing any substantive limits on the activity of the members.[24] This phase of the agreement was carried out as a coordinated research and monitoring program known as Med Plan, developed by the UN Environment Program. Peter Haas, in the definitive work on the subject, says that "actual studies were conducted by laboratories nationally. Virtually no joint studies were undertaken ... The lead laboratories consolidated these nationally generated findings into reports, with the support of international agencies."[25]

As with LRTAP, considerable effort was devoted to the development of "common styles of pollution monitoring" and "intercalibration." Again the result was the creation of "a scientific consensus which demonstrated the need to treat a broad range of sources, channels and types of pollution."[26] Like EMEP's reports on acid rain, this process was effective in generating scientific consensus. The ensuing report on land-based sources of pollution in the Mediterranean, presented in September 1977, "compellingly demonstrated the need for dealing with land based pollutants and pollution transmitted by rivers."[27] And also as in the acid rain case, national policy coordination came before international standard setting. According to Haas, national pollution control policies "began to converge" around more comprehensive marine pollution controls, especially where members of the "epistemic community" of marine scientists and ecologists were favorably placed in national bureaucracies: "Governments adopted increasingly more comprehensive pollution control legislation and many of their control practices focus on broader and more stringent forms of control than before the Med Plan was adopted."[28] This in turn led to the first new regulatory action under the convention, the Protocol for the Protection of the Mediterranean Sea against Pollution from Land-Based Sources, signed in May 1980.

Generalizing from these two cases, LRTAP and Med Plan, the authors of *Institutions for the Earth* propose as one of their principal recommendations that environmental institutions should foster an open-ended process of knowledge creation and dissemination to enhance their effectiveness.[29]

Maritime inspections. The Memorandum of Understanding on Port State Control was signed by fourteen European states in 1982.[30] Each signatory agreed to inspect no fewer than 25 percent of the ships entering its harbors for compliance with various safety and environmental regulations of the International Maritime Organization (IMO). A ship that is found free of deficiencies cannot be inspected again for six months. The parties also agreed to notify each other in real time, via a computerized network, of the ships they have inspected and the results of the inspections. Using this information, ports visited by the ship later in its voyage can focus their inspection effort on other ships that have not previously been inspected, or on difficulties turned up by prior inspection. As a result, each state can optimize the use of its limited enforcement resources. In the aggregate, a large proportion of the ships visiting the member ports are inspected yearly, and since a very large part of the world's commercial fleet passes through the ports of these fourteen countries, the overall enforcement effort for IMO safety and environmental rules is greatly enhanced.[31]

Nonproliferation. A more centralized coordination function is illustrated by the operation of the International Atomic Energy Agency safeguard system. The system enables parties to the Nuclear Non-Proliferation Treaty to coordinate their actions so as to comply with two of the core obligations of the treaty: (1) not to assist non–nuclear weapon states to acquire nuclear weapons, and (2) not to deny their access to nuclear energy and technology for peaceful purposes.[32] As noted in Chapter 4, the system evolved from the U.S. Atoms for Peace initiative of the 1950s. States receiving assistance from the United States for their peaceful nuclear programs signed bilateral agreements under which they agreed to submit the equipment or material to periodic U.S. inspections to ensure against diversion to military uses. Later, by agreement between the United States, the purchasing country, and the IAEA, the agency took over the inspection responsibilities. Other nuclear exporters adopted the same policy. Potential suppliers do not provide nuclear facilities or materials to a country unless a safeguards agreement is in effect under which the agency conducts periodic inspections to ensure that none of the exported materials or equipment has been diverted to military uses.[33] By this means, exporting states coordinate their actions so as to implement the treaty obligation not to assist non–nuclear weapons states in the acquisition of nuclear weapons, while at the same time providing access to peaceful nuclear energy and technology.

Debt reduction. The International Monetary Fund has gone a step further, granting what is in effect a "seal of approval" to countries seeking to restructure their debt, even in cases where the fund is not itself contributing new money. The IMF staff conducts "enhanced surveillance" of the debtor to determine its economic position and decide on an appropriate adjustment program. Until the fund has approved an adjustment program to accompany the restructuring, public and commercial lenders will not proceed. Once it has signaled its approval, the creditors ordinarily go forward without further ado. In fact, the lenders have pressed the IMF to undertake this function. Coordination of the actions of hundreds of public and private creditors on issues of large political and economic significance has been accomplished by means of data collection and analysis by the IMF.[34]

Conventional arms limitation. The UN Register of Conventional Arms is perhaps the most ambitious effort to achieve coordination by information dissemination. The register was established by a General Assembly resolution calling on states to voluntarily record their sales of conventional arms of certain categories.[35] The hope was that the publicity would begin to induce states to moderate their arms sales programs, at least with respect to certain, presumably more dangerous, buyers. In the first registration in April 1993, seventy-two countries reported, including the "big six" (China, France, Germany, Russia, the United Kingdom, and the United States) and most other major exporters. Performance on the importing side was less satisfactory.[36] There is no sign of abatement in conventional arms sales, but supporters of the register see it as a long-term project that may provide a basis for future discussion on conventional arms limitation, much as the transparency measures in LRTAP and Med Plan led first to coordinated national policies and then to positive law regulations. This looks to be a case, however, where the incentives for independent action are too strong to be constrained by transparency alone.

The Need for Reassurance

It is sometimes said that in a pure coordination situation, the actor has no incentive to depart from the rule.[37] It may be true that the actor has no preference whether the rule is "drive on the left" or "drive on the right," so long as everyone knows the rule and abides by it. But unless everyone else conforms, it is not necessarily true that the individual actor has no incentive not to comply. If other drivers are driving at random, then the actor had better forget about the rule and drive so as to avoid oncoming traffic. Indeed, even if there is a single "defector" approaching, the actor may be well advised to abandon the rule. The absence of an incentive not to comply is a reflection of the expectation that everyone else *will* comply.

The pure coordination situation is a strong case of the broader proposition that cooperative action in general, and the special case of compliance with rules, is a function at least in part of the expectation that others will also comply. As Carlisle Runge argues, in problems involving the provision of public goods, where benefits and costs are a function of the total action of the group, the decision of each actor to contribute or not (and how much) is necessarily affected by expectations about the decisions of others.[38] In a situation where the actor's benefits will exceed the value of his contribution if, but only if, everyone in the group contributes, then he will contribute if he expects everyone else to do so, and not otherwise. Since no real-world situation will conform precisely to these conditions, "incentives exist to free ride if this behavior is expected of others, but . . . the assurance that others will contribute their fair share increases the likelihood that one will contribute too."[39]

Reassurance Generated by the Norm System Itself

As we argued in Chapter 5, the existence of the norm itself increases the expectation that others will behave in accordance with it. These expectations alone may be enough to ensure compliance in situations that are not pure coordination games, in which where the actor's incentives to behave differently or the costs to the actor of another's defection are small. The treaties banning deployment of nuclear weapons on the seabed,[40] in outer space,[41] and in Antarctica[42] were concluded with little difficulty in the early days of the cold war, because these environments were uniformly regarded as unpromising for military activity. Although the seabed and antarctic treaties have inspection provisions, they are not seriously exercised, as we discuss in Chapter 8. Yet there has been no reported deviation from the requirements of these treaties over a period of four decades.

It is true that the incentive to deploy weapons in these environments was originally low, but it is not inconceivable that, in the absence of the treaties, one or the other superpower, for some reason—supercaution, perhaps—would have begun thinking about and even experimenting with deployments in one or more of them. There were certainly people in the United States who advocated "seizing the high ground" with deployments in outer space.[43] Such actions would have generated pressure for the other side to begin a counterdevelopment. It is thus not hard to imagine that in the absence of the treaty on outer space, for example, even without any strong incentive, an arms race looking toward deployments in outer space might have developed. The presence of the treaty, embodying a norm of nondeployment, may have been enough to prevent this outcome. Why? Arguably because it generated expectations in each party, even if weak ones, that the other would abide by the norm.

In a somewhat harder case, the same factors may operate to induce compliance by the industrialized states with the Montreal Protocol for the Protection of the Ozone Layer, which (as amended) bans the production of chlorofluorocarbons and other some ozone-depleting chemicals beginning January 1, 1996.[44] At the time the protocol was written, in 1987, only five major chemical companies operating in a small number of countries produced CFCs.[45] Neither the CFC-producing states nor the companies had strong incentives to break the treaty, since the same companies also controlled the likely substitutes and, in a number of countries, the alternative to an effective international regime was unilateral domestic prohibition. It was clear that everyone would suffer the consequences of destruction of the ozone layer, and that destruction could be avoided only through a universally observed ban. It may be that the treaty by itself provided companies with sufficient assurance that all the others would get out of the market to keep each producing state in compliance.

For the future, however, the situation looked much less stable. China and India were seen as major potential markets for CFCs in the fields of refrigeration and air conditioning, and the manufacturing technology is relatively simple and readily available. If China and India were not satisfied in some other way, it seemed unlikely that the protocol by itself would prevent their development of indigenous CFC production. The result was Article 10 of the London Amendments, drawn up in 1990, according to which the developed countries undertook to cover the "agreed incremental costs of compliance" for developing countries.[46]

Reassurance Generated by Monitoring the Compliance Behavior of the Parties

To this point, our claim has been a limited one: there are situations that are not pure coordination cases where the mere existence of the rule, and the expectations of compliance generated by it, will provide sufficient reassurance to overcome incentives to defect. In most situations, however, the incentives to break the rule are stronger or the costs of defection to the regime are higher, and the actor will need more reassurance than is provided by the mere existence of the rule. Information about the actual behavior of others will be needed. Transparency thus becomes a key to reassurance, and to compliance.

The situation in which the results are better for everyone if all cooperate than if all defect, but each actor has overriding incentives to go his own way, has come to be known as prisoners' dilemma. The reason it is a dilemma is lack of transparency. The conditions of the game specify that the parties cannot communicate with each other and that they have no information about each other's moves. It can be shown that transparency converts the prisoners' dilemma into an assurance game.

In the classic prisoners' dilemma, two prisoners each have the choice of confessing or remaining mute. They are confined in separate cells and cannot communicate. They know that if neither confesses, both will get a short jail term—say, one year. If both confess, they will both get a significantly higher term—five years. But if one confesses and the other does not, the one who confesses will go free, and the other will get ten years. The dilemma is that although it would obviously be better for both if both held out, the incentives are such that each will confess and both will go to jail for five years.

Assume now that the actions of each prisoner are fully known to the other. Then, so long as prisoner A holds out and refuses to confess, it is in prisoner B's interest to hold out also, for then they will both reap the best result—a one-year sentence. With complete knowledge, the possibility that prisoner A could confess and get off scot-free is nonexistent. So is the risk that prisoner B will get a ten-year term, since if prisoner A confesses, prisoner B will know about it and will certainly also confess to protect himself. So long as each prisoner knows that the other is refusing to confess, each will continue to hold out himself. The standard presentation of two-person prisoners' dilemma games in the form of a four-cell matrix suggests that the decisions are made simultaneously, but there is nothing in the original specifications of the game that requires the decisions of the two prisoners to be simultaneous. Simultaneity is simply a way of enforcing nontransparency the lack of knowledge about the other's action.

Thus, the same "payoff structure" that produced mutual defection in the absence of knowledge about the other's actions produces cooperation under conditions of transparency.[47] By the same token, although it is said that in prisoners' dilemma an agreement to cooperate would not work, because in the absence of outside enforcement each prisoner would have an overwhelming incentive to break it,[48] with transparency, an agreement (or a rule) prohibiting confession would be self-enforcing. Merely making the agreement or promulgating the rule would not by itself be enough to induce compliance, but the agreement plus the continuing assurance that the other prisoner is complying will do the trick. A number of analysts, beginning as early as Amartya Sen in 1967, have warned against the tendency to view all collective action problems as prisoners' dilemmas.[49] The same injunction applies to international relations and treaty compliance problems. The actors' incentive structures—and thus the "rational" responses—in all these situations depend on available information and expectations about the performance of other participants.

The strategic relationship between the United States and the Soviet Union during the cold war can be, and indeed was, conceived as a gigantic prisoners' dilemma.[50] The advantages of mutual restraint were obvious. The consequences of continuing buildup on both sides were regarded as bad, but not as bad as the other side's gaining a decisive advantage. That might happen, it was thought, if one side exercised restraint and it was not reciprocated.[51] For the United States (and perhaps the USSR as well) expectations that the other side would reciprocate were low. True to the game theorists' predictions, the two countries ran a forty-year arms race, at a cost of trillions of dollars, that ended with one side bankrupt and even the winner approaching exhaustion.

Yet within this conflictual setting, the two parties were able to agree on rules establishing islands of stability in some of the most dangerous areas: ending the most threatening forms of nuclear testing,[52] capping arsenals of strategic nuclear weapons,[53] and in effect prohibiting ABM systems.[54] The rhetoric of the U.S. debates on verification of these arms control agreements demanded certainty that the other side was not "cheating."[55] As is developed in Chapter 8, the systems that evolved never came close to achieving the desired level of certainty. Relying primarily on national technical means of verification (NTM), their main function from the U.S. point of view, even during the cold war, was to provide reassurance that the Soviet Union was substantially complying with the obligations it had undertaken. On this basis, the United States, like the prisoner in the assurance game, could continue to cooperate—to comply with existing treaties and try to negotiate new ones. The reassurance function became more explicit and open as the cold war wound down, and the Soviet Union for the first time accepted on-site inspection as a means of verifying compliance with treaty obligations (see Chapter 8).

The pursuit of confidence- and security-building measures (CSBMs), which became an important focus of conventional arms control efforts in Europe during the late 1970s and early 1980s, was a conscious attempt to establish the dynamic of reassurance here described. The idea was to put in place a system that would assure all of Europe that neither NATO nor the Warsaw Pact was preparing for a surprise attack on the other. In the Helsinki Final Act, signed by all European states, East, West, and neutral, the parties agreed to notify each other of military maneuvers occurring within 250 miles of the East-West border and involving more than 25,000 troops. They also agreed to "invite other participating States, voluntarily and on a bilateral basis, in a spirit of reciprocity and good will ... to send observers to attend military maneuvres."[56] Between the conclusion of the Final Act in 1975 and the beginning of the next negotiation in Stockholm in 1984, NATO and the neutral countries announced thirty-nine major maneuvers under these provisions, inviting observers to thirty-one of them. The Warsaw Pact notified twenty-two major maneuvers, inviting observers to seven. According to Jonathan Dean,

> CSBMs are pure transparency measures. They differ from classic arms control, which consists of reduction and limitation of armed forces.

Confidence building measures are intended in the first instance to contribute to the flow of information about the armed forces of the participating countries, increasing visibility and diminishing secrecy of routine military activities, thus providing participants with assurance that preparations for attack are not under way.[57]

Negotiations to strengthen these measures began almost at once and culminated, at Stockholm in 1984, with the establishment of a continuing Conference on Confidence- and Security-Building Measures and Disarmament in Europe (CDE). The Stockholm Act, signed in September 1986, expanded the notification requirements, with coverage "from the Atlantic to the Urals"; made the attendance of observers obligatory for most notifiable events; and prescribed elaborate procedures for the host country to ensure that the observation is meaningful.[58] More important, it gave any party the right to conduct an inspection on the territory of another, where "compliance with the agreed confidence- and security-building measures is in doubt."[59] According to one careful observer, "the overall effect of the CSBM regime adopted at Stockholm is to make it impossible for a state to mass forces for any reason without being subject to prompt inspection and accountability among all other 34 CDE participants."[60]

There is no way of evaluating this CSBM effort. There was no surprise ground attack across the East-West line in Europe after 1975, but then there were none between 1945 and 1975 either. (It is doubtful that these measures would have provided protection against the Soviet invasion of Hungary in 1956 or Czechoslovakia in 1968.) The Stockholm Act, although it perhaps laid the groundwork for the Treaty on Conventional Forces in Europe, was soon overtaken by the massive changes in East-West relations that began with the Gorbachev era.[61] But the point remains that, even at the height of the confrontation, the security establishments on both sides of the divide were prepared to invest heavily in a pure reassurance system as a way of reducing the likelihood of a European conflict.

If reassurance works for arms control, where stakes are highest, it is not too surprising to discover the same process at work in more mundane settings. Elinor Ostrom's study, *Governing the Commons,* shows that reassurance about compliance is central to the successful management of common-pool resources. Garrett Hardin's enormously influential article, "The Tragedy of the Commons," presented this problem in terms of a classical prisoners' dilemma. He evoked what has become an almost mythical image of a group of herdsmen, each responding to individual incentives for gain, relentlessly increasing the number of cattle on the common pasture, knowing the inevitable outcome but unable to stop until the common is exhausted and the whole band deprived of the means of subsistence. "Therein is the tragedy. Each man is locked into a system that compels him to increase his herd without limit—in a world that is limited. Ruin is the destination toward which all men rush, each pursuing his own best interest in a society that believes in the freedom of the commons."[62]

The historical record does not bear out Hardin's gloomy forecast, however. Common-property agricultural systems, including commons for grazing, were standard in medieval Europe. In England, the common was destroyed not by overgrazing but by the rapacity of landowners who enclosed them for commercial agriculture in the sixteenth and seventeenth centuries. And, according to Runge, common-property grazing systems among nomadic peoples in much of the developing world were relatively stable until recently, when the impact of population growth, technological change, and rapid climate change undermined traditional institutions.[63]

Ostrom examines the circumstances under which, pace Hardin, a stable system for managing the commons can emerge. In such situations, rules governing the rights of members of the group who have access to the common resource emerge from practice or from some form of positive lawmaking. The members pursue a "contingent strategy": they will follow the rules so long as most others similarly situated also. "Making a contingent rule-following commitment requires that individuals obtain information about the rates of rule conformance adopted by others."[64] With access to this information, their implicit commitments are "safe, advantageous and credible."[65] In other words, transparency is critical to the success of the strategy.

Ostrom's work draws on Axelrod's theoretical model of "the evolution of cooperation" in iterated prisoners' dilemma games.[66] As discussed in Chapter 5, tit for tat, the preferred strategy that emerged from the Axelrod experiment, is a contingent strategy. Each move depends on the immediately preceding move of the other player. A priori, however, there is no reason to suppose that either party's first move will be cooperative, and if it is not, a series of retaliatory defections may well ensue. With a rule in place encoding Axelrod's advice to be "nice, retaliatory, forgiving, and clear"[67] the likelihood of initial cooperative moves that can evolve into stable cooperation (rule following) should be considerably higher.

Axelrod's model assumes that the parties have complete information about the moves and outcomes in past rounds, and thus a basis for future expectations. But he gives little consideration to the methods and costs of generating such information. Ostrom notes that these monitoring services are typical public goods presenting a typical collective action problem, so it is not obvious that they will be provided.[68] Ostrom's empirical studies suggest that systems with relatively few participants, where all are in close proximity, have built-in incentives for mutual monitoring by the parties.[69] In the bilateral arms control case, those incentives lent support to a multibillion dollar NTM programs on both sides. Ostrom's result is consistent with the argument of Mancur Olson, among others, that collective action problems can be solved in groups that are small enough for the members to keep tabs on one another. In larger communities, however, he believes that the incentives for defection are too strong and the penalties too small for the cooperative solution to be stable in the absence of systematic enforcement procedures.[70] Ostrom's empirical examination of reassurance mechanisms in larger systems tends to belie this conjecture.

A domestic example is offered by the groundwater systems of the West and Central Basins of Los Angeles, where monitoring is "obvious and public."

> Every year, each party reports total groundwater extraction [to the watermaster] and receives a report listing the groundwater extractions of all other parties (or anyone else who has started to pump). The reliability of these records is high. Several agencies cross-check the records . . . Given the accuracy of the information and its ease of access, each pumper knows what everyone else is doing, and each knows that his or her own groundwater extractions will be known by all others. Thus the information available to the parties closely approximates the "common knowledge," so frequently a necessary assumption for solution to iterated dilemma games.[71]

This reporting system provides high confidence to all participants that their restraint is not being taken advantage of by others. The result is a durable and effective arrangement for use of a common-pool resource.

The watermaster, moreover, much like the typical international organization, does not operate as "an active policing agency" but rather as "a neutral monitoring agency." "It is our policy not to take affirmative action against any party since this would place us in the position of being an active party in the action. Our policy has been to inform the active parties of any infringements and leave affirmative action up to them. We want to stay as neutral as possible in order to gain as much voluntary cooperation as possible."[72]

It is true that the Los Angeles water basins operate under a court order, based on negotiations among the parties, and that violations of the rules could presumably be redressed in court. Nevertheless, because of the effective transparency of the system, the rules allocating rights in the reservoir are in practice self-enforcing, and judicial oversight has never been invoked against original parties to the settlement.[73]

What have common-pool resources and Los Angeles water basins got to do with international treaty compliance? Like these systems, international regimes produce collective goods. The problem, as always, is to induce cooperation among independent (but interdependent) actors, when the possibilities for external sanctions are limited if not nonexistent. The work just discussed suggests that reassurance as to the complying behavior of the other parties is the key to the solution of some, perhaps many, of these international collective action problems.

The treaty regimes we have discussed—for example, the ITU, LRTAP, the Montreal Protocol, the Stockholm Act—are essentially reassurance mechanisms that operate by establishing transparency. They embody an agreed set of rules defining cooperative behavior, sometimes with procedures for further specifying the performance required.[74] Since widespread compliance is necessary to achieve the desired benefits, the likelihood that any party will comply is affected by the likelihood that others will comply. The rules themselves focus and crystallize expectations of compliance. Many of the treaties go further, to provide continuous information about the performance of the parties in addition to publicizing and defining the applicable rules. If the conditions of the assurance problem hold—that is, if the benefits to a state exceed its costs of contributing to the regime on the assumption that others also comply—transparency in these international treaty regimes supplies the reassurance necessary for the parties to make safe, advantageous, and credible commitments to follow the rules.

These conditions are not as demanding as they may seem. For a party to continue to cooperate, it does not necessarily require assurance of universal compliance by the other parties to the agreement. As we suggested in Chapter 1, most regimes can and do tolerate a significant level of noncompliance or free riding. In this respect, the NPT, for example, contrasts sharply with the Framework Convention on Climate Change (FCCC). A few defectors from the NPT detract seriously from the overall benefits of the regime, and the demand for universality is so strong that defection may threaten to unravel the whole enterprise. In the climate change context, at least for some years, most of what can be achieved will be accomplished by a fairly small group of industrialized states that account for by far the largest proportion of greenhouse gas emissions. This distinction in responsibility and obligation is in fact explicitly recognized in the FCCC, which requires more exacting reports and commitments from developed than developing countries.[75] The International Convention for the Regulation of Whaling, discussed in Chapters 4 and 5, is an intermediate case. That regime might survive as an effective protector of whales against extinction despite the defection of Iceland, Norway, and even Japan, if those countries confined their takings to relatively low levels, as they appear to be doing. Other potential whaling countries continue to have strong incentives, based in domestic politics, to remain within the convention.

Michael Taylor discounts the possibility that, in these circumstances, a stampede might begin, with each country trying to commit itself irrevocably to noncompliance so that the burden and cost of producing the collective goods would be shunted to the hindmost.[76] In cases like ozone-protection, the parties whose participation is necessary to achieve the benefits are identifiable. All of the major industrialized countries will have to be in the complying group to achieve significant benefits. None of them can free ride, because the achievement of the collective good depends on the participation of this entire subset of the parties. Thus, according to the rational actor assumptions of game theory, they will continue to comply, regardless of defections, so long as the benefits to each of them exceeds the costs, and even if the defectors cannot be excluded from the benefits.[77] Free riding in these cases is not as big a problem as is commonly supposed.

Deterrence

Deterrence is in a sense the obverse of reassurance. Each acts at the opposite end of the transaction. A party disposed to comply needs reassurance. A party contemplating violation needs to be deterred. Transparency supplies both. The probability that conduct departing from treaty requirements will be discovered operates to reassure the first and to deter the second, and that probability increases with the transparency of the treaty regime. The efforts of treaty organizations to provide information about the compliance of members thus has a deterrent as well as a reassurance effect.

Deterrence theory was the principal focus, if not the obsession, of strategic analysts during the cold war period. The doctrine held that a Soviet attack on the United States or Western Europe could be deterred only if the Soviets expected that such an attack would be met by a retaliatory U.S. nuclear strike on their homeland. The problem was to make such a threat credible, since it was apparent that, if an attack should occur, carrying out the threat and escalating to the level of strategic nuclear exchange would be much worse for the United States than not. Reams of paper and billions of dollars were spent in a fruitless attempt to solve this logical dilemma. As a historical matter, the USSR was deterred—if in fact it ever contemplated such an attack.

In the standard analysis, for deterrence to work, the expected value of the adverse reactions must outweigh the short-term benefit that is the fruit of noncompliance. In the U.S.-Soviet case, the expected value was thought to turn on the likelihood that the threat would be carried out. Since this was low, deterrence was continuously thought to be fragile.[78] Similarly, we argue that, in the case of ordinary treaty violations, the likelihood of significant formal sanctions or even seriously coercive collateral sanctions is extremely low. So the case for deterrence on this score is limited.

But costs come in many forms. The most obvious is loss of the anticipated benefits of the bargain. In bilateral treaties or where the impact of the violation is sharply focused, as in trade cases, the response of the aggrieved party to a serious violation may infect other aspects of the relationship between the parties. The treaty violator may also suffer more diffuse responses from states and even private groups or individuals with a stake in the treaty regime. As we noted in Chapter 4, pressures and expressions of disapproval of various kinds are the daily fare of diplomatic intercourse. More subtle and perhaps more menacing, in an increasingly interdependent world where not many states can achieve many of their objectives by their own exertions, are various kinds of reputation effects. And to these may sometimes be added political trouble at home. The expected value of these negative responses to defection depends on the probability of detection, which is in turn a function of the transparency of the regime. According to Oran Young,

> the prospect of being found out is often just as important, and sometimes more important, to the potential violator than the prospect of becoming the target of more or less severe sanctions of a conventional or material sort. There are, in other words, many situations in which those contemplating violations will refrain from breaking the rules if they expect that their non-compliant behavior will be exposed, even if they know the probability that their violations will be met with sanctions is low.[79]

Young argues that the forces of "social opprobrium" and "the sense of shame or social disgrace" will work to induce treaty compliance. We will return to a consideration of these sorts of effects in Chapter 10.

Transparency operates more directly to deter where, as is the case with most arms control agreements, the treaty is designed to affect the benefit side of the actor's calculation. The ABM treaty is illustrative. The main purpose of the treaty is to prevent either party from deploying a nationwide ABM system. It accomplishes this goal by prohibiting precursor activities—development and testing of systems and components—thus creating "a buffer zone so that neither party [can] come close enough to deployment to be worrisome to the other."[80] If one party discovers that the other is engaged in these activities, it will have ample time for an offsetting response. Since the prohibited activities are clearly visible to each side's NTM, the likelihood of discovery is high, and the possibility of obtaining a unilateral advantage through deployment of an ABM system is correspondingly low. For a party deliberately contemplating violation, the high probability of discovery reduces the expected benefits rather than (or as well as) increasing the costs, and would thus deter violation regardless of the prospect of sanctions.

Prohibitions of testing and precursor activities in other arms control agreements have a similar effect. The party contemplating defection is in the same position as the actor in the prisoners' dilemma when there is complete transparency. Defection would be met with counterdetection, erasing any possible gain and triggering the very arms race the treaty is designed to prevent. It is not surprising, then, that such arms control agreements have proved very stable in practice.

It is obviously hard to measure these kinds of cost and benefit factors, and it is partly for this reason that they are often heavily discounted by analysts, and sometimes by decision makers as well. Even if properly weighed, they would not always be sufficient to dissuade the state from violating its undertaking in pursuit of more immediate gains. And when a state does decide to violate a treaty, it is hardly surprising that the negative responses are often ineffective to reverse that decision. They have already been weighed in the balance, together with the expected costs of more formal sanctions, and have been found inadequate to offset the benefits. Prospectively, however, both the measure of the costs and the likelihood that they will be imposed are uncertain. In these circumstances, the state, at least if it is risk averse, may give the threat more weight than our skeptical appraisals of the actual experience with sanctions would seem to warrant.

For all of these reasons, it is hard to demonstrate in any particular case that these sorts of considerations operated to deter a state from violating its treaty commitments. The motivations for state action are always multiple, and in the case of deterrence there is the additional difficulty of proving a negative. However, under standard theories of rational behavior, it can hardly be denied that these consequences of violation are matters that the actor should take into account. Even on rational-actor premises, therefore, it follows that at least in some cases they must tip the balance in favor of compliance.

7

Reporting and Data Collection

Reassurance, as was seen in Chapter 6, requires a continuing flow of information on the parties' performance of their treaty obligations and on the general situation in the regime's field of operation. Independent data collection by a central organization is costly, intrusive, and by no means error-free, as U.S. experience with the decennial census demonstrates. In the international arena, with its sensitivity to issues of sovereignty and coercion, the obstacles to centralized data collection are even greater. Therefore, international treaty regimes often rely in the first instance on self-reporting by member states for needed information. International treaty makers seem to have gotten the message that transparency is the key to compliance. The incidence of reporting requirements is so high that they seem to be included almost pro forma in many agreements, with little concern about cost or implementing capacity.

International bureaucratic reports are no less tedious to write (and write about) or read (and read about) than the domestic variety. Nevertheless, reporting is central to compliance systems in international regulatory regimes, as it is to many domestic regulatory programs.[1] The stated purpose of reporting is to generate information about the policies and activities of parties to the treaty that involve treaty compliance and regime efficacy. Thus the transparency of the regime as a whole is crucially dependent on the nature and scope of the reporting requirements and the quality of the response to them. More broadly, reporting is the point at which the national bureaucracies are first engaged by the treaty regime. It is there that domestic officialdom begins to translate the treaty into the daily work of administration and to define the level of commitment to it.

Reporting thus can be a kind of early warning system for substantive compliance problems. It identifies parties that have deficits in domestic capability and similar barriers to compliance. It turns up problems of ambiguity and interpretation. As with North Korea and the Nuclear Non-Proliferation Treaty or many of the reporting failures under human rights agreements, the refusal to report is often the first intimation of serious political resistance to compliance with basic treaty norms, and it begins the mobilization of counterpressures. Reporting requirements are often cumbersome. The quality of the responses varies widely, as does the effectiveness with which the information is analyzed and used. Nevertheless, some familiarity with the variety of reporting requirements, and their problems, is essential to an understanding of compliance.

The widespread use of self-reporting raises the general question of the reliability of the information reported, either for the construction of a database or as a measure of compliance. Why would a state report information that shows it to be out of compliance with its obligations?[7] The principal issues are, first, the failure to report or to report fully and on time, and second, the accuracy of the data that are reported.

Failure to Report

In the past several years there have been some spectacular instances of deliberate misreporting. Iraq's failure to disclose the full scope of its nuclear and chemical weapons programs as required by the Gulf War cease-fire resolution is discussed more fully below. A more recent and totally unexpected instance was the revelation of the Soviet Union's massive and systematic falsification of reports to the International Whaling Commission. The Russian government is still investigating the full scope of the reporting failure, but in the 1961–62 season the total catch of humpback whales reported by the Soviets was 270, whereas in reality a single ship, out of four in operation in the Antarctic, had killed 1,568. In 1963–64, the Soviets reported 74 blue whale kills; in fact, the *Sovietskaya Rossia* alone (again one ship out of four) had taken 530. The estimated 1993 population of blue whales in the southern hemisphere was 700. The USSR's false reporting was so drastic and pervasive that some experts believe it accounts for the persistent inaccuracy of the IWC Scientific Committee's forecasts of whale populations, on which the catch limits were based.[3] Similar if less egregious defaults occur under fisheries conventions that rely on catch reports made by the fishers themselves. It takes little imagination to see that such reports are likely to seriously understate the size of the catch. The unreliability of these reports no doubt contributes to the recurrent failure of these regimes to provide effective management of the resource.

Nevertheless, despite these high-profile cases, nonreporting or incomplete reporting seems to be the chief deficiency of international data collection systems. How full the glass is varies widely among parties and treaties. The range of performance and response is illustrated by the contrast among the reporting results under three important regulatory treaties: the International Convention for the Prevention of Pollution from Ships (MARPOL), the International Labor Organization, and the Montreal Protocol on Substances That Deplete the Ozone Layer (the Montreal Protocol).

MARPOL

The MARPOL agreement, which came into force in 1983, and its predecessor the International Convention for the Prevention of Pollution of the Sea by Oil (OILPOL), dating from 1954, requires states to report annually to the International Maritime Organization (IMO) the number and results of prosecutions for violations of the conventions.[4] Studies of the reporting performance uniformly conclude that compliance with this requirement has been low, although there is some variation among the figures because of differences in methodology. A U.S. General Accounting Office (GAO) survey of reporting activity under seven environmental treaties found that only thirteen of fifty-seven parties (23 percent) filed any report in 1990.[5] A Friends of the Earth study in 1992 found that

> only six Contracting Parties have submitted reports for each year since the entry into force of the MARPOL Convention. These reports do not always comply with the reporting format given by the IMO in MEPC/Cir. 138. [Three additional countries have submitted reports in every year but one.] . . . More than 30 Contracting Parties have never submitted a report to IMO. The other Contracting Parties have submitted (often incomplete) reports for one or a few years only.[6]

Analysis of the IMO data collection system suggests some reasons for this unimpressive record. Information on the number and results of prosecutions is at best only indirectly related to regime efficacy and is not very significant in the administration of the treaty. The IMO secretariat makes little effort to facilitate reporting. For most of the lifetime of the regime, it had not developed a standard form nor even specified the items that should appear in the report. After almost two decades, a requirement for reporting "in a form standardized by the Organization" was finally incorporated in the text of the MARPOL agreement, negotiated in 1973. Nevertheless, the secretariat did not complete the form until 1985.[7]

In addition, "IMO's analysis of reports on enforcement has been infrequent and of poor quality."[8] Only twice in the history of the two conventions has it prepared analyses of enforcement reports, and these were brief and uninformative. In other years, it duplicated the national reports as submitted and circulated them at annual meetings without comment or analysis. Members at IMO meetings do not review or discuss the reports and do not censure failures to report. In such circumstances, it is no wonder that reporting is lackadaisical.

International Labor Organization

In contrast, the ILO places great emphasis on the importance of its reporting requirements, and although the obligation is complex and burdensome, its record of compliance is good, running to well over 80 percent in every year of the organization's existence, except during World War II. The ILO is essentially a forum for negotiating conventions concerning terms and conditions of employment to be established under the domestic law of the parties. The organization also promulgates official Recommendations, which are directed to all members but do not constitute binding obligations.

Every four years (two years for the most important conventions), members are required to report (1) measures taken to implement each convention that has been ratified, (2) the submission of new conventions and recommendations to the appropriate national authorities for action, and (3) the application of recommendations and unratified conventions.[9] The ILO has an elaborate compliance procedure that culminates in a decision to blacklist a member in "cases where special and persistent problems seem to have prevented the discharge of obligations."[10] Four of the seven categories of infraction that warrant blacklisting are failures to comply with reporting obligations.

In 1979 there was a proposal to list reporting failures separately from other blacklisted actions, since they were likely to be due to administrative and technical difficulties, and thus less serious than deliberate violations. The ILO rejected the suggestion on the ground that reporting was so essential to the compliance process that it would be unwise to do anything that might appear to diminish the significance of reporting failures.[11] The performance of ILO parties in fulfilling their reporting obligations seems to reflect this concerted organizational emphasis.

The Montreal Protocol

As with the ILO, reporting plays a central role in the implementation of the Montreal Protocol in at least two respects: the reductions in consumption of chlorofluorocarbons and other controlled substances mandated by the treaty are to be measured against the reported 1986 baseline, and parties with consumption of less than .3 kilogram per capita (essentially, the developing countries) have a ten-year grace period for compliance with the limitations.[12] Both measurements must be based on self-reported information.

The protocol requires parties to report baseline data on consumption, production, imports, and exports of CFCs for 1986 and current data beginning with 1989. As of June 1991, only about half of the forty-eight parties had reported complete data. About half of the failures were developing countries. The parties established an Ad Hoc Group of Experts on Reporting even before the protocol came into force.[13] This group recognized immediately that the developing country delinquents were, for the most part, simply unable to comply without technical assistance from the organization, and it made a variety of proposals for providing it.[14] Of special importance was the decision that technical assistance for reporting would be eligible for financing out of the "ozone fund," established to help defray compliance costs for developing countries.[15]

The experts' analysis of the reporting process exposed other defects. As with MARPOL, the formats were complex and confusing. Much of the information requested was not clearly relevant to treaty compliance. Standard customs classifications did not coincide with treaty-controlled chemicals. All of these issues, which made it difficult even for developed countries to comply, were addressed by the Ad Hoc Group.[16]

In August 1992, the UN Environment Program issued another lengthy and detailed report on the status of data reporting. The results were a marked improvement over the 1990 figures. Of the 78 parties required to report baseline data, 47 filed complete reports. That amounted to 60 percent of the parties, accounting for upwards of 90 percent of world consumption. Another 12 filed incomplete reports.[17] The UNEP secretariat noted somewhat severely that "three reminders to report were sent in 1989 and two reminders were sent each year in 1991 and 1992. The format to be used for reporting data was also sent to the Parties." The intensity of the focus on the reporting issue left no doubt about the priority attached to it by the treaty regime. As the number of parties adhering to the treaty has expanded (to 114 in 1994), so has the number of reports. Reporting by developing countries continues to be a problem, although it is still attributed to a deficit of capacity rather than will. Increased emphasis on reporting in the Implementation Committee, including regional workshops on reporting, produced first-time reports from 11 developing countries in early 1994 and still more by the annual meeting in October. Nevertheless, at that point more than 40 countries had still not reported baseline data, and only 46 had reported consumption figures for 1993.[18]

Experience in Other Treaty Regimes

The foregoing examples give some sense of the range of states' responses to reporting requirements and some of the characteristic problems, but there is no comprehensive survey of reporting behavior under international treaties. Available evidence on particular treaties or groups of treaties tends to bear out common-sense suppositions that, aside from deliberate refusals, the level of reporting will depend on a variety of factors, most prominently the importance of the subject matter, the effectiveness of the secretariat or other central treaty institutions, and the capacity and resources of the reporting state.

Environmental Treaties. In a large class of cases, particularly environmental treaties and others with high technical or scientific content, failure to report is disproportionately high among developing countries, primarily because of limitations on the financial, scientific, and bureaucratic resources of the reporting government. The GAO report on environmental treaties is peppered with comments about how the widespread failure of developing countries to report reflects their lack of personnel, resources, technical capability, and the data themselves. We have already noted the ILO's judgment that reporting failures were generally due to administrative and technical difficulties and personnel changes.[19]

Of the seven environmental treaties surveyed by the GAO's the most impressive record was for the Nitrogen Oxides Protocol to the Convention on Long-Range Transboundary Air Pollution: sixteen out of seventeen parties submitted reports in 1990. All of the parties are industrialized European states, although some are from Eastern Europe. In two other treaties a substantial majority of the parties reported, but the results are much more qualified.[20] According to the GAO count, under the Montreal Protocol, fifty-two of the sixty-five parties (80 percent) had filed reports on their baseline CFC consumption as of October 1990, but only twenty-nine of those were complete. Seven states reported that they had no relevant data. The 1989 reporting to the IWC on whale harvests registered 100 percent, but during that year the moratorium on whaling was in effect except for aboriginal subsistence hunting or scientific research. Only six states engaged in these activities and all of them reported in full.

Reporting in the other four conventions was much less satisfactory. In addition to the 23 percent response rate for MARPOL already noted, only 25 of the 104 parties (24 percent) to the Convention on International Trade in Endangered Species reported; only 22 out of 47 reports were submitted for the International Tropical Timber Agreement (many of which were incomplete and inaccurate); and only 19 of 64 parties (30 percent) reported to the London Convention. Only 2 developing countries reported under the London Convention and MARPOL, [21] and only 15 of 78 reported under CITES.[22]

The secretariat of the London Convention complained that "over the years, only 50% of the Contracting Parties [have responded] to the [reporting] requirements," despite "the continuous efforts made by the Secretariat."[23] The fault did not lie entirely with the parties. The same IMO secretariat handles both the London Convention and MARPOL, and there was a similar lag in developing a reporting format for the London Convention. Although the convention was concluded in 1972, the first year a standard set of procedures and forms for reporting dumping activities was sent to the parties was 1993, and it was sent along with the quoted report. It was not exactly unpredictable that there should be "a lack of confidence concerning the control and enforcement procedures of the Convention."[24]

These reporting deficiencies are disappointing but not surprising. Apart from the capacity deficiencies in developing, and even some developed, countries, preparing reports to a remote international organization is understandably not the most urgent priority for small and overworked national bureaucracies. Environmental treaty secretariats tend to be small and overworked as well, with little capacity to follow up when reports fail to arrive.[25]

Security Treaties. Arms control treaties, as would be expected, rely less on current reporting and more on post hoc verification than do other types. But where baseline reporting is called for, the parties insist on strict fulfillment of the obligation. North Korea waited seven years after adhering to the NPT before signing a safeguards agreement and filing an initial declaration of its peaceful nuclear facilities. The delay was unprecedented and was met by a series of intensifying pressures. The United States and other Western powers took the lead, but Russia and China were also involved. In the end, North Korea responded with a declaration more voluminous and detailed than had been expected, although serious questions remained about its complete-ness.[26] Subsequent events showed that the refusal to report was only a har-binger of more serious substantive problems with North Korea's adherence to the nonproliferation regime and of the international response. As we discuss in Chapter 8, concern with the reliability and completeness of reported data is likely to intensify under multilateral arms control agree-ments and as treaty-limited items become harder to detect.

Human Rights. At the opposite end of the spectrum from security are the treaties on human rights. A survey by the UN secretary general of reporting under seven major human rights conventions as of September 1, 1992, reveals an abysmal record. The conventions typically require a basic report within one year of adherence and periodically thereafter, at four- or five-year inter-vals. Of the 164 states parties to one or more of the treaties, substantially all were delinquent on at least one report, most were in arrears on several, and 27 were behind on ten or more. The situation was somewhat better (though by no means satisfactory) for the two principal treaties: for the International Covenant on Civil and Political Rights, slightly more than half (59 of 113) were up to date; and for the International Covenant on Economic, Social, and Cultural Rights, somewhat less than half were (46 of 116).[27]

Like the ILO, some of the human rights bodies make public a list of nonreporting states, and the Committee on Economic, Social, and Cultural Rights adopts specific decisions identifying serious delinquents by name. Neither of these expedients seems to have improved the situation much. A meeting of the chairs of human rights bodies urged that the supervisory committees should "follow, as a last resort . . . the practice . . . of scheduling for consideration the situation in States parties that have consistently failed to report or whose reports are long overdue . . . [A] persistent and long term failure to report should not result in the State party concerned being immune from supervision while others, which had reported, were subject to careful monitoring."[28]

Among the countries listed in the secretary general's report, many are too small, poor, and disorganized to address the reporting requirement seriously, but the report also shows a number of flagrant human rights violators among those most seriously in arrears on reporting. The complaint of the chairper-sons suggests that in many of these cases, nonreporting is deliberate and is to be taken not as a reporting failure but as a refusal to make a minimal gesture toward compliance with the treaty obligations.

*   *   *

The experience with reporting under a variety of international agreements shows that even the first step toward transparency is not an easy one. Routine reports on routine matters, whether domestic or international, rarely move to the top of bureaucratic agendas. Nevertheless, the ILO and ozone-treaty cases suggest that considerable improvement can be made through fairly straightforward measures to facilitate reporting and instill a sense of urgency about the need for the information. Given that reporting is the least intrusive method for achieving transparency and getting some measure of early warning of violations, it is worth the investment of human and financial resources to improve the lackluster record that exists in many areas.

Reliability

Self-reporting is only the beginning, not the end of the data-gathering process. Since reporting is closely related to treaty compliance, a major focus of the systematic efforts to verify compliance with arms control treaties and other agreements is checking and evaluating national declarations and reports. These formal verification activities are discussed at length in Chapter 8. There is, however, a substantial network of more informal methods for corroborating data reported by treaty parties.

In the bilateral arms control cases, assurances of the reliability of the reported data are built in. The pattern was set in the Strategic Arms Limitation Treaty (SALT II), in which the parties established an "agreed data base," to be updated regularly, on the numbers of strategic weapons each party deployed in categories covered by the treaty.[29] It consisted of a Memorandum of Understanding, a couple of pages long, appended to the treaty. It is said that when the Soviet negotiator turned over his report disclosing the numbers of Soviet weapons, he remarked, "You realize, you have just repealed 400 years of Russian history."[30] The agreed database accompanying the Intermediate-Range Nuclear Forces (INF) Treaty, concluded less than ten years later, had swelled to fifty-six printed pages, to be updated every six months.[31]

The numbers are supplied in the first instance by the parties, but the database must be "agreed." In the SALT II negotiations, the Soviets argued that the word "agreed" was redundant, because data are a matter of objective fact. The United States, however, "wanted to make it explicit that the data base must be mutually agreed so that [it] could challenge any information it could not independently confirm."[32] If a party challenges the accuracy of the figures submitted by its treaty partner, they are not taken into the database until agreement is reached.

The formal provision simply codified the formidable incentives for accurate reporting that would exist in any case. Each side knew that the other had detailed knowledge about its deployments, based on intense and continuous surveillance by national technical means of verification and national intelligence. The declarant could not be sure what gaps, if any, there were in the other's knowledge. Any discrepancies between the reported figures and the numbers derived unilaterally would, at a minimum, have to be resolved to the satisfaction of the objecting party. In the worst case, an inaccurate report could sour the whole treaty process. For example, when the Soviet Union failed to report certain infantry units subject to reduction under the Conventional Forces in Europe Treaty, arguing that they were "naval infantry" and thus exempt, it raised serious issues in Congress in connection with ratification of the Strategic Arms Reduction Treaty (START).[33] In such a situation, the incentives for telling the truth are high and the possible gains from misreporting are small.

An extreme example of the process of checking a national declaration is seen in the UN inspections of Iraq at the end of the Gulf War, pursuant to the cease-fire resolution of the Security Council.[34] The resolution, like the bilateral arms control agreements, required Iraq to declare all its nuclear, chemical, biological, and missile weapons and facilities, to provide the starting point for the inspection process. The first Iraqi declarations pursuant to this obligation were checked against information supplied by U.S. and other Western intelligence services and found wanting. A series of increasingly intense exchanges produced much improved disclosures by Iraq. Indeed, an iterative process of interchange leading to more complete and detailed Iraqi disclosures continued throughout the inspection period.[35] Similarly, it seems clear that the International Atomic Energy Agency made use of U.S. satellite observations in verifying North Korea's declaration of its peaceful nuclear materials.[36]

Although not all treaties are monitored with the level of commitment and technological sophistication that marks the security area, external checks are often available against which national reports can be tested. Other states and nongovernmental scientific groups make their own measurements of atmospheric conditions, for example, or ozone depletion or species populations. National governments, business groups, and private organizations generate and publish a wide range of economic data for a variety of purposes.

Ernest Haas's authoritative study shows that the ILO Committee of Experts bases its review of national reports on information received from a variety of sources, including national official documentation, press reports, complaints from trade unions, information furnished by national ILO correspondents, conversations with visiting national officials, reports from returning technical assistance experts, and other information in the possession of the ILO secretariat, with which the committee maintains a close liaison.[37] In addition, the reports of the Expert Committee reveal extensive reliance on other UN agencies, such as the Economic and Social Council and the Human Rights Committee.

In the 1970s, NGOs began to play an increasingly important role in crosschecking the accuracy and completeness of governmental reporting in many areas. Human rights organizations have been particularly active in producing information to challenge reports filed by parties to human rights treaties. Indeed, one of the principal activities of these organizations is to provide information to the various supervisory committees established under human rights conventions, against which they can evaluate the national reports submitted in accordance with those treaties.

> The United Nations is virtually completely dependent on human rights data collected and presented by NGOs for their own activities in the area of supervision and monitoring, since generally these are the only readily accessible data available (a notable exception in this respect is the US State Department's annual reports on human rights practices, a compilation of country reports which can be compared, as far as its scope is concerned, with Amnesty International's yearbook). Information about the human rights situation in a specific country is important for the treaty-based supervising bodies when they have to evaluate the periodic reports submitted by a government in conformity with its reporting obligation under the convention concerned.[38]

In the environmental field, too, national claims face a constant challenge from nongovernmental organizations. All environmental treaty secretariats testify to the importance of the information and auditing activities of NGOs. Trade in endangered species is monitored on a continuing basis by Traffic, an affiliate of the World Wildlife Fund, and the results are so highly regarded that they have become virtually replaced national reporting as the primary source of compliance data.[39] Much of the information that national governments fail to report to the International Maritime Organization is provided by a few dedicated NGOs. The IMO secretariat also gets information from the "gray" literature, seminar proceedings, and other indirect data sources.[40] The chemical industry itself checks on official reports of CFC consumption, along with other organizations that provide information where official reporting is weak.[41] The industry and NGOs provide reports of illegal hazardous waste traffic to the Basel Convention secretariat.[42]

Even in the security-shrouded world of arms control, advocacy NGOs like the Federation of American Scientists and research organizations like the Stockholm Institute of Peace Research and the International Institute for Strategic Studies have developed impressive credentials as independent sources of authoritative information against which national representations can be measured.

At the same time, some reporting systems seem to be designed to make it difficult for outside agencies and parties to verify the accuracy and completeness of required reports. National economic and financial information provided in the course of IMF country studies or surveillance is available to the representatives of the parties on the Executive Directors, but it is otherwise confidential, as is much of the national reporting to the Organization for Economic Cooperation and Development. Under the Montreal Protocol, only "consumption" data are provided to the public, not data on production, imports, and exports, assertedly because national reports contain information from which production levels of private corporations could be deduced.[43] Similarly, only aggregated data are made public under the Convention to Protect the Rhine against Chemical Pollution.[44] National findings in the assessment component of the Barcelona Convention for the Protection of the Mediterranean Sea[45] were amalgamated into ten regions, so that no single country could be targeted as a major polluter and to protect states' reputations with respect to fish exports and tourism.[46]

The Iraq case shows that deliberate misreporting can occur as a result of a high-level political decision, even when the probability of discovery is high. Similar instances can probably be found in human rights and other politically and economically sensitive areas. But reports under international treaties are not usually written by heads of state or even foreign ministries. For most regulatory treaties, the relevant functional ministry—labor for the ILO, finance for the IMF, the environmental ministry for the Montreal Protocol, and so on—rather than the foreign office, has the principal reporting responsibility. It is noteworthy that the Soviet misreporting of whale kills required "a military style operation lasting 40 years" run by the ministry of fisheries with the cooperation of the KGB.[47]

Ordinarily reports will be prepared routinely by middle- or lower-level officials. This bureaucratic setting has its own problems, as we have noted, but it provides some insulation against deliberate misreporting. Reliable statistical data are important for everyday policy-making and administration.

Many countries take special precautions to insulate statistical services from political influences. National data collection activities are increasingly automated and computerized, making it harder to "cook the books." Whistleblowers abound. The immediate political salience of the reported matters is not ordinarily high, so the potential gains of misreporting may be limited. Officials filing reports to be scrutinized by knowledgeable colleagues have their personal reputation to consider. All of these factors combine to provide some warrant for the belief that routine reports actually submitted under international treaties will be as accurate as the time and data available to the reporting officials permit. Nevertheless, if the official responsible for reporting is also in charge of the relevant substantive program, there will be incentives to make the performance look good. Keeping operational and reporting responsibilities separated to some extent would be a useful designing rule of thumb in reporting systems.

Varieties of Reporting

Reporting takes many forms. Frequently it is a vehicle for collection, collation, and dissemination of statistical information in the field regulated by the treaty. A principal function of the IMF is to "act as a centre for the collection and exchange of information on monetary and financial problems."[48] Members are obligated to furnish extensive reports on their external transactions, and these are the basis for the fund's monthly publication, *International Financial Statistics,* which runs back over four decades, an invaluable historical source for balance of payments information. International commodity organizations collate members' reports to develop general statistical data on their industries.[49] Almost all environmental treaties of the past two decades include extensive reporting and data collection provisions of this kind.[50] Indeed, as was the case with LRTAP, the establishment of a database can be a primary object of a framework-type agreement that initiates international cooperation in a particular environmental field.[51]

More directly related to compliance is reporting on measures taken to implement a treaty. As early as the International Slavery Convention in 1926, parties undertook "to communicate to each other and to the Secretary General of the League of Nations any laws and regulations which they may enact with a view to the application of the present Convention."[52] Similar provisions for reporting applicable laws and regulations are ubiquitous.[53] They reflect in fact that for many modern regulatory treaties, compliance is not solely a matter of government action but depends primarily on the behavior of individuals and private companies, so that the country must adopt appropriate legislation or administrative regulations to translate the treaty requirements into domestic law.

Equally common are provisions that require the parties to report their actual success in achieving treaty-imposed standards. For example, the Montreal Protocol requires each party to report current consumption of CFCs and other regulated substances,[54] and the Chemical Weapons Convention (CWC) requires a party to make declarations "regarding the implementation of its plans for destruction" of chemical weapons and manufacturing facilities.[55] The International Covenant on Civil and Political Rights requires the parties to disclose "the progress made in the enjoyment of those rights," as well as measures adopted.[56]

Where performance is to be measured against some previous level of activity, as is the case with environmental agreements regulating emissions, national reporting is also the initial recourse for establishing the baseline.[57] As has been noted, even in high-stakes arms control agreements, once they began to get more complicated than the Limited Test Ban Treaty and SALT I, self-reported baseline data have been the starting point for the verification system. The CWC has perhaps the most elaborate and detailed disclosure requirements to date. Under Article III, a state must declare the number, type, location, and composition of existing as well as old or abandoned chemical weapons within its jurisdiction; transfers or receipts of chemical weapons since January 1, 1946; and chemical weapons production facilities in its territory or under its jurisdiction since that date.[58] Details of the required declarations are spelled out in five pages of the annex.[59]

From our perspective, the most interesting development is a growing tendency to require reports on a party's proposed future policies and programs that fall within the purview of treaty obligations. The roots of this development can perhaps be traced to the early days of the IMF. It is also a characteristic tool of the OECD and more recently has been adopted by the GATT and the World Trade Organization (WTO). Similar reporting requirements have made their appearance in current environmental treaties and, not least, in the arms control field with the CWC. The party responding must submit more than historical data, it must engage in a strategic planning effort in the relevant policy area, subject to review and evaluation within the treaty organization. In this way, policy and program reporting can become a powerful instrument for managing compliance. We discuss this at length in Chapter 10.

Other Methods of Data Generation

Although self-reporting is the primary means of collecting information and creating transparency under international agreements, it is by no means the only one. The range includes advance notification with respect to particular regulated activities, various kinds of targeted inquiries, and the use of materials developed by national governments, scientific and industrial organizations, and NGOS.

Notification

An inherent attribute of the classical notion of sovereignty is that the state need not ask or obtain advance permission for actions it contemplates (although it may have to make amends for any harm it may cause). By extension, it is under no obligation to notify parties that may have an interest in the matter. This austere legal position is considerably modified in practice, but mostly as a matter of grace and reciprocal diplomatic courtesy. The basis of the resistance to an *obligation* to notify is that it may be thought to imply a further obligation to consult and even to take the other party's interests into account.

The issue of advance notification has a history in the field of transboundary pollution, that dates at least to the Lake Lanoux arbitration in 1957, which held that a state undertaking activities that might harm the environment of a neighbor was under no customary international law obligation to give advance notice.[60] An effort to include such a requirement in the 1972 Stockholm Declaration on the Environment failed.[61] Finally, the Rio Declaration on Environment and Development, adopted at the Earth Summit in 1992, incorporated a notification provision: "States shall provide prior and timely notification and relevant information to potentially affected states on activities that may have a significant adverse transboundary environmental effect and shall consult with those States at an early stage and in good faith."[62] Numerous recent pollution conventions contain provisions on notification of activities or incidents affecting shared resources.[63]

In the Basel Convention, notification of transboundary movements of hazardous waste is the central element of the control structure. Exports of hazardous wastes are prohibited except with the specific written consent of the importing state. The exporting state must notify the importing state in advance of any shipment, providing details of composition, packaging, and transport. The shipment cannot proceed unless there is an official consent in writing containing assurance of "environmentally sound management of the wastes in question" at the importing end.[64] The London Guidelines on trade in toxic chemicals employ a similar system.[65] There is a basis for concern, however, particularly in the case of the London Guidelines, that without a strong central secretariat, individual developing countries will not be able to process the information effectively, and the system will break down in a snarl of bureaucratic red tape.

Similar notification provisions have been employed to monitor compliance with other international agreements regulating trade, both in the environmental field and elsewhere, but they have had similar problems. The CITES control mechanism is based on the requirement that a certificate accompany all permitted exports of specimens of listed species, and that there be a matching import certificate for the most endangered species.[66] Although the parties make summary biennial reports to the CITES secretariat on the issuance of permits, the treaty does not require real-time central processing of these certificates. Experience suggests that the certification requirement has not been very effective.[67] The GAO reported that some countries did not even have the resources to print the certificates.[68] The International Coffee Agreement at first required that each export of coffee be accompanied by a certificate, with a copy sent to the organization, which would verify that the shipment was within quota. The secretariat was simply unable to perform the monitoring function within the time available in the fast moving international coffee trade.[69]

The GATT has numerous notification requirements, for example, when a member state plans to take an escape-clause action or to enter into a customs union or free trade area. As with the environmental agreements, the purpose is to permit consultation with affected parties with a view to reaching resolution of the problem in advance, including compensation for any concessions that may be withdrawn or modified in the course of the contemplated action.[70]

Another variant in the economics field, the OECD Guidelines for Officially Supported Export Credits, contains rules on such matters as interest rates, down payments and repayment schedules for government financing assistance to exporters. For any particular transaction, a state may provide credit terms more favorable than those specified in the rules, provided it gives notice in advance, in which case the other members are free to match or underbid the offer. Since notification of a derogation is likely to lead to a competitive offer and possibly even the loss of the sale, the notice requirement tends to ensure compliance.[71]

Advance notification of regulated actions also has an important role in modern arms control agreements. A provision for advance notification of missile launch tests, was included in SALT II and was carried forward to START.[72] But failure to ratify the first and delay in concluding the second led to a separate agreement between the United States and the USSR, requiring that "Each Party shall provide the other Party notification, . . . no less than twenty-four hours in advance, of the planned date, launch area, and area of impact for any launch of a strategic ballistic missile."[73]

On a multilateral level, the Conference on Security and Co-operation in Europe's confidence-building measures (CSBMS), as discussed in Chapter 6, include prior notification of a wide range of military activities and exercises (above specified quantitative thresholds) conducted by any of the parties within Europe. The notification provides extensive information on the time, place, and size of the proposed activity and must include an invitation to other parties to observe the exercise. A calendar of military exercises must be provided a year in advance.[74]

The CSBMS are, as their name implies, designed to provide reassurance about the overall intentions and military posture of the parties, but like all notification provisions, they are also closely involved with inducing compliance with substantive limitations contained in the treaty. A failure to notify is, ipso facto a serious violation. Beyond that, the missile test notification provisions permit the other party to alert and calibrate its monitoring system so as to obtain an accurate understanding of the technical characteristics of the missile being tested. The ability to gain such detailed information makes it difficult if not impossible to evade the stringent treaty limitations on the development of "new" missiles.[75]

Active Data Collection

There are a variety of more active ways in which treaty organizations can gather information from their members about compliance. The time-honored international method is a questionnaire circulated to the treaty parties. For example, the IMO and its predecessors have circulated questionnaires from time to time on the availability of adequate reception facilities for oily wastes in ports of member states, although the conventions seem to put the obligation to report on the parties. Ronald Mitchell concluded that, in many situations, this was a more effective method. "Mailing out a survey annually or less frequently . . . places an item in a bureaucrat's in-box, certainly eliciting more response than a standing requirement for a report for which no prompting reminder arrives."[76]

Human rights committees have developed the practice of appointing a rapporteur for a particular problem, who has broad powers to gather evidence and information from all available sources, often including country visits to view the problem firsthand.[77] The ILO's "direct contacts" and the IMF's country reviews also involve a good deal of time on site by the international staff. Many organizations have regional or local offices that, among other things, perform an information gathering function. And there is much informal back and forth between working bureaucrats at the national and international level. Members of environmental secretariats believe that they have a handle on the state of compliance with their treaties, even with a good deal less than universal fulfillment of national reporting obligations.[78]

Nongovernmental Sources of Data and Information

National reporting or notification is the usual method of producing information, but treaty organizations, secretariats, and interested parties are of course also free to consult the myriad additional sources of information in a data-rich world. Often a secretariat will piggyback on the efforts of private or national organizations, or will farm out parts of its data-collection function to them.

- The International Council for the Exploration of the Seas (ICES), a public coordinating body made up of scientists from the littoral states of the North Sea, has been conducting scientific studies of fisheries in the North and Baltic Seas since 1902. It provides basic data on fish populations and pollution to environmental bodies operating in that area, such as the Oslo, Paris and Helsinki Commissions and the North Sea Fisheries Commission.[79]
- In the 1920s, the whaling industry and the Norwegian government established a Bureau of International Whaling Statistics, which provides essential statistical data for commercial whaling.[80]
- The World Conservation Union (WCU) (formerly the International Union for the Conservation of Nature) has for many years published a "red book" on the status of threatened and endangered species, that is the authoritative source of information for CITES. The International Council of Scientific Unions (ICSU) coordinates transnational scientific research on a range of important environmental questions and its committees have provided the database for international action in these fields.[81]
- Under MARPOL, self-reporting and responses to questionnaires failed to produce adequate information on the availability of reception facil-

ities where tankers can discharge oily ballast water. As a result, that IMO relies on, and sometimes helps to finance data collection by, the International Chamber of Shipping or INTERTANKO a private association of tanker owners.[82]

Very few international regimes have in-house research capability. For broader problem assessment, they turn of necessity to governmental and nongovernmental scientific and technical organizations. The research that discovered the ozone hole was sponsored by a consortium of the UN Environment Program, the World Meteorological Organization, and NASA, among others, but was conducted by national scientific organizations. The Antarctic Treaty is backed up by ICSU's Special Committee on Antarctic Research (SCAR). The ICSU has also performed catalytic information development and processing functions in connection with other environmental issues. The scientific and technical preparation for the Framework Convention on Climate Change was carried out by the Intergovernmental Panel on Climate Change (IPCC), organized by UNEP and WMO at the request of the UN General Assembly.[83] The IPCC was deliberately established as an *intergovernmental* body, with representatives appointed by governments, to preempt private transnational scientific groups that had begun to generate strong political pressure for far-reaching efforts to limit greenhouse gases. After the adoption of the FCCC at the Rio Summit, the IPCC was continued.[84]

Conclusion

Provisions for the gathering and dissemination of information appear with great regularity in major multilateral agreements, from the Act for the Suppression of the Slave Trade to the INF Treaty. So common and embracing are these provisions that they risk information overload, in which reports, studies, notices, requests for information far outstrip the ability of national and international bureaucracies to produce or to process and assimilate the product. The foregoing account of the experience under these provisions is less than comforting. Except for a few areas where heavy emphasis is placed on the reporting process, the response of treaty parties is for the most part disappointing.

There are mitigating factors. Nonreporting does not necessarily equate with noncompliance with the substantive obligations of the treaty.[85] The inadequacy of available resources—including resources of energy and attention—accounts for a very large part of the reporting deficit, particularly in developing countries. All gaps in a database are not created equal: failure to report a nuclear missile is more important than failure to report a whale kill. Moreover, although omitting of a report is the nonfulfillment of a treaty obligation, it is generally thought to be of a different order of seriousness than nonperformance of the substantive requirements, and it is so regarded even in domestic legal systems. Nevertheless, the transparency of a treaty regime depends in large part on how effectively the information and data collecting functions of this multifaceted reporting process are fulfilled. National reports are essential management tools, and thus, as we discuss in Chapter 10, are crucial to inducing compliance with treaty obligations. There is some basis for the belief that the importance of reporting for regime maintenance is becoming more widely recognized. Surveys of reporting practice, like those conducted by the GAO, the UN secretary general on human rights reporting, the Montreal Protocol secretariat, and the IMO, all evidence a new seriousness of focus on what is, after all, the dullest of tasks.

At the treaty drafting level, reporting provisions no longer seem to be included as boilerplate but are the subject of more serious attention. The two conventions adopted at the Rio Earth Summit provide an instructive contrast. The Biodiversity Convention has one short and limited article calling for reports "at intervals to be decided by the Conference of the Parties . . . on measures taken for the implementation of the provisions of this Convention." The Climate Change Convention much more elaborately and specifically requires developed (though not developing) countries to "communicate":

(a) A detailed description of the policies and measures [they have] adopted to implement [their] commitments . . .; and

(b) A specific estimate of the effects that the policies and measures . . . will have on anthropogenic emissions by sources and removal by sinks [by the end of the present decade].[86]

Although many other considerations no doubt were in play, it is more than plausible that these variations reflect a more sophisticated appreciation of the role of transparency in generating pressures for treaty compliance. This new understanding of the significance of reporting requirements needs to be matched by the seriousness of purpose and adequacy of resources to implement them.

8

Verification and Monitoring

Verification is the most demanding aspect of achieving transparency. Although it may begin with self-reporting, it can become far more costly and intrusive. The concepts and requirements for verification were developed primarily for cold war arms control agreements, when the U.S.-Soviet relationship was characterized by hostility and suspicion, and fears of nuclear confrontation were seriously entertained. A high degree of transparency was thought essential to persuade parties that their vulnerability would not be increased unacceptably by treaty limits on weapons deployment.[1] To that end, the United States organized a costly system of surveillance, relying on complex advanced technology developed for both verification and intelligence purposes. Methods of verification achieved great technological precision and sophistication in an era when costs were not a major issue. The large body of Western verification literature, both technical and political, is dominated by this context.[2]

The cold war experience continues to color approaches to verification today, even though the context has changed. Therefore, this chapter begins with an attempt to understand those earlier dynamics. But the focus of discourse about verification has begun to shift to emerging multilateral arms limitation arrangements, particularly for the control of weapons of mass destruction, and to regulatory initiatives in other substantive areas, such as environmental, economic, welfare, and human rights regulation.[3] And with the growing role of international peace enforcement efforts aimed at controlling regional, cross-border, and civil conflict, new forms of verification are needed to help assure that cease-fire agreements are maintained and that military surprise does not shatter a hard-won truce.[4]

These new arenas pose issues of cost-effectiveness and intrusiveness. While aspects of the cold war paradigm have continuing value—especially in the nonproliferation of dangerous weapons, where the issue involves elements of deterrence as well as reassurance—the legacy of elaboration and thoroughness, premised on extreme caution and low financial constraint, is less compelling for the management of verification in all the varied international arrangements that now require it.

Verification in Cold War Arms Control Agreements

Bilateral U.S.-USSR Agreements

From the late 1950s, when arms control negotiations began in earnest, until the late 1980s, when the relationship between the United States and the Soviet Union changed dramatically, the two superpowers were able to reach a number of cooperative legal arrangements to limit or reduce weapons. Although the overall political relationship remained primarily adversarial, characterized by extreme mistrust, suspicion, and hostility, these agreements operated to reduce the costs and uncertainties of the arms race, while limiting the military risks of relying on an untrusted treaty partner.

Reassurance and Deterrence. Because the parties were deeply suspicious of each other, they required continuous assurance against "breakout," the possibility that the other party was preparing a devastating surprise by building prohibited weapons systems clandestinely. There were two paths to this end. First, the military posture on each side, even after agreed reductions, was kept so robust that a breakout could not achieve a critical military advantage. Second, the arms control arrangements were designed to provide warning long enough in advance to permit an adequate military response.[5] Thus, the ABM Treaty not only limited deployment but also prohibited development and testing of ABM systems that were not land based.[6] Verification procedures were designed to monitor these precursor activities as well as actual deployments to ensure that any attempted breakout would be detected in time to allow for appropriate countermeasures.

The same system that provided reassurance against breakout also contained a strong element of deterrence. Since the prospects of discovery were high and the possibility of achieving a significant military advantage was low, there was little to be gained from violation. Exposure could spark the very spiral the agreement sought to forestall. Not only would both parties lose the benefit of their bargain, but a general and dangerous deterioration in the bilateral relationship might also ensue.

In the United States, this verification philosophy was broadly shared by both Democratic and Republican administrations. When in 1977 Congress enacted a requirement of "adequate verification" for arms control agreements, Secretary of Defense Harold Brown testified: "The relevant test is not an abstract ideal, but the practical standard of whether we can determine compliance adequately to safeguard our security—that is, whether we can identify attempted evasion if it occurs on a large enough scale to pose a significant risk, and whether we can do so in time to mount a sufficient response. Meeting this test is what I mean by the term 'adequate verification.'"[7]

The Reagan administration rhetoric, substituting the term "effective" for "adequate," seemed to imply a more exacting standard, but in fact it came to essentially the same thing. Ambassador Paul Nitze stated, in defining effective verification for the INF treaty: "If the other side moves beyond the limits of the Treaty in any militarily significant way, we would be able to detect such a violation in time to respond effectively and thereby to deny the other side the benefit of violation."[8]

During the cold war, the rhetoric of deterrence overshadowed the importance of ongoing reassurance. In the future, the mix of deterrence and reassurance must be appropriate to the context of the agreements at issue. Potential military threats remain so long as the proliferation of weapons of mass destruction and the widespread dissemination of advanced military technology are not checked. Military vulnerability occurs anywhere that one party develops weapons capable of inflicting serious damage on its neighbors who have phased them out or agreed not to develop or acquire them. Elements of deterrence, requiring sufficiently early warning to permit a timely response will therefore remain in contemporary security regimes, despite the change in status of the former Soviet Union. Although the possibility of nuclear holocaust has subsided, at the regional level, uncertainty and danger may be greater than when the superpowers could rein in excesses of nationalism and ethnic violence.

National Technical Means of Verification. Because neither party was willing to trust the other, the early bilateral arms control agreements relied primarily on national technical means of verification, with heavy emphasis on satellite observation, to monitor and evaluate treaty behavior. From the time of the Baruch Plan in 1946[9] until 1987, the USSR persistently refused to accept either emplacement of passive technical monitors or on-site inspections, dismissing them as thinly veiled opportunities for espionage. The test ban negotiations in the early 1960s came close to breaking this pattern. The Soviets offered two to three on-site inspections, but the position of the United States was that the number necessary to verify a comprehensive test ban covering underground testing was seven.[10] As a way out of the impasse, the parties settled for a Limited Test Ban Treaty, prohibiting only tests in the atmosphere, outer space, and under water, which could be verified by NTM, and excluding underground tests, which arguably could not. Thereafter, until the INF agreement at the end of the cold war, arms control agreements between the superpowers were tailored to unilateral technical verification capabilities.[11] During this era, the increasing capabilities of NTM provided the confidence that permitted the parties to accept some limited agreements to stabilize and limit nuclear force levels as an alternative to the costs and risks of an uncontrolled arms race. The arms limitation agreements, in turn, made some aspects of military planning and intelligence less demanding, since they provided a certain predictability—neither side would be likely to engage in open or extensive violations.[12]

Monitoring by NTM alone, however, could not provide fully satisfactory verification of compliance. Even where the weapons controlled were large and highly visible, evidence was often ambiguous and required clarification and explanation. Thus, despite the mistrust and suspicion, a considerable degree of cooperation in verification evolved over the course of the relationship. In 1972, SALT I established the Standing Consultative Commission as a forum "to consider questions concerning compliance with the obligations assumed and related situations which may be considered ambiguous."[13] The SALT I agreement contained other rudimentary cooperative elements, as well. The parties undertook not to interfere with each other's NTM and not to take measures of deliberate concealment.[14] The SALT II treaty, which was signed but never ratified, moved to a still greater degree of cooperation. It established an "agreed data base," thus, as was noted earlier, "repeal[ing] 400 years of Russian history."[15] A variety of counting rules facilitated the operation of NTM. In sum, even though reliance on unilateral monitoring by NTM remained the primary source of assurance of compliance, the usefulness of cooperative measures was increasingly recognized.[16]

The Politics of Cold War Verification. During the cold war, basic U.S. policy was to insist on detailed accountability for every provision and timeline of the verification procedures. Most Americans who participated in the process, in whatever administration, proceeded on the assumption that the Soviet

Union would take advantage of any loopholes or ambiguities, and would "salami slice" to see what the United States would permit.[17] Military caution alone cannot explain these demands for exactitude and full technical compliance with the detailed verification schemes. The cold war had deep roots in the national consciousness. From the 1960s through the 1980s, a large American domestic constituency had doubts about the value of arms control altogether. They had to be satisfied that there was substantially no risk. Their assumption was that the Soviets would not honor agreements but would attempt to take advantage of them. This ideological framework gave credibility to even partial and uncertain evidence of Soviet violations, putting political pressure on U.S. officials to draw worst-case conclusions from ambiguous observations. No administration could risk the perception that it had been duped. This, in turn, reinforced the negative public image of the Soviet Union. The result was an attitude of hypervigilance, rooted neither in military necessity nor in the requirements of normal political relationships, but in these ingrained ideological attitudes.

A driving assumption was that relatively small changes in the size or structure of nuclear forces could directly affect the military balance and endanger American security. Failure to maintain a precise military balance, it was thought, would encourage the Soviets to pursue expansionist goals, because the United States would be too weak to deter them. After the SALT I ratification debate, this approach was enshrined in the concept of parity.[18] The Senate enacted the Jackson Resolution, establishing a requirement of "substantial equivalence" in all further U.S.-Soviet arms control treaties.[19] The effect was to make parity a surrogate in popular debate for the superpower arms balance.

The parity requirement attributed significance to even marginal differences in selected quantitative dimensions of strategic arsenals. Crude numerical comparisons became the basis for political attacks on proposed agreements, regardless of military realities. As a result, verification measures, too, had to be designed to detect any minute departure from parity, whether or not it was militarily significant.[20]

The Reagan administration was even more suspicious of Soviet behavior than its predecessors. Beginning in 1984, the president issued annual Noncompliance Reports to Congress that chronicled even the smallest and most questionable alleged violations of treaties in force (and some that remained unratified), leading to public confrontation on issues of violation that, even if true, were quite trivial.

Shards of these fears remain.[21] Despite the disintegration of the Soviet

Union, the beginnings of democratization in its successor states, and the radical change in relationships with the Western democracies, the insistence on parity (at a minimum) has not disappeared either from the American scene or from the minds of the successors to the Soviet military. It matters less today than it did in 1990 that Russian factories not disguise SS-20 missiles as SS-25s. It is now accepted that "core deterrence" is not easily unbalanced.[22] But the insistence on rigorous verification remains.

A Look at Early Post–Cold War Arms Control Verification. Despite the echoes of the old ways, the confrontational style of cold war bilateral verification began to give way to greater cooperation and openness in the Intermediate-Range Nuclear Forces negotiations. In a remarkable shift, the Soviet Union accepted on-site inspection for the first time, and the parties agreed to a complex protocol establishing joint procedures for carrying out these inspections.[23] As U.S.-Russian relations became even more cooperative and less adversarial, the breakthrough in the INF Treaty was extended to the more complex agreement on conventional arms in Europe (CFE) and the strategic nuclear weapons (START) agreements.[24] Indeed, all subsequent arms control treaties, including START II and the Chemical Weapons Convention (CWC), follow the INF pattern in authorizing extensive on-site inspections to verify compliance with their provisions.[25] The same model is being urged for the a renegotiated Biological Weapons Convention (BWC).[26]

All of these treaties have lengthy verification annexes that run to scores of pages of requirements and procedures and contain unprecedented cooperative measures. Separate types of inspections are matched to particular treaty obligations. Initial baseline inspections verify the agreed database. Where elimination of a weapon system or production is called for, close out inspections are required.[27] Where production is prohibited, exemplar facilities are subject to continuous portal monitoring.[28] A number of random or challenge inspections may be specified in addition to those conducted on a routine basis.[29] The treaties also contain elaborate measures to ensure that the inspections are not obstructed. The inspected state must provide escort teams for the inspectors and special transportation, including helicopters, for certain inspections. The cold war caution has by no means been relaxed in this environment of increased cooperation.

National technical means of verification continue to play an important role, particularly with regard to troop movements and where treaty-limited items or facilities are large and visible to overhead inspection.[30] The Open Skies Treaty, signed by twenty-nine states in March 1992, enhances the potential of cooperative NTM by authorizing substantial quotas of overflights in the territory from the Atlantic to the Urals. These will be useful for observing not only troop movements but also other items regulated by a number of treaties. Thus far the parties have continued to insist on meticulous compliance with these requirements.[31]

A Parallel Model

An alternative model for assuring compliance—one that also had its beginnings in the cold war period—relies on verification and inspection by an international organization, rather than by the treaty parties themselves. It operated first in the field of nuclear proliferation, where the interests of the United States and the Soviet Union were more closely aligned. The instrument was the International Atomic Energy Agency, created in 1958 to promote the peaceful use of atomic energy while safeguarding against the diversion of nuclear materials and technology to weapons development. As the assumed gateway to the hoped-for wonders and benefits of the nuclear future, it was a broadly based international agency from the beginning, with 81 original members (expanded to 122 by 1995), and a Board of Governors of 35.[32] In 1956 the United States had embarked on the Atoms for Peace program to export nuclear facilities and materials for peaceful purposes. Recipients under the program were required to agree to inspection to ensure against diversion for military use. When the IAEA was established, these bilateral agreements were renegotiated, and the IAEA assumed the inspection function. As other nations began to enter the export market for atomic energy, they too agreed to the inspection procedures established by the IAEA. Inspection, as codified by the Board of Governors in a publication called Information Circular (INFCIRC) 68, was limited to the particular materials that were the subject of the import-export transaction and did not extend to indigenous production. Thus, for example, Israel's Dimona reactor never came under IAEA inspection.

In the Nuclear Non-Proliferation Treaty of 1968, the non-nuclear parties agreed not to acquire nuclear weapons, and to verify compliance with that obligation, they also agreed to accept safeguards on all their peaceful nuclear facilities.[33] Although the treaty does not directly confer inspection rights on the IAEA, the agency has assumed the safeguards function. Non–nuclear weapon states negotiate agreements providing for all nuclear facilities to be declared and open to inspection, whether indigenous or imported. These requirements are codified in INFCIRC 153 (1971) and are known as "full-scope safeguards."[34] The regulations required each party to declare and provide current, detailed accounts of all its peaceful nuclear materials and facilities. The agency conceived of its responsibility as limited to verifying that there was no diversion from civil use, based on its inspection of declared facilities. Its procedure was to audit each facility's materials balances to ensure that there was no "significant" nuclear material unaccounted for. The yardstick for what was significant was the approximate quantity needed to manufacture a single nuclear weapon—twenty-five kilograms of U-235 or eight kilograms of plutonium.[35] Thus it was theoretically possible for a country to divert enough material from each facility to produce a nuclear weapon without objection under the safeguards procedures.

Even more important, the IAEA did not search for undeclared facilities or materials or even probe suspicious circumstances, such as the construction by Iraq of new large installations close to declared facilities.[36] Indeed until the Gulf War, the agency maintained that it had no authority to do so. The situation uncovered in Iraq by the UN Special Commission, which exercised virtually unlimited powers of inspection under Security Council Resolution 687, highlights the inadequacy of the routine inspection procedure as conceived by the IAEA until that time.[37] The initial inventory submitted by Iraq in April 1991 pursuant to Resolution 687 showed that it possessed 27.6 pounds of highly enriched uranium that had been under IAEA inspection and 22 pounds of lightly enriched uranium that had been supplied by the Soviet Union for the Al Tuwaitha research center. It listed twenty-four installations engaged in nuclear activity, and revealed that Iraq had received six tons of depleted uranium from an undisclosed source.[38] In June, intelligence information provided by a defecting Iraqi scientist indicated that Iraq had greatly understated its nuclear weapons program and the amount of weapons-grade nuclear material in its possession.[39] New inspections ordered by UNSCOM ultimately uncovered conclusive evidence of an extensive nuclear weapons development program designed to produce an implosion-type nuclear weapon and linked to a surface-to-surface missile project.[40]

Based on this experience, the IAEA has decided that in the future it should conduct "special" inspections where it has reason to believe there are undeclared facilities or materials. The director general, with the approval of the Board of Governors, construed INFCIRC 153 as authorizing such inspections, another example of the acceptability of intrusive verification after INF, CFE, and START I.[41] The first test of the new authority came in North Korea, when the director general requested a special inspection after an initial inspection in February 1993 raised some suspicions. The basic INFCIRC 153 provision permits special inspections "with the consent of the party," and the IAEA was stymied when North Korea refused to give its consent.[42] As the inspection procedure had been originally conceived, this refusal of consent was itself treated as a serious departure from acceptable conduct. The director general formally brought the matter before the Board of Governors, which has the authority to refer it to the Security Council for further action if it is not settled by negotiation. In the summer of 1994, after extended negotiations, North Korea agreed to a standstill in the refueling of its existing reactors (with the effect of stopping any potential bomb program), to be monitored by the IAEA. In return, the United States and South Korea agreed to supply North Korea with a light water reactor, much less susceptible to diversion for weapons purposes. The standstill went into effect as planned, but the negotiations for the supply of the reactor proved long-drawn-out and difficult. They had not been completed by mid-1995. Neither had the special inspection.[43]

At the same time, the IAEA was developing an elaborate program for strengthening the safeguards system to cover detection of undeclared activities in states that have accepted full-scope safeguards. The new program includes an Expanded Declaration, covering not existing but planned nuclear programs, together with broad access inspections to all nuclear and nuclear-related locations, to give increased assurance that there are no undeclared activities. The inspections would be made on a regular though not routine basis, and could be conducted without advance notice as to timing, activities, or location. In June 1995 the IAEA Board of Governors decided to bifurcate implementation of its new safeguards system. While the first stage was implicitly approved, the second stage, negotiations with individual states, was pending separate legal authority at the next board meeting, in December.[44]

The CWC avoids this problem by providing that a party may demand a challenge inspection "for the sole purpose of resolving any questions concerning possible non-compliance" with the convention.[45] Throughout most of the negotiations, the United States pushed for no-notice "anytime, anywhere" inspections, but it had second thoughts when the conference appeared to be on the verge of agreeing to this. In an ironic reversal, the United States began to appreciate the virtues of protecting classified and proprietary information. It moved to a less demanding concept of "managed access" and modified its negotiating position accordingly.[46] It was decided that challenge inspections will be conducted by the Technical Secretariat of the new Organization for the Prevention of Chemical Warfare (OPCW), and that the inspected state must provide full access to the inspected installations on a short timetable. The inspected state has a minimum of twelve hours' notice before the inspection team arrives at a designated entry point, and an additional thirty-six hours before it must get the team to the perimeter of the suspect site. It has a right to have an observer present at the inspection. Negotiations about the perimeter of the area to be inspected must be completed within the first twenty-four hours. The host country may refuse inspection to safeguard constitutional requirements with respect to proprietary rights or search and seizure. In such cases, the host state is obligated "to demonstrate compliance" by alternative means.[47]

The internationalization of verification under the cwc makes U.S. experts somewhat nervous, given the long history of U.S. concern with high levels of verification and its traditional skepticism of the iaea.[48] The loss of control involved in internationalization may seem also to entail a lowering of standards. But broadly inclusive multilateral agreements are likely to be the pattern of the future, and they will of necessity move to multilateral verification and cost sharing, as the cwc has done. The United States and a few other countries may continue to exercise their ntm, but parties to multilateral security arrangements are unlikely to accept unilateral on-site inspections by another state.

The new types of security agreements will be both cooperative and intrusive, and will require imagination and careful exploitation of advanced verification technology. The limitations on cooperation, heretofore political, may now be more a matter of resource availability and the kind of security and industrial interests that emerged in the cwc negotiations. The agreements of the early 1990s appear to be transitional, reflecting the caution and precision of the past and the uncertainty of the future.

The Need for Reassurance in Other Regulatory Agreements

The experience with verification of security agreements, and particularly with superpower arms control agreements, cannot be transferred wholesale to other areas. Verification of compliance in environmental regimes and similar areas does not seem to have the same urgency. The stakes are not seen to be so high nor the consequences so immediate nor the tolerance for error so low. Even the terminology is different. "Monitoring," the term most often used in these areas, covers only some of the concerns addressed in the arms control verification literature. In particular it is much less focused on the detection of every individual violation. Some aspects of the classic model of security verification, however, may be adaptable to other contexts. The role of technical monitoring, including forms of satellite surveillance, is increasing in environmental regulation. On-site inspection, as it has developed in arms control from inf on, will also find applications in environmental monitoring, and where available, has been used to good effect in human rights and peace enforcement as well.

By the same token, experience in regulatory regimes can feed back into the security field. The requirements and constraints of multilateral nonproliferation agreements more closely parallel other regulatory regimes, even though higher risks may be involved. Bilateral arms control is traditionally preoccupied primarily with state action, while the efficacy of other regulatory areas depends more heavily on the behavior of private actors. But that distinction has blurred. Efforts to control weapons proliferation also find it necessary to monitor private activity. New methods are required to deal with activities less directly under state control and more difficult to measure, in security and regulatory agreements alike.

Verification of Environmental Agreements

Environmental regulation relies primarily on self-reporting to generate data on compliance, with little by way of independent, official confirmation of the accuracy and completeness of the information. In most treaties, there is a general injunction to review the reports,[49] but neither the conference of the parties nor the secretariat is likely to have the resources or technical capability to do so systematically.[50] For the most part, limited internal analysis and cross-checks of reports, supplemented by the "triangulation" possibilities offered by nongovernmental organization reports and independent technical assessments, form the only basis for inferential judgments on the accuracy of reported data.[51]

Monitoring Environmental Conditions. As already noted, where monitoring is more systematic, the primary concern is to ascertain the overall status of the environmental system subject to regulation. The issue is not party compliance but the effectiveness of existing regulation and the need for tighter standards. The monitoring effort facilitates the coordination of national policies, as discussed in Chapter 6. It informs policy-making at national and international levels and in many situations helps to generate the political impetus needed to forge new agreements or to strengthen weak ones. Indeed, if a current agreement is not ameliorating the problem, the characteristic response—and maybe the most effective one—seems to be to try to raise standards generally, rather than to track down one or two violators.

For example, from 1954 to 1978, the International Maritime Organization kept tightening the limits on permissible oil pollution from tankers under the International Convention for the Prevention of Pollution of the Sea by Oil,[52] even though available oil content meters were not accurate enough to enable tanker operators to measure compliance with the discharge standard.[53] Similarly, when, after the conclusion of the Montreal Protocol, monitoring revealed continuing depletion of the stratospheric ozone layer, it was decided that existing controls would be inadequate to deal with the problem. The parties expanded the list of controlled substances and amended the control provisions from a cutback of 50 percent to a phaseout of most controlled substances by the year 2000. Two years later, in Copenhagen, the phaseout date for many substances was advanced to January 1, 1996.[54] Individual party compliance with intermediate cutback targets became almost irrelevant.

In Chapter 6, we described how the fruits of cooperative monitoring under the European Monitoring and Evaluation Program credibly established the existence of acid rain damage to northern European forests and lakes and provided the impetus for concerted action to reduce emissions.[55] With consensus on the nature and extent of the problem, parties could more easily reach agreement on regulation.[56] Under Med Plan[57] and the Convention for Protection of the Rhine against Chemical Pollution, cooperative monitoring networks also function as part of an early warning system with respect to environmental hazards.

Monitoring Compliance. Party performance is not ignored altogether. Cooperative monitoring mechanisms developed to identify problems may also be used to monitor the impact of regulation. The EMEP has continued to perform the "dual role" of scientific research and compliance monitoring for the parties to the Convention on Long-Range Transboundary Air Pollution. It produces such a comprehensive matrix of information that states are not tempted to report inaccurate national data, and this provides both reassurance and deterrence. Peter Sand remarks that "few other international agreements can be said to come equipped with verification instruments of this caliber."[58]

The IMO finally solved the problem of oil pollution from tankers by requiring segregated ballast tanks, which physically prevent the intermixture of oil with the discharged ballast water. This was costly to tanker operators but easily monitored by shipping authorities in the course of routine inspections of incoming tankers. Moreover, private marine insurers now refuse to certify noncomplying vessels. Compliance with the equipment standard has been close to 100 percent, and the discharge of oil from the new ships is substantially nil. A dismal record of compliance has been transformed into a near perfect one.[59]

Again, after more than twenty years of consideration, the International

Convention for the Regulation of Whaling was amended in 1977 to authorize the establishment of an International Observer Scheme (IOS).[60] The IOS is akin to on-site inspection systems. It provides for voluntary bilateral exchanges of observers on whaling ships and at land stations. The observers submit reports to the International Whaling Commission noting any infractions, although these are normally accompanied by satisfactory explanations. The scheme is voluntary—facilitated but not required by the IWC And the bilateral exchanges are largely between whaling nations. Nevertheless, the IOS provided some additional reassurance of compliance.[61]

The Antarctic Treaty employs a more characteristic on-site inspection system. The treaty freezes (without recognizing) existing territorial claims on the continent and prohibits military activities of all kinds.[62] It further provides that, on notice, any party may inspect the installations of any other party in the Antarctic region. The Soviets accepted this arrangement, presumably because the inspections were not on any nation's territory and the treaty was only partly related to security matters. The United States, on the other hand, hoped that the Antarctic system of inspection would set a benign precedent for more serious arms control agreements. Although that expectation was disappointed, the inspection system has helped to prevent activities that might have been threatening environmentally or militarily. Ten inspections were conducted up to 1983 (half by the United States, the rest by New Zealand, Australia the United Kingdom, and Argentina). Thereafter, with the intensification of environmental concerns, the number of inspections has risen dramatically to 113 between 1983 and 1992 (again, about half by the United States; others by Australia, Chile, France, Germany, New Zealand, the United Kingdom, and the Soviet Union). Greenpeace, taking advantage of the openness of the Antarctic system, gained access to a French base and discovered that a number of Adelaide penguins had been killed during the construction of a new airstrip there. The Greenpeace photographs forced the consideration of the issue by the Antarctic Treaty Consultative Meeting, and France commissioned an environmental impact assessment as required by the Agreed Measures for the Conservation of Fauna and Flora.[63] Stricter notice, inspection, and impact assessment requirements are included in the new Antarctic Treaty Protocol on Environmental Protection.[64]

A more recent entry in the on-site inspection field is the Convention on Wetlands (the Ramsar Convention). Under a monitoring procedure established in 1989, more than twenty on-site inspections have been conducted. Parties to the treaty voluntarily list wetlands within their territory for which they propose to provide protection. Inspections are prompted by information in national reports or from independent sources suggesting that a protected wetland may be threatened. Usually a secretariat representative and a technical expert visit the site to discuss the activities that are threatening the wetland. The tone of these visits is not adversarial but highly cooperative, and the emphasis is on finding solutions.[65]

Finally, the Implementation Committee established under the Montreal Protocol is authorized "to undertake, upon the invitation of the Party concerned, information-gathering in the territory of that party for fulfilling the functions of the Committee."[66]

Despite these examples, however, environmental regimes do not display the obsessive concern with meticulous compliance that marks the security field. A number of considerations account for this difference. First, ecological systems are very complex and not well understood, and so the phenomena involved often are not susceptible to precise measurement. If the monitoring technology is not sufficiently accurate to provide evidence of noncompliance, the regime must rely on indirect measures. Carbon dioxide emissions may be inferred from fossil fuel consumption, for example, but the resulting estimate would be a shaky predicate for harsh compliance measures. Emissions of other major greenhouse gases, such as methane, cannot be estimated with even this degree of reliability, and the performance of sinks, such as forests and large bodies of water, is even less well understood. The development of an adequate methodology and technology for performance monitoring itself involves cost-effectiveness trade-offs.

Second, if monitoring is to serve verification purposes, the treaty must mandate either quantitative standards or specific technologies, such as scrubbers in smokestacks or the separate ballast tanks designed to reduce oil pollution. But the uncertainty we have noted feeds into political resistance to such well-defined constraints. In the Mediterranean Action Plan, a serious issue between the developed and developing countries was whether standards for control of land-based sources of pollution should be based on ambient levels or emissions. Industrialized states, already suffering from serious coastal pollution, wanted emissions standards, which could be readily monitored at the source. Less developed countries favored ambient standards, arguing that the strict standards were inappropriate for them, since their coasts were better able to assimilate pollution. It is, of course, almost impossible to pinpoint a single source responsible for a transgression of ambient standards. The compromise was to apply emission standards to a short "black list" of the most serious pollutants and ambient standards to other controlled pollutants.[67] In the antidumping protocol to the Barcelona Convention, a major dispute between France and Italy over the inclusion of titanium dioxide was resolved by prohibiting dumping of "acid and alkaline compounds of such composition and in such quantity that may seriously impair the quality of the sea water."[68] Positive verification of this standard is also impossible. Perhaps the most notorious invocation of scientific uncertainty was the Bush administration's refusal to accept quantitative limits on CO_2 emissions in the climate change convention. As a result, the Framework Convention on Climate Change had to settle for a vaguer undertaking by developed countries to adopt policies "with the aim of returning . . . to their 1990 levels these anthropogenic emissions of carbon dioxide and other greenhouse gases."[69] Whatever else may be said for this standard, it is inherently not susceptible to strict performance monitoring. The issue was revisited, in the first Conference of the Parties in March 1955, but it will take a long time to reach measurable specificity.[70]

Third, free rider problems have not seemed so urgent in practice as in the theoretical literature. As the foregoing examples illustrate, the objective of environmental treaties is not so much to achieve a particular end state as to manage the environmental resource over time, by setting in motion trends that will reverse its current decline or depletion. Even fairly significant individual deviations from prescribed standards may not entail immediate dire consequences, as was thought to be the case in the security area. Thus, there is time for managerial efforts to induce compliance. Retaliation in kind, the usual prescription for free riding, is an even less attractive option in environmental contexts than elsewhere. It would itself result in further deterioration of the resource, and often the retaliator would face the same international and domestic pressures as an original defector.

Fourth, developing countries in particular are treated leniently. As yet they make only a small contribution to many global environmental problems, and there seems to be a general recognition that they lack technical and political capabilities needed for full compliance. The result is a considerable tolerance for noncompliance or partial compliance with both reporting and substantive requirements, and often a more leisurely schedule for achieving compliance. The ozone agreements, for example, expressly authorize free riding for developing countries by providing a grace period of ten years before the control obligations apply to them.[71] Both the FCCC and the Biodiversity Convention concluded at the Rio summit, establish a lesser level of obligation for developing countries, but neither of these conventions contain quantitative performance standards.[72]

This relatively complacent view might change under certain circumstances.

If the perceived environmental threat were immediate and devastating, no doubt efforts to monitor the individual performance of important contributors would intensify. It is a fair prediction that the phaseout of controlled substances under the ozone agreements at the end of 1995 will be closely monitored, in view of the general consensus on both the high probability and serious consequences of further ozone layer depletion.

Another development that might generate a requirement for more meticulous performance monitoring would be the use of tradable emission permits as a regulatory instrument. According to some current models for such a scheme, the parties to the climate change treaty would agree on some global cap for greenhouse gas emissions, and emissions permits would then be allotted by some formula to participating countries (or perhaps to private polluters). These allotments would be tradable. A country that could reduce its emissions at low cost would reduce below its assigned limit and be able to sell a portion of its allotment to countries with higher reduction costs. It is hoped that the agreed global cap would be achieved more efficiently this way than if each country had to make the required reductions on its own.[73] As has been suggested, the global climate system might well tolerate moderate deviations from established emission limits from time to time. But under a tradable permit system, accurate verification that the seller had indeed reduced its emissions as promised would still be required, to ensure that the buyer got what it paid for. Similar verification issues would arise under many "joint implementation" schemes—as, for example, when a country supplying financing would get credit for the emissions reduction achieved in the country of the investment.

In general, however, even grave concerns about individual violators or free riders would not necessarily lead parties to undertake a costly performance monitoring program instead of pursuing other strategies to enhance compliance. Significant violators may be discovered without systematic verification procedures. Thus far, diplomatic and economic pressures, shaming, appeals to domestic constituencies, and economic incentives have been employed in such cases to achieve acceptable compliance (see Chapter 10).

Current Issues

As the hypervigilance of the cold war recedes, the potential role of verification in managing compliance in such areas as weapons proliferation and environmental degradation becomes more problematic. An important issue is how much of the scarce resources available for implementation overall should be allocated to monitoring and verification, especially in view of its high cost and intrusiveness.

One plausible rule of thumb would seem to be to allocate verification resources in at least rough proportion to the perceived risk.[74] Sensitivity to differences in risk might explain, for instance, the sharp contrast between the simple IOS system of the Whaling Convention and the elaborate on-site inspection schemes of INF, CFE, and START I. Nevertheless, this simple correlation is not borne out by past experience. Even in bilateral nuclear arms control, the insistence of the United States on meticulous compliance was disproportionate to a realistic assessment of potential U.S. vulnerability to Soviet violations, in our view. By contrast, the total absence of verification provisions in the 1975 Biological and Toxin Weapons Convention (BWC) may have seriously underestimated both potential vulnerabilities and the parties' ability to respond to noncompliance. At the time, it was argued that moral stigma and questionable military value combined to make such weapons unusable, although the concerns raised during the Reagan administration about "yellow rain" in Vietnam and Afghanistan and particularly about the outbreak of anthrax in Sverdlovsk in Russia indicate that certain officials believed biological weapons were being produced and used by the Soviet Union.[75] A U.S. official said that at least ten nations were working to produce both previously known and futuristic biological weapons.[76] After years of neglect, the UN is slowly moving to strengthen the verification provisions of the BWC. The Chemical Weapons Convention has finally remedied the absence of verification provisions in its predecessor, the Geneva Protocol. But the pace has been slow, especially given evidence of actual use in the Iran-Iraq war.[77]

Hypervigilance is unlikely to dominate verification policy as new security challenges call for new approaches. Environmental regulation still faces a lack of consensus about the immediacy and irreversibility of many threats. In both areas, the primary determinants of verification systems are more likely be intrusiveness and cost.

Intrusiveness

The potential for routine inspection of private facilities under the CWC is staggering. It is estimated that there are 20,000 establishments subject to inspection in the United States alone and another 40,000 to 60,000 elsewhere in the world. Undoubtedly some form of randomization will be employed, so not all of these sites will be subject to regular inspection. Nevertheless, the scope of international intrusion into private business activities will be unprec-

edented, and important questions of the protection of proprietary and confidential business information are involved.

Confidentiality has also become an issue in the Montreal Protocol. Under
the current arrangement, the secretariat publishes "consumption" data for
each individual substance. Consumption is defined as "production plus
imports minus exports."[78] To keep production figures confidential, only the
parties to the agreement may access one another's production, import, and
export figures—the components of the calculation—and only if they agree to
maintain confidentiality.[79] The procedure is awkward, and it is also an
obstacle to participation in the verification process by scientific and academic
groups, NGOS, and other international organizations.

Confidentiality problems are likely to increase in number and importance
as environmental agreements like the Climate Change Convention and the
Biodiversity Convention begin to implicate a broad range of industrial activities and processes.

Costs

During the cold war, each superpower footed the bill for its own verification
activity, much of which was in any case justified by intelligence requirements.
In the future, international verification systems will be limited by the willingness of the members of the relevant treaty regimes to pay—in practice, the
willingness of industrialized states to fund the operation of the system. In
addition, developed states may have to finance technical, legal, and administrative assistance developing countries that are unable to implement verification mechanisms.[80]

The High Costs of Reliable Verification. Issues of both absolute cost and cost-
effectiveness permeate any evaluation of the thoroughness and intrusiveness
of verification systems. Some sense of the magnitudes involved can be had
from the early experience under recent arms control agreements. According
to the General Accounting Office, INF inspections cost the United States about
$105 million per year in the first four years of operation, including equipment,
travel, and personnel.[81] Annual expenditures dropped as baseline inspections
were completed, and the On-site Inspection Agency (OSIA) estimated annual
operating costs, including military service costs, to be in the vicinity of $29
million for the fiscal years 1993, 1994, and 1995.[82] The Congressional Budget
Office estimated in 1990 that the costs of verifying START I will be in the range
of $100 million to $290 million annually, in addition to one-time costs from
$410 million to $1.83 billion. Later estimates by OSIA were at the low end of

that range—$140 million for fiscal year 93, dropping to $110 million in subsequent years. The range of OSIA estimates for one-time costs of all the new treaties taken together—START I, CFE, CWC, the Threshold Test Ban Treaty, and the Treaty on Peaceful Nuclear Explosions (PNE Treaty)—is from approximately $600 million to $3 billion, and annual costs are estimated at approximately $350 million to double that amount.[83] While these costs are not staggering in the context even of a shrinking U.S. military budget, they are large in absolute terms.

For the multilateral agreements, IAEA's annual safeguards budget has run in the neighborhood of $75 million.[84] Some idea of the demands of a more intrusive system are given by the costs of UNSCOM's operations in Iraq: $61 million for the period from January 1991 to July 1994.[85] The budget for the CWC verification system has not yet been developed, but a cadre of more than three hundred officials is contemplated, the great majority of whom will be involved in inspection and verification.[86]

Cooperation in Verification and Monitoring. Cooperation has been a fact of life in verification and monitoring since SALT I, the early European confidence-building measures,[87] and especially the regimes involving inspections. For INF and START I, detailed requirements for notifications, escort rules, timetables, and the like are specified in the applicable verification protocol, and adjustments have been made on the ground to smooth the inspection operations further.[88] One important development in OSIA has been the elaboration of the right under the protocol "to request clarifications in connection with ambiguities." From the early days of INF inspections, the teams asked for clarification and attempted to settle disputes over interpretation in the field. "Ambiguity" became a term of art for a potential violation, and the recording or even photographing of a potential ambiguity became an event to be avoided by negotiation.[89] This degree of cooperation in the process of verification has enhanced reassurance and created a climate of cooperation for the entire regime.

As indicated, multilateral regimes inherently involve cooperation, if only in the sense that some of the verification tasks will be performed by international organizations. There has been considerable discussion of the potential efficiencies of an integrated international verification agency that would serve a broad spectrum of treaties.[90] Yet this idea is not without its problems, especially in the security area. Although the potential savings are obvious, nations with advanced military intelligence technology have concerns about exposing intelligence sources and methods and their transfer to potentially hostile nations. The use of national intelligence sources also raises the possibility that information would be manipulated by the supplying state for its own purposes. The effort to secure approval for use of information provided by national intelligence establishments in connection with IAEA "special inspections" ran into resistance on these grounds.[91] To ensure that reliance on such information would be based on the careful, neutral evaluation of data gathered in pursuit of national purposes and policies, the director general established a small intelligence evaluation unit in his own office.[92]

Nevertheless, it seems likely that national intelligence will play a role in the verification activities not only of the IAEA but of other nonproliferation regimes as well. The level of resources necessary for an effective intelligence agency—to say nothing of the level of secrecy—could not be duplicated at the international level. The track record of neutrality and fairness in the use of national intelligence by the IAEA and other international nonproliferation organizations might help at some future date to overcome some of the concerns that make the notion of a more generic international verification agency politically difficult now. At some point the obvious synergy of such an approach, and the avoidance of duplication, will make it a matter for careful consideration.

Cooperative monitoring of the environment presents much less of a problem and is in fact is under way in a number of areas, such as the activity of EMEP discussed earlier. Yet the extent to which cooperation will mean internationalization remains a contentious issue in situations where reliability requirements are high.[93]

New Methods and Technologies of Verification. High costs of verification in the security area drive a search for new, cost-effective, and relatively unintrusive techniques. The unclassified U.S. budget for verification research and development, has not diminished significantly in the post–cold war years and is currently set at approximately $315 million.[94] The future context for technical monitoring will be very different from that of the cold war. Budgetary constraints will pinch even more, and technical challenges are likely to remain high, though they will be of a different order. Conspicuous weapons installations and development facilities may be a relatively minor problem as arms control turns to issues of the proliferation of more easily concealed materials and weapons, and agreed reductions and changes in conventional force postures. New approaches to regional security may also require innovation in verification technology. The concept of "cooperative security" offers reassurance through preventive measures such as the reconfiguration of conventional forces for purely defensive purposes, restraints on military investment and expenditures, and broader measures of regional transparency.[95] Peace-keeping and peace enforcement operations will impose similar demands for monitoring and verification when and if the budgets for such operations begin to approximate realistic requirements.

Among the most promising new technologies for verification requirements are ground and airborne sensors and "tags." They are used to detect troop movements, tanks and other heavy vehicles, aircraft movements, chemical composition, and radiation. Spectral analysis of seismograms is coming close to determining not only a vehicle's direction and speed but its type as well.[96] These technologies are in varying states of development and refinement. Early operating cost estimates average $1 million per point controlled, which does not compare unfavorably with the personnel costs of conventional verification methods.[97] One problem is that although such devices could provide early warning, they might not produce dispositive evidence of non-compliance. But while that might have been an insurmountable obstacle under hypervigilance, it may be a necessary trade-off in a time of budgetary stringency and continuing concerns about intrusiveness.

Tags can be used to identify items limited by treaty. They range from very sophisticated electronic devices to simple epoxy paint with mica flakes in it. They may be attached or "intrinsic," using some feature of the item itself as a unique marker. Any untagged item would be presumptively in excess of treaty limits. Other new technologies include remote sensing through on-site deployment of infrared or X-ray scanners. In Iraq and North Korea, the IAEA has used continuous monitoring by tamperproof cameras located on site. Tamperproof gauges have long been proposed for providing continuous real-time data on materials balances in nuclear reactors.[98]

The emerging and adapted technologies are expensive, and their cost-effectiveness should be examined on a case-by-case basis. But there is little justification for carrying over the hypervigilance of the cold war into these new missions.

Trade-offs and Alternatives. For agreements in which the costs and dangers of free riding are much less than those associated with nuclear arms control agreements among major powers, the high costs of technology are likely to focus attention on alternative approaches to the problem of securing adequate compliance with agreements.

For example, all nonproliferation regimes depend to a very large degree on technology denial through national export control systems that have proved uncomfortably leaky, as Iraq and North Korea have demonstrated.[99] Yet the solution may not be simply to tighten up the controls, but to develop a more imaginative system of end-use assurances for dual-use items. Today purchasers of such items are required to provide end-use assurances, but there is little effort to police them. If the seller had civil and criminal responsibility under its domestic law for continuous verification of end-use assurances, and the purchaser were required as a condition of the sale to grant the seller continuous access to carry out this responsibility, the incentives and penalties would be placed on those who most benefit from the permitted trade. This technique is not foolproof, but for many items it is likely to be more effective than the present system of denial, and it would shift some of the public costs of verification to the private sector. The Chemical Weapons Convention combines outright trade prohibitions for the most dangerous class of chemicals, a phaseout of trade in precursor chemicals, and end-use certification for dual-use chemicals.[100]

Again, the IAEA considers itself bound to conduct inspections on all safeguarded facilities every six months, to maintain a wholly nondiscriminatory stance among its members. As a result, about 89 percent of its safeguards budget is expended on inspections in Japan, Germany, Canada, Holland, Belgium, and Sweden, where there is no real concern about compliance.[101] The IAEA's director general believes that greater reliance on "special inspections," not necessarily involving suspect activity, would permit it to reduce the number of routine inspections that now exhaust its budget.[102]

The cost of meeting their obligations under the START agreements is a major issue for Russia and the two other former Soviet republics with nuclear weapons. It has been difficult to spend the funds provided under the Nunn-Lugar Bill and in any case, the costs will exceed any realistic level of American assistance.[103] Given both the proliferation and environmental dangers of inadequate storage, these compliance tasks warrant the highest priority, and traditional verification may have to take a backseat. At the same time, hands-on U.S. assistance in weapons destruction performs a verification function in itself. The proposed U.S. purchase of highly enriched uranium (HEU) from nuclear weapons destroyed by Ukraine and Russia is another case where assistance and verification are complementary.[104]

The trade-off between verification and compliance costs also appears in the environmental field, where contemporary treaties recognize for the first time a legal obligation of the regime to provide financial and technological assistance for compliance by developing countries. The Montreal Protocol led the way with the "ozone fund" to finance "the agreed incremental costs of compliance,"[105] and similar arrangements are provided for in the FCCC and the Biodiversity Treaty.[106] Since these regimes entail enforcement against private actors at the domestic level, "incremental cost" has to include the domestic infrastructure for surveillance and enforcement in terms of both technical capacity and trained officials. As international regulatory agreements proliferate, the overall costs of compliance will continue to increase, perhaps at an accelerating rate. The need for funds to compensate less affluent nations for their compliance costs will become even more acute. At the end of the day, the choice will be assuring compliance through verification or by paying for it.

Conclusion

The superpowers, with only a few arms control treaties to temper their cold war military buildup, could afford the extreme caution and associated high costs that characterized the verification process. But in the changed world of multiple and multilateral opportunities and threats, hypervigilant verification policies and procedures are out of place. It may be that new security arrangements or urgent responses for severe environmental degradation will require the commitment of significantly larger resources to monitoring and verification. But the search for absolute assurance is illusory. Ultimately, no system of verification, no matter how abundantly endowed, will be able to verify completely all the activities subject to regulation. No matter how sophisticated the verification program, there will be uncertainties and disagreements about the state of the information that is developed. Both the cold war arms control experience and a careful consideration of the problems of compliance with new types of regulatory treaties caution against placing too heavy a burden on the verification element in securing regime transparency.

9

Instruments of Active Management

This chapter discusses three instruments of active management: capacity building, dispute settlement, and the adaptation and modification of treaty norms. Our survey indicates that these instruments are used and useful in bringing about compliance with complex and difficult treaty obligations. Together they comprise three elements of a strategy for active management of the compliance process. In our view, even though, in the settings where they are now employed, some of them are rudimentary and others not fully realized, they are worth close examination, because they are the building blocks of what could become a sophisticated and comprehensive management strategy.

Capacity Building and Technical Assistance

Technical assistance is an explicit or implicit objective of many treaty regimes. In most it is administered by the secretariat under budgetary and broad policy constraints established by the political organs.[1] In such organizations as the World Health Organization, the Food and Agricultural Organization, and the World Meteorological Organization, the provision of technical assistance may be the main programmatic activity. The International Atomic Energy Agency spends half of its budget on technical assistance to developing countries for the peaceful uses of nuclear energy.

A major by-product of the International Monetary Fund surveillance process has been the enhancement of the technical and professional capacity of the finance ministries and central banks of its members. Sir Joseph Gold, the legal adviser to the IMF during most of its first three decades, has remarked that one of the fund's most important accomplishments was improving the professional quality of finance bureaucracies in developing countries. Training occurred informally through the interaction of IMF staff and local officials in preparing the frequent staff studies and reports on local economies involved in the IMF process. Promising young economists in developing countries were selected by the international financial institutions for graduate education in industrialized countries, primarily the United States and England, where they were instructed in the reigning economic ideas underlying IMF policies. Often they served for several years on the IMF staff, learning not only the personalities but also the mores and ways of doing things, before returning to the finance ministries of their own countries.[2] That these programs involve an element of indoctrination in the goals and philosophy of the fund does nothing to dilute their effect on compliance with fund norms.

Even where there is no express conditionality in technical assistance grants, it follows from the organization's inherent commitment to the treaty that there will be pressure for conformity to treaty goals. However, in the environmental area, technical assistance is increasingly being provided explicitly for purposes of enabling compliance with treaty obligations. An entire chapter of *Agenda 21,* adopted at the 1992 Earth Summit at Rio, deals with "national mechanisms and international cooperation for capacity building in developing countries."[3] In *Saving the Mediterranean,* Peter Haas describes the UN Environment Program's policy of channeling research funds, equipment, maintenance, and training to laboratories in the less-developed-country members of Med Plan, to enable them to participate fully in the program. Indeed, UNEP chose to upgrade those labs, rather than concentrate its contracts in the more sophisticated and efficient establishments in France.[4]

The Montreal Protocol formally acknowledges that capacity building is central to the compliance process. Despite a ten-year grace period for developing countries before they must comply with the control provisions, the treaty recognizes that compliance will be impossible for those countries in any event unless they receive technical and financial assistance. Article 10 provides that "the Parties shall . . . taking into account in particular the needs of developing countries, co-operate in promoting technical assistance to facilitate participation in and implementation of this Protocol." The protocol as amended in London establishes a Multilateral Fund, with resources contributed by the developed countries, to "meet all agreed incremental costs of [developing country] Parties in order to enable their compliance with the control measures established by the Protocol."[5] It extends beyond technical assistance to the provision of funds for the incremental compliance costs of actual development projects.

The notion of "agreed" costs implies that the Multilateral Fund's financial obligation is not open-ended. The budget for the first three years was set at $160 million, with another $80 million available when China and India adhered. The fund has a complex management structure reflecting an intricate set of compromises between developing and developed country negotiators. It is administered by the World Bank (to satisfy donor demands for responsibility) with the assistance of UNEP and the UN Development Program (to satisfy developing country demands for friends at court). The three "implementing agencies" operate under the supervision of an Executive Committee made up of seven developed and seven developing country parties to the protocol, acting by a two-thirds overall majority that must include a majority of each subgroup.

Eligibility for funding is not determined project by project but only in the context of a comprehensive country compliance program.[6] Technical assistance for the preparation of the program may be provided by the implementing agencies, and funding is available from the Multilateral Fund. The completed program is reviewed by the implementing agencies and approved by the Executive Committee. At that point, individual projects contained in the program are eligible for funding.[7] The Executive Committee approves all requests in excess of $500,000, and a country whose application for a smaller grant is denied can appeal to the Committee.

The chairman of the Executive Committee reported enthusiastically to the Conference of the Parties in November 1992 that

> the initial critics had been proved wrong, as representatives of the developed and developing countries worked side by side, adopting all decisions by consensus and taking into consideration the concerns of all members. To date, 60 projects had been approved for the phase-out of more than 30,000 tonnes of ozone-depleting substances, which represented 20 per cent of the total consumption of the developing countries party to the Protocol . . . As at October 1992, it had allocated funds for the preparation of 39 country programmes, 9 of which had already been approved . . .
>
> . . . all nine approved programmes aimed at the phase-out of controlled substances, and most countries involved committing themselves to phasing out the substances according to the same schedule as that followed by [developed country] Parties . . . With the approval of the

China country programme, strategies would have been developed to eliminate more than half of current consumption of controlled substances in developing countries party to the Protocol.[8]

Making allowances for the chairman's pride in the performance of his committee, it remains a very substantial achievement.

The actual implementation of projects has been much slower, and only fifteen projects, eliminating 1,037 tons of CFCs, had been completed by December 1994. The November 1993 meeting of the parties in Bangkok authorized funding for the second three years of the fund in the amount of $510 million, but developed country contributors have not been prompt in meeting their obligations.[9]

Both the Framework Convention on Climate Change and the Convention on Biological Diversity contain provisions for similar funds to finance capacity building and compliance.[10] The treaties specifically recite that the commitments of the developing country parties are contingent on the provision of resources by the developed countries to meet the full agreed incremental costs of compliance.[11] The resource requirements in these areas are potentially much larger than for ozone, and controversies about the level of contributions, administration, and decision making are correspondingly more acute. For the FCCC, interim arrangements for the first three years provide that funds are to be funneled through the Global Environmental Facility (GEF), with the World Bank, UNDP, and UNEP acting as implementing agencies. Global Environmental Facility funding for the period has been set at $2 billion, to be divided among climate change and three other environmental areas. The arrangement is subject to a complicated governance process. A committee of thirty-two members (fourteen developed, sixteen developing, and two countries in transition), many representing "constituencies" of several of the members of the GEF, makes final decisions on projects and programs to be funded, subject to the policy guidance of the Conference of Parties of the FCCC. The committee acts by a 60 percent majority of the members representing at least 60 percent of the total contributions to the fund, giving the developed country members a veto, despite their inferior numbers.[12] The first meeting of the Conference of the Parties in March 1995 adopted policy guidance to the GEF, giving priority to "enabling activities undertaken by developing country Parties such as planning, endogenous capacity building including institutional strengthening, training, research and education, that will facilitate implementation, in accordance with the Convention, of effective response measures."[13] These capacity-building issues were a major focus of the preparatory committee in anticipation of the first meeting of the Conference of the Parties.

Dispute Settlement

If, as we suggest in Chapter 1, ambiguity about the meaning of treaty obligation or the actual character of a state's conduct is a significant source of potential deviance from treaty norms, then managing compliance requires some method of addressing these differences. Treaty negotiators know that such disputes are likely to arise during the life of the agreement and often make provisions for their settlement. In contemporary regulatory agreements, this is almost a matter of routine.[14] The canonical sequence of methods recognized by international law for the peaceful settlement of disputes is found in Article 33 of the UN Charter: "negotiation, inquiry, mediation, conciliation, arbitration, judicial settlement." These methods, whether provided for by the treaty or developed informally, are part of the standard tool kit for the management of a working regime. But there is widespread disagreement about the benefits and drawbacks of the different approaches. Strangely, this debate and the dispute resolution provisions themselves often seem disconnected from the subject matter of the treaty and responsive to a different set of conceptions, as if the primary motive is not so much to assist in securing compliance with the treaty as to vindicate the "legal" character of the arrangement.

Most international disputes, like most disputes within states, are settled informally by negotiation, sometimes among disputants, and often with the assistance of some form of intermediation.[15] Treaties commonly provide for consultation and negotiation between the parties to the dispute as a prerequisite to other dispute settlement mechanisms.[16] It is the first rung in the stepladder of dispute settlement processes listed in UN Charter Article 33. The question is, what happens if negotiation fails? The dilemma is how to achieve effective resolution of issues of interpretation and application that, if left to fester, would undermine the treaty regime, while not forcing unwilling parties into dispositive processes that will be either avoided or unenforceable, thus also undermining the treaty. The philosophical (or perhaps disciplinary) divide is between those who press for a process of formal adjudication and those who believe that disputes will be settled better through a more flexible, nonbinding, mediative process.

Dispute Settlement by Formal Adjudication

A major objective of the international legal community during the past century has been to expand the range and quantity of international disputes submitted to formal adjudication, preferably in an international court, but if not, then by binding arbitration. The objective has been realized in a manner of speaking. The Permanent Court of International Justice (PCIJ), established in 1920, and its post–World War II successor, the International Court of Justice (ICJ) are visibly courts, recognizable as such by participants in any of the world's legal systems. Under the original impetus of Secretary of State Elihu Root, a leader of the American bar, a network of bilateral arbitration treaties links the advanced industrial states.[17] And increasingly, international agreements provide for reference to the ICJ or to arbitration (usually on a voluntary basis) to settle disputes over the interpretation of their terms. But the triumph of the legalists, if such it is, has been a hollow one. The settlement institutions are for the most part inert, and the treaty provisions remain dead letters. The practical business of adjusting disputes in the process of managing treaty compliance is accomplished otherwise.

The ICJ and its predecessor have long been regarded by international lawyers as the juridical crown jewels of the international system. The court is designated by the UN Charter as the "principal judicial organ of the United Nations."[18] Yet the ICJ seems to be the only court in the world to have solved the problem of docket congestion. In its almost half century of existence, it has decided fewer than a hundred cases, many of which have been disposed of on jurisdictional grounds.

The jurisdiction of the court is consensual, not compulsory, and draws on two principal sources. Under Article 36(2) of the ICJ Statute, a state may accept the jurisdiction of the court generally. About fifty states have done so, most of them with more or less extensive reservations, excluding disputes involving national security or other categories of cases. Of the permanent members of the Security Council, only the United Kingdom accepts the general jurisdiction.[19]

The second and, for present purposes, more relevant basis of the court's jurisdiction is "all matters specially provided for . . . in treaties or conventions in force."[20] The *Yearbook* of the court lists more than two hundred fifty treaties between 1933 and 1992 containing such compromissory clauses.[21] In most of them, recourse to the court requires agreement of the parties. But some are compulsory: the provision for ICJ adjudication in the Vienna Convention on Diplomatic Privileges and Immunities[22] was the basis for the U.S.

suit against Iran for detaining hostages in 1980,[23] and the suit by Nicaragua against the United States was based in part on the jurisdictional clause in the bilateral Treaty of Friendship, Commerce, and Navigation (FCN) between the two countries.[24]

Overall, resort to provisions for judicial settlement of treaty disputes is almost vanishingly small. The ICJ and its predecessor, the PCIJ, have decided, on average, about one treaty dispute a year in their entire seventy-five-year joint history, almost half of them by advisory opinions. There were a number of early decisions under the Treaty of Versailles, mostly dealing with technical questions arising out of the ILO Constitution,[25] and some under the postwar treaties providing for the rights of minorities.[26] Otherwise, except for the UN Charter, no agreement has been the subject of ICJ adjudication more than twice.

Many of the specialized UN agencies provide for reference to the ICJ or an arbitral tribunal for settlement of disputes involving questions of interpretation of the basic treaty, either in the first instance or after failure to reach a settlement through the organs of the agency itself. A 1972 study found, however, not only that recourse to the ICJ under these provisions was insignificant but also that alternative adjudicative procedures were equally unused.

ILO:

> Infrequent use has been made of the formal machinery for settling disputes. Six cases were brought before the Permanent Court; no cases before the International Court. The tribunal provided for in Article 37(2) has not been established . . .
>
> [T]he formal machinery contained in Articles 26–34 of the Constitution has been invoked on only three occasions.[27]

UNESCO:

> The formal machinery prescribed for settlement of disputes (the International Court or an arbitral tribunal) is rarely invoked. Instead, the Legal Committee of the General Conference has been empowered to express an opinion on a disputed or obscure point.[28]

ICAO:

> So far, no appeal has been made from a decision of the Council to an ad hoc tribunal, the International Court or the arbitration procedure formulated in Article 85 . . .
>
> So far there has been no occasion for a decision of the Council under

Article 84 of the Convention, as no case of dispute has been presented to the Council under that provision, . . . One may note that up till now no dispute under an air transport agreement has been referred to the Council of ICAO.[29]

FAO:

Recourse has never been had to the International Court or an arbitral tribunal.

Disputes and questions of interpretation involving the Constitution or Conventions adopted under Article XIV of the Constitution are usually referred to the Committee on the Constitution and Legal Matters.[30]

IMCO:

Under this Article [providing for the settlement of "legal questions" by reference to the ICJ], IMCO has already requested an opinion from the International Court. Other questions involving a dispute have been dealt with by the Assembly or by the Council.[31]

WMO:

In practice, disputes and questions of interpretation are usually determined by the Congress instead of being referred to arbitration.[32]

WHO:

In practice not many disputes have arisen and none of them have been referred to the International Court.[33]

The constitution of the Universal Postal Union provides that disputes between members "shall be settled by arbitration"[34] by the traditional tripartite panel of two party-selected arbitrators, with a third chosen by the first two or by the International Bureau (the UPU secretariat) if the two cannot agree. The UPU departs from most of the other specialized agencies in omitting any provision for reference to the ICJ. Its experience, however, parallels that of the other agencies. Since 1874, when the union was founded, fewer than thirty cases have been arbitrated.[35]

We have not made a systematic study, agency by agency, of the period since 1972, but a quick survey of agency records and the ICJ's docket confirms that there has been no significant change.[36]

While most of the cases that go to the ICJ are almost by definition polit-ically salient, a few have dealt directly or peripherally with sensitive security issues. Some of these were outside the ambit of a treaty regime, such as the *Corfu Channel* case and the suit of Australia and New Zealand to end French nuclear testing in the Pacific.[37] More recently, a number of highly political cases involving treaty interpretation have been decided by the court, among them the *Iran Hostages* case and *Nicaragua v. United States.*[38] Still pending as of mid-1994 are the shooting down of the Iran Airbus, Libya's suit against Great Britain and the United States growing out of the Lockerbie bombing, and *Bosnia and Herzegovina v. Former Republic of Yugoslavia,* under the Genocide Convention.[39]

Whatever one thinks of the law the court made in these sensitive cases, the outcomes were not very satisfactory for any of the parties. In many of them, the respondent state did not participate fully, and in most it formally ignored the judgment of the court. As a result of the *Nicaragua* case, the United States withdrew its acceptance of the compulsory jurisdiction of the court.

United Nations secretary general Boutros Boutros-Ghali, in his *Agenda for Peace,* urged greater use of the ICJ in settling disputes among nations under the UN Charter: "It remains an under-used resource for the peaceful adju-dication of disputes." He proposed greater use of advisory opinions and asked members to withdraw reservations and accept the general jurisdiction of the court. He characterized such a development as an "important contri-bution to United Nations peacemaking."[40] Whether this will have any more impact than the countless similar exhortations that have preceded it may well be doubted. A century of experience with international adjudication leads to considerable skepticism about its suitability as an international dispute set-tlement method and, in particular, as a way of securing compliance with treaties.

Like other forms of litigation, it is slow, costly, cumbersome, and inflex-ible. It is risky and unpredictable. The great American judge Learned Hand said that he would dread a lawsuit beyond almost anything "short of sickness and death."[41] Adjudicative procedures intensify the confrontational and adversarial aspects of a dispute, which are likely to be even more dysfunc-tional in international than in domestic disputes. These disadvantages have led to increasing resort to alternative forms of dispute resolution even in a bastion of legalism like the United States and, more recently, in Europe.

However it may arise, a dispute between nations turns out in the end to be about the exercise of sovereign power, always a delicate matter and hard to resolve within the winner-take-all framework of adjudication.[42] International controversies present an additional problem in that, whoever "wins," the relationship between the parties must continue. Therefore the outcome must be in some sense satisfactory to both sides. On the whole, the record of compliance with ICJ decisions has been good. In a number of important cases, however, of which the *Nicaragua* case is the most spectacular, the respondent refused to heed the court's judgment. This adds to the ordinary risks of litigation.

Adjudication seems even less appropriate for interpretation and application of a multilateral treaty. There the controversy is more likely to be about the requirements and functioning of the regime, rather than whether one party has wronged the other and is obligated to make reparations. Students of complex domestic litigation in the United States have recognized for twenty years that if the tribunal is called on to deal with many parties and a complex interacting set of issues, the bilateral, adversarial model is not useful, and in fact is not applied. The issues cannot be disposed of once and for all in a sweeping court judgment but must be managed over time, in a more flexible and mediative process.[43] Some have argued that these characteristics disqualify "polycentric" controversies for adjudication, even in domestic legal systems.[44] The objections are even more telling in the international sphere.

Perhaps for these reasons, the United States, despite its well-advertised legalistic culture and frequent rhetorical invocation of the virtues of international judicial settlement, has been at best ambivalent about relinquishing sovereignty to a non-American adjudicative forum. Keith Highet states:

> The idea of submitting American sovereignty and independence to [the International Court of Justice] has never been fully accepted. To this extent, the "commitment" of the United States to the International Court of Justice has been both qualified *and* illusory. The deep-seated nature of the "inherent ambivalence" has now come out in the open again, as a result of the first, and the only, significant reversal suffered by the United States the *Nicaragua* case] . . . a reverse that did not take place until almost forty years—two full generations—after the United States adhered to the Statute of the Court.[45]

The skepticism is not confined to the United States. The sparse use of treaty provisions for settlement by an arbitral or judicial body suggests that concerns about sovereignty, particularly if the issues in question are politically sensitive, are widely shared. The ICJ surely has a significant role in the international legal system, most importantly in pronouncing and elaborating general principles of international law.[46] But neither the court nor other instruments of binding adjudicative settlement have shown themselves adaptable as instruments for the settlement of the stream of routine disputes that necessarily arise under a regulatory treaty regime.

Informal Dispute Settlement

Juxtaposed to adjudication are a variety of negotiating and mediative processes. An important function of international regimes is the promotion and assistance of these processes, and the performance of this function is a major instrument for managing the regime so as to induce acceptable levels of compliance.

Security and Arms Control Agreements. Even in the sensitive area of security, states have increasingly recognized the value of institutionalized negotiations and, in the multilateral case, a significant if not fully admitted role for mediation by the organization and its subsidiary bodies. In the cold war setting, neither the Soviet Union nor the United States was prepared to relinquish any influence over dispute settlement to a third party, but, as noted in Chapter 8, they created the Standing Consultative Commission under the SALT I agreements, to serve as the official forum for resolving disputes and making adjustments under those agreements. During the détente of the mid-1970s, the SCC succeeded in clarifying some ambiguities and disputed situations. In 1973, for example, the United States observed activity on existing Soviet intercontinental ballistic missile (ICBM) sites that it thought might indicate the construction of new launchers in violation of SALT I. The Soviets explained that the installations were hardened launch-control facilities and provided supporting information and data. Satellite surveillance by the United States confirmed the Soviet explanation.[47] In the early Reagan years, the SCC became a rhetorical battleground that not only reflected an increasingly hostile relationship generally but to some extent also contributed to an atmosphere of heightened confrontation. Even then, however, the parties were able to negotiate in the SCC forum a series of understandings on the meaning of "testing in an ABM mode," which had been unresolved in the original treaty negotiations.[48]

The Reagan administration's hostility to the SCC was so great that the 1987 INF Treaty created a parallel but totally distinct body, the Special Verification Commission (SVC), to perform the same functions.[49] Experience in this new forum was good from the outset, no doubt because the political climate changed after the Soviet Union broke up, and Russia sought to establish a cooperative relationship with the United States. In fact, as described in Chapter 8, most compliance problems involving interpretation of the INF Treaty are worked out in the field between the leaders of the inspection teams, with the SVC acting as a kind of appellate body when they cannot reach agreement.

Multilateral security arrangements are also respectful of sovereign sensitivities. The Chemical Weapons Convention remits disputes about the interpretation and application of the agreement to consultation between the parties or "other peaceful means of the parties' choice, including recourse to appropriate organs of this Convention and, by mutual consent, referral to the International Court of Justice."[50] However, the convention does not leave disputes in the hands of parties completely. Article XIV empowers the forty-one-member Executive Council to "contribute to the settlement of a dispute by whatever means it deems appropriate." It also provides that the Conference of the Parties shall consider disputes, either by itself or through appropriate subsidiary organs. Both the Conference and the Executive Council are authorized to request advisory opinions from the ICJ, subject to approval of the UN General Assembly, a procedure that is unlikely to be invoked.

Of a good deal more importance, the Executive Council is also given responsibility for managing the related process of clarifying "any matter which may cause doubt about compliance with this Convention, or which gives rise to concerns about a related matter which may be considered ambiguous."[51] Article IX provides an elaborate scheme of information exchange and fact-finding that culminates in the right of a party to request a challenge inspection, with procedures for its execution described in detail.[52] This pair of closely connected responsibilities gives the council a mandate for managing compliance disputes, at least on paper. The apparatus is in place for the full panoply of mediative efforts, with the challenge inspection to back them up.[53] The ultimate recourse "in cases where serious damage to the object and purposes of this Convention may result" is for the conference to recommend collective measures to states parties "in conformity with international law" or, "in cases of particular gravity," to refer the matter to the Security Council.[54]

Other Multilateral Treaty Organizations. In multilateral regimes outside the security context, similar institutionalized processes provide scope for the secretariat or uninvolved parties to play a mediative role. The experience of International Civil Aviation Organization is typical. The Chicago Convention commits the decision of disagreements about its interpretation or application to the council of the organization.[55] Many bilateral air traffic agreements also provide for dispute settlement by the ICAO council. Since the thirty-three-member council is an awkward body for carrying out judicial functions, the predominant mode of settlement is by informal conciliation. Thomas Buergenthal, a leading expert on ICAO, concludes that "in dealing with disputes arising under the Chicago Acts, the ICAO Council has been guided by a policy that favors settlement by political and diplomatic rather than judicial means."[56] Occasionally, a difference of view about the interpretation of a provision of the convention will be referred to the Legal Committee, a standing committee of the organization.[57]

The same mediative approach is used for complaints under air transport agreements. "The primary role which the Council thus performs ... is to provide a forum where difficulties between Contracting States can be ironed out," usually "by getting the parties to reestablish the status quo ante."[58] Buergenthal thinks that "the very existence of this adjudication procedure has been a contributing factor in encouraging the Contracting States to resolve their differences without resorting to it." But he laments the almost universal resort to conciliation in this context, because, unlike adjudication, it does not generate "a body of case law upon which states could draw in drafting or adopting [air transport agreement] clauses."[59]

Continuous opportunities for conciliation and mediation also arise in connection with the interpretative activities discussed in the following section.

Authoritative Interpretation of Treaty Provisions

In regimes managed by international organizations, the preferred alternative to adjudication for the resolution of disputes involving legal issues is authoritative or semi-authoritative interpretation by a designated body of the organization, often the secretariat or a legal committee. Not only is this a far less contentious method for dealing with disputes about the meaning of treaty provisions, but it also may help to prevent disputes, and in some situations stem potentially noncompliant behavior before a party has committed itself to engage in activity that might clash with the goals of the regime. A state is not likely to ignore the answer to a question it has itself submitted. And the nonadversarial context is conducive to working out the difference or misunderstanding that led to the request, either by the parties themselves or with the help of the interpretative body. In addition, the interpretative process provides the continuous clarification and elaboration of the governing legal rules that courts or administrative agencies perform in domestic legal systems. At the extreme, "interpretation" can be a way of adapting the norms to radically changed circumstances.

Our scan of the treaties in the appendix shows that more than half have some sort of provision for nonjudicial treaty interpretation. Often the power is implied even when not specifically granted. From an unsystematic examination of the practices of some of the governing organizations, it appears that, unlike adjudication, the interpretation process, is widely used. A more complete and less anecdotal sample would be worth developing, but the experience of a variety of regulatory regimes, summarized here, indicates that the power to interpret is an important management tool in treaty implementation and may help avoid some of the contentiousness of a more adversary dispute resolution mechanism.

The International Monetary Fund. Perhaps the most far-reaching use of the interpretative power is found in the IMF. Article XVIII of the original Articles of Agreement (entitled "Interpretation") provides that "any question of interpretation of the provisions of this Agreement arising between any member and the Fund or between any members of the Fund shall be submitted to the Executive Directors for their decision."[60]

An early exercise of this power was to resolve a fundamental issue left open in the Bretton Woods negotiations. The British, led by Lord Keynes, maintained that members should be entitled to draw up to the maximum of their fund quotas unconditionally. The United States, which would be supplying most of the money, argued that the fund should be able to impose conditions to ensure that the advances were not dissipated by unsustainable monetary and fiscal policies of the drawer. The difference was deliberately papered over: Article V provided that "a member shall be *entitled*" to use the Fund's resources if it "*represents* that [they are] presently needed for making . . . payments which are consistent with the provisions of this Agreement," but only up to 25 percent of its quota in any one year. The fund was empowered to waive this limitation "on terms that safeguard its interests."[61] When the IMF came into operation, the executive directors resolved this Anglo-American dispute with a categorical interpretation, reflecting, not surprisingly, the dominance of the United States both in postwar international economics and in the fund's weighted voting scheme: the purpose for which IMF resources could be used was "to give temporary assistance in financing balance of payments deficits on current account."[62] "The word 'represents' . . . means 'declares'. . . . But the Fund may, for good reasons, challenge this declaration, on the grounds that . . . the payments will not be consistent with the provisions of this agreement."[63] When, after the end of the Marshall Plan, the fund began actual lending operations, the directors, by another "interpretation," gave further precision to the concept of "temporary assistance": "The period should fall within an outside range of three to five years." The fund's "attitude" toward a member's request for a drawing would "turn on whether . . . the policies the member will pursue will be adequate to overcome the problem within such a period."[64]

By this series of generalized interpretations, the fund converted the broad statements of purpose concerning international monetary cooperation, exchange stability, a multilateral system of payments, and orderly adjustment of balance-of-payments disequilibrium into a set of precise rules for the use of its funds, well understood by the members and the staff: you must repay within five years, and before you can borrow you must satisfy us that your overall economic policies are such as to assure that you will be able to do so![65] The invention of standby arrangements, also a creature of executive directors' interpretative decision, provided occasions at annual intervals for checking whether the policies were indeed accomplishing the intended result.[66] These interpretations provided the foundation for the whole subsequent structure of "conditionality" in the use of IMF resources. They were incorporated in the IMF Agreement when it was amended in 1978.[67]

Similarly, when the fixed exchange-rate system established at Bretton Woods collapsed in 1972, the shift to a floating exchange-rate system was accomplished by a series of interpretative decisions. In 1978 these were embodied in Article IV of the amended IMF Articles of Agreement, requiring that the fund should exercise "firm surveillance" of the monetary policies of members, to ensure that they were consistent with the principles of monetary conduct set forth in the agreement. Again, the executive directors translated these general injunctions into a code of norms of monetary conduct, to be continuously applied in the fund's review and assessment of members' performance.[68]

Thus, in the two primary areas of the fund's responsibility—the use of its resources and monetary policy—the operative norms were not to be found initially in the Articles of Agreement, but in interpretations delivered by the executive directors under the authority of Article XVIII.

The International Coffee Organization. The International Coffee Agreement also expressly grants authority to interpret its terms to the governing body. Article 61 (entitled "Disputes and Complaints") provides that "any dispute concerning the interpretation or application of the Agreement which is not settled by negotiation, shall, at the request of any Member party to the dispute, be referred to the [International Coffee] Council for decision."[69] A majority of members, or members holding not less than one-third of the total votes, may require the council to seek the opinion of an "advisory panel" on the issues in dispute. "The opinion of the advisory panel and the reasons therefor shall be submitted to the Council which, after considering all the relevant information, shall decide the dispute."[70]

In 1965 the council exercised this power to achieve a fundamental change in the structure of the agreement. Newly independent African entrants in the coffee market were expanding their trade rapidly and sought an increase in their quotas to give them a higher share of the global quota relative to the established and dominant South American producers. The Coffee Agreement permitted adjustments of the global quota to meet the ups and downs of supply and demand, but only by "altering the basic export quota of each Member by the same percentage."[71] The dispute between Brazil, the Latin American protagonist, and the African producers paralyzed the 1965 meeting of the council. To escape the impasse, the council convened an advisory panel under Article 61 to consider whether a "selective quota system" would be consistent with the agreement. The panel submitted a unanimous report to a waiting council, opining that a selective quota system, as envisioned by the African exporters, could not legally be adopted by a resolution of the council but would require amendment of the agreement.[72]

Less than two weeks after the panel rendered its decision, the council adopted Resolution 92, which authorized the granting of special "waivers" of quota limits for types of coffees grown principally in Africa.[73] The effect of the decision was to establish a selective quota system, albeit one of limited duration and application. At its 1966 meeting, the council adopted Resolution 115, a "System for Selective Adjustment of Supply of Coffee."[74] Although swathed in an elaborate new taxonomy, the arrangement constituted, in effect, a selective quota system adopted despite the panel's remonstrance. There were only a few dissents, and in fact the decision satisfactorily resolved the underlying dispute.

The parties were able to alter the fundamental obligations of the treaty through a process of interpretation, in the face of a contrary opinion issued by a panel of legal experts. The denouement provides a striking contrast between the adjudicative and the interpretative methodologies. The panel was perhaps legally correct, whatever that means, but its decision threatened the continued viability of the organization. Indeed, there is some reason to believe that the Brazilians had understood this, and that they agreed to the panel procedure because they expected the panel to come out the other way, thus allowing them to accept a selective quota system despite strong pressure from domestic constituencies. The council, by avoiding the words "selective quota" and inventing a variety of special allotments with other labels, was able to satisfy all the parties to the dispute, not least Brazil, which, as the largest producer, had the most to lose if the agreement collapsed.

Arms Control and Security. Although the Standing Consultative Commission established by SALT I was primarily a negotiating body, it performed interpretative functions as well.[75] Since the agreements were between superpowers, any interpretation had to be negotiated and agreed between them, which seemed like a recipe for impasse. Nevertheless, the SCC was able to issue some authoritative interpretations, occasionally even when the relationship was dominated by confrontational tactics. An early example was the elaboration of procedures for dismantlement and destruction of weapons prohibited under the agreement.

As mentioned earlier, the most important instance was the interpretation of the meaning of "testing in an ABM mode," prohibited by Article VI. The United States was concerned during the treaty negotiations that the Soviet Union might try to upgrade defensive surface-to-air missile (SAM) systems to give them anti ballistic missile capability. If they were able to do so, the large numbers and wide distribution of these air defense installations would provide the very nationwide ABM system that the treaty prohibited. Any such upgrade would require testing against ICBMs in flight. Soviet colocation of SAMS at ICBM test sites, and their practice of testing the SAM radars concurrently with ICBM reentry, fueled American suspicion. The United States sought to achieve a precise stipulation prohibiting this practice in the treaty negotiations, but the Soviets refused. The United States then spelled out its position in a Unilateral Statement appended to the treaty that detailed the joint operations of the SAM systems and ICBMs that it would regard as prohibited testing.[76] Thereafter, when it observed the Soviet Union continuing the practice, it brought the issue up in the SCC as a violation of the treaty. In 1978, after lengthy negotiations, the SCC worked out an agreed interpretation of prohibited practices under Article VI that, in effect, gave the United States the interpretation it had been unable to negotiate in the treaty, although the text remains classified. However, that did not solve all the problems of concurrent testing of ICBMs with air defense components, since the United States continued to observe concurrent operations of missile testing with SAM radar tracking. In 1985, when superpower relations were at their testiest, the SCC negotiated a second interpretation, also classified, that further refined the interpretation and moved the problem closer to resolution.[77]

The INF goes further than SALT I and expressly authorizes the svc to "agree upon such measures as may be necessary to improve the viability and effectiveness of this Treaty."[78] This has been characterized as a "non-amendment procedure."[79] The authorization is repeated in the Inspections Protocol and the Elimination Protocol, with the stipulation that "such measures shall not be deemed amendments to the Treaty."[80]

As of 1992, six different nonamendment interpretations had been negotiated and implemented pursuant to the INF. The first three were relatively minor, establishing operating procedures for the svc, and creating verification regimes for the missile facilities at Votkinsk and Magna, Utah.[81] The most significant was the Memorandum of Agreement (MOA),[82] signed on December 21, 1989, which not only provided detailed procedures to fill in gaps in the INF Treaty documents, but also departed in some respects from the original text of the inspections and elimination protocols. For example, the MOA substituted new types of inspection aircraft for those specified in the treaty. In adopting these modifications, the MOA specifically cited the "viability and effectiveness" language of the protocols. In April 1991, the parties amended the MOA to incorporate two further modifications of the INF implementation procedures.[83]

This approach has since become widespread. The START agreement provides that

> The Parties may agree upon such additional measures as may be necessary to improve the viability and effectiveness of the Treaty. The Parties agree that, if becomes necessary to make changes in this Protocol that do not affect substantive rights or obligations under the Treaty, they shall use the Joint Compliance and Inspection Commission to reach agreement on such changes, without resorting to the procedure for making amendments set forth in Article XVIII of the Treaty.[84]

Similar language was introduced by protocol into the two testing treaties, the Treaty on Underground Nuclear Explosions for Peaceful Purposes (PNE Treaty) and the Threshold Test Ban Treaty,[85] and appears in the multilateral Treaty on Conventional Armed Forces in Europe, but there has been no practical experience with any of these procedures.[86]

The GATT. The question of the interpretative powers of the GATT Council did not arise until recently, when the issue of adjustments in GATT rules to meet competing environmental requirements emerged. John Jackson argued that under Article XXV of the original GATT agreement, which authorizes the contracting parties to "meet from time to time for the purpose of giving effect to those provisions of this agreement which involve joint action and, generally, with a view to facilitating the operation and furthering the objectives of this agreement," the council had the power to interpret definitively the provisions of the agreement.[87] The new World Trade Organization agreement resolves the issue by granting to the Ministerial Conference and the council, acting by a three-fourths majority, the "exclusive authority to adopt interpretations of this agreement."[88]

A more muted form of interpretation was performed by the GATT council through the adoption of dispute settlement panel reports. Although panel reports adopted by the council were legally binding only on the parties to particular disputes, they carried considerable precedential weight in subsequent panel proceedings, and, more generally, as source materials for interpretation of the agreement. It is hard to distinguish this from other forms of interpretation.[89] It seems likely that under the binding dispute settlement provisions of the WTO, discussed later in this chapter, panel decisions and especially decisions of the Standing Appellate Body will come to resemble common law development even more closely.

Other Specialized Agencies. The use of interpretative mechanisms in the familiar UN specialized agencies is pervasive. The ILO Governing Body has assumed the responsibility for interpretation, often in response to a conference resolution or request.[90] With the multiplication of labor conventions, the International Labor Office has offered hundreds of opinions to member states on the interpretation of labor conventions. "It is now well established that informally the International Labour Office will advise a State on a question involving interpretations [of international labor conventions] So far [1972], the Labour Office has given over 150 such opinions."[91] The ILO states that such opinions have no official standing, but they are seldom if ever challenged in practice. MacMahon and Akehurst conclude that "potential disputes are anticipated and doubts resolved before they crystallize in the form of a dispute by the Governing Body of the International Labour Office."[92]

In the UPU, where, as noted, compulsory arbitration has been very infrequent, the constitution also provides that the International Bureau can give opinions on matters in dispute (or other matters) at the request of the parties.[93] In the period from 1965 to 1990, when only two disputes were submitted for arbitration, there were nine requests for an opinion of the bureau "in disputed matters" and forty-four "inquiries" that were also handled by bureau opinion before they were formally in dispute.[94]

The study of the specialized agencies discussed earlier in this chapter is to the same effect. The Legal Committee of the UNESCO General Conference gives opinions on disputed matters of interpretation.[95] Disputes and questions of interpretation involving the constitution or conventions of the FAO are usually referred to the Committee on Constitution and Legal Matters,[96] and in WHO to the Committee on Administration, Finance, and Legal Matters (Committee B).[97] In the WMO, they are usually handled by the World Meteorological Congress.[98]

The Human Rights Committee established under the International Covenant on Civil and Political Rights, composed of nongovernmental experts, is authorized by Article 40(4) of the covenant to "transmit its reports, and such general comments as it may consider appropriate to the States Parties." On this slender textual basis, the committee has begun to develop a practice of issuing authoritative interpretations of the covenant, at first elaborating the procedures and content of the required reports from parties, but more recently addressing the substantive content of the obligations.[99]

And, as noted in Chapter 8, the confirmation of the IAEA's authority to conduct "special inspections" came in the form of an interpretation of the relevant provision of INFCIRC 153, the regulation governing safeguards for NPT countries, announced by the chairman in summarizing a general debate on the issue by the Board of Governors.[100]

Unlike the often found but little used reference of disputes to the ICJ, interpretative mechanisms, whether they consist of the parties themselves or a subcommittee or a standing committee of legal experts, appear to function as intended. The decisions carry weight and at least help to eliminate specious interpretations. They are a part of the continuing management of treaty compliance, adjusting both individual differences and the details of the norm structure to meet the shifting needs of the regime.

A Return to Adjudication?

Despite the long record of reluctance to submit to adjudication and the almost universal practice of resort to more informal mechanisms, there are signs of a resurgence of interest in dispute resolution that culminates in binding, judicial-type decisions. This may simply be a case of international lawyers doing what comes naturally, but in a world increasingly dependent on the reliable performance of international regimes, states and their citizens may also be less willing to rest content with either negotiation or the hope that some ad hoc arrangement to umpire a dispute will be set up in the event of an impasse. In any case, within the past decade a number of important new regulatory treaties or adaptations of old ones have emerged with either full-blown adjudicative mechanisms or some other form of fairly powerful compulsory third-party intervention.

The Law of the Sea Convention. An early instance of this turn is the disputes chapter of the Law of the Sea Convention (UNCLOS III), which was negotiated from 1974 to 1981 and went into force in November 1994. The UNCLOS III treaty is complex, involving politically charged issues as well as a myriad of technical and commercial relationships. In particular, a number of provisions extend the jurisdiction of coastal states into their adjoining waters. The treaty establishes a 200-mile exclusive economic zone (EEZ) seaward from territorial waters, and special regimes for straits and archipelagic waters. The convention grants a complicated mix of powers to coastal states in these areas, covering, broadly speaking, regulation of environmental matters, scientific research, and, in straits and archipelagos, some aspects of navigation. The powers are subject to the condition that they be exercised "reasonably" or "consistent with generally accepted international practices," phrases that leave considerable room for regulations trenching on traditional navigational rights. As Louis Sohn, the architect of the UNCLOS dispute resolution chapter, says, "It is one of the prerogatives of sovereign equality that in the absence of an agreement on impartial third-party adjudication, the view of one state with respect to the interpretation of the Convention cannot prevail over the views of other member states. Each party can claim forever that its view alone is correct, but another party can make the same claim, resulting in an impasse."[101]

The maritime powers, led by the United States, were unwilling to entrust their navigational rights to the unilateral decisions of coastal states, and made acceptance of the treaty contingent on binding resolution of disputes regarding the exercise of these new jurisdictional powers. The UNCLOS III dispute resolution procedures were developed by a separate negotiating committee (Negotiating Group 7). Professor Sohn describes the procedure as "at the same time simple and complex." "Its simplicity," he writes, "is due to the fact that the Convention accepts as its guiding principle that in general the will of the parties to a dispute shall prevail and that the parties may by agreement select any dispute settlement they wish. The more complex provisions apply only if the parties do not agree upon a dispute settlement method."[102] On the side of flexibility, the parties, if they can agree, can choose the forum and procedure they believe most likely to settle the dispute, selecting from a varied menu of dispute resolution methods, binding and nonbinding, meditative and adjudicatory. But, with some notable exceptions, the drafters insisted on binding determination of disputes if other means of settlement fail. Even at this stage, the parties have a range of choice. They may opt for the ICJ, a regional body, or a new permanent Tribunal for the Law of the Sea to be located in Hamburg. But if they cannot agree on one of these, the issue goes to binding arbitration according to procedures spelled out in the convention.[103]

Only a few categories of disputes were exempt from this array of procedures. Some issues involving marine research within the EEZ were either exempt or subject only to compulsory, nonbinding conciliation.[104] Parties can opt out for certain categories of sea boundary disputes, and military activities are totally exempt, as are issues being dealt with by the UN Security Council.[105] On seabed mining, the issue that caused President Reagan to reject the convention, a patchwork of procedures was developed, including a special Seabed Chamber of the Law of the Sea Tribunal.[106]

Whether the formal provisions will be widely used or informal processes of settlement will generally prevail as under other treaties is a matter of conjecture. It is perhaps significant that, during the decade before the treaty came into force, the United States accepted the new regulatory authority of the coastal state as a matter of customary international law, without benefit of the dispute resolution provisions.[107]

The General Agreement on Tariffs and Trade and the New WTO. Of all the international regimes, the GATT has the most developed and most active system of formal dispute settlement. In the period from 1948 through 1989, 207 complaints were processed through this system.[108] The dispute resolution process has gone through periods of disuse and discredit as it slowly adapted. Robert Hudec identifies four periods corresponding roughly to the four decades of GATT's existence. In the 1950s, the details of the procedures were worked out, but, because the participants were primarily members of the "GATT club" of diplomats and trade officials who had negotiated the original agreement, "legal rulings were drafted with an elusive diplomatic vagueness" often expressing "an intuitive sort of law, based on shared experiences and unspoken assumptions."[109] During this period, 53 legal complaints were filed. In the 1960s, with the advent of the European Economic Community and the accession of more than forty new developing country members, there was a significant falling off in formal dispute settlement activity. Only 7 complaints were filed, 6 of them before 1963. Hudec characterizes it as "a period when GATT more or less suspended its legal system while it tried to sort out, by negotiation, the legal and economic adjustments that were needed to accommodate its new members and its new agenda."[110]

The 1970s marked a return to formal dispute resolution, with 32 new cases filed. The Tokyo Round of negotiations, concluded in 1979, was supposed to develop a new and improved dispute resolution procedure, but it succeeded only in reducing the existing practice to writing, with minor clarifications. On the other hand, it produced nine substantive codes adhered to by subsets of the greater GATT membership and dealing with such subjects as trade in dairy products, civil aircraft, and bovine meat. Each of these established its own dispute settlement mechanism, tighter and more legalistic but subject now to jurisdictional challenge and a new set of delays. The 1980s was the climactic decade of GATT legal activity with 115 complaints filed, more than in the previous three decades together. But, as Hudec remarks, "the steadily increasing ambitions of the legal system eventually brought an increased number of failures in their wake."[111]

Articles XXII and XXIII of the GATT, which are carried over into the WTO, set out in general terms the procedures for dispute resolution. Article XXII is a requirement of consultation "with respect to any matter affecting the operation of this Agreement." Under Article XXIII, a member considering that its expected benefits under the agreement are being "nullified or impaired" must first consult with the other party "with a view to the satisfactory adjustment of the matter." If a settlement cannot be worked out, the Contracting Parties are to investigate the matter and make appropriate recommendations. If the circumstances are "serious enough," they may authorize the complainant to suspend concessions or other obligations to the other party. Very early, the practice grew up of submitting such complaints to an ad hoc panel of three or five experts from nations other than those of the disputants, acting in their individual capacities, to assist the Contracting Parties in the premises. The panel system was thus an internal GATT innovation. It was consistent with, though not specifically mandated by, the underlying agreement.

From the beginning, the panel process was judicial in tone. The disputants submitted their legal and factual case in writing and make oral presentations, much as they might before a court. Panels came to issue written reports explicating the legal issues and the reasons for their recommendations, which are increasingly relied on as precedent. But although the formal process has many of the marks of adjudication, in the first decades the panels also acted in a mediative capacity, trying to assist the parties to reach settlement.[112]

Unlike a judicial decision, the panel report was a recommendation to the

Contracting Parties and was not binding until adopted by the GATT council. Since the council operated by consensus, there was the possibility that a party adversely affected by the recommendation could block the adoption of a panel report. Although the average length of time from a complaint to the adoption of a report may not seem long by the standards of U.S. court litigation, there were inevitably cases, often the most explosive ones politically, that took much longer, and this became a focus of concern.

Except for a short period in the late 1960s, the United States argued for increased judicialization of the GATT process, while the Europeans have traditionally preferred a more negotiated and diplomatic approach. The United States spearheaded the Tokyo Round effort to tighten up dispute resolution procedures, but delay and strategic inaction remained a problem. By the mid-1980s, however, the Europeans, who had until then been primarily defendants, began assuming the role of complainants more frequently. They joined in a series of incremental moves to speed up the dispute resolution timetable and eliminate occasions for stonewalling.[113] But until the Uruguay Round, the bottom line remained that a dissatisfied litigant could block the adoption of a panel report, although the formidable pressures available were able to reduce this power in most cases from a veto to a delaying tactic.[114]

The Uruguay Round's Understanding on Rules and Procedures Governing the Settlement of Disputes fundamentally changed the previous dispensation. The panel's recommendations are not to be adopted automatically, unless there is a consensus on the council to the contrary, so that now a single dissenting vote can ensure rather than block adoption. Appeals on questions of law can be taken to a Standing Appellate Body of seven persons "with demonstrated expertise in law." In case of disagreement as to the value of compensatory concessions offered by the losing party, the issue goes to compulsory arbitration. The understanding establishes a strict timetable, and the process from the time of the request to action on the panel report is not to exceed nine months, or twelve months where an appeal is taken.[115] These procedures went into effect provisionally by the agreement of the parties in 1992 and are now embodied in the constitution of the new World Trade Organization.[116] The effect is that trade disputes under the WTO will be subject to binding adjudication in an institution that looks quite a bit like an international court.[117]

While all this was going on in GATT, the Canadian-American Free Trade Agreement adopted provisions for binding adjudication by binational panels to review national decisions on antidumping and countervailing duties.[118] The North American Free Trade Agreement followed suit, and added the possibility of binding determinations of disputes under the provisions of side agreements on environmental and labor regulation.[119] It remains to be seen whether all these new procedures will be flexible enough to deal with highly political trade disputes.

A Middle Ground: Mandatory Nonbinding Mediative Procedures

The Conference on Security and Co-operation in Europe. A persistent effort spearheaded by Western European jurists to install formal adjudicative mechanisms for settlement of disputes in the Conference on Security and Co-operation in Europe was ultimately unsuccessful, but the outcome was a new emphasis on compulsory third-party intervention that may be a portent of future developments.

The CSCE was constituted under the Helsinki Final Act, signed in 1975 in the context of the brief cold war détente. The act, which was not legally binding, enunciated broad principles of peaceful coexistence accompanied by a political commitment to deal with some of the most divisive and sensitive issues in Europe and the Soviet Union at the time—most notably human rights and the inviolability of borders.[120] Fifteen years later, after the face of Europe had changed, the November 1990 Charter of Paris for a New Europe called for "appropriate mechanisms for the peaceful resolution of any disputes that may arise," undertaking to "seek new forms of cooperation," and singling out the desirability of "mandatory third party involvement," though not necessarily in the form of adjudication.[121]

The European states mounted a continuing campaign to prescribe a formal set of mandatory procedures, culminating in binding adjudication, to resolve disputes among CSCE members. The Swiss, for example, proposed a highly formal draft convention[122] intended to ensure that every type of dispute would be submitted to a formal process, the details of which had been worked out with watchmakers precision, down to the term and age limits of tribunal members.[123]

The United States took a very different position from Switzerland. Influenced by the increasing use of flexible alternative dispute resolution processes to resolve domestic disputes, its objective was to create a dispute resolution mechanism that would offer a forum for dialogue among disputants who could not negotiate a resolution unaided, and would increase the likelihood that parties would come to the table.[124] While European jurists sought elegance in a structure that prescribed an increasing degree of intervention at each step, the Americans felt that by establishing a simple principle of mandatory third-party intervention, with no requirement that it be binding, a workable process could be developed by the parties ad hoc.

A month-long meeting of legal experts in early 1991 at Valletta in Malta, after heated and protracted debate, rejected the European approach entirely but did not embrace the U.S. alternative either. Instead, the final report adopted by the CSCE at the June 1991 meeting of the Council of Ministers in Berlin[125] provides that if the parties fail to agree on a settlement procedure, either party may request the establishment of a CSCE "Dispute Settlement Mechanism"[126] of one or more members selected from an established roster "to assist the parties in identifying suitable procedures for the settlement of the dispute." If that fails, any party "may request the Mechanism to provide general or specific comment on the substance of the dispute," which "the parties will consider in good faith and in a spirit of cooperation."[127] At its Stockholm meeting two years later, the CSCE rounded out this package with a Convention on Conciliation and Arbitration within the CSCE and a voluntary set of provisions for a CSCE Conciliation Commission. The convention is only operative as between countries that ratify it. Twenty-nine members signed at the Stockholm meeting, including France and Russia but not the United States or the United Kingdom. In any case, the arbitration procedure requires agreement between the parties to the dispute. The Conciliation Commission is mandatory if one party requests it, but it is nonbinding.[128] The most draconian element of the new package is the Provisions for Directed Conciliation, under which "the Council of Ministers or the Committee of Senior Officials may direct any two participating States to seek conciliation to assist them in resolving a dispute that they have not been able to settle within a reasonable period of time."[129]

Simultaneously with this almost frenzied legal activity, the most violent and brutal European disputes in recent memory were proceeding in the former Yugoslavia and some of the successor states to the Soviet Union. None of the elaborate settlement machinery developed under CSCE auspices has been invoked, as might be predicted in light of the experience described earlier in this chapter. Instead, the CSCE has sent ad hoc teams of intermediaries on missions to some of the most serious political trouble spots. And the creation of a High Commissioner on National Minorities in 1993 provided another flexible, informal channel for dealing with minority rights questions. Each of these devices has had some modest successes, although not in the former Yugoslavia, where a "mission of long duration" in Kosovo was expelled after almost a year. Formal legalism created the illusion that acceptable and effective dispute resolution mechanisms were in place to deal with politically charged situations, but when the time came for action, the need was for far more flexible and voluntary ways of dealing with compliance and interpretive issues.[130]

Contemporary Environmental Treaties. In environmental treaties of the past decade, the concern for reliable dispute settlement has led to compulsory reference to nonbinding third-party mediation or conciliation, as the United States recommended for the CSCE. The Vienna Convention for the Protection of the Ozone Layer provides for mandatory submission to a conciliation commission that must, in the absence of agreement, "render a final and recommendatory award, which the parties shall consider in good faith."[131] The 1991 Amendments to the Montreal Protocol add a more developed "non-compliance procedure." Under this procedure, "Reservations" regarding a party's performance of its obligations are brought before a five-member Implementation Committee that hears the case "with a view to securing an amicable resolution." The committee reports to a meeting of the parties, which may, "taking into consideration the circumstances of the case, decide upon and call for steps to bring about full compliance with the Protocol."[132]

The Framework Convention on Climate Change has a Subsidiary Body on Implementation and authorizes the establishment of a "multilateral consultative process . . . for the resolution of questions regarding the implementation of the Convention."[133] But it also directly embraces compulsory conciliation for dispute settlement. After setting out the usual range of settlement options available on a voluntary basis, Article 14 provides that "if after twelve months following the notification by one Party to another that a dispute exists between them, the Parties concerned have not been able to settle their dispute . . . the dispute shall be submitted, at the request of any of the parties to the dispute, to conciliation."[134] Article 14 also sets out the basic procedures for activating the process. The Biodiversity Convention, also adopted at Rio, has a substantially identical dispute resolution provision.[135]

The critical element in all these procedures is that, in the absence of an agreed settlement, the conciliation committee is authorized to make a recommendatory award. That award will represent a considered, neutral, and informed judgment of what, all things considered, would be an appropriate settlement of the dispute. Although in no sense binding, and perhaps even less "legal" than the old GATT panel reports, such a recommendatory award will radically change the bargaining positions and exert heavy pressure on the parties to comply. There is as yet no experience with any of these new conciliation institutions, and it may well be that they are destined for the obscurity that has dogged other treaty-based dispute mechanisms. Nevertheless, as Sohn points out, states may need to know that at the end of the day a genuine dispute over the meaning or application of treaty provisions can be laid to rest. Given sensitivities about submission to adjudication, compulsory conciliation may be a more workable path.

The most interesting thing about this survey is the effectiveness of the ubiquitous procedures—most of which have grown up informally—for treaty interpretation by the parties or some specialized organ, without all the trappings of a formalized adversary proceeding. It is probably better to agree on a dispute mechanism ex ante, even though informal processes are likely to spring up. But it is a lot easier to manage the regime if the mechanisms provided are usable, emphasizing flexibility rather than formal legalization.

American domestic experience with mediation and dispute settlement through the 1990s can bring a richness and variety to international forums. The mediator, whether formal or informal, is capable of developing options, clarifying underlying interests and values, examining the alternatives to settlement, cutting through the posturing that may defeat resolution, and helping the parties reach creative solutions that offer joint gains. The record of ad hoc mediations of international conflict is sufficiently impressive to encourage supporters of a flexible, nonbinding process, especially where national stakes are very high, as opposed to formal adjudication, which has not been able to provide solutions for issues affecting national security and sovereignty.

We do not conclude that adjudicative methods of dispute settlement are useless. In regimes like UNCLOS and the GATT, where there is a strong normative consensus and which generate a stream of sharply bilateral disputes with high legal content, well-defined remedies, and limited stakes, binding judicial settlement may meet the needs of and be acceptable to the parties. Experience shows, however, that in most cases the struggle on the part of treaty negotiators to impose binding procedures is not worth the candle, since they are unlikely to be used anyway.

At the same time, for the critically important treaties regulating environmental and economic relations that are not limited, technical, and straightforwardly "legal," a mediative process that is wholly malleable may be too slow, uncertain, and inefficient to deal with a predictable stream of disputes. Mediation also encompasses more formal and evaluative procedures that create pressures for settlement, even though the process remains consensual.

When a neutral expresses an opinion on the merits of the dispute, generally after presentations by the disputants,the process becomes adjudicatory in tone, if not in fact. Such quasi-adjudication may be particularly useful for agreements that coordinate activity essential to modern life, where the incentive to defect is blunted and the impetus to cooperate is strong.

Treaty Adaptation

If a treaty regime is to endure and continue to serve its basic purpose over time, it must be adaptable to inevitable changes in technology, shifts in substantive problems, and economic, social and political developments.[136] Much of this adaptation can be accomplished in the course of the elaboration or interpretation of treaty norms But sometimes the necessary changes are more drastic or more detailed than can be accomplished within the accepted leeways of the interpretative process. A management strategy must be designed to foresee and accomplish these necessary changes.

The traditional way to change treaty obligations is by amendment or by the addition of a protocol. Almost all treaties contain provisions for amendment and in any case could be changed by agreement of the parties.[137] The amendment process is generally cumbersome, however. And, of course, any amendment must be ratified in accordance with the formalities provided by domestic law. In the United States, this means the political pitfalls of submission to the Senate for advice and consent, and similar, if not quite so formidable, political obstacles exist in other parliamentary governments. The ABM Treaty originally provided that each party could deploy a limited number of missiles at two sites, but the number was reduced to one by a protocol signed at the Moscow summit in 1974. The protocol, a comparatively simple exercise, did not come into force until almost two years later. Moreover, parties that do not ratify the amendment are not bound by it, so there is a possibility that parties to a multilateral treaty would be subject to differing sets of obligations.

Despite these problems, a number of regulatory treaties rely heavily on amendments or protocols to adapt treaty obligations to new needs. The International Telecommunication Union makes frequency allocations by treaty, although the text is incomprehensible to anyone but electrical engineers. In the environmental field, the "framework-protocol" format has often been used. The initial treaty is drafted in very general terms, often establishing no more than a regime of cooperation in scientific research and data exchange. It is anticipated that as scientific and political consensus grows, more detailed regulatory "protocols" will follow. The Vienna Convention on Protection of the Ozone Layer is the exemplar of this format. The Montreal Protocol followed in two years, prescribing a phasedown of CFCs by the year 2000. This deadline has since been advanced twice and the number of controlled substances extended by treaty amendment—at London in 1990 and at Copenhagen in 1992—with phaseouts for most substances now scheduled for January 1, 1996.[138] The framework-protocol approach has also been used successfully in LRTAP and in the Barcelona Convention. It has been adopted for climate change and biodiversity, although it is too soon to say whether these frameworks will be supplemented by binding protocols as in the earlier treaties.

This kind of evolving treaty is one response to the need for adaptation and flexibility in a regulatory regime. It permits a treaty embodying general principles to come into force and a cooperative regime to get under way where the consensus necessary for a more detailed agreement is lacking. It does not, however, avoid the burden of repeated negotiation and ratification of the protocols. These problems were not serious in the ozone case, because the sense of imminent danger was strong.

Absent such urgency, and particularly with a loosely denominated category of "technical" or "administrative" changes, the long slow route of treaty making and amending is likely to be too rigid and unresponsive for the requirements of adaptation. To this end, treaty lawyers have developed ways to deal with the problem of adaptation without seeking formal amendment. Often the governing body is given a kind of rule-making authority, analogous to that found in domestic regulatory agencies, to make rules and regulations within the area of treaty concern. Thus, the ICAO council can "adopt . . . international standards and recommended practices" covering the whole range of safety and operational requirements including aircraft noise and emissions.[139] The International Maritime Organization has similar authority. The ITU establishes technical specifications for telephone communications by adopting recommendations drafted by specially convened industry groups.[140] The International Coffee Agreement and most other commodity agreements give the plenary body authority to establish and adjust quotas.[141] The OECD adopts "recommendations" and "guidelines" governing a wide range of economic activity that are treated as all but binding in the absence of some urgent reason for departure. As we have noted, arms control treaties, beginning with the Inspection Protocol to the INF, have contained provisions permitting the parties to "agree upon such measures as may be necessary to improve the viability and effectiveness" of the agreement, which measures "shall not be deemed amendments to the Treaty."[142] The U.S. Senate was informed that the provisions applied only to "technical changes."[143]

A similar and frequently used device is to place regulatory provisions in an annex or appendix to the treaty that can be changed without reference back to legislatures. Trade in specimens of species listed in Appendix I of CITES is prohibited, and less stringent regulations are imposed with respect to species listed in Appendix II. Species are initially listed and thereafter moved from one appendix to another by vote of the Conference of the Parties. A number of other conventions regulating dangerous or hazardous activities differentiate between severely regulated activities and those under less stringent control by means of appendix that can be altered by party vote.[144] So with whaling quotas under the ICRW. The parties to the Montreal Protocol may decide "whether any substances, and if so which, should be added to or removed from any annex to this Protocol." They are also empowered to decide "the mechanism, scope and timing of the control measures that should apply to those substances."[145] Changes in the Annex on Chemicals of the CWC related to "matters of an administrative or technical nature" are also within the power granted to the Conference of the Parties.[146]

The procedures by which these powers can be exercised vary. Almost all require the vote of a special majority, usually two-thirds but in the case of whaling quotas, three-fourths. Some treaties, like the CWC, permit the change to go into effect on the recommendation of an executive body, unless a party objects. Many of the provisions permit a dissenting party to opt out of the decision. As discussed in Chapter 5, however, the opt-out right is often illusory.

In sum, within these areas of delegated authority, treaty bodies exercise what is in substance legislative power. They act by majority vote with binding effect, in practice, on the parties to the treaty, very often with consequences for private actors and activities.

Conclusions

This review of some of the instruments used to induce compliance with treaties demonstrates that compliance activity for the most part involves assisting and organizing the efforts of willing, or at least nonrecalcitrant, parties to move toward increasingly complete fulfillment of their obligations. Technical assistance, research, information and education, and capacity building are the primary instruments. Efforts at precipitate or preemptory enforcement of determinate obligations are foreign to this enterprise and seem to be regarded by the parties as counterproductive. Taken together, these features lead to a reconception of the compliance problem in complex regulatory regimes. The treaty and the regime in which it is embedded are best seen not as a set of prohibitory norms, but as institutions for the management of an issue area over time. Bringing the separate compliance instruments together in a coherent strategy for this purpose is increasingly seen as the function of systematic review and assessment procedures, to which we now turn.

10

Policy Review and Assessment

Recent "institutionalist" accounts of regimes based on rational choice theory stress their function in facilitating cooperation by reducing transaction costs and uncertainties. In the words of Robert Keohane, a pioneer of this line of inquiry, "international regimes perform the function of establishing patterns of legal liability, providing relatively symmetrical information, and arranging the costs of bargaining so that specific agreements can more easily be made."[1] Much of this book to this point has been an expansion and elaboration of these insights. But in our view they do not go far enough. The basic conception of the regime underlying the institutionalist analysis is that of a switching system, facilitating the independent interactions of independent states. Much observed regime activity can be explained within that framework, but not all. Moreover, these explanations are directed primarily to the formation and persistence of regimes. They say little about the compliance problem. In our view, what is left out of this institutionalist account is the active role of the regime in modifying preferences, generating new options, persuading the parties to move toward increasing compliance with regime norms, and guiding the evolution of the normative structure in the direction of the overall objectives of the regime.

In this chapter, we describe an emerging and potentially powerful process for performing these more active functions—systematic review and assessment of individual members' performance in relation to treaty obligations, with a view to defining steps to improve performance where it may be lagging. Data for review and assessment come from country reports as well as other available sources: for example, independent analysis by secretariats, NGOS and scholarly studies. When questions about performance emerge, the review explores the shortfalls and problems, works with parties to understand the reasons, and develops a program for improvement. In the course of this process, the compliance instruments described in the last chapter are deployed as necessary. Differences about the content and applicability of the governing norms are resolved. Technical and sometimes financial assistance is provided.

We have characterized this process as essentially managerial rather than enforcement. As in other managerial or administrative settings, the approach is not primarily accusatory or adversarial. In the first instance, it accepts that all are engaged in a common enterprise and that the objective of the assessment is to discover how individual and system performance can be improved. The dynamics of dialogue and accountability are central. States are given ample opportunity to explain and justify their conduct. The reasons advanced to excuse noncompliant conduct point to avenues for improvement and correction. The state concerned can hardly avoid undertaking to act along the indicated lines. As the review is reiterated over time, these promises of improvement contain increasingly concrete, detailed, and measurable undertakings.

Although in comparison with sanctions these procedures are noncoercive, they exert strong pressures on parties to comply with their obligations. For the most part they rely on persuasion, but there may be considerable muscle behind the jawboning. In some cases, of which the International Monetary Fund is the salient example, the possibility of a denial of access to financial or other resources, even if remote, cannot be discounted entirely by a state dependent on them. But even in the absence of such material inducements, the threat of exposure or shaming is a powerful spur to action. In an interdependent and interconnected world, a reputation for reliability matters. And in the last analysis, the ability of a state to remain a participant in the international policy-making process—and thus its status as a member of the international system—depends in some degree on its demonstrated willingness to accept and engage the regime's compliance procedures.

The roots of this development can be traced at least as far back as the early days of the International Labor Organization, the first of the modern international regulatory agencies. It reaches its highest polish to date, perhaps, in the practices of the IMF. But it is finding new applications in the World Trade Organization and in the environmental field, and it is still evolving. In some cases, it remains little more than an exceptional action triggered by an episode of suspected noncompliance. The CITES review of imports of lizard and crocodile skins by the Italian shoe industry is one such example.[2] Increasingly, however, review and assessment has evolved from an ad hoc process to part of the regular administrative routine and a systematic implementation and compliance strategy; from review and assessment of past discrete actions to the shaping of future plans, policies, and programs.

We do not provide a rigorous demonstration of the effectiveness of the review and assessment process (taking refuge in the traditional call for further research). We pursue the usual case study format, first examining three treaty regimes that have practiced review and assessment policies over several decades—the ILO, the IMF, and the Organization for Economic Cooperation and Development. In each case, the impressionistic evaluation is favorable, though not unqualifiedly so. The ILO has achieved a high level of compliance with reporting requirements, but its success is less clear on the more difficult problems of inducing states to adopt internal legislation and, when they do, ensuring that the law in action conforms to the law on the books. The IMF has often achieved its goals of compliance with the norms of monetary policy set forth in its Articles of Agreement, but, alone among the major international treaty organizations, it disposes of substantial resources to induce performance. The review process has been a major instrument in the OECD's long history of successful harmonization of economic policies over a broad range of program areas, from export credits to payments liberalization to environmental policy. But it consists of politically and economically homogenous states with a long tradition of effective cooperation. After these three fairly extended studies, we turn to more recent applications and developments of the process in the General Agreement on Tariffs and Trade and environmental treaties, and to some general conclusions.

The International Labor Organization

The foundations of the ILO review and assessment process are the reporting obligations discussed in Chapter 7. As there noted, compliance with these requirements has ranged above 80 percent in every year except during World War II. The organization has established an elaborate procedure for assessing these reports and a finely calibrated series of responses to indications that a party has failed to comply with its obligations.

The process begins in the Committee of Experts on the Application of Conventions and Recommendations (Committee of Experts). The members are recognized experts in labor law and practice, sitting as individuals rather than as representatives of their countries.[3] The Committee of Experts reviews the country reports in detail. It transmits "observations" on unsatisfactory reporting and failures to implement obligations directly to the states concerned, together with suggestions for corrective action. Although the committee has no investigatory powers, it can request a state to provide specific information, and the state is bound to reply. The reporting formats of the committee have grown increasingly detailed over the years, its observations more pointed, and its suggestions for remedial action more specific. Beginning as a relatively passive advisory body, it now makes critical observations, acknowledges and refutes or comments on government responses, and makes suggestions to reporting governments.[4] Ordinarily, there is a two-year grace period before the committee publicizes a failure to implement treaty obligations, to afford time for the International Labor Office and the committee itself to work with the country to bring it back into compliance. The period can be extended if the effort seems to be bearing fruit.[5]

The Committee of Experts reports annually to the Conference Committee on the Application of Conventions and Recommendations (Conference Committee), which is made up of delegates to the International Labor Conference—government, worker, and employer representatives from each member state.[6] The report includes specific observations on a country-by-country basis regarding serious or long-standing cases of failure to apply ILO conventions.

The Conference Committee takes up the more serious violations reported by the Committee of Experts in a "discussion" at which a representative of the country involved must appear and defend its position. The committee's ultimate sanction is to place a non-complying state on a special list—a "blacklist"—in its annual report to the International Labor Conference. Seven categories of offense can warrant blacklisting. Most of these are concerned with failure to report or to appear at committee discussions. The one substantive category is *continued* failure to implement a convention. The notion of continued nonimplementation entails strong elements of intransigence or willful flouting of organizational processes, and this category is infrequently used.

Two stages intervene before a country reported for non-implementation by the Committee of Experts is blacklisted by the Conference Committee. First, the state may request "direct contacts"—a site visit by representatives of the ILO staff to try to work out the problem on the ground. The second intermediate stage is listing in a "special paragraph," which is in effect a notice to the delinquent country that it risks being blacklisted if it does not mend its ways. Special paragraphs have emerged as a prominent tool to prod the deviant into compliance. Usually they identify steps that the country can take to avoid blacklisting.[7] It is evident from the Conference Committee discussions that states are anxious to avoid being listed in a special paragraph or being black-listed on grounds of continued failure to implement. The special paragraph has become a long-term holding pen for recalcitrant states, where, rather than being written off as defectors, they remain subject to continued pressure within the ILO in the annual discussions of the Conference Committee. During the 1980s, twenty-three states were listed in special paragraphs (none more than four times), but only three—Iran, Guatemala, and the USSR—were ulti-mately blacklisted for continued failure to implement.[8]

The Conference Committee review has many attributes of an adjudication, at least on the surface. It begins with a kind of complaint from the Com-mittee of Experts, the accused state is given an opportunity to appear and defend, and it culminates in the imposition of a kind of sanction, if only reputational. It would be a mistake, however, to conclude that the procedure is essentially judicial. The "complaint" emerges only after an extended review of routine country reports carried out by the Committee of Experts in dia-logue with the country concerned. In the course of this interaction, which stretches over at least two years, most problems are worked out by discussion or staff assistance. Only serious or long-standing cases of failure to comply are reported to the Conference Committee. The proceedings in that forum are carefully labeled "discussions," as opposed to something more suggestive of a trial. The Conference Committee's two-phase procedure is a further effort to weed out cases of misunderstanding, differences of interpretation, or feasibility problems, and to induce voluntary adjustment of behavior. The country that fails to correct its conduct through this long succession of opportunities to do so stands exposed as a willful and deliberate violator.[9] Few states are willing to put themselves in this position.

It is not easy to measure with confidence how effective this process is in securing compliance. The only formal obligation of the members is to submit conventions drafted in the organization to the appropriate domestic author-ities for ratification. The United States, for example, has actually ratified only 11 of the 172 ILO conventions, but it is not in violation of any obligation on that account.[10] Even when a convention is ratified, "implementation" requires, in the first instance, only the enactment of conforming domestic legislation. What actually happens on the ground is harder to assess, although much of the reporting and review activity covers actual performance. Earlier studies recorded impressionistic judgments that the reporting process has a positive effect on compliance.[11] But as the organization moved into the sensitive areas of freedom of association and related human rights issues, the appraisal, in the United States at least, was considerably more reserved. As discussed in Chapter 3, these differences were part of the circumstances that led to the temporary U.S. withdrawal from the organization in the mid-1970s. In these cases, however, the practices at issue were deeply embedded in the ideological commitments of the states concerned, so that far more than labor policy was implicated in any corrective action. The ILO, nevertheless, became one of the important forums for confronting such practices. In its "functional" area of labor relations, the continued commitment of representatives of labor, management, and government to the review procedures is at least some evidence of their importance in promoting the evolution of practice in the directions set by the ILO constitution and conventions.

The International Monetary Fund

There is little doubt that over the first half century of its existence the IMF has massively influenced many of its members, for good or ill, to adopt monetary and fiscal policies in conformity with the norms of monetary conduct defined and elaborated under the IMF Agreement. Its impact on developing countries increased throughout the period, and it was felt by industrialized countries at least through the 1970s. It is now poised to play a similar role with the countries of Eastern Europe and the former Soviet Union.

Much of the commentary among regime theorists on the effectiveness of the international monetary regime emphasizes the incentive/coercive measures at the fund's disposal.[12] It is of course true that in these activities the IMF carries a big stick. But in actual practice, the sanctions are much less real than they would seem. Like all ultimate weapons, the IMF's power to cut off funds is not easy to use. What is perhaps surprising is how closely, in the concrete setting of standby decisions, the fund is confined to the instruments of dialogue and persuasion and how much freedom the most destitute of borrowers are able to maintain. The conception of the fund's activities that emerges from its history and practice is rather different from the conventional picture of the IMF as an effective wielder of carrots and sticks.

The fund was established after World War II as an organization for international cooperation in monetary policy. Members contribute to a pool of currencies according to a quota roughly proportionate to their relative economic importance. A member may draw against the pool only to provide funds to tide it over the period of adjustment when it is in balance-of-payments difficulties.[13] Article XIV of the original IMF Agreement permitted countries to maintain exchange restrictions in derogation of the obligations of currency convertibility during "the postwar transitional period." To ensure that the restrictions were removed as soon as feasible, the agreement required that "any member still retaining [such] restrictions . . . shall consult the Fund [annually] as to their further retention."[14] In 1952, after the Marshall Plan, when the IMF actually began lending operations, this same pattern of consultations on future policies and programs was adapted for vetting requests of members for drawings against the fund's resources or for standbys (tantamount to a line of credit). In the 1970s, the fixed exchange-rate system contemplated at Bretton Woods gave way to a "flexible" system, with "strict surveillance" by the fund over the monetary policies of its members.[15] The same basic methodology was employed for all three functions: an intensive review of the country's performance, conducted at regular intervals, based on a report concerning the country's past and future monetary policies prepared by the fund staff with the assistance of national officials. Although a number of states are still in the "transitional period," Article XIV consultations are now merged in one of the other two review and assessment processes.

Surveillance of Exchange Rate Policies

The IMF exercises "firm surveillance over the exchange rate policies of members"[16] by conducting routine consultations with each member, usually at eighteen-month intervals, and special consultations at the instance of the managing director if developments seem to warrant it. The substantive obligations imposed by the agreement are very general: "to collaborate with the Fund and other members to assure orderly exchange arrangements and to promote a stable system of exchange rates" and, in particular, to avoid "manipulating exchange rates."[17] Under this broad mandate, successive decisions of the Executive Directors and the Board of Governors have elaborated criteria of acceptable exchange rate practices and established a systematic surveillance procedure.[18]

The first step is a staff study of the member's overall economic position, giving special emphasis to monetary and balance-of-payments elements. Officials of the member's government cooperate in the development of the study, which typically involves extended staff visits to the member's capital, followed by review and revision at IMF headquarters in Washington. The executive director representing the member presents the final report at a meeting of the Executive Directors, where the discussion includes comments, criticism, and suggestions for policy changes. The managing director summarizes the discussion for the record. Though the summary is given orally, the language is usually carefully prepared in advance.

Neither the country studies nor the Executive Directors' discussions nor the summaries are made public, so it is not possible to draw any precise conclusions about their content or impact. There seems to be little "enforcement" atmosphere about the process. The emphasis is on getting a clear picture of developments in the member's monetary and overall economic situation and identifying potential or emerging problems in time to take corrective action. The methodology is professional analysis, argument, and persuasion about what are treated as technical issues of economic policy. At the same time, the IMF, through frequent statements of the managing director and otherwise, makes it clear that it attaches great importance to the surveillance process.[19] Particularly for developing countries that may need to draw on the fund's resources or need its approval for access to other credit markets, and therefore must remain in its good graces, there is considerable pressure to act on the recommendations and suggestions that emerge from these reviews.[20]

The impact of Article IV surveillance on national policy is illustrated by the recent efforts of the IMF (in coordination with the World Bank) to bring military expenditures into the economic and fiscal review.[21] Traditionally, discussion of members' military expenditures was taboo in these consultations, on national security and sovereignty grounds. In 1989, IMF managing director Michel Camdessus began speaking out publicly about the impact of military expenditures on developing-country economic development and stability. The campaign intensified through 1991,[22] culminating in Camdessus's closing address at the IMF annual meeting in October of that year, where he said: "As regards military spending, I was impressed by the broad support for our aim to study more carefully the problem. An immediate priority must be to collect full and accurate information, and analyze the economic implications."[23] In the carefully modulated language of the IMF, this was clear notice that the existing norms of monetary conduct were changing. The Executive Directors instructed the staff to include the subject of military expenditures in Article IV consultations. Thenceforth military spending would be viewed as an economic as well as a strategic/political issue. Military spending decisions would be dealt with on the same footing as other fiscal decisions. Trade-offs would be examined more systematically so as to achieve a sounder balance among military, monetary, and development priorities.[24]

The IMF has insisted that this is a "policy dialogue" confined to Article IV surveillance, and that it will not apply military-related conditions to drawings against the fund's resources. Even if this distinction is maintained, however, the dialogue can influence policy in a variety of ways. The first is in capacity building: educating government officials about the desirability of better military budgeting practices and the benefits of greater transparency with respect to military expenditures. In countries where the military plays a strong role in internal politics, "merely discussing the importance of treating the military budget in the same fashion as other portions of the budget is a significant event. Reviewing military spending, even if available only in aggregate terms, will not only provide lenders with data but will also be a first step toward making military-related data available to other departments of the government and, ultimately, the public."[25] Second, governments are not monolithic. There are almost always elements supporting compliance, in this case, perhaps, civilians interested in reducing military expenditures in favor of other priorities or simply competing for power. Review and assessment gives them a basis for raising the issue with their armed forces, and the necessity of defending the level of military expenditures in an outside forum strengthens their hand in internal debates.[26] Finally, without addressing military expenditures directly, the IMF can set targets in other sectors so as to squeeze the military.[27] In 1991 the fund may have gone further and linked support to India and Pakistan more directly to reductions in military spending.[28] This new policy appears to have had some effect on the military budgets of several countries. Besides India and Pakistan, for example, in June 1992 Uganda announced a plan for deep cuts in military spending, which had accounted for one-third of the national budget, after aid institutions had urged lower military spending.[29]

Use of the Fund's Resources

The procedure on a request for a drawing (or more usually now a "standby arrangement")[30] is much the same in broad outline. The central element of the consultations, however, is not a general appraisal of the applicant's monetary policy but a negotiation between the fund and the member about the economic policy requirements that the IMF will attach as a condition of approving the drawing.[31] "The negotiations may be protracted and involve several staff missions, trips to the IMF in Washington, D.C., by country technicians and representatives and even direct negotiations between the Managing Director and the country's finance minister or head of government."[32] There is one other significant difference: the negotiated conditions are embodied in a "letter of intent" executed by the member and often containing undertakings as to monetary and fiscal targets expressed in precise quantitative terms.[33] Thus, although past performance of the drawing member will necessarily be reviewed, the exercise is, in the main, *future oriented.*

Like the country studies in the surveillance process, the letters of intent are not public documents (although drawing members sometimes release them),[34] so it is hard to make any precise statements about their content. In general, however, they have embodied relatively orthodox deflationary policies, emphasizing, in particular, reduction in public-sector expenditure and elimination of subsidies.[35] Needless to say, the enthusiasm of economists and political leaders for both the analysis and the policy prescription is less than universal.

For present purposes, the question is not whether these policies are sound or not, but whether and how the fund is able to secure compliance with undertakings in the letters of intent. It would seem that the problem is fairly straightforward. The IMF is one of the few international organizations that has a real carrot and stick at its disposal. Drawings are paid out in installments, and a standby remains on call (in the usual case, for a year) until the member decides it needs to use it. If the member does not meet the agreed targets, the IMF can presumably cancel the arrangement and refuse to disburse the funds when called upon. The threat of cancellation should powerfully concentrate the debtor's mind.

As it turns out, the matter is not that simple. Jeffrey Sachs asserts that "compliance with Fund programs has long been mediocre . . . [and] seems to be getting worse over time."[36] The drawing member may fail to meet the conditions in its letter of intent for any number of reasons other than simple disinclination. Often economic events are simply beyond the party's control. Export prices may slide or the cost of essential imports—oil—rise precipitously. Bureaucratic and administrative incapacity is endemic. And national politics in developing countries, as elsewhere, are notoriously resistant to economic austerity measures. In the 1970s the IMF developed new arrangements, such as the Extended Fund Facility, that go beyond balance-of-payments financing and are "designed to help countries adopting 'comprehensive' adjustment programs."[37] These programs are inherently slower to implement, less susceptible to quantitative measurement, and thus harder to evaluate. A central economic instrument within the direct responsibility of the finance ministry—say, the interest rate—is much easier to control than a change in agricultural policies and practices. Policy prescriptions are contestable and contested, and the fund cannot always insist on them.

The fund itself is not blameless. Because of the disparity of initial bargaining power, in many instances it exacts conditions for theoretical, political, or internal bureaucratic reasons that it knows are unrealistic, given the economic plight of the drawer.[38] All this means that the IMF cannot insist rigidly on full compliance with undertakings made in such programs.[39]

As a result, when a drawing member fails to meet its undertakings, what ensues is a series of renewed exchanges with the fund—a major negotiation usually leading to revised targets and undertakings.[40] "Many countries have complied only partially with IMF conditions and have entered into drawn-out negotiations with the Fund (and the Bank), among them Brazil, Mexico and Kenya."[41] The fund's principal weapon is "jawboning"—argument, advice, influence, and persuasion—to induce a policy response from the debtor government.[42] As a part of the exercise, it may occasionally cancel the drawing or standby, but this is usually a formality. In the period from 1954 to 1984, the IMF canceled fifty-six standby or extended arrangements with developing countries. In all but nine of these, it established a new arrangement within one month of the cancellation.[43] In the course of the iterated negotiations between the parties, the terms of the letter of intent may begin to reflect more closely the realistic political and economic capabilities of the member government.

One careful study concludes that "as IMF programs are seldom implemented fully as negotiated and the penalties for partial compliance are not great, ... debtor countries have more flexibility in imposing austerity measures and the economic constraints are less binding on politicians than often assumed."[44]

In the end, states using IMF resources are members of the organization, and the fund feels a kind of fiduciary obligation to them. Although it tries to keep the pressure on, it could not simply turn its back on an exigent country, without at least making sure that all other possibilities had been exhausted.[45] Thus, as Peter B. Kenen points out, "the Fund faces a dilemma. If it cuts a member off, particularly one that has large debts, it may precipitate a crisis of confidence. If it fails to cut the member off or agrees too readily to modifications in the country's policies, it may tarnish its seal of approval."[46]

The Brazilian experience is representative. After the military coup in 1964, the government applied for a standby arrangement, which was granted and renewed annually in varying amounts until 1972.[47] Brazil drew against the arrangement only twice, in 1965 and again in 1968. In other years, however, the availability of the standby was nonetheless important for Brazil's overall credit standing in international financial markets and with other public funding agencies, particularly the U.S. Agency for International Development (AID).

The standbys were accompanied by the usual letters of intent containing constraints on exchange control policies and targets for international monetary reserves, the size of the public-sector deficit, credit expansion, foreign indebtedness, and the like. As early as 1965, Brazil failed to meet these targets, and a series of renegotiations ensued during that year to keep the credit in operation. Nevertheless, the IMF renewed the standby each year.[48] Overall compliance with these conditions during the period from 1965 to 1972 has been characterized as "not bad."[49] But monetary and credit expansion was always higher than indicated, limits on reserve requirements for commercial banks and lending from central banks were generally not met, and progress was spotty on other fronts. Only once, in 1970, was a standby canceled.

Although the arrangement was renewed within a month, the political "stigma" resulting from this experience helped to preclude any Brazilian government from resorting to the fund again until March 1983. At that time a new two-year standby of SDR 4.2 billion was granted in connection with the rollover of Brazil's commercial debt. By May, the IMF had suspended the second installment of the loan, arguing that Brazil had failed to meet its deficit reduction undertaking. Despite new austerity measures, which led to protest demonstrations and serious riots, Brazil continued to fall short of its targets. As a result there were a succession of renegotiated letters of intent and periodic suspensions of disbursements until February 1985, when, after two years of a three-year standby, the IMF suspended disbursement of the remaining $1.5 billion of the loan.[50]

Can the overall results of this consultation process be characterized as "acceptable compliance"? Jeffrey Sachs has a straightforward answer: "The evidence presented in the IMF's 1988 review of conditionality also suggests that, since 1983, the rate of compliance has been decreasing sharply, down to less than one-third compliance with performance criteria in the most recent years. Of course, given the secrecy surrounding IMF programs, it is impossible to evaluate the seriousness of the breaches or the reasons for them (e.g., internal policy failures versus external shocks)."[51]

Peter Kenen presents a different view: "It is virtually impossible to measure the effectiveness of conditionality. The debate on the subject will continue, because the participants do not agree on the ways in which policy instruments work, and because they cannot know what governments would have done if they had not made policy commitments to the Fund."[52]

Perhaps the conflict between these two highly respected economists, both more than ordinarily knowledgeable about the work of the IMF, is more apparent than real. A closer look suggests that they may be answering somewhat different questions. Sachs addresses an issue capable of objective resolution, like compliance with the speed limit: have the quantitative targets in letters of intent been met? Kenen asks whether the policy goals have been achieved. Sachs is talking about "compliance," Kenen about "effectiveness."

Yet at a deeper level the contradiction between the two appraisals remains. Kenen's approach suggests that to treat targets and policy commitments as a basis for on-off judgments of compliance misconceives the nature of the normative process and the policy context. Sachs himself recognizes this point to a degree when he implies that it would make a difference whether the shortfall was due to "internal policy failures" or "external shocks." And that does not exhaust the range of relevant possibilities.

This analysis suggests that IMF activity in administering drawings and standbys can best be understood not as an attempt to enforce policy commitments but as an effort to ratchet up the borrower's performance by monitoring what are essentially best-efforts undertakings. The letter of intent is a tool in an ongoing process of negotiation that exerts continuing pressure to bring developing country monetary and economic policy into line with the fund's notions of what is desirable. The continuous consultations give rise to a relationship extending over time, shifting its focus with the transaction or problem currently on the agenda, but without a sharp beginning or ending. The superior bargaining power of the fund in this ongoing negotiation helps to ensure that the policy movement is in what it regards as the desired direction. There is little doubt that many developing countries have adopted deflationary and austerity policies in the face of serious domestic political resistance—and even at the cost of real suffering for their own people.

A cut off of funds transforms the relationship between the IMF and the drawing member from cooperative to confrontational. The likely result is a rupture that reduces the fund's ability to influence the country's policy for a considerable time. Although the fund may make threatening noises, it is unlikely to contemplate this recourse so long as continued dialogue holds out even minimal prospects for further progress.[53] (Of course, even countries that broke with the fund—Peru, Zambia, Brazil—ultimately had to make their peace with it.) It not only controls access to its own large resources, but in general it also acts in concert with its sister institution, the World Bank. Moreover, in the 1980s, regional development banks, bilateral aid donors, and private lenders all took their cue from the fund. Thus it essentially controlled all sources of new credit for a straightened country. Yet when the prodigal returned, the IMF never failed to welcome it with visions of future possibilities rather than past sins.

Critics insist with considerable force that IMF monetary surveillance and conditionality are paternalistic, if not worse. And whether the prescriptions are "correct" in the sense of improving the overall economic status of the fund's developing country clients is of course a highly contestable and sharply contested matter. But if it can be said that these norms reflect the wishes and interests of the United States and other dominant members of the IMF, it remains true that the major economic powers have operated in significant part through the instrumentality of the fund and could hardly have achieved the same results without it. The indifferent record of the Group of Seven in coordinating economic and monetary policies among the major economic players is testimony to the need for a more formal and structured organization and process. Most would agree, moreover, that the managing director and staff of the IMF, by their strong professional competence, their close relationships with national finance ministries and central banks, and their apparent independence from national direction, have achieved a considerable degree of autonomous influence in the field within broad guidelines established by the membership.

It is not easy to tell, in the end, just how much of the IMF's success in influencing the policies of its developing country members is attributable to its control over resources and how much to the managerial techniques of policy dialogue. But from the fund's perspective, the dominant conception is of an essentially cooperative and consensual effort to achieve generally agreed goals of monetary policy.

The Organization for Economic Cooperation and Development

The OECD consists of all the advanced industrial states. It was formed in 1960 to deal with problems of coordinating and harmonizing economic policy.[54] It normally operates through committees in such areas as environment, development assistance, multinational enterprise, export credits, and the like. The committees develop guidelines or codes on particular problems within their jurisdiction, and these are ultimately promulgated by the OECD council as recommendations or occasionally as binding decisions. The committees supervise compliance and performance under these instruments using a policy review procedure similar to the IMF's. Unlike the IMF, however, the OECD has no bag of goodies with which to back up its normative decisions.

Liberalization

The OECD Codes of Liberalization of Capital Movements and Invisible Transactions, adopted early in the history of the organization, are a clear example of the use of the review technique to ratchet up performance without any coercive element. The codes prohibit the parties from imposing restrictions on foreign participation in specified categories of financial transactions. Although they were adopted as binding decisions, as in many other treaties a member may opt out of particular code requirements by taking a "reservation," or it may make more general "derogations" to its obligations, subject to review by the Committee on Capital Movements and Invisible Transactions.[55] A state is selected for review (usually on an ad hoc basis, determined primarily by its actual performance in liberalization). It makes a report to the OECD secretariat on its economic situation, the justification for any existing restrictions, and its plans for removing current reservations and derogations from code requirements. The secretariat distributes an analysis of the report to committee members in advance of the meeting, usually suggesting issues on which the committee "may wish" to examine the state under review. The state may submit an addendum to its report in response to the secretariat's comments. Review sessions, which are held quarterly, last for several days. Again, as with the IMF, although the process begins as a review of past performance, it quickly turns to the future. Over the course of the review, the state often makes significant withdrawals or modifications of existing reservations or undertakes to do so in the future. For example, Turkey, in its initial report for its 1990 review, offered to withdraw or modify twenty-five of the forty-five reservations it had maintained since adhering to the codes in 1986. In its addendum after the secretariat's analysis was circulated, it upped the ante to complete withdrawal of 24 reservations and modification of twelve others; in the examination before the committee, it agreed to withdraw two additional reservations.[56] At the end of the examination, the committee reports (through the secretariat) to the council, identifying any additional steps toward liberalization it thinks the state might take, and the council ordinarily embodies this report in formal recommendations to the state concerned.[57]

Periodically, when existing reservations have been substantially eliminated, the OECD adds additional categories to the list covered by the codes, often leading to new reservations, and the whole process starts again. Despite this continuous moving of the goal posts, the OECD has published charts showing a generally downward trend in the overall percentage of items covered by reservations and derogations from 1964 to 1990.[58]

Environment

In January 1991 the OECD environment ministers launched as a major new initiative a program for environmental policy review of member countries.[59] After a transitional period, the program was launched in November 1993. By

the end of the first year, reviews of five countries had been completed—
Iceland, Germany, Portugal, Norway, and Japan—with Italy and the United
Kingdom in process. Reviews of four to five countries a year are contem-
plated, with the whole membership being reviewed every five or six years.

The format follows that worked out by the OECD in its peer reviews of
members' economic, agricultural, fisheries, and energy policies. It begins
with a study conducted by a peer review team made up of nongovernmental
experts nominated by reviewing governments, outside consultants hired by
the secretariat, and a few secretariat officials. The topics to be covered are
agreed in advance with the country under review. The team conducts site
visits, consulting with environmental NGOs, union representatives, business-
people, and academics, as well as the relevant government ministries. The
final report is circulated to the members conducting the review, along with
a list of thirty to forty recommendations and a discussion paper prepared by
the secretariat. At the meetings, representatives of all the relevant ministries
of the government under review appear to defend and justify their policies
before their peers. The debate is active and mixes praise and criticism, with
criticisms tending to be more frequent and sharper as experience with the
process has grown. One country solicited criticism for use against bureaucratic and political opponents at home.

A major topic in all reviews is compliance with international commitments. Attention is focused on failure to ratify environmental agreements,
adequacy of implementing legislation and policies, particular violations of
specific commitments, and follow-up planning. Questions and comments
from the secretariat and the reviewing members elicit undertakings for
improved performance.

The OECD Environmental Performance Review Program is still too new to
be evaluated. The members, however, have expressed strong satisfaction with
the program. Candidates for countries to sit in review are plentiful, and
although the reviews are voluntary, the secretariat is confident that there will
be no opt outs. By the end of the first full year's program, more than
two-thirds of the membership had signed up to be reviewed.

The General Agreement on Tariffs and Trade

After four decades of watching the policy review processes of its fellow
economic organizations, the GATT decided to follow suit. As a result of the
Tokyo Round commitments on notification and surveillance of trade policies, the GATT secretariat began to assemble its own data on national trade

restrictions, published annually as the *Review of the Developments of the Trading System.*[60] At the midterm review of the Uruguay Round in April 1989, this was expanded into the Trade Policy Review Mechanism (TPRM), modeled closely on the IMF and OECD procedures.[61] Under the mechanism, the council is to examine, at periodic special meetings, the impact of each member's trade policies and practices on the multilateral trading system. Each country is to be reviewed not less than once every six years, and as often as biennially for the more important trading countries.[62] As of mid-1993, thirty-three countries (counting the European Community as one) had undergone policy reviews; of these, the United States, Japan, the European Community, and Canada had been reviewed twice.[63] The TRPM was formally embodied in the Uruguay Round agreements, which incorporate the practice as it grew up under the GATT.[64]

As with the OECD policy reviews, TPRM began with a report from the member under review on its overall economic situation, together with a detailed analysis of its trade policies and practices. The GATT secretariat provided a separate report focusing on special areas of concern.[65] These two documents formed the basis of the review, which took place at a special day-long meeting of the GATT council. There was extended and often lively exchange between members of the council and the country representative. The discussion was not narrowly confined to compliance with GATT obligations. Indeed, the WTO agreement recites that the review "is not intended to serve as a basis for the enforcement of specific obligations under the Agreement or for dispute settlement procedures." Its function "is to examine the impact of a Member's trading policies and practices on the multilateral trading system."[66] Policy reports necessarily look to the future to some degree, and states tend to emphasize future performance in order to show good faith, to mitigate a less than stellar record, and to minimize troublesome present practices. During the reviews, these general assurances have often been converted into specific undertakings as to the timetable for particular reforms.[67] Inevitably, however, much of the interchange has revolved around the applicability of GATT norms to current practices. Comments from Council members on specific practices have repeatedly raised the issue of consistency with GATT requirements, and if there was an argument that the policy was consistent with the agreement, that was the state's first line of defense to criticism.

In the new arrangement, the reviews will be conducted by a Trade Policy Review Body, which will be a committee of the whole membership. Country reports, the secretariat report, and the minutes of the meeting are to be published and forwarded to the Ministerial Conference.[68] In the past, the summaries of the meetings have observed the diplomatic amenities and have found something to praise in each state's performance. But the bulk of each summary has been devoted to a fairly pointed discussion of the unsatisfactory aspects of the country's trade policies, under such headings as "Concerns," "Some Questions," or "Clarification."[69] The state's response have been noted in detail, and the chair's conclusion restates the key points of the discussion.

It is too early to evaluate the effectiveness of the TPRM, but it is significant that it was established after extended efforts tighten up the GATT's traditional dispute settlement mechanism. The reviews are infrequent and do not include the intense interaction between country officials and the secretariat that give ILO review and IMF surveillance much of their bite. At a minimum, TPRM provides an opportunity for focused and public exposition, criticism, and justification of a state's overall trade policy in terms of GATT norms, in an expert and concerned forum of colleagues engaged, in some part, in a cooperative enterprise. The experience to date seems to have been good enough that the members included review committees of various kinds to monitor activities under many of the subsidiary agreements concluded in the Uruguay Round.[70]

Environmental Agreements

Recent environmental conventions display an increasingly self-conscious recourse to policy review mechanisms as the principal device for regime management. At the same time, there has been something of a backlash, reflecting a growing awareness of the power of the instrument.

Long-Range Transboundary Air Pollution

The original LRTAP treaty called for exchange of information through the Executive Body on "policies and strategies for the control of sulphur compounds and other major air pollutants."[71] In the 1985 sulphur dioxide protocol, the provision was amplified to require that the parties "develop without undue delay national programmes, policies and strategies which shall serve as a means of reducing sulphur emissions . . . and shall report thereon as well as on progress in achieving the goal to the Executive Body."[72] Although the reporting requirements are taken seriously, the reports are not systematically reviewed as such. According to Marc Levy, "they are simply collated and published. There is no effort to ascertain whose measures place them in compliance with either specific protocols or broader norms. Nor is there any effort to fill in missing information or to correct misleading information. In fact, there is a conscious attempt on the part of the secretariat not to embarrass parties in these reports."[73] Major reviews of national policies and strategies are conducted every four years, however, and updated annually. Levy cites frequent instances of states voluntarily providing clarification and justification of their policies in the meetings of the Executive Body, and even undertaking firm targets for future emissions reduction.[74] The practice thus corresponds to that of the other organizations discussed. It is not confrontational, and it is not directed to identifying particular violations or punishing violators. Instead, the reports lay the basis for policy reviews in a problem-solving mode that generate pressure for cooperative action to improve overall regime effectiveness.

Climate Change

The negotiation and development of the reporting and review requirements in the Framework Convention on Climate Change is a complex story the outcome of which is still unclear as of mid-1995. The issue is so sensitive, particularly among developing countries, that the words "report" or "reporting" do not appear in the convention. Instead, the parties are required to submit "communications" covering inventories of greenhouse gasses and policies and measures designed to implement emission reduction and other treaty commitments.[75]

The convention contains no firm obligations to limit greenhouse gas emissions, but the developed countries agree to adopt policies "with a view to" reducing emissions to 1990 levels by the year 2000.[76] By the same token, and in line with the "common but differentiated responsibility" proclaimed by the convention as between industrialized and developing countries,[77] industrialized countries are subject to a much more stringent policy and program reporting obligation than developing countries. The communications of industrialized countries, which were due on September 21, 1994, six months after the entry into force of the convention, were required to contain, in addition to an inventory of greenhouse gas emissions,

(a) A detailed description of the policies and measures that [they have] adopted to implement [their] commitment . . .; and
(b) A specific estimate of the effects that the policies and measures . . . will have on anthropogenic emissions by [their] sources and removals by [their] sinks [by the end of the present decade].[78]

The developing countries need report only "a general description of steps taken or envisaged . . . to implement the Convention," and need file their initial report only within three years of entry into force, as compared to six months for the industrialized countries.[79]

The convention is deliberately ambiguous on whether an intensive individualized review is contemplated, also reflecting a growing awareness of the effectiveness of review and assessment as a control instrument.[80] The FCCC provides that the Conference of Parties (COP) is to "assess, on the basis of all the information made available to it in accordance with the provisions of the Convention, the implementation of the Convention by the parties, the overall effects of the measures taken pursuant to the Convention . . . and the extent to which progress towards the objectives of the Convention is being achieved."[81]

Nevertheless, the preparation for the first meeting of the Conference of Parties, scheduled for the spring of 1995, proceeded on the basis that a fairly thorough review of the reports will take place. As noted in Chapter 9, the Global Environmental Facility has been told to give priority to funding developing-country reporting capacity, and there is some indication that funding will be available only to projects that grow out of broader programs for emission reduction that would be communicated to the COP. The preparatory committee has drawn up detailed guidelines for the content and organization of the communications. At the instance of the United States, the Netherlands, and Canada, the OECD secretariat, in cooperation with the Intergovernmental Panel on Climate Change (IPCC), developed technical criteria for communications to ensure that they are full, meaningful, and comparable. The Conference of the Parties at its first meeting in March 1995 adopted the OECD-IPCC recommended criteria.[82]

Chemical Weapons

The CWC reflects this development in the arms control field. The required declaration as to chemical weapons must include the state's "general plan for destruction" of chemical weapons or chemical weapons production facilities that "it owns or possesses . . ."[83] Each party must also submit annual plans for the destruction of weapons 60 days before an annual destruction period begins[84] and 180 days before the destruction of the facility begins.[85] The plans are subject to review and critique by the Technical Secretariat and ultimately by the parties.

Conclusion

The review and assessment process is a vehicle for bringing together all the compliance measures and instruments discussed in the earlier chapters in a single coherent compliance strategy. As such, it has a compelling dynamic, engaging the parties in an increasingly detailed and comprehensive dialogue, not only to identify areas where compliance is unsatisfactory but also to develop ways of improving performance in the future. The states party to the treaty are, of course, the key interlocutors in this dialogue. But they are not the only ones. Review and assessment provide a major point of access to the compliance process for nonstate actors. Indeed, in its developed forms, the review process depends heavily on the participation of NGOs and international organizations for its effectiveness. The final two chapters are devoted to a survey of their increasingly prominent role.

11

Nongovernmental Organizations

It is a measure of the stubborn persistence of the state-centered view of international affairs among academic and public figures that the first ten chapters of this book treat primarily the role and activities of states. States, however, are not opaque and unitary entities, nor are they the only actors in the international arena. Especially in democratic societies, nongovernmental organizations play a large and growing role in many treaty regimes. We have discussed their activities in passing in earlier chapters. Here we give a more extended account of their role and impact.

The extensive involvement of NGOs in international affairs begins with the emergence of economic and social issues on the international agenda after World War I.[1] A generation later, at the end of World War II, 1200 organizations came to San Francisco to participate in the proceedings on the adoption of the United Nations Charter. Their main objective was to ensure that the Charter would not be confined to international security matters but would include provisions dealing with economic, social, and cultural issues.[2] They are credited by some with securing the inclusion of human rights provisions in the Charter.[3]

In the early post-war decades, arms control organizations like Strike against Nuclear Energy (SANE) and Mothers Strike for Peace were prominent, and the nuclear freeze movement ballooned as late as the 1980s. With the adoption of the basic human rights covenants in 1966, organizations in that field began to proliferate, and as of 1993 they numbered close to five hundred.[4] Similarly, environmental NGOs have grown spectacularly since some four hundred NGOs went to the UN Conference on the Environment in Stockholm in 1972.[5] There they invented the device of an NGO conference running parallel to the intergovernmental meeting, which is now a feature of UN conferences on all subjects and often of meetings of treaty organizations as well. At the UN Conference on Environment and Development (UNCED) in Rio twenty years later, the number of registered NGO participants had risen to 1,400.[6] At the end of the century, internationally oriented NGOs number in the many thousands[7]—to say nothing of the many businesses, academic organizations, and professional and trade associations that are active on the international scene. The *Yearbook of International Organizations* lists ninety-nine subject matter areas for more than twelve thousand international NGOs, ranging from agriculture to vehicle science and technology. Most of the NGOs are based in the United States, but a growing number are found in other countries as well.[8]

Nongovernmental organizations perform parallel and supplementary functions at almost every step of the strategy for regime management we have begun to identify. They are independent sources of information and data that can be used by the regime. They help to check and verify party reporting. In many cases, they provide the basic evaluation and assessment of party performance that is the fulcrum of the compliance process. They have provided technical assistance to enable developing-country parties to participate in treaty negotiation and administration and to comply with the reporting and sometimes the substantive requirements of the treaty. They perform mediating and facilitating services. Where there is noncompliance, they are key to public exposure, shaming, and popular political response. In a real sense, they supply the personnel and resources for managing compliance that states have become increasingly reluctant to provide to international organizations (see Chapter 12).

This burgeoning array of NGOs is the one element of the system that is not even in theory subject to governmental control. They define their objectives, generate resources, and make commitments through their own internal processes. They have their own vision of compliance that may or may not coincide with that of the parties. They remain free to critique or attack the regime managers, national or international. It is therefore not surprising that they are not always appreciated by the states and international organizations that have official responsibility for managing the regime.

The NGOs vary enormously. The choice of targets includes the group's own government, foreign governments, international organizations, and the public at large. The object may be to change the target's own policies on compliance matters or to induce it to put pressure on other states or international organizations. These strategies are by no means mutually exclusive.

Although some organizations tend to concentrate on a particular approach—litigation, for example, in the United States—the same NGO may take different tacks on different issues and sometimes simultaneously on the same issue. Often a number of NGOs will form an alliance on a particular issue, each pursuing its own preferred tactics or constituency. Whatever the target, tactics range along a spectrum from confrontation through persuasion to more or less neutral provision of information.

Although NGOs work directly with national governments and international organizations in an attempt to shape their policies and actions, they exert their major influence through the domestic political process. In democratic systems, NGO activities are a part of normal interest group politics, and the sources and vectors of their influence differ little from those of other private groups. Like the others, they mobilize voters, lobby legislators, endorse candidates, disseminate information (more or less accurate), bring lawsuits, seek to persuade interested publics, and badger journalists, academics, and other opinion leaders. They have to make up in quality and persistence what they lack in money and membership, but they have access to all levels of the system through the normal workings of civil society in a democratic country. As will appear, however, even in countries without strong democratic traditions, shifting alliances of domestic and international NGOs can mount significant pressures on the government through "shaming" campaigns organized around the norms of international agreements.

This multitude of groups is so disparate and varies along so many dimensions—size, organization, objectives, location, staffing, funding sources, membership, strategy, life cycle—that it is hard to generalize about their activities or impact. Systematic scholarly work is really just beginning. Indeed, even efforts to define NGOs in a way that distinguishes them sharply from other private actors in civil society have not been very impressive. In general, they are thought of as organizations (usually not for profit) of people united by their orientation toward a particular public policy issue rather than their "selfish" individual interests.[9] Obviously, other private-sector actors—corporations, unions, trade associations—carry out very similar programs.

Because of all these differences, we content ourselves in this chapter with presenting a sample of cases in the human rights and environmental fields, where NGO activity has been particularly dramatic in recent years. Compliance with the governing instruments in these fields has always been an NGO priority, but the organizations do not limit themselves to that objective. They also deploy the same strategies in an effort to influence substantive policy—usually to increase the level of protection. Although it is, thus, difficult to sort out the activities aimed specifically at compliance, the cases are nevertheless unusually instructive as to the impact and modus operandi of the NGOs in securing compliance with existing regulations.

Human Rights

Among the purposes of the United Nations is "to achieve international cooperation . . . in promoting and encouraging respect for human rights and for fundamental freedoms for all, without distinction as to race, sex, language, or religion."[10] The newly formed organization turned promptly to this task, establishing a UN Commission on Human Rights with Eleanor Roosevelt as chair that in 1948 produced the Universal Declaration of Human Rights, adopted without a dissenting vote by the General Assembly. Although initially intended as hortatory and aspirational, it has become the foundation for a truly impressive growth of international human rights law, comprising not only customary international law but also a growing number of treaties. The central instruments are the International Covenant on Civil and Political Rights and the International Covenant on Economic, Social, and Cultural Rights, both promulgated in 1966. Since then, the treaty structure has been elaborated with a number of specialized treaties (dealing with, for example, racial discrimination, torture, genocide, the rights of women, the rights of the child); regional treaties in Europe, Latin America, and Africa; and various nonbinding declarations, such as specific General Assembly resolutions and the Helsinki Act. Although NGOs and their members are obviously motivated by moral and political aims that go beyond the strict terms of these instruments, the network of treaties provides the legal framework about which their activities are organized.

Civil Liberties Organization: Behind the Wall

Sometimes a single organization in a single country can generate powerful pressure for the enforcement of international norms. In 1987, two Nigerian lawyers founded the Civil Liberties Organization (CLO) to represent common prisoners held without charges or trial for extended periods. Within a year, CLO's strategy of representing individuals evolved first to class actions on behalf of groups of detainees and then to public reports on individual prisons in the system.[11] Each action drew some official response. The government released substantial numbers of prisoners and shut down one especially pestilent prison. In 1990, the government established a Committee on Prison Reforms, chaired by a former justice of the Nigerian Supreme Court.[12]

The CLO's activity culminated in the publication in 1992 of *Behind the Wall,* a comprehensive report on Nigerian prison conditions.[13] The organization's staff and volunteers carried out the fact-finding, including visits to fifty-six of the country's prisons. Each of the report's thirteen chapters begins with citations to the relevant provisions of the international legal framework: the Universal Declaration of Human Rights, the International Covenant on Civil and Political Rights, the UN Standard Minimum Rules for the Treatment of Prisoners, and the Body of Principles for the Protection of All Persons under any Form of Detention or Imprisonment.[14] The report received wide publicity in the Nigerian press and was distributed to government officials and the Commission on Prison Reforms.

The CLO reports that shortly after the publication of *Behind the Wall,* 5,300 prisoners were granted amnesty.[15] The prison budget, the number of prison doctors, and the inmates' food allowance all more than doubled. Although these figures may perhaps be discounted as self-interested, the minister of internal affairs wrote a letter of commendation, listing policy changes already under way and proposing a new CLO study of the Nigerian court system. The CLO's success stimulated the organization of many other Nigerian human rights groups, including some that continue to address prison conditions. And once the report was published, a number of international human rights groups began to interest themselves in Nigeria.

Chile

In September 1973, the constitutional government of Chile was overthrown in a military coup that culminated in the assassination or suicide of the president, Salvatore Allende. The reign of terror that followed galvanized international human rights organizations and provided a first test of new UN Economic and Social Council procedures for monitoring human rights violations that were established in 1971.[16]

In February 1974, the Soviet Union and its allies, which normally had little use for UN human rights activities, brought charges against Chile before the UN Human Rights Commission for violations of the most fundamental provisions of the international human rights instruments for the protection of the security of the person—the prohibitions against arbitrary arrest and detention, torture, and disappearances. The charges were based largely on documentation supplied by NGOs, led by Amnesty International and the International Commission of Jurists (ICJ), which had been gathering information about conditions in Chile since shortly after the coup.[17] The first proceeding ended in an official telegram from the Human Rights Commission to the government of Chile, demanding "the immediate cessation of any kind of violation of human rights" and the release of a number of named political prisoners.[18] In 1974 it was a strong move for an organization made up of states, many of them with less than perfect human rights performance, to call directly on another state for specified actions that might easily be regarded as within its "domestic jurisdiction" and thus off-limits for the UN. "The Commission had gone further than the United Nations had dared to go previously (except in the case of South Africa) in demanding changes in the internal behavior of a sovereign government."[19]

Reports of torture, mass arrests, and killings in Chile continued. The Subcommission on the Prevention of Discrimination and the Protection of Minorities conducted hearings on the Chilean case in the summer of 1974. A representative of the ICJ raised, apparently for the first time, the idea of an investigation of the situation to be conducted by the UN itself. The subcommission's report endorsed this proposal and invited information on violations from all sources, specifically including nongovernmental organizations.[20] As a result, at the next meeting of the Commission on Human Rights in February 1975, NGOs were able for the first time to appear in their own name, rather than acting merely as suppliers of information to member governments. Several had sent teams of investigators to Chile and had direct evidence to report. Thirty-six nongovernmental organizations presented statements to the commission, and seven NGO representatives testified orally. In the end, the commission took another unprecedented step by establishing an Ad Hoc Working Group to investigate the situation and report back both to the Commission and to the General Assembly.[21] Chile at first agreed to cooperate with the Working Group but at the last minute withdrew permission for it to enter the country. Nevertheless the Working Group continued to pursue its assignment, relying now primarily on contacts and information supplied by the NGOs, who "funnel[ed] all material unofficially to the Working Group which then prepare[d] its official report on the basis of our information."[22] Its interim report led to a General Assembly resolution condemning Chile for "constant, flagrant violations of human rights."[23] After the final Working Group report, the Human Rights Commission again denounced the Chilean violations, singling out the secret police organization, Dirección de Inteligencia Nacional (DINA), for special condemnation.

Chile was increasingly on the defensive in all UN forums. It felt itself under the necessity of responding to the accusations, and sought, unsuccessfully, to justify its actions and discredit the evidence. In the course of these efforts, it eventually had to address the NGO charges directly, but its response was unconvincing and failed to stem further UN action.[24] Changes were occurring in Chile as well as in New York. In 1975 the junta adopted a decree requiring medical examinations for all prisoners at the time of arrest and release, assertedly to prove that they had not been tortured. Beginning in 1976, human rights activists began to observe some slackening of cases of torture. In August 1977, after the assassination of former Chilean ambassador Orlando Letelier in Washington, DINA was dissolved. In 1978, when the state of siege expired, the junta decreed a general amnesty for offenses committed since the coup and announced a transition to a "new institutionality." During the 1980s, a UN special rapporteur, replacing the Working Group, reported continuing and widespread violations, but he also noted slow improvement in the situation, culminating in the plebiscite on return to civilian rule, constitutional amendments, and free elections in 1988.[25]

These developments were slow and halting, and many of the actions were primarily cosmetic. For example, the DINA was replaced by a new Central Nacional de Informaciones (CNI), which carried out many of the same functions, and the state of seige was supplanted by a new antiterrorism law. Events in Chile did not occur in a vacuum but corresponded to a widespread shift to democratic government throughout Latin America and elsewhere. In any case, the changes can hardly be ascribed solely to the work of the human rights NGOs. Nevertheless, these organizations, working with courageous counterparts within Chile, kept up a steady stream of documentation establishing the continuation of human rights violations despite the denials of the regime, frequently correcting the special rapporteur's overly sanguine appraisals.[26] It seems clear that they supplied much of the evidence for the strong and continuous condemnation of the junta by the UN Human Rights Commission, ECOSOC, and the General Assembly, which in turn provided the basis for intensifying governmental pressures on the regime. Finally, the Chile case established a precedent for similar action by the UN commission elsewhere, beginning with Argentina, Uganda, and Mozambique shortly after the first report of the pathbreaking Ad Hoc Working Group for Chile.

Helsinki

Even in the Soviet Union, dissident groups, particularly after the adoption of the Helsinki Final Act in 1975, invoked international legal instruments embodying human rights norms as a major fulcrum for pressure on the government. Beginning in 1965, after the end of the Khrushchev era, a number of dissident organizations systematically measured Soviet official action against domestic and international legal requirements. The *Chronicle of Current Events,* published in samidzat from 1965 through 1968, printed on its masthead Article 19 of the Universal Declaration on Human Rights, which guarantees "the right to freedom of opinion and expression."[27] The text of the *Chronicle* consisted simply of accounts of Soviet actions juxtaposed with the relevant provision of the Universal Declaration. The Human Rights Committee, organized in 1970 by Valeri Chalidze and Andrei Sakharov, announced that it "would be guided by the humanistic principles of the Universal Declaration of Human Rights."[28] When Sakharov assumed the leadership of the committee, his first appeal to the Supreme Soviet "called for legislation which would deal with the question [of freedom to choose one's country of residence] in the spirit of Article 13 of the Universal Declaration."[29] Publications of the committee referred frequently to the Universal Declaration and, to a lesser extent, to the covenants on human rights.

With the adoption of Helsinki Final Act, a systematic effort at shaming the Soviet Union for its human rights performance began in earnest. Although at first the dissidents greeted détente and Helsinki with some skepticism, they soon recognized that the Soviet signature on the document made it possible to call their government to account for violations. The Moscow Helsinki Group, founded by Yuri Orlov, took the lead. Orlov said, "It was a weak document, weaker than the Universal Declaration of Human Rights, but it was more important . . . If the Soviet government said was important, it was, in fact important. It was the Soviet government itself that gave us something to work with."[30]

By the terms of the Final Act, signatory governments were required to publish its text, and President Leonid Brezhnev, eager to promote détente, was true to his word. The impact was unexpected: "Soviet citizens, reading the text of the Final Act in the papers, were stunned by the humanitarian articles; it was the first they had heard of any kind of international obligations in the human rights field of their government. A spontaneous reaction was to refer to the Helsinki Accord when appealing to Soviet officials in cases where they refused to satisfy a vital need of the petitioner."[31]

The objective of the Moscow Helsinki Group was to hold the government to its word. Its tactics were surprisingly legalistic. Of 140 appeals, protests, letters, and other documents produced by the group between 1975 and 1982, all but four referred directly to the Helsinki Act, and many also cited the covenants on human rights, which had been signed by the Soviet Union in 1973 and entered into force in 1976.[32]

The Helsinki Act, and in particular the periodic review process it established, provided, for the first time, a basis for systematic outreach by the dissidents. They targeted Soviet citizens beyond the circle of the Moscow intelligentsia and foreign audiences, especially the burgeoning human rights movement in the United States and the West. In the first thirty-eight days after the formation of the Moscow Helsinki Group, it dispatched almost two thousand pages of documentation on human rights abuses to thirty-five foreign heads of state.[33]

The Final Act contained a section entitled "Follow-up to the Conference," Article 2 of which called for periodic meetings to conduct "a thorough exchange of views both on the implementation of the provisions of the Final Act and of the tasks defined by the Conference." This provision was thought to be of little account at the time, and the United States in fact opposed it, but it became the lever for the "Helsinki process." The first review session was held in Belgrade in 1977, two years after the signing. It lasted through 1979. The second, in Madrid, began in 1980 and continued through 1983. In the 1980s, according to Andrew Moravcsik, "Helsinki review [became] a permanent feature of the European diplomatic landscape."[34] The Moscow Group aggressively exploited the review conferences. For the Belgrade review in 1977, it prepared 26 documents delineating Soviet violations of the act. At the 1980 Madrid conference, the total had risen to 138, divided by themes corresponding to the humanitarian provisions of the Final Act.[35] Similar groups oriented to monitoring the performance of their governments against the standards of Helsinki sprang up in Poland and other Eastern bloc countries. Much of their work was targeted on the review conferences. Charter 77, the Czechoslovak group, took its name in part because 1977 was the year of the first Helsinki review conference. A plethora of U.S. organizations, including Helsinki Watch, the American Council for Soviet Jewry, traditional human rights organizations, and others, supported the efforts of the Soviet and Eastern European NGOs, both by protesting directly to those governments and by bringing pressure on the United States.

According to Joshua Rubenstein, a student of the Soviet human rights movement, "the [Moscow] group's primary strategy was to raise an echo in the West."[36] In this it was successful. At the Belgrade review, the United States was not of a single mind as to how hard to press on human rights issues, and the Europeans were at best lukewarm. As already noted, traditional international law or diplomatic practice did not countenance official criticism of another government's human rights performance, because this was an aspect of its "internal affairs." The Helsinki review process itself was one of the principal developments that were changing all that. By 1980 in Madrid, with Ambassador Max Kampelman heading the American delegation and under pressure from the fully mobilized U.S. human rights movement, the United States and its allies subjected Soviet and East European policies to almost continuous and withering critique throughout the three years of the exercise. Thirty-five of the Helsinki signatories publicly condemned Soviet and Eastern European violations at the Madrid meeting. Kampelman believed that "history would proclaim the Helsinki Final Act of 1975 as a 'moral tuning fork' and one of the most important milestones on the path to peace. It proved to be significantly more. Its distinction is that it established a set of Western values agreed to by thirty-five sovereign nations as standards by which to judge responsible international behavior."[37] Many other observers with less personal involvement concur.[38] Moravcsik believes that "the shaming process may create a symbolic environment that stimulates domestic opposition in non-complying governments" and that, in the case of the Helsinki Accord, it "had a dramatic and unexpected impact in various countries behind the Iron Curtain ... [by] offering a focal point, source of legal language and provisions for legal reforms."[39]

Despite some hyperbolic evaluations of the impact of Helsinki, there can be no doubt that the Helsinki process and Soviet human rights violations ultimately became a major element in Western cold war strategy. For a U.S. foreign policy establishment that had traditionally been hostile to human rights efforts, this took some convincing. It is unlikely that it would have happened without the voice of the Soviet dissidents and their organizations, backed up by continuous pressure from their U.S. NGO counterparts.

Environmental Issues

International Maritime Organization

The intervention of NGOs to expose and shame states for noncompliant behavior is not always as long drawn out as the Helsinki process. In October 1993, Russia dumped hundreds of tons of low-level nuclear waste into the Sea of Japan.[40] Although the level of radioactivity was low enough that the action was not prohibited by the London Convention, it violated a moratorium then in effect. Greenpeace International revealed the Russian action, which was all the more embarrassing because it took place only a few days after a state visit by President Boris Yeltsin to Japan.[41] As a result of the adverse publicity, Russia called off announced plans for a second discharge,[42] and in response to a U.S. initiative, a permanent ban on all nuclear waste dumping was adopted at the IMO meeting in November 1993.[43]

Beginning with the Stockholm Conference on the Human Environment in 1972, international environmental regulation has been much more transparent to NGOs than other aspects of international policy-making. Significant NGO participation in the negotiation and drafting of the major environmental agreements evolved naturally into the monitoring, on a continuing basis, of organizational activity, compliance by members with treaty obligations, and overall regime effectiveness.[44]

As in the human rights area, it sometimes happens that a single NGO or even a single person in it can have a decisive impact on the compliance policy of an international organization. As noted in Chapter 7, reporting by IMO members on prosecutions and convictions for violation of marine oil pollution regulations was at best desultory during the first three decades of the organization's life.[45] Nonperformance stemmed from the usual problems: low priority, organizational indifference, and impenetrable reporting requirements. Gerard Peet, a staff member of Friends of the Earth, the only environmental representative at the IMO, conducted his own study of reporting over the history of the organization, establishing both the reporting failure and the official neglect of the issue.[46] Reporting returned to the IMO agenda, and for the first time the secretariat promulgated a comprehensible reporting form. Compliance jumped significantly, and then improved further after NGO publication of reporting compliance.[47]

The Association of Small Island States

One of the most unusual products of NGO activity is the Association of Small Island States (AOSIS), a coalition that originated in the international negotiations on climate change. As the issue of climate change moved to the head of the international environmental agenda in the late 1980s, the special vulnerability of small island states to the possibility of rising sea levels caused by global warming became an important area of concern. Several conferences, mostly sponsored by the UN Environment Program, drew attention to the problem and provided scientific information.[48] In 1989, the Ford Foundation made a grant to the Centre for International Environmental Law (CIEL), consisting of two London environmental lawyers, to provide legal, tactical, and research assistance to small island states in the forthcoming world climate negotiations. The organizers got CIEL invited to anticipatory conferences of regional organizations in the South Pacific and the Caribbean, and ultimately the Caribbean Ministers of Environment requested it to act as "advisors for the Caribbean Community Regional Group (CARICOM) at the

Second World Climate Conference in Geneva and thereafter in any convention process that followed."[49]

Operating from this base and building on prior contacts among the major island groups, CIEL presided over the organization of AOSIS at the Second World Climate Conference in Geneva in 1989. The coalition consisted of thirty-seven island states, mostly developing countries, and represented all major ocean areas. The CIEL lawyers drafted the group's six-point policy statement. In general, the statement echoed the position of the developing countries on climate change issues, with the addition of a demand for "adequate financial resources and mechanisms, including insurance, which recognize the need to assist small island and low-lying coastal developing countries, some of whose very existence is placed at risk by the consequences of climate change."[50]

Representatives of CIEL attended the sessions of the climate change negotiations as advisors to AOSIS, and CIEL invited Greenpeace to participate as scientific advisor. Before every session of the International Negotiating Committee (INC), the two organizations put together an extended briefing for AOSIS members at which they presented background papers on key issues. During the negotiating sessions, CIEL conducted daily meetings to help AOSIS keep abreast of developments and to coordinate positions and strategy. Since most AOSIS delegates operated under only the most general instructions from their government, the substantive positions of the group on issues arising during the negotiations were worked out in these meetings. One effect of this concentrated activity was to educate the AOSIS delegates and improve their performance in the negotiations.

On the technical side, CIEL prepared a draft treaty to be tabled at the first negotiating session, and, as the negotiations proceeded, drafted changes in the negotiating texts for use by members of AOSIS. The CIEL lawyers were actually attached to some delegations so that they could participate in the formal negotiations, but in any case they were continuously present on the floor to advise the coalition and coordinate its work. Finally, at the instance of CIEL, AOSIS campaigned for a significant formal role within INC and secured the election of Ambassador Robert Van Lierop of Vanuatu, the AOSIS chair, as cochair of one of the two INC working groups.

The Association of Small Island States was organized to participate in the negotiation of the climate change treaty, but the coalition continues its existence in the implementation phase, and CIEL (now renamed as the Foundation for International Environmental Law and Development) continues as its advisor. Its almost forty members quickly ratified the convention and are recognized as responsible for its early entry into force in March 1994. It is actively engaged in the preparatory work for the implementation of the convention, and the small island states were the subject of their own UN conference in April and May 1994.[51]

The projection of NGO influence from negotiating to implementing a treaty is illustrated also by the Chemical Weapons Convention. The Quaker United Nations Center in Geneva performed general facilitative functions during the final years of the CWC negotiations, convening informal meetings to discuss sticky negotiating issues that could not be resolved in formal sessions. The Chemical Manufacturers Association, the U.S. industry trade association, provided crucial assistance by helping to organize national test inspections to demonstrate the feasibility of the verification requirements. The Harvard-Sussex Project, consisting primarily of two well-placed professors of chemistry, one at each institution, established a close working relationship with the negotiating process and provided technical and political advice to delegates. After the convention was signed, the Provisional Technical Secretariat, formed to prepare for the convention's entry into force, invited the Harvard-Sussex Project, with the help of others, to prepare a series of handbooks and other educational and instructional materials to assist signatories in implementing the convention. The subjects include not only the history and background of the CWC and summaries of its main provisions but also detailed guidelines on the domestic legal and administrative arrangements that the parties will have to carry out to bring themselves into compliance.

Since 1970, there have been very few major international conferences without a swarm of NGOs as a significant part of the negotiating environment, establishing contacts in the delegates' lounge, distributing briefing papers, advancing suggestions and drafts on contentious points, exerting pressure, or facilitating interchange among the delegates. Commitments of resources and relationships established during the treaty negotiations commonly continue into the implementation phase, and the same NGO figures are to be found lobbying the secretariats and attending the meetings of the parties.

Wildlife Protection

Nongovernmental organizations were the driving force in the two most visible campaigns of the 1980s for the protection of animal species—those for the whales and the elephants. In many parts of the United States, the Save the Whales bumper sticker became a symbol of the entire environmental movement. As early as 1976, the New Zealand commissioner to the International

Whaling Commission maintained that "like it or not, the whale is now a symbol of mankind's failure to manage the world's resources responsibly."[52]

Both whales and elephants are under the protection of international regimes. The International Whaling Commission dates back to 1946, and the Convention on International Trade in Endangered Species was concluded in 1973, shortly after the Stockholm Conference on the Human Environment.[53] Both organizations make periodic decisions on the level of protection to be accorded to species within their responsibility, the IWC by setting quotas and other regulations on the taking of whales, and CITES by regulating commercial trading in the most severely endangered species. In their approach to these organizations, NGOs have used tactics covering the entire range—from grassroots work with domestic constituencies to sophisticated mass-media campaigns, various kinds of direct action, and lobbying at both the domestic and international levels.

Whales. As noted in Chapter 4, in the immediate postwar decades whaling regulation under the International Convention for the Regulation of Whaling had failed to prevent serious declines in the populations of many whale species, particularly the larger ones. The idea of a complete moratorium on whale hunting first emerged at the Stockholm Conference in 1972, where NGOs floated a huge inflated model of a blue whale outside the conference hall, "expressing rising concern about the future of planetary life in general and of the living ocean in particular."[54] Largely under pressure from the parallel NGO conference, the official Conference on the Human Environment adopted a recommendation for a complete moratorium. During the 1970s, the primary theater of action was in the United States, where, U.S. NGOs were able to secure the enactment of the Packwood-Magnuson and Pelly Amendments, authorizing trade sanctions against countries that were "diminishing the effectiveness" of a conservation regime.[55] Although the U.S. government did not enforce these sanctions as vigorously as some had hoped, it became a leading advocate of the moratorium in the IWC from the mid-1970s on.

The IWC finally voted a moratorium in 1982. Thereafter the NGOs began to target individual noncomplying or opt-out countries.[56] Inflatable whales reappeared—on Valentine's Day in 1982 at the Japanese consulate in Boston[57] and when Greenpeace activists stuffed hundreds of them into Japan Airlines offices in 1985.[58] Again in 1988, the whale, draped with a banner in Japanese that read, "Research whaling is an abuse of science," was deployed to block a Japanese whaling ship ready to sail.[59] In 1990 Greenpeace sent a 125-foot inflated humpback and a 30-foot minke whale on tour across the

United States and eventually to Japan, where Japanese environmental groups presented the minke model (with more than 7,000 signatures on its surface) to the prime minister, in support of a petition to stop "research" whaling.[60] Nongovernmental organizations in the United States continued to press for the application of statutory sanctions to noncomplying states. Consumer boycott was also a frequent tactic. In 1980, at the urging of Greenpeace, German supermarkets, the Nordsee Fish Company in Iceland, and New England school districts all canceled contracts for Iceland's fishery products. A 1989 boycott of Iceland was estimated to have cost it $50 million in fish exports. The minister of fisheries promised not to conduct research whaling the following year.[61] A major campaign to boycott Norwegian fish products and even the Norwegian Cruise Line followed Norway's refusal to abide by the one-year renewal of the moratorium in 1992.[62]

Greenpeace also indulges in less playful types of direct action. Members of the group have chained themselves to harpoons aboard whaling vessels and confronted whalers at sea.[63] In 1980, small boats from the *Rainbow Warrior* surrounded a Spanish whaler to interpose themselves between the ship and any whales that appeared.[64] In 1984, members of the group boarded a Soviet ship, and similar operations were launched against Norway in 1986.[65] Another organization called Sea Shepherd has actually rammed and used electric mines to sink whalers.[66] All these forays were carefully calculated with a view to maximum media impact and were closely coordinated with television news enterprises.[67]

Meanwhile, international NGOs, led by the International Union for the Conservation of Nature (IUCN), the World Wildlife Fund (WWF) and Greenpeace, mounted a crescendo of pressure in the international forum. The number of NGOs at IWC meetings rose from five in 1965 to twenty-four in 1978 and more than fifty in the 1980s, and their "links to the management of marine resources were—by traditional standards—no longer as clear as they had used to be."[68] Moreover they were now permitted to participate directly in the meetings, rather than having to remain silently on the back benches as observers.

> These organizations have contributed to the change of the very atmosphere and climate surrounding the IWC meetings. The IWC meetings were no longer confined to discussing technicalities and difficult scientific issues far away from the attention of the public and the media. The non-whaling nations and the environmental organizations were the agenda setters and media attention was one way of achieving their aim of stopping commercial whaling.[69]

Increasingly since 1978, NGOs have commissioned and presented research studies designed to demonstrate the inadequacy of the scientific basis of the management system on which existing quotas were based.[70] They have investigated violations of existing regulations both in support of stronger compliance efforts and to demonstrate the ineffectiveness of the sustained-yield regime.[71] As in other international organization meetings, at the IWC they provide technical and tactical assistance to delegations, particularly those from developing countries that lack expertise or personnel, and publish a daily newsletter, *ECO,* for circulation among the delegates. In the United States, NGOs confer with representatives from the Departments of State and Justice before every IWC meeting, and similar meetings are held in the United Kingdom and Australia.[72]

In the whaling case, however, the NGOs seem to have gone further. The IWC takes decisions on quotas by a three-fourths majority. Until the end of the 1960s, IWC membership remained a "whalers' club" of about fifteen countries, all of them with whaling industries. Then some of the existing members began to abandon whaling and new countries began to join. Some of the newcomers were whaling states pressured by the United States to join so that their activities would be subject to the restraints of the regime. But many were nonwhaling states. The NGOs mounted a "membership drive" to recruit developing countries, many with little direct interest in whales. The avowed objective was to achieve the three-fourths majority necessary to vote the moratorium.[73] The NGOs paid the annual dues and expenses of attendance at IWC meetings for some of these countries. Greenpeace is said to have gone still further, drafting and submitting the required membership documents and assigning Greenpeace members to represent these "states of convenience" at IWC meetings.[74] The Seychelles, a leader in the movement for the moratorium, on first addressing the IWC in 1979, felt obliged to insist that it was not speaking "as a client state for any strong cause without a country."[75] On the other hand, Steinar Andresen points out that

> Politically the IWC was an arena where the voice of the developing countries could be heard. Especially so after the increasing tendency—among non-whaling developing and developed countries alike—to look on whales as the "common heritage of mankind" ...
>
> ... For developed and developing countries alike, participation in the IWC on the conservationist side was also a relatively "politically cheap" way of giving your country an "environmentalist" profile; most countries had nothing to lose economically by protecting the whales and at the same time they had something to gain politically.[76]

The drive went over the top at the 1982 meeting at Brighton, England. Sixteen new members, almost all developing countries, had joined since 1980. They provided the three-fourths majority needed to vote a ten-year moratorium on all commercial whaling, beginning after a three-year phase-in period in 1986.[77] The Greenpeace vessel *Cedarlea* was in the harbor as a warning to states that voted no.[78]

As discussed in Chapter 5, it is not clear that the moratorium strategy has been wholly salutary. During the 1980s, whaling by the principal whaling nations continued, mostly under reservations or the rubric of "research whaling." And when the IWC renewed the moratorium in 1992, Iceland left the organization and Norway began whaling again. The question as to which principle—"no whaling," or "sustained yield whaling"—will result in the least whaling remains open.

Elephants. The objectives and timing of the fifteen-year campaign to protect the elephants were largely dictated by a few nongovernmental organizations. The IUCN and the WWF, together with a few other organizations, seem to have been in charge from the beginning of the effort in 1976 to its culmination with the ban on ivory trade in 1989. Familiar NGO tactics reappear. There were major media events, like the public burning of twelve tons of contraband ivory by Daniel arap Moi, the president of Kenya, in July 1989.[79] Consumers were asked to boycott ivory. And in Lausanne, as the CITES Conference of the Parties met to consider a ban on commercial ivory trade, children masked in tusks paraded through the meeting hall on one day, while on another, schoolchildren trooped in with an inflated elephant floating above them.[80]

Unlike the IWC, CITES has always been a wide-open organization, in 1994 numbering more than one hundred parties. Not all of them, of course, are equally concerned with species preservation. The convention regulates trade in specimens of all species "threatened with extinction which are or may be affected by trade" (listed in Appendix I to the convention), and of species which "may become so unless trade in specimens of such species is subject to strict regulation" (listed in Appendix II).[81] For Appendix I species, commercial trade is generally prohibited.[82] For Appendix II specimens, the exporting country must certify that the export will not be detrimental to the survival of the species and that it is not in contravention of the laws of that state.[83] A species is placed in an appendix or moved from one to the other by a two-thirds vote of the Conference of Parties, subject to the right of dissenters to opt out by filing a reservation within ninety days.[84] The relationship between the IUCN, the WWF and CITES has been close and continuing. For a considerable period the IUCN performed secretariat services for CITES, and the IUCN's "Red Book" is, in effect, the CITES database.[85] The CITES secretariat still relies on the WWF's publication, *Traffic,* as a primary means of communicating with its constituency.

The IUCN's Survival Service Commission established an Elephant Group as early as 1976, to study the situation and prepare an action plan. In 1977 the African elephant was placed in Appendix II.[86] Although there was concern about declining elephant populations in East Africa, a 1982–83 study by the U.S. Fish and Wildlife Service attributed the decline to habitat loss.[87] As the end of the decade approached, however, the focus of concern shifted to poaching, which seemed susceptible to correction by means of trade regulation, while habitat loss was not. In 1986, CITES established a quota system for exports,[88] but a study commissioned by the WWF (in cooperation with the EC) indicated that East African elephant populations continued to fall at alarming rates.[89] The author, Ian Douglas-Hamilton, was adamant in his conclusion that "drought and human encroachment [were] not killing the animals"—poachers were.[90] Other NGOs joined the chorus, and the report received wide publicity.[91]

But even Douglas-Hamilton rejected the idea of a total ban on ivory trade, and the NGO community followed suit. "In the spring of 1988, it would have been hard to find a scientist or conservationist with experience in Africa who did believe in a total ban as the solution to elephant poaching."[92] The situation was complicated because South Africa, Botswana, Zimbabwe, and other southern African states had excellent management programs under which the herds were thriving. The income from meat, hides, and tusks of culled animals was used to support the conservation program, and poaching was minimal. Even the African Wildlife Foundation, when it called for a consumer boycott on ivory purchases in the spring of 1988, did not support an official ban. "We felt that it would be arrogant and inappropriate for outsiders to tell Africa what to do about a natural resource of theirs."[93] As late as February of 1989, a meeting of the African Elephant Coordinating Group, consisting of governments and leading NGOs in the field, concluded that a trade ban would not be helpful, because it would mainly serve to drive the trade underground (as had happened in the case of the black rhino). Instead the group endorsed an action plan calling for rational use and management of the existing herds.[94]

Within six months, all this had changed. On June 1, 1989, Wildlife Conservation International and the WWF called for an immediate worldwide ban on ivory imports.[95] A spokesman for Friends of Animals, however, expressing the view of other NGOs in the field, maintained that leaders of the WWF were "the last ones to jump on the bandwagon . . .; they only flip-flopped after they saw that the rest of the world had already changed." Within days the United States and the European Community imposed national bans.[96] In July, President Daniel arap Moi of Kenya set $3 million worth of ivory on fire (an event staged by a Washington lobbying firm) to symbolize Kenya's support of a total ban on ivory trade.[97] "By the time of the CITES vote," says Raymond Bonner, "it was hard to find a conservationist who was willing to speak out publicly against the ban."[98] Although the southern African states continued their opposition, the vote at the Lausanne conference was overwhelmingly for moving the African elephant to Appendix I.

Changes in the situation in East Africa were cited in support of this reversal. A new study conducted by Douglas-Hamilton for the Ivory Trade Group (an NGO consortium) concluded that half the African elephants had been wiped out since 1979 and that "all attempts to control the ivory trade had proved futile."[99] A television report on illegal ivory trade produced by an English NGO, the Environmental Investigation Agency, was released to coincide with Tanzania's call for a trade ban. East African states, like Kenya and Tanzania, endorsed the ban, as did Kenya's new wildlife conservation director, the widely respected Richard Leakey.[100]

But Bonner had a short answer to the question, why the change—"public emotion and money."[101] In his view, the NGOs drove the policy, and the demands of fund-raising and membership drove the NGOs. The African Wildlife Foundation, the International Wildlife Coalition, and others saw their receipts and membership increase as their advertising took an increasingly categorical tone.[102] "We rode on the backs of elephants and rhinos for years," said the director of South Africa's Endangered Wildlife Trust.[103] The debate within the WWF was particularly intense. Although professional Africanists and conservationists on the staff favored sticking to the organization's traditional sustainable-use principles, the argument that carried the day was that "failure to endorse a ban . . . would have 'a seriously detrimental effect on our membership.'"[104] Bonner is not alone in his view. After the Lausanne vote, the delegate from Gabon remarked bitterly that "the chief economic benefit of the elephant was its ability to generate income for conservationists in developed countries."[105]

The ban proved to be a success, however. Japan abstained on the final vote on the moratorium, but on the last day of the conference it announced that, "respecting the overwhelming sentiment of the international community," it would not take a reservation.[106] As a Japanese diplomat had said earlier in the year, "We don't want another whale."[107] It had been made clear that

Japan would not be chosen to host the following year's CITES conference if it reserved.[108] The United Kingdom, somewhat surprisingly, entered a reservation for Hong Kong, but only for six months, to permit it to run down stocks. The southern African states also reserved, but announced that they would not exercise their rights until the issue was reexamined at the 1992 conference. When the ban was renewed at that time, the southern African states withdrew their reservation.[109] Surveys indicate that poaching is down, and many ivory workers are unemployed. The price of ivory has dropped on both the legal and the black market.[110]

The Impact of the NGOs

In all these cases, the activities of the NGOs made a difference. The development and elaboration of norms and states' policies on compliance with existing norms cannot be explained without attributing significant causal power to the activities of the NGOs.

The members of the International Maritime Organization went along comfortably for years without paying much attention to the reporting requirements, until Gerard Peet, on behalf of Friends of the Earth, called attention to them. Even if the small island states on their own had managed to form a coalition in the climate change negotiations, it would have been looser, less informed, and less effective without CIEL. It is hard to account for the position of the United States, the United Kingdom, Australia, and other Western supporters of the ban on whale hunting and ivory trading under traditional conceptions of state interests.

The same is true of the human rights cases. There is no reason to suppose that Nigeria would have improved its prisons without the prod of CLO. The UN campaign against Chile was fueled by the ardor and evidence of the human rights organizations, and they exploited the institutional precedents forged against Chile to pursue other violators. The United States hung back from exploiting the Helsinki process until activated by Soviet and U.S. NGOs.

A good part of the NGO effect can be explained by opening up the model of the unitary state actor to take account of the role of domestic politics in determining state interests and policies.[111] But not all. In some circumstances, NGOs seem to be able to go over the heads of governments to mobilize a process of public shaming and reputational pressure unrelated to vote getting or other aspects of domestic political power. In the Chile case, over time the junta was forced to bend to international human rights norms, although apart from the UN pronouncements driven largely by the NGOs, it was never the target of strong economic or diplomatic pressure. Indeed, in the 1980s the United States voted against General Assembly and Human Rights Commission condemnation of Chile and for World Bank loans to it. Nigeria was never in internal or external political danger because of its prison conditions. Japan went against strong internal constituencies in accepting the ban on ivory trade, because it didn't want "another whale."

The international organizations themselves are in uneasy partnership with the NGOs. National governments, as we discuss in Chapter 12, are increasingly unwilling to invest substantially in intergovernmental organizations. The deficiencies in resources and information are often made up by the nongovermental organizations. Most important, the NGOs are responsible, to a large extent, for the public awareness that determines the position and importance of the international organization on the international stage. From this point of view, the NGOs are an important asset to the compliance strategies of the international bureaucracy, just as they are for sympathetic elements in the domestic governmental establishment. At the same time, the NGOs can raise problems for international as well as domestic foreign policy officials. Their agendas and timing almost never coincide exactly with that of the international organization and can complicate the delicate task of trying to influence national governments while not offending them.

Even from a more detached perspective, their influence is not always positive. Sometimes their efforts to improve a regime can backfire. "Packing" the IWC with controlled votes is not self-evidently justified by the objective of banning whale hunting. There may be good reasons for overriding the needs of the effective southern African sustained-yield programs for managing elephant herds, but NGO funding requirements is not one of them. Even in the human rights area, the title of largely white, Western, affluent, and liberal NGOs to control both the priorities and the content of the norms is not universally acknowledged. In the environmental and human rights fields, states have begun to try to rein in the NGOs. At the insistence of China and other Asian states, they were excluded from the drafting committee at the 1993 UN Conference on Human Rights in Vienna, and their participation privileges under the FCCC are narrower than under the Montreal Protocol.[112]

These maneuvers testify to the growing power of NGOs to influence policy and force compliance with treaty norms, and it is unlikely that NGOs will be brought under control or that their influence will decline. International issues like human rights and environmental affairs, among others, strike too deeply at the concerns of ordinary people to be left entirely in the hands of diplomats.

12

Revitalizing International Organizations

In the preceding chapters we have discussed the instruments available to international regimes to induce compliance with treaty obligations—the normative framework, reporting and transparency, verification, review and assessment, dispute settlement, and interpretation—and we have considered to what extent they are and how they might be combined into a coherent compliance strategy. These processes do not arise and operate spontaneously, of course. Their effectiveness depends heavily on the institutional setting in which they are deployed. States parties to treaties, acting unilaterally or in concert and with the occasionally unwelcome assistance of nongovernmental organizations, can sometimes activate these instruments. This loose and decentralized model is appealing in an era of extreme skepticism about the capacities of governmental and bureaucratic institutions. Peter Haas, Robert Keohane, and Marc Levy, while stressing the importance of international institutions "as magnifiers of concern, facilitators of agreement, and builders of capacity," hasten to reassure their readers that these "do not require large administrative bureaucracies."[1] But it is no coincidence that the regimes with the most impressive compliance strategies—ILO, IMF, OECD, GATT—are operated by substantial, well-staffed, and well-functioning international organizations.

International organizations occupy an important place throughout this book, and in Chapter 5 we gave a more extended account of their role in the development of treaty norms. In this chapter we first examine the paths and patterns of influence by which international organizations can affect national decision making. International organizations are supposed to be the creatures of their member states. How does it happen that "faceless international bureaucrats," unelected and without the power of purse or sword,[2] can affect the decisions of these members to comply with treaty obligations? Finally, we revisit the question of the institutional capabilities that will be required in an international system that makes increasing demands for cooperative regulation of major common problems.

Although there were a few multinational organizations in the nineteenth century, mainly in Europe, "the move to institutions" began decisively with the League of Nations and its satellite bodies after World War I. A generation later, at the end of World War II, an extraordinary burst of institutional architecture brought into being not only the United Nations and its subsidiary organs but also the Bretton Woods institutions, as well as organizations to regulate fields like international civil aviation, maritime transport, telecommunications, food and agriculture, health, meteorology, labor, and international trade. Today there are literally hundreds of these institutions of every stripe and variety.[3]

An international organization typically consists of decision-making organs made up of representatives of member states, a secretariat with a seat, specific locations in time and space, identifiable resources, and personnel with defined roles and power relationships. These bureaucratic characteristics make the organization an entity apart from the sum of its members and with a degree of autonomy from them.[4] An account of their activities in securing compliance with international obligations must draw on theories of bureaucratic organization and behavior. The international organizations operate primarily from the top down, through their interaction with national bureaucracies, rather than (like the NGOs) as actual participants in national politics. The governments that are members of the organization typically assign responsibility for matters concerning the treaty to appropriate components of their own bureaucratic establishments.[5] The relationships and interactions between these international and domestic bureaucracies are major factors in implementing compliance strategies. We examine this impact along two dimensions—political and bureaucratic.

Political Bargaining

International organizations are political institutions—arenas for political interaction among the members, their representatives, and the staff. Like all politics, this involves persuasion (appeals to norms, interests, policy analysis) and power. There is also an important element of political bargaining, generating a continuous exchange of commitments among the participants.[6] The management strategy described in the preceding chapters can be seen in part as just such a bargaining process, eventuating in commitments, as to future performance under the agreement. The organizational setting conduces strongly to carrying out these commitments. Keohane argues that international organizations enhance the credibility of commitments because they "raise the costs of deception and irresponsibility."[7] Commitments made within an organizational framework are visible to the participants, and they are part of a stream of favors, promises, and patronage exchanged over time. Lisa Martin emphasizes the importance of "the array of issue-linkages generated by international institutions": "These structures provide benefits to states across a range of issues and these benefits depend on members demonstrating that they can be trusted to live up to their institutional commitments."[8] Martin's work is concerned with eliciting cooperation in the imposition of sanctions, but the same mechanism should operate even more strongly to promote compliance with the substantive regulatory norms of the organization to which the parties have agreed.

By issue linkage, Martin seems to have in mind a straightforward kind of logrolling. Her prime example is the Falklands/Malvinas war, where Great Britain, in order to gain European Community support for sanctions against Argentina, conceded on a number of unrelated issues being contested within the EC. But in international organizations, as in other political settings, specific reciprocity is not the only or even the most important form of exchange. When a member of an organization goes back on a commitment, it compromises in some degree its reputation as a reliable partner and jeopardizes its ability to continue to reap organizational benefits.[9] Moreover, the organizational process generates a continuous flow of transactions, most of them of small intrinsic importance yet capable of serving as counters in a unending game of political bargaining. Votes on resolutions of varying sponsorship and importance, procedural matters, scheduling, membership on committees and working groups, organizational offices, even excusing or overlooking incidents of noncompliance all represent, in one aspect, inducements or disbenefits that can be calibrated to reinforce a party's commitment to the treaty norms.

Keohane goes beyond this "running account" concept in emphasizing "the interests of continuing satisfactory results for the group . . . as a whole" as motivating compliance with these commitments. In the conditions of the new sovereignty, the stakes are even higher, because the state's position in both the particular organization and the system at large is continuously under scrutiny.

It is not only the reputation of the state that counts but also that of the persons who represent it. Political exchanges in international organizations take place among diplomats, who are, of course, understood to be agents presenting the positions and decisions of their principals. Yet the diplomats' reputations—even acting in a representational capacity—for candor, promise keeping, and inducing their government to live up to its commitments is an important professional asset, not lightly put at risk. Despite a reservoir of professional sympathy, it remains difficult to explain before an audience of sophisticated and informed colleagues with whom you are engaged in trying to promote and enhance a regulatory regime that your government has found it impossible to comply with one or another of its undertakings. Delivering the message during the negotiations for the Montreal Protocol that the United States had revoked its earlier commitment to contribute ozone fund resources "additional" to existing foreign aid flows was, according to Ambassador Richard J. Smith, the hardest thing he had ever had to do.[10] This, of course, is how diplomats earn their pay, but "policy-makers, like private individuals, are sensitive to the social opprobrium that accompanies violations of widely accepted behavioral prescriptions. They are, in short, motivated by a desire to avoid the sense of shame or social disgrace that commonly befalls those who break widely accepted rules."[11]

Bureaucracy

Students of bureaucracy tell us that these organizations act to advance their own interests, expand their role in policy making, and enhance their own power and prestige, conceived primarily in terms of the size of staff and budget.[12] Unlike its members, the international organization is an entity whose raison d'être is the treaty. At least presumptively, it will be committed to treaty compliance.[13] Likewise, the process by which the treaty is negotiated and adopted means that the responsible domestic bureaucracies will also have a strong commitment to the objectives and policies of the treaty, and thus to compliance.[14] At the same time, a domestic bureaucracy must respond to domestic interests and constituency pressures, which will include some mix of supporters, opponents, and those for whom the treaty does not carry a high priority. Moreover, although treaty negotiations and relations with other treaty partners are generally conducted under the supervision of the foreign ministry, the bureaucratic or legislative bodies with responsibility for implementation at the domestic level may or may not be part of the foreign policy–making apparatus.[15] In the United States, for example, arms control matters are dealt with by the foreign affairs bureaucracy—the State Department, the Defense Department, and the Arms Control and Disarmament Agency (ACDA). Trade issues are the province of the U.S. trade representative (USTR) in the Office of the President, as well as the International Trade Commission and the Commerce Department. Environmental enforcement is a matter for the Environmental Protection Agency (EPA). Thus the responsibility for treaty negotiation and treaty implementation is often diffused among a number of agencies and, in a federal state like the United States or Canada, among a number of governments.[16] How does the international organization operate to change the mix and the policy vectors that emerge from the balance of domestic considerations in the direction of treaty compliance?

Control of the Agenda

At its most basic, the international secretariat influences action through its control of the organizational routine. We have already noted the role of organizational secretariats in the review and assessment process. But more generally, the life cycle of an international organization consists of periodic meetings of its various organs and working groups that make policy decisions. Graham Allison and Richard Neustadt have taught the importance of such meetings in the domestic context in setting deadlines and providing occasions for decision.[17] The content of these meetings is framed by jurisdictional assignments as well as instructions and decisions of prior meetings or superior bodies. Within these broad limits, a strong secretariat will prepare the agenda, the documentation, and the initial drafts of instruments in which decisions will be recorded. Thus the bureaucracy has considerable sway over what the members of the organization talk about and over the informational base of their decisions.

Control of the agenda is one of the classic sources of power in decision-making bodies.[18] In the international context, Mustapha Tolba, the executive director of the UN Environment Program, an agency with a very small budget and no formal powers, was able to define the agenda for environmental treaty making during the 1970s and 1980s. The regional seas program—which spawned subsidiary organizations and treaties for the Mediterranean, the Baltic, the Caribbean, and other basins—the Vienna Convention on the Protection of the Ozone Layer and its subsequent protocols, the Tropical Forest Action Plan, the Basel Convention on Hazardous Wastes, and the Framework Convention on Climate Change, among others, were in whole or part products of his entrepreneurial initiative.[19]

The actions of Director General Hans Blix to strengthen the International Atomic Energy Agency safeguards system in the wake of the disclosures about the Iraqi nuclear program illustrate the impact that control of the agenda can have in the context of implementation and compliance. Blix proposed a series of actions to the Board of Governors to improve and strengthen the safeguards system. They included an official interpretation of the safeguards agreement to permit "special inspections" of undeclared nuclear facilities in certain circumstances, permission to use information supplied by national intelligence agencies to evaluate the need for such inspections, and the first steps toward the introduction of a comprehensive system of reporting on imports, exports, and domestic production of nuclear materials and facilities.[20] By simply placing the items on the agenda, the director general was able to force some kind of action on all of these contentious issues, which many of the members would no doubt have preferred to avoid. A similar and more regularized example of the power of agenda control in an international bureaucracy is seen in the European Commission, which, by adopting a proposed directive or regulation, can force the member governments of the European Community to vote on far-reaching economic regulations when they may have neither the desire nor the ability to secure favorable action from their own legislatures. By contrast, Ronald Mitchell argues that the failure of the International Maritime Organization secretariat to give reporting issues a prominent place on the agenda at annual meetings was an important cause of the members' neglect of reporting requirements.[21]

Carrots and Sticks

Of the more direct forms of influence, international bureaucrats, unlike their domestic counterparts, never have authority to impose punitive sanctions. We have already shown that coercive sanctions are infrequently provided for in regulatory treaties and even less frequently invoked. When they are, it is a matter of the highest politics, and the decision is made directly by the members. Similarly, although economic incentives bulk large among instruments available to domestic bureaucracies, few international treaty organizations dispose of significant financial resources. The one important exception is the IMF, which dispenses more foreign economic assistance than all bilateral aid programs combined. There, the managing director and staff play a major, if not dominant, role in negotiating and renegotiating the performance conditions to be imposed on members using the fund's resources and in determining whether the conditions have been met.

The environmental field is a new area in which the possibility of financial reward may be available to promote compliance. As already noted, the ozone fund established under the London Amendments to the Montreal Protocol amounted to $240 million over the first three years and was increased to $510 million in the second triennium.[22] The FCCC and the Biodiversity Convention also establish funds to meet incremental compliance costs, although the amounts have yet to be settled.[23] In these treaties, the obligations of the developed countries to contribute is given point by a warning that "the extent to which developing country parties will effectively implement their commitments under the Convention will depend on the effective implementation by developed countries of their commitments related to financial resources and transfer of technology."[24] For most international organizations, however, technical assistance is almost the only material incentive they can provide, and even this is falling victim to shrinking budgets and waning commitment to the foreign aid enterprise. Sometimes the organization provides the funds to finance the attendance of developing country delegations to meetings, as UNEP did during the ozone negotiations.

Nevertheless, these organizations manage to influence the policies of their members. A particularly impressive example is the World Health Organization's activities with respect to international population programs. A careful study concluded (as of 1976) that "neither the member governments of WHO nor the empirical findings of scientific research have dictated the particular courses of action WHO pursued in the population field. Rather . . . the critical decisions in this area have been made largely by the WHO bureaucracy and determined by the organizational and professional values that prevail in the WHO Secretariat."[25]

At first, to stave off dissension and perhaps withdrawals by member countries with large Catholic populations, WHO officialdom maintained that population growth and family planning were primarily social and economic matters outside the purview of medicine and public health. With increased international concern about population growth, this position became untenable, however. The WHO shifted, but demanded that family planning activities be integrated "as part of an organized health service, without impairing its normal preventive and curative functions."[26] The effect was to discourage population control policies unrelated to health services, such as numerical targets for reducing fertility, mass sterilization programs, and delivery of family planning services through mobile units, all of which were strongly supported by most proponents of vigorous population limitation efforts.

When WHO's control of the turf was threatened in the 1970s by the establishment of the UN Fund for Population Activities (UNFPA), the secretariat mobilized its formidable constituency of health ministries, medical groups and NGOs to persuade governments and the international community to maintain the integration of family planning and health under the control and supervision of the health sector.[27] The authors describe the policy-making process as follows:

> Although WHO member governments made the formal decisions, WHO officials played a highly influential role in determining WHO policies in the population field. In the process of formulating WHO's population mandate, the Secretariat participated in drafting the resolutions for the World Health Assembly, provided the necessary background documentation, and was actively involved in building consensus in support of the resolutions. The influence of WHO's permanent staff members has been even more pronounced in the interpretation and application of WHO policy to specific country settings. WHO officials and the experts they have consulted have developed guidelines covering all aspects of family planning programs, including leadership, organization, training, and evaluation. A prime objective of the Secretariat has been to assure that national family programs are administered within health ministries and to prevent attempts to give them greater autonomy even within health systems.[28]

Bureaucratic Alliances

The interpenetration of international organizations and their domestic bureaucratic constituents is far more extensive and subtle than a quid quo pro for technical assistance or other perquisites. Two decades ago, Joseph Nye and Robert Keohane pointed out that "when the same officials meet recurrently, they sometimes develop a sense of collegiality, which may be reinforced by their membership in a common profession, such as economics, physics, or meteorology . . . [T]ransgovernmental elite networks are created, linking officials in various governments to one another by ties of common interest, professional orientation, and personal friendship."[29] These recurrent meetings often take place at or under the aegis of the international organization and are serviced by the international secretariat, whose members are in fact part of the network.

This phenomenon is strikingly illustrated in the early experience of the GATT in the decade or so immediately after World War II. The agreement was negotiated by senior trade officials of the participating countries as a part of broader negotiations for the aborted International Trade Organization. The first GATT director general, Wyndham Lewis, had been a leading spirit in the negotiations. Most of his small staff was drawn from officials who had participated. Delegates and representatives sent by members to routine GATT meetings also tended to come from among the negotiators. The result was a group of both national and international bureaucrats heavily invested in the success of the organization. They were, in the literal sense, an "interpretive community"[30] who knew what the provisions of the agreement meant, since it embodied their own intentions as negotiators. They shared the policy ideals and goals of the GATT, the more so since its creation had been one of the most important professional experiences of their careers. They were the keepers of the flame. Observers have attributed an asserted decline in GATT compliance in the late 1960s and 1970s in part to the replacement of these officials by younger successors who had not been "present at the creation."[31] A similar development marked the post–World War II ILO under David Morse.

In a number of organizations, the international secretariat worked consciously to create such a "transgovernmental elite network." As noted in Chapter 10, the development of professionally sophisticated and sympathetic national economic bureaucracies has been an important byproduct of IMF surveillance and lending activities.[32] Similarly, a major objective of the WHO secretariat was the development of public health personnel and administrators in developing countries. Its activities focused on "the problems of the developing countries in health planning, health manpower, and the integration and extension of preventive and curative health services." The secretariat supported activities that "left behind . . . a permanent 'infrastructure' of personnel and facilities capable of dealing with other health problems."[33] In the elaboration of population policy discussed above, an important objective was to protect WHO's special relationship with health ministries in developing countries.

> No relationship is more important to WHO: national health administrators from these countries are the major clientele for WHO assistance; they constitute the major pressure group for expanding the program and budget of WHO; and they represent their governments in the World Health Assembly . . . The Secretariat is therefore conscious that its most dependable allies in recommending growth in the organization's resources are health ministries from the Third World.
>
> . . . [I]ts alliance with national health ministries has remained its overriding commitment—a commitment that health ministries regard as equally advantageous to them.[34]

Mutatis mutandis, the description would fit many if not most well-developed international organizations. These transnational bureaucratic networks are essentially coalitions in support of the international organization's objectives. Keohane and Nye were quick to recognize the role of international organizations as incubators of such coalitions.

> One of the important but seldom noted roles of international organizations in world politics is to provide the arena for sub-units of governments to turn potential or tacit coalitions into explicit coalitions characterized by direct communication among the partners. In this particular bit of political alchemy, the organization provides physical proximity, an agenda of issues on which interaction is to take place, and an aura of legitimacy. Informal discussions occur naturally in meetings of international organizations, and it is difficult, given the milieu, for other sub-units of one's own government to object to these contacts.[35]

The implication, at least, is that the international organization helps shield these "sub-units"—the domestic bureaucracies with responsibilities within the area of concern—from the control of central foreign policy–making authorities and from other pressures that might militate against compliance with the organization's mandate. And vice versa: a characteristic use of the GATT is to shield the foreign office against domestic demands for protection against imports. The characteristic division of national bureaucracies into smaller units with differing priorities and emphasis provides many opportunities for the international organization to find domestic allies to help forward its programs and priorities, as against countervailing forces within national governments and political processes. Thus, the Cambridge-trained economists in developing-country finance ministries provided a cadre of support for the IMF's norms of monetary behavior.

So with the Med Plan. Mostafa Tolba and the UNEP secretariat used their minuscule technical assistance budget to forge a "transnational alliance with regional marine scientists," who then provided advice to their governments consistent with UNEP's own preferences. By using a number of LDC institutions as lead laboratories for the Med Plan monitoring projects, he was able to attract their allegiance to UNEP away from their own governments, who were not forthcoming with research funds.[36] The result at the international level was a comprehensive set of arrangements going further and taking a broader view of pollution than the initial interests of any of the individual governments, and at the national level it was increased support for Med Plan and for enforcement of its protocols.[37] As might be expected, pressures for compliance generally came from environmental ministries, many of which had been strengthened by UNEP's assistance and staffed by its scientific allies.[38]

Based on his study of Med Plan, Peter Haas advances a more general theory of "epistemic communities" to explain the coordination of state policies in the environmental area. Although designed for different purposes, the relevant parts of this approach support the analysis of transnational bureaucratic interaction we have developed.

An epistemic community, according to Haas, is "a network of knowledge-based experts"—"professionals with recognized expertise and competence in a particular domain or issue area."[39] Haas locates epistemic communities, at least initially, outside governments and more specifically in academia. His theory is essentially an explanation of how innovations and new ideas developed in the academy come to affect governmental policy.[40] His answer: through "the political infiltration of an epistemic community into governing institutions" as officials or advisors, who then use their positions of power to implement the shared beliefs and policy orientation of the community.[41]

Haas's interest is in international policy coordination, and the epistemic communities of interest to him are transnational in scope. The diffusion of new ideas throughout the international system, so as to provide the basis for coordination in adoption and implementation of policy, is his primary interest. Although this diffusion can occur through normal scientific and academic channels, public and official bodies often play a key role.

> A transnational community's ideas may take root in an international organization or in various state bodies, after which they are diffused to other states via the decision makers who have been influenced by the ideas. As a result, the community can have a systemic impact. Because of its larger diffusion network, a transnational community's influence is likely to be much more sustained and intense than that of a national community.[42]

Once the epistemic community has insinuated itself into the policy-making process,[43] the account of how it influences policy coordination is necessarily in large part a story of interactions within and among the bureaucracies that implement the policy, as well as with the NGOs and other allies in the political community. And as Haas himself realizes, the bureaucracy may play a more active role than simply as a conduit of ideas generated outside its walls. On the contrary, bureaucrats may use the community for their own purposes: to pursue "the political goal of building domestic or international coalitions in support of their policies" or to "legitimate package deals."[44] In describing the influence of Keynesian economists on the post–World War II economic settlement, G. John Ikenberry emphasizes that they "did not really stand alone outside of government. The efforts of government officials in Britain and the United States to get postwar planning started helped to stimulate the thinking and give organizational form to the experts."[45] In any event, at the stage of policy implementation—of treaty compliance, in our terms—bureaucratic alliances and practices assume the principal role. "Even if community members were initially consulted to clarify policy alternatives in a given domain, rather than to identify state interests, once their ideas are assimilated and institutionalized, they continue to influence state practice in that domain through institutional habit and inertia."[46]

Future Prospects

The foregoing may be thought an excessively roseate account of international bureaucracies. Throughout the 1970s and 1980s, the countries that pay most of the freight, led by the United States, became seriously disaffected by UN organizations and sought to impose more stringent budgetary and policy discipline on the international secretariats.[47] In part this new skepticism may have been a response to the very success of the international organizations in establishing a degree of policy autonomy. It is certainly true, for example, that the U.S. withdrawal from the UN Education, Scientific, and Cultural Organization, discussed in Chapter 3, reflected a distaste not only for "wasteful spending" but also for the unwillingness of the secretary general to accept the policy priorities of the United States and the West. More broadly, many of the specialized agencies, as exemplified by WHO, regard the developing countries as their principal clients, and secretariats tend to cater to their needs and interests. In fact universal international organizations, because of their one country one vote and consensus voting rules, are forums where countries less well endowed with the traditional accoutrements of power can press their agenda. Political disenchantment was confirmed by academic studies criticizing both the efficiency and effectiveness of the international bureaucracies.[48] They seemed to manifest the same dank and impacted characteristics as their domestic counterparts, perhaps to a heightened degree because of the attenuated political accountability on the international scene.

This changing attitude continues to manifest itself in the shrinking budgets of existing agencies and in an extreme resistance to the creation of new ones on the traditional model of the 1950s and 1960s. The IAEA, established in

1968, may be the exemplar of this pattern.[49] Even in the environmental field, where new and complex international agreements have proliferated, there is hostility to well-endowed international organizations. The UN Environment Program, the organizational product of the Stockholm Conference, was designed as a "program" not an "organization." It was conceived as a low-budget, small-scale entity with catalytic and coordinating functions rather than operational responsibilities. In subsequent environmental treaties, the operating arm is the Conference of the Parties, not only nominally but in actual practice. Special committees or working groups staffed by country representatives do much of the preparatory and staff work. It appears that any new financial assistance under these treaties will be administered by the Global Environmental Facility, which, like the ozone fund, is essentially a consortium headed by the World Bank with the assistance of the UN Development Program and UNEP.[50] The secretariats of recent environmental treaties consist of a few officials, too small to be capable of much in the way of policy initiative. The last budget for UNEP was $64 million for fiscal year 1992. The plans for the FCCC secretariat for the years 1996 and 1997 contemplate an annual operating budget of $18.5 million.[51] The Commission on Sustainable Development, which emerged after the Rio Conference of 1992 as an umbrella unit to oversee implementation of international environmental agreements, seems likely to continue this pattern.

This design is already leading to concerns about "institutional overload."[52] The demand for intensive and extensive party participation strains the resources of even the largest and most dedicated foreign policy establishments. Haas, Keohane, and Levy cite a recent Swedish study showing that 180 different international environmental bodies demanded some active involvement by the Swedish government.[53] In the climate change negotiations and later in the work of the FCCC preparatory committee, developing country representatives insisted that the number of working groups be limited to two and that intersessional meetings be banned, because the smaller states simply did not have the personnel or funds to cover more. But of course in the new organizational design, it is these working groups and committees that are relied on to provide staff work and analysis, without which the plenary organs will not be able to function. The annual meeting of the Conference of the Parties of these organizations, which lasts perhaps two or three weeks, permits consideration of only the most urgent management items. And a small group of environmental diplomats in each country does the main work under all the treaties.[54]

The tasks facing the new regulatory regimes in environment, nonproliferation, and similar areas are among the most complicated and challenging ever undertaken by institutions of government. If the antibureaucratic reaction (or overreaction) is not modified, the prospects that these tasks will be fulfilled are poor. Implementation, compliance, enforcement are the quintessential responsibilities of bureaucracies in all organizations[55] Reducing the resources available will not improve compliance. On the contrary, as Stanley Hoffmann saw more than a decade ago, collective management "implies a reinforcement of regional and international institutions." Whatever else it means, reinforcement "surely means an increase in resources and powers."[56]

It is true that bureaucratic institutions are not universally efficient and effective—rather the opposite, on the whole. This recognition has powered the move to deregulation, decentralization, and the search for "market-based instruments" on the domestic as well as the international level. But these approaches have their own deficiencies, and there seems little doubt that the effective operation of major international and transnational regimes will require some combination of both approaches. The problem of bureaucratic capability will not go away.

The demand for collective management is rising steeply. Problems suppressed during the cold war or regulated as an aspect of the bipolar division of power are asserting themselves with new urgency. The response of the international system to these new demands has been diffuse and hesitant. Yet in some areas—trade, weapons proliferation, the global environment—the outlines of a substantive response are emerging in the array of new multilateral treaties that have provided most of the grist for this book. Nevertheless, however well-conceived substantively, the response will fail without effective implementation. An essential component will be robust, active, well-endowed institutions to manage the intricate network of political and social interactions required for implementing complex regulatory treaties.

It should not be beyond the abilities of the international community to create new organizational arrangements that are lean, effective, and politically responsive. Some established international institutions have proven capable of assuming tasks of the necessary magnitude. It is obvious that all international organizations cannot and should not be cut to the same measure. Different tasks and functions require different institutional arrangements. The common characteristic of the successful organizations, however, is that they combine expert management and staff with extensive party involvement at a high level. The most obvious examples are the major international financial institutions. The IMF and the World Bank have a history of distinguished senior management, professional staffs of high quality, and large-scale involvement of responsible officials of the member states. The IAEA—for all its limitations, a major policy actor in the field of nuclear nonproliferation—also has a record of outstanding directors general, highly qualified technical staff, and continuous involvement of influential officials from national nuclear energy programs.

This pattern is apparently being followed in the arrangements contemplated for the administration of the Chemical Weapons Convention, signed in January 1993. The Preparatory Committee is planning for a substantial Organization for the Prevention of Chemical Warfare, with a staff of several hundred and an annual budget of upward of $100 million. This may simply reflect the higher degree of seriousness with which the international system approaches arms control issues, but perhaps it is also an indication of a new awareness of the organizational requirements for effective international regimes.

Once before, at the end of World War II, the international system experienced a burst of institution building after a long period of exclusive concentration on security problems. This effort was by no means a failure. Those organizations are alive and performing essential functions today. If they were not, we would have to invent them. A comparable effort is needed now to provide the institutional capacity to manage compliance with the most demanding regulatory problems the international system has yet addressed.

Appendix: List of Treaties

This appendix lists treaties and other international instruments, with their official citations and popular names or acronyms, in the following categories:

- Arms control/security/defense treaties
- Economic/trade treaties
- Treaties regulating the environment or natural resources
- Miscellaneous treaties

The listing for each treaty includes a citation from one official source (in order of preference: *United States Treaty* [UST], *International Legal Materials* [ILM], *United Nations Treaty Series* [UNTS], *Arms Control and Disarmament Agreements, 1982* [ACDA], other document source). Date of entry into force (EIF) is given where applicable.

Arms Control/Security/Defense Treaties

Agreement on International Energy Program, Including Establishing of the International Energy Agency, 27 UST 1685, 1974, EIF Jan. 19, 1976	IEA Treaty
Agreement on Notification of Launches of Intercontinental Ballistic Missiles and Submarine-Launched Ballistic Missiles, 27 ILM 1200, 1988, EIF May 31, 1988	
Conference on Security and Co-operation in Europe, Final Act, 14 ILM 1292, 1975	Helsinki Final Act
Convention on the Prohibition of the Development, Production, and Stockpiling of Bacteriological and Toxin Weapons, and on Their Destruction, 26 UST 583, 1972, EIF Apr. 10, 1975	BWC

Convention on the Prohibition of the Development, Production, Stockpiling and Use of Chemical Weapons and on Their Destruction, 32 ILM 800, 1993, EIF Jan. 13, 1993 — CWC

General Treaty Providing for the Renunciation of War, 46 Stat 2343, 1928, EIF July 24, 1929 — Kellogg-Briand Pact

Geneva Protocol for the Prohibition of the Use in War of Asphyxiating Poisonous or Other Gases, and of Methods of Warfare, 26 UST 571, 1925.

Inter-American Treaty of Reciprocal Assistance, 21 UNTS 77, 1947, EIF Dec. 3, 1948 — Rio Treaty

• Inter-American Treaty of Reciprocal Assistance Amendments, II Applications, Basic Instruments of the Organization of American States (Washington, D.C.: General Secretariat, Organization of American States, 1981)

North Atlantic Treaty, 34 UNTS 243, 1949, EIF Aug. 24, 1949 — NATO

Statute of the International Atomic Energy Agency, 8 UST 1093, 1956, EIF July 29, 1957 — IAEA

Strategic Arms Limitation Talks — SALT I

Interim Agreement between the USA and the USSR on Certain Measures with Respect to the Limitation of Strategic Offensive Arms, and Protocol, 23 UST 3462, 1972, EIF Oct. 3, 1972 — Interim Agreement

Treaty between the USA and the USSR on the Limitation of Anti–Ballistic Missile Systems, 23 UST 3435, 1972, EIF Oct. 3, 1972 — ABM Treaty

• Memorandum of Understanding Regarding the Establishment of a Standing Consultative Commission, 24 UST 238, 1972, EIF Dec. 21, 1972

• Protocol Establishing and Approving Regulations Governing Procedures and Other Matters of the Standing Consultative Commission with Regulations, 24 UST 1124, 1973, EIF May 30, 1973

- Protocol to the Treaty of May 26, 1972, on the Limitation of Anti–Ballistic Missile Systems, 27 UST 1645, 1974, EIF May 24, 1976

Treaty Banning Nuclear Weapons Tests in the Atmosphere, in Outer Space, and under Water, 14 UST 1313, 1963, EIF Oct. 10, 1963	Limited Test Ban Treaty (LTBT)
Treaty between the USA and the Russian Federation on General Reduction and Limitation of Strategic Offensive Arms, U.S. Treaty Doc. 103-1, 1993, EIF Aug. 26, 1993	START II
Treaty between the USA and USSR on the Elimination of Their Intermediate-Range and Shorter-Range Missiles, with Memorandum of Understanding and Protocols, 27 ILM 90, 1987, EIF June 1, 1988	INF

- Agreement regarding Inspections Relating to the Treaty between the USA and the USSR on Elimination of Their Intermediate-Range and Short-Range Missiles, 27 ILM 190, 1987, EIF June 1, 1988   — INF Inspection Protocol
- Memorandum of Understanding regarding Establishment of the Data Base for the Treaty between the USSR and the USA on Elimination of Their Intermediate-Range and Short-Range Missiles, 27 ILM 98, 1988

Treaty between the USA and the USSR on the Limitation of Strategic Offensive Arms, 18 ILM 1112, 1979	SALT II
Treaty between the USA and the USSR on the Reduction and Limitation of Strategic Offensive Arms, Washington, D.C.: U.S. Arms Control and Disarmament Agency, 1991, EIF Oct. 1, 1992	START I

- Protocol on Inspections and Continuous Monitoring

Treaty between the USA and the USSR on Underground Nuclear Explosions for Peaceful Purposes and Protocol, ACDA 173, 1976	PNE Treaty
Treaty between the USA and the USSR on the Limitation of Underground Nuclear Weapon Tests and Verification Protocol, ACDA 167, 1974, EIF Dec. 11, 1990	Threshold Test Ban Treaty (TTBT)

- Protocol to the Treaty of July 3, 1974, on the Limitation of Underground Nuclear Weapon Tests, 29 ILM 971, 1990, EIF Dec. 11, 1990

Treaty for the Prohibition of Nuclear Weapons in Latin America, 22 UST 762, 1967, EIF Apr. 22, 1968 — Tlatleloco Treaty

Treaty for the Prohibition of Nuclear Weapons in the South Pacific, 24 ILM 1442, 1985 — South Pacific Nuclear Free Zone Treaty

Treaty on Conventional Armed Forces in Europe, 30 ILM 1, 1990, EIF Nov. 9, 1992 — CFE

Treaty on the Non-Proliferation of Nuclear Weapons, 21 UST 483, 1968, EIF Mar. 5, 1970 — NPT

Treaty on the Prohibition of the Emplacement of Nuclear Weapons and Other Weapons of Mass Destruction on the Seabed and the Ocean Floor, 23 UST 701, 1971, EIF May 18, 1972 — Seabed Treaty

Economic/Trade Treaties

Agreement Establishing the Asian Development Bank, 17 UST 1418, 1965, EIF Aug. 22, 1966 — ADB Agreement

Agreement Establishing the Inter-American Development Bank, 10 UST 3029, 1959, EIF Dec. 30, 1959 — IADB Agreement

Agreement Establishing the International Fund for Agricultural Development, 28 UST 8435, 1976, EIF Nov. 30, 1977

Articles of Agreement of the International Bank for Reconstruction and Development, 2 UNTS 134, 1945, EIF Dec. 27, 1945 — IBRD Agreement (World Bank)

Articles of Agreement of the International Monetary Fund, 2 UNTS 39, 1945, EIF Dec. 27, 1945 — IMF Agreement

• IMF Amendments, 29 UST 2203, EIF Apr. 1, 1978

Amended Constitution of the International Rice Commission, 13 UST 2403, 1960, EIF Nov. 23, 1961

Convention on the Organization for Economic Cooperation and Development, 12 UST 1728, 1960, EIF Sept. 30, 1961 — OECD Agreement

Fourth African, Caribbean and Pacific Countries European Economic Community Convention, 29 ILM 783, 1989, EIF Mar. 1, 1990	LOME IV
Free Trade Agreement between the USA and Canada, 27 ILM 281, 1988, EIF Jan. 1, 1989	
General Agreement on Tariffs and Trade, 55 UNTS 194, 1947	GATT
International Coffee Agreement, Cmnd. 8810, 1982, EIF Sept. 11, 1985	
Multilateral Trade Negotiations: Final Act Embodying the Results of the Uruguay Round of Trade Negotiations, 33 ILM 1125, 1993, EIF Jan. 1, 1995	Uruguay Round
• Multilateral Agreement on Trade in Goods, 33 ILM 1154	
• Agreement Establishing the Multilateral Trade Organization, 33 ILM 1144	WTO Agreement
• General Agreement on Trade in Services and Annexes, 33 ILM 1167	
• Agreement on Trade-Related Aspects of Intellectual Property Rights, 33 ILM 1197	
• Understanding on Rules and Procedures Governing the Settlement of Disputes, 33 ILM 1226	Dispute Settlement Understanding
• Trade Policy Review Mechanism, Annex 3 (Geneva. GATT Secretariat, 1994)	TPRM
• Plurilateral Trade Agreements, Annex 4 (Geneva: GATT Secretariat, 1994)	
North American Free Trade Agreement, 32 ILM 289, 1992, EIF Jan. 1, 1994	NAFTA
• North American Agreement on Environmental Cooperation, 32 ILM 1480, 1993	NAFTA Environmental Side Agreement
• North American Agreement on Labor Cooperation, 32 ILM 1499, 1993	NAFTA Labor Side Agreement
• Agreement concerning Establishment of a Border Environment Cooperation Commission and a North American Development Bank, 32 ILM 1545, 1993	NADBANK

Wheat Trade Convention, 19 UST 5499, 1986, EIF July 1, 1986

Treaties Regulating the Environment or Natural Resources

Agreement concerning Pollution of the North Sea by Oil, 704 UNTS 3, 1969, EIF Aug. 9, 1969

Agreement for the Establishment of the Indo-Pacific Fisheries Council, 13 UST 2511, 1961, EIF Nov. 23, 1961

Agreement on the Conservation of Polar Bears, 27 UST 3918, 1973, EIF May 26, 1976 — Polar Bear Agreement

Convention for the Conservation of Antarctic Seals, 29 UST 441, 1972, EIF Mar. 11, 1978

Convention for the Prevention of Marine Pollution by Dumping from Ships and Aircraft, 11 ILM 262, 1972, EIF Apr. 7, 1974

Convention for the Prevention of Marine Pollution from Land-Based Sources, 13 ILM 352, 1974, EIF May 6, 1978

Convention for the Protection and Development of the Marine Environment of the Wider Caribbean Region, and Protocol, Treaties and Other International Acts no. 11085, 1983, EIF Oct. 11, 1986

Convention for the Protection of the Mediterranean Sea against Pollution, and Protocols, 15 ILM 290, 1976 — Barcelona Convention

- Protocol for the Prevention of Pollution of the Mediterranean Sea by Dumping from Ships and Aircraft, UNEP/GC.16.Inf.4, 1976
- Protocol concerning Co-operation in Combating Pollution of the Mediterranean Sea by Oil and Other Harmful Substances in Cases of Emergency, UNEP/GC.16.Inf.4, 1976
- Protocol for the Protection of the Mediterranean Sea against Pollution from Land-Based Sources, UNEP/GC.16/Inf.4, 1980
- Protocol on Specially Protected Areas, UNEP/GC.16/Inf.4, 1982

Convention for the Protection of World Cultural and Natural Heritage, 27 UST 37, 1971, EIF Dec. 17, 1975 — World Heritage Convention

Convention on Assistance in the Case of a Nuclear Accident or Radiological Emergency, 25 ILM 1377, 1986, EIF Feb. 26, 1987

Convention on Biological Diversity, 31 ILM 818, 1992 — Biodiversity Convention

Convention on Early Notification of a Nuclear Accident, 25 ILM 1370, 1986, EIF Oct. 27, 1986

Convention on International Trade in Endangered Species of Wild Fauna and Flora, 27 UST 1087, 1973, EIF July 1, 1975 — CITES

Convention on Long-Range Transboundary Air Pollution, 18 ILM 1442, 1979, EIF Mar. 16, 1983 — LRTAP

- Protocol on Long-Term Financing of the Co operative Programme for Monitoring and Evaluation of the Long-Range Transmission of Air Pollutants in Europe, 27 ILM 698, 1984, EIF Jan. 28, 1988
- Protocol to the 1979 Convention on Long-Range Transboundary Air Pollution on the Reduction of Sulphur Emissions or Their Transboundary Fluxes by at Least 30 Percent, 27 ILM 698, 1985, EIF Sept. 2, 1987 — Sulphur Protocol
- Protocol to the 1979 Convention on Long-Range Transboundary Air Pollution concerning Control of Emissions of Nitrogen Oxides or Their Transboundary Fluxes, ECE/EB.AIR/18, 1988, EIF Feb. 15, 1991 — NOX Protocol
- Protocol concerning the Control of Emissions of Volatile Organic Compounds or Their Transboundary Fluxes, 31 ILM 568, 1991 — VOX Protocol

Convention on the Conservation of Antarctic Marine Living Resources, 33 UST 3476, 1980, EIF Apr. 7, 1982

Convention on the Control of Transboundary Movements of Hazardous Wastes and Their Disposal, 28 ILM 649, 1989, EIF Mar. 5, 1992 — Basel Convention

Convention on the Prevention of Marine Pollution by Dumping of Wastes and Other Matter, 26 UST 2403, 1972, EIF Aug. 30, 1975 — London Convention

Convention on the Protection of the Marine Environment of the Baltic Sea, 13 ILM 546, 1974, EIF May 3, 1980	Baltic Sea Pollution Convention
Convention on the Protection of the Rhine against Chemical Pollution, 16 ILM 242, 1975, Feb. 1, 1979	Rhine Pollution Convention
Convention on the Regulation of Antarctic Mineral Resource Activities, 27 ILM 859, 1988	
Convention on the Wetlands of International Importance Especially as Waterfowl Habitat, 996 UNTS 245, 1971, EIF Dec. 21, 1975	Ramsar Convention
Convention regarding Fishing and Living Resources, 17 UST 138, 1958, EIF Mar. 20, 1966	
Framework Convention on Climate Change, 31 ILM 849, 1992, EIF Mar. 21, 1994	Climate Change Convention (FCCC)
Inter-American Tropical Tuna Commission, 1 UST 230, 1949, EIF Mar. 3, 1950	IATTC
International Convention for the Conservation of Atlantic Tuna, 20 UST 2887, 1966, EIF Mar. 21, 1969	
International Convention for the Prevention of Pollution from Ships, 12 ILM 1319, 1973, EIF Oct. 2, 1983	MARPOL
• Protocol of 1978 Relating to the International Convention for Prevention of Pollution from Ships, Cmnd. 5748, 1978, EIF Oct. 2, 1983	
International Convention for the Prevention of Pollution of the Sea by Oil, 12 UST 2989, 1954, EIF July 26, 1958	OILPOL
International Convention for the Protection of New Varieties of Plants, 33 UST 2704, 1978, EIF Nov. 8, 1981	
International Convention for the Protection of Plants and Plant Products, 23 UST 2767, 1952, EIF Apr. 3, 1952	Plant Protection Convention

International Convention for the Regulation of Whaling, 161 UNTS 72, 1946, EIF Nov. 10, 1948	Whaling Convention (ICRW)
International Convention on Civil Liability for Oil Pollution Damage, 9 ILM 45, 1969, EIF June 19, 1975	
International Convention Relating to Intervention on the High Seas in Cases of Oil Pollution Casualties, 26 UST 765, 1969, EIF May 6, 1975	Oil Pollution Intervention Convention
International Tropical Timber Agreement, UNCTAD Doc. TD/Timber/11, 1983, Apr. 1, 1985	ITTA
Rio Declaration on the Environment and Development, 31 ILM 874, 1992	Rio Declaration
Stockholm Declaration of the United Nations Conference on the Human Environment, 11 ILM 1416, 1972	Stockholm Declaration
United Nations Convention on Fisheries, 17 UST 138, 1958	
Vienna Convention for the Protection of the Ozone Layer, 26 ILM 1516, 1985, EIF Sept. 22, 1988	
• Montreal Protocol on Substances That Deplete the Ozone Layer, 26 ILM 1541, EIF Jan. 1, 1989	Montreal Protocol
• Adjustment and Amendments to the Montreal Protocol on Substances That Deplete the Ozone Layer, 30 ILM 537, 1990, Mar. 7, 1991	London Amendments to the Montreal Protocol
• Adjustments and Amendments to the Montreal Protocol on Substances That Deplete the Ozone Layer, 32 ILM 874, 1992	Copenhagen Amendments to the Montreal Protocol

Miscellaneous Treaties

Vienna Convention on the Law of Treaties, 1155 UNTS 331, 1969, EIF Jan. 27, 1988

Vienna Convention on the Law of Treaties between States and International Organizations or between International Organizations, 8 ILM 679, 1969, EIF Jan. 27, 1980

Convention on the Recognition and Enforcement of Foreign Arbitral Awards, 21 UST 2517, 1958, EIF June 7, 1959	New York Convention

United Nations and Specialized Agencies

Charter of the United Nations, 59 Stat 1031, 1945, EIF Oct. 24, 1945	UN Charter
Constitution of the Food and Agriculture Organization, 12 UST 980, 1945, EIF Oct. 16, 1945	FAO
Constitution of the International Labour Organization, 49 Stat 2712, 1919	ILO
Constitution of the United Nations Educational, Scientific and Cultural Organization, 4 UNTS 275, 1945	UNESCO
Constitution of the Universal Postal Union, 16 UST 1291, 1964, EIF Jan. 1, 1966	UPU
Constitution of the World Health Organization, 14 UNTS 185, 1946, EIF Apr. 7, 1948	WHO
Convention Establishing the World Intellectual Property Organization, 21 UST 1749, 1967, EIF Apr. 26, 1970	WIPO
Convention for the Protection of Literary and Artistic Works, 12 Martens (2d), 1886, EIF Dec. 5, 1887	Berne Convention

  • Universal Copyright Convention and Protocols and
    Revision, 6 UST 2731, 1952, EIF Sept. 16, 1955
  • Universal Copyright Convention (Revised), 25 UST
    1341, 1971, EIF July 10, 1974

Convention of the World Meteorological Organization, 1 UST 281, 1947, EIF Mar. 23, 1950	WMO
Convention on International Civil Aviation, 15 UNTS 295, 1944	ICAO (Chicago Convention)
Convention of the Intergovernmental Maritime Consultative Organization, 9 UST 621, 1948, EIF Mar. 17, 1958	IMCO

International Telecommunications Convention and Optional Protocol, 28 UST 2495, 1973, EIF Jan. 1, 1975 — ITU

Statute of the International Court of Justice, Treaty Series 993, 1945

Transportation and Communication

Agreement Relating to the International Telecommunications Satellite Organization, 23 UST 3813, 1971, EIF Feb. 12, 1973 — INTELSAT

Convention concerning Customs Facilities for Touring, 8 UST 1293, 1954, EIF Sept. 11, 1957

Convention for the Unification of Certain Rules Relating to International Transportation by Air, Treaty Series 876, 1933, EIF Feb. 13, 1933

Convention on Road Traffic, 3 UST 3008, 1949, EIF Mar. 26, 1952

Convention on the International Maritime Satellite Organization, 31 UST 1, 1976, EIF July 16, 1979 — INMARSAT

Convention on the International Regulations for Preventing Collisions at Sea, 2 UST 3459, 1972, EIF July 15, 1977

International Convention for the Safety of Life at Sea, 3 UST 3451, 1948

- International Convention for the Safety of Life at Sea, 16 UST 185, 1960
- International Convention for the Safety of Life at Sea, 32 UST 47, 1974, EIF May 25, 1980

International Convention on Load Lines, 18 UST 1857, 1966, EIF July 21, 1968 — Load Line Convention

International Convention on Safe Containers, 29 UST 3707, 1972, EIF Sept. 11, 1957

International Regulations for Preventing Collisions at Sea, 28 UST 3459, 1972, EIF July 15, 1977

Statutes of World Tourism Organization, 27 UST 2211, 1970, EIF Jan. 2, 1975

Human Rights

Conference for Security and Co-operation in Europe: Final Act, 14 ILM 1292, 1975	Helsinki Final Act
Constitution of the Intergovernmental Committee for Migration, 6 UST 603, 1953, EIF Nov. 30, 1954	
Convention for the Protection of Human Rights and Fundamental Freedoms, 213 UNTS 221, 1950, EIF Sept. 3, 1953	European Human Rights Convention
General Act for the Repression of the African Slave Trade, 27 Stat 886, 1890	
Geneva Convention for the Amelioration of the Condition of the Wounded and the Sick in the Armed Forces in the Field, 75 UNTS 31, EIF Oct. 21, 1950	Geneva Protocols
Geneva Convention for the Amelioration of Wounded, Sick and Shipwrecked Members of the Armed Forces at Sea, 75 UNTS 85, 1949, EIF Oct. 21, 1950	Geneva Protocols
Geneva Convention Relative to the Protection of Civilian Persons in Times of War, 75 UNTS 287, 1949, EIF Oct. 21, 1950	Geneva Protocols
Geneva Convention Relative to the Treatment of Prisoners of War, 75 UNTS 135, 1949, EIF Oct. 21, 1950	Geneva Protocols
Inter-American Convention on Human Rights, 8 ILM 679 (1969), 1969, EIF July 18, 1978	Inter-American Human Rights Convention
International Covenant on Civil and Political Rights, 999 UNTS 171, 1966, EIF Mar. 23, 1976	Civil and Political Rights Covenant

International Covenant on Economic, Social and Cultural Rights, 993 UNTS 3, 1966, EIF Jan. 3, 1976

Economic, Social and Cultural Rights Covenant

International Slavery Convention, 46 Stat 2153, 1926

Supplementary Convention on the Abolition of Slavery, the Slave Trade, and Institutions and Practices Similar to Slavery, 18 UST 3201, 1955, EIF Apr. 30, 1957

Protocol Relating to the Status of Refugees, 19 UST 6233, 1967, EIF Oct. 4, 1967

Universal Declaration of Human Rights, GA Res. 217A(III), UN GAOR, 3rd Sess. 71, UN Doc. A/810 (1948)

Universal Declaration

Diplomatic Matters

Convention between the USA and Other American Republics on the Status of Aliens, Treaty Series 815, 1928, EIF Aug. 29, 1929

Convention concerning the Exchange of Official Publications and Government Documents between States, 19 UST 4467, 1958, EIF May 30, 1961

Vienna Convention on Consular Relations, 21 UST 77, 1963, EIF Mar. 19, 1967

- Optional Protocol to Vienna Convention on Consular Relations concerning the Compulsory Settlement of Disputes, 596 UNTS 487, 1963, EIF Mar. 19, 1967

Vienna Convention on Diplomatic Relations, 23 UST 1728, 1961, EIF Apr. 24, 1964

- Optional Protocol to the Vienna Convention on Diplomatic Relations concerning the Compulsory Settlement of Disputes, 23 UST 3374, 1961, EIF Apr. 24, 1964

Criminal Matters

Convention for the Suppression of Unlawful Acts against the Safety of Civil Aviation, 24 UST 564, 1971, EIF Jan. 26, 1973

Convention for the Suppression of Unlawful Seizure of Aircraft, 22 UST 1641, 1970, EIF Oct. 14, 1971

Convention on Offenses and Certain Other Acts Committed on Board Aircraft, 20 UST 2941, 1963, EIF Dec. 4, 1969

Convention on Psychotropic Substances, 32 UST 543, 1971, EIF Aug. 16, 1976

Convention on the Prevention and Punishment of Crimes against Internationally Protected Persons, Including Diplomatic Agents, 28 UST 1975, 1973, EIF Feb. 20, 1977

Convention to Prevent and Punish Acts of Terrorism Taking the Form of Crimes against Persons and Related Extortion That Are of International Significance, 27 UST 3949, 1971, EIF Oct. 16, 1973

Single Convention on Narcotic Drugs, 18 UST 1407, 1961, EIF Dec. 13, 1964

Special Domains

Antarctic Treaty, 12 UST 794, 1959, EIF June 23, 1961 — Antarctic Treaty

- Protocol on Environmental Protection to the Antarctic Treaty, 30 ILM 1455, 1991

Convention for the International Council for the Exploration of the Sea, 24 UST 1080, 1964, EIF July 22, 1968 — ICES

Treaty of Principles Governing the Activities of States in the Exploration and Use of Outer Space, Including the Moon and Other Celestial Bodies, 18 UST 2410, 1967, EIF Oct. 10, 1967 — Outer Space Treaty

- Agreement on the Rescue of Astronauts, the Return of Astronauts, and the Return of Objects Launched into Outer Space, 10 UST 7570, 1968, EIF Dec. 3, 1968
- Convention on International Liability for Damage Caused by Space Objects, 24 UST 2389, 1972, EIF Sept. 1, 1972
- Convention on Registration of Objects Launched into Outer Space, 28 UST 695, 1974, EIF Sept. 15, 1976

United Nations Convention on the Law of the Sea, 21 ILM   UNCLOS III
1261, 1982, EIF 1994

Educational and Cultural Matters

Agreement on the Importation of Educational, Scientific and
Cultural Materials, 17 UST 1835, 1950, EIF May 21, 1952

Convention for the Protection of Producers of Phonograms
against Unauthorized Duplication, 25 UST 309, 1971, EIF Apr.
18, 1973

Convention for the Protection of World Cultural and Natural   World
Heritage, 27 UST 37, 1971, EIF Dec. 17, 1975   Heritage
                                                                Convention

Patent Co-operation Treaty, 28 UST 7645, 1970, EIF Jan. 24,
1978

Statutes of the International Centre for the Study of the Preservation and Restoration of Cultural Property, 22 UST 19,
1956, EIF May 10, 1958

Western Hemisphere Matters

Charter of the Organization of American States, 119 UNTS 3,   OAS
1948, EIF Dec. 13, 1951

Constitution of the Postal Union of the Americas and Spain, 23
UST 2924, 1971, EIF July 1, 1972

Notes

Official citations for most treaties referred to in the text and notes may be found in the appendix.

1. A Theory of Compliance

An earlier version of this chapter appeared as Abram Chayes and Antonia Handler Chayes, "On Compliance," *International Organizations*, 47 (Spring 1993): 175–205.

1. In the course of the work, we refer to more than 125 treaties, in some cases at considerable length, sometimes in passing. They are listed alphabetically by subject in the appendix, together with their full official citations and their common names or acronyms. The list is not a systematic selection. It is mainly drawn from a scan of the multilateral treaty section of *Treaties in Force: A List of Treaties and Other International Acts of the United States in Force on January 1, 1994* (Washington, D.C.: USGPO, 1994) and is thus weighted in favor of multilateral treaties to which the United States is a party. The principal bilateral treaties considered are the U.S.-Soviet arms control agreements of the cold war period. A few significant regional agreements are added. Although the selection is in no sense scientific, we are confident that all of the principal regulatory agreements of the categories listed above are included.

2. "Nuclear Tests Case *(Australia v. France)*, Judgment," *ICJ Reports* (1974): 253, and "Nuclear Tests Case *(New Zealand v. France)*, Judgment," *ICJ Reports* (1974): 457.

3. The now-classical definition of an international regime appears in Stephen D. Krasner, "Structural Causes and Regime Consequences: Regimes as Intervening Variables," in Stephen D. Krasner, ed., *International Regimes* (Ithaca, N.Y.: Cornell University Press, 1983), p. 2: "Regimes are sets of implicit or explicit principles, norms, rules, and decision making procedures around which actors' expectations converge in a given area of international relations." Regime theorists find it hard to say the "L-word," but "principles, norms, rules, and decision-making procedures" are what international law is all about.

4. A shift in emphasis from coercive to cooperative strategies is also becoming apparent in contemporary domestic law enforcement. See Malcolm Sparrow,

Imposing Duties: Government's Changing Approach to Compliance, (Westport, Conn.: Praeger, 1994).

5. Niccolò Machiavelli, *The Prince,* ed. Q. Skinner and Russell Prince (New York: Cambridge University Press, 1988), pp. 61–62. For a modern instance, see Hans J. Morgenthau, *Politics among Nations: The Struggle for Power and Peace,* 5th ed. (New York: Alfred A. Knopf, 1978), p. 560: "In my experience [states] will keep their bargains as long as it is in their interest."

6. See, e.g., George Stigler, "The Economics of Information," *Journal of Political Economy,* 69 (June 1961): 213; G. J. Stigler and G. S. Becker, "De Gustibus non Est Disputandum," in K. S. Cook and M. Levi, eds., *The Limits of Rationality* (Chicago: University of Chicago Press, 1990), pp. 191, 202; Charles E. Lindblom, *The Policy Making Process* (Englewood Cliffs, N.J.: Prentice-Hall, 1968), p. 14; Oran R. Young, *Compliance and Public Authority: A Theory with International Applications* (Baltimore: Johns Hopkins University Press, 1979), pp. 16–17.

7. Herbert Simon, *Models of Man: Social and Rational; Mathematical Essays on Rational Human Behavior in a Social Setting* (New York: John Wiley and Sons, 1957), pp. 200, 204. See also James G. March and Herbert A. Simon, *Organizations* (New York: John Wiley and Sons, 1958), p. 169. "Rules constitute an essential feature of bureaucracies and . . . routinized compliance with rules is a deeply ingrained norm among bureaucrats." Young, *Compliance and Public Authority,* p. 39. For an example of this model of organizational behavior applied to the analysis of international affairs, see Graham T. Allison, *The Essence of Decision: Explaining the Cuban Missile Crisis* (Boston: Little, Brown, 1971), chaps. 3–4.

8. Oran R. Young, *International Governance: Protecting the Environment in a Stateless Society* (Ithaca, N.Y.: Cornell University Press, 1994) pp. 24, 38–46, 81.

9. This is the central teaching of contemporary negotiation theory. See Roger Fisher and William Ury, *Getting to Yes: Negotiating Agreements without Giving In* (Boston: Houghton Mifflin, 1981) pp. 41–57; David A. Lax and James K. Sebenius, *The Manager as Negotiator* (New York: Free Press, 1986), pp. 63–87.

10. Phillip R. Trimble, "Arms Control and International Negotiation Theory," *Stanford Journal of International Law,* 25 (Spring 1989): 543, 549.

11. John Newhouse, *Cold Dawn: The Story of SALT* (New York: Holt, Rinehart and Winston, 1973); Gerard C. Smith, *Doubletalk: The Story of SALT I* (Lanham, Md.: University Press of America, 1985); Strobe Talbott, *Endgame: The Inside Story of SALT II* (New York: Harper and Row, 1979); Strobe Talbott, *Deadly Gambits: The Reagan Administration and the Stalemate in Nuclear Arms Control* (New York: Alfred A. Knopf, 1984; distributed by Random House); Raymond L. Garthoff, *Détente and Confrontation: American-Soviet Relations from Nixon to Reagan* (Washington, D.C.: Brookings Institution, 1985); John McNeill, "U.S.-U.S.S.R. Arms Negotiations: The Process and the Lawyer," *American Journal of International Law,* 79 (1985): 52. Although knowledge of the process in the former Soviet Union is less detailed, the sources cited above, among others, suggest that it was not fundamentally dissimilar, making allowances for a more compartmentalized bureaucratic structure.

12. Richard Elliot Benedick, *Ozone Diplomacy: New Directions in Safeguarding the Planet* (Cambridge, Mass.: Harvard University Press, 1991), pp. 51–53. The Domestic Policy Council, which established a special senior-level working group to ride herd on the process, consists of nine cabinet secretaries, the director of the Office of Management and Budget (OMB), and the U.S. trade representative (USTR). At the time, it was chaired by Attorney General Edwin Meese. Other states, at least in advanced industrialized societies, exhibit similar—if perhaps not as rococo—internal practices in preparation for negotiations. Developing countries, with smaller resources to commit to bureaucratic coordination, may rely more on the judgment and inspiration of representatives on the scene.

13. See Benedick, *Ozone Diplomacy*, p. 57, describing the emphasis on Congress, industry, and environmental groups in the development of the U.S. strategy to build support for the Montreal Protocol. See also Robert O. Keohane and Joseph S. Nye, *Power and Interdependence*, 2nd ed. (Glenview, Ill.: Scott, Foresman and Company, 1989), p. 35, for a discussion of how governments "organize themselves to cope with the flow of business generated by international organizations" in an international political system of "complex interdependence."

14. Robert D. Putnam, "Diplomacy and Domestic Politics: The Logic of Two-Level Games," *International Organizations*, 42 (Summer 1988): 427.

15. See James K. Sebenius, *Negotiating the Law of the Sea* (Cambridge, Mass.: Harvard University Press, 1984). See also William Wertenbaker, "The Law of the Sea," *The New Yorker*, Aug. 1, 1983, p. 38 (part 1), and Aug. 8, 1983, p. 56 (part 2).

16. As early as 1975, UNEP funded a World Meteorological Organization technical conference on implications of U.S. ozone-layer research. But the immediate precursor of the Vienna Conference came in March 1977, when UNEP sponsored a policy meeting of governments and international agencies in Washington, D.C., that drafted a "World Plan of Action on the Ozone Layer." Benedick, *Ozone Diplomacy*, p. 40.

17. The Intergovernmental Panel on Climate Change was set up by UNEP and the WMO after the passage of G.A. Res. 43/53, A/RES/43/53, Jan. 27, 1989, "Resolution on the Protection of the Global Climate."

18. See Richard N. Gardner, *Sterling-Dollar Diplomacy in Current Perspective: The Origins and Prospects of Our International Economic Order* (New York: Columbia University Press, 1980).

19. David Colson, "U.S. to Sign Seabed Mining Agreement of the Law of the Sea Convention," *U.S. Department of State Dispatch*, 5 (July 18, 1994): 485; Steven Greenhouse, "U.S., Having Won Changes, Is Set to Sign Law of the Sea," *New York Times*, July 1, 1994, p. A1, col. 5.

20. Susan Strange, "Cave! Hic Dragones: A Critique of Regime Analysis," in Krasner, ed., *International Regimes*, p. 353.

21. Systems in which compliance can be achieved only through extensive use of coercion are rightly regarded as authoritarian and unjust. See Michael Barkun, *Law without Sanctions: Order in Primitive Societies and the World Community* (New Haven, Conn.: Yale University Press, 1968) p. 62.

22. International law recognizes a limited scope for abrogation of an agreement when there has been a fundamental change of circumstances at the time of performance. See the Vienna Convention on the Law of Treaties, Art. 62. Generally, however, the possibility of change is accommodated by provisions for amendment, authoritative interpretation, or even withdrawal from the agreement. See, for example, the withdrawal provisions in the ABM Treaty, Art. XV(2), and the Limited Test Ban Treaty, Art. IV. None of these actions poses an issue of violation of legal obligations, though they may weaken the regime of which the treaty is a part.

23. "'Treaty' means an international agreement concluded between States in written form and governed by international law, whether embodied in a single instrument or in two or more related instruments and whatever its particular designation." Vienna Convention on the Law of Treaties, Art. 2(1)(a).

24. According to Young, "'Obligation' encompasses incentives to comply with behavioral prescriptions which stem from a general sense of duty and which do not rest on explicit calculations of costs and benefits . . . Feelings of obligation often play a significant role in compliance choices." Young, *Compliance and Public Authority*, p. 23. See also Richard Fallon, Jr., "Reflections on Dworkin and the Two Faces of Law," *Notre Dame Law Review*, 67 (1992): 553, 556, summarizing H. L. A. Hart's concept of a law as a social rule: "From an internal point of view—that of an unalienated participant of the social life of the community—a social rule is a standard that is accepted as a guide to conduct and a basis for criticism, including self-criticism." See also M. Rheinstein, ed., *Max Weber on Law in Economy and Society* (New York: Simon and Schuster, 1954), pp. 349–356; Friedrich V. Kratochwil, *Rules, Norms and Decisions: On the Conditions of Practical and Legal Reasoning in International Relations and Domestic Affairs* (Cambridge: Cambridge University Press, 1989), pp. 15, 95–129.

25. We use "norm" as a generic term that includes the concepts of principles, precepts, standards, rules, and the like. For our present purposes, it is adequate to think of legal norms as norms generated by processes recognized as authoritative by a legal system. Compare H. L. A. Hart, *The Concept of Law* (New York: Oxford University Press, 1961). See also Chapter 5.

26. Vienna Convention on the Law of Treaties, Art. 26: "Every treaty in force is binding upon the parties to it and must be performed in good faith." See also Arnold Duncan McNair, *The Law of Treaties* (Oxford: Clarendon Press, 1961), chap. 30.

27. U.S. Constitution, Article VI.

28. See William Eskridge, Jr., and G. Peller, "The New Public Law: Moderation as a Postmodern Cultural Form," *Michigan Law Review*, 89 (1991): 727, 787–789.

29. Elinor Ostrom, *Governing the Commons: The Evolution of Institutions for Collective Action* (Cambridge: Cambridge University Press, 1990).

30. Robert C. Ellikson, *Order without Law: How Neighbors Settle Disputes* (Cambridge, Mass.: Harvard University Press, 1991).

31. Frederick F. Schauer, *Playing by the Rules: A Philosophical Examination of Rule-Based Decision-Making in Law and Life* (Oxford: Clarendon Press, 1991).

32. Kratochwil, *Rules, Norms and Decisions,* pp. 95–129. See also Sally Falk Moore, *Law as Process: An Anthropological Approach* (London: Routledge and Kegan Paul, 1978).

33. Jon Elster, *The Cement of Society: A Study of Social Order* (Cambridge: Cambridge University Press, 1989), p. 15. See also Margaret Levi, Karen S. Cook, Jodi A. O'Brien, and Howard Faye, "Introduction: The Limits of Rationality," in Karen Schweers Cook and Margaret Levi, eds., *The Limits of Rationality* (Ithaca, N.Y.: Cornell University Press, 1990), p. 1.

34. See German chancellor Theobald von Bethman-Hollweg's remark to the British ambassador when Germany invaded in 1914, about the treaty guaranteeing Belgian neutrality, quoted in *Encyclopaedia Britannica,* 14th ed. (Chicago: Encyclopaedia Britannica, 1972), s.v. Bethman-Hollweg, Theobald von. For an example of the U.S. response, see letter of Theodore Roosevelt to Sir Edward Grey, the British foreign secretary, January 22, 1915, quoted in Hans J. Morgenthau, *Politics among Nations: The Struggle for Power and Peace,* 4th ed. (New York: Alfred A. Knopf, 1967).

35. Robert Kennedy, *Thirteen Days: A Memoir of the Cuban Missile Crisis.* (New York: W. W. Norton, 1971), p. 99. See also Abram Chayes, *The Cuban Missile Crisis: International Crises and the Role of Law* (New York: Oxford University Press, 1974). This was the advice Kennedy heard from his lawyers, and it was a thoroughly defensible position. Nevertheless, many international lawyers in the United States and elsewhere disagreed, because they thought the action was inconsistent with the UN Charter. See, e.g., Quincy Wright, "The Cuban Quarantine," *American Journal of International Law,* 57, (1963): 546; James S. Campbell, "The Cuban Crisis and the UN Charter: An Analysis of the United States Position," *Stanford Law Review,* 16 (1963): 160; W. L. Standard, "The United States Quarantine of Cuba and the Rule of Law," *American Bar Association Journal,* 49 (1963): 744.

36. "U.S. Compliance with Commitments: Reciprocity and Institutional Enmeshment," unpublished paper prepared for PIPES Seminar, University of Chicago, Oct. 24, 1991, p. 35. Robert O. Keohane surveyed two hundred years of American foreign relations history and identified only forty "theoretically interesting" cases of "inconvenient" commitments, where there was a serious issue of whether or not to comply.

37. Vienna Convention on the Law of Treaties, Art. 26. See L. Oppenheim, *International Law: A Treatise,* ed. Hersch Lauterpacht, 8th ed. (London: Longmans, 1955), vol. 1, p. 956; McNair, *The Law of Treaties,* p. 465.

38. See Abram Chayes and Antonia Handler Chayes, "Living under a Treaty Regime: Compliance, Interpretation, and Adaptation," in Antonia Handler Chayes and Paul Doty, eds., *Defending Deterrence: Managing the ABM Treaty Regime into the 21st Century* (Washington, D.C.: Pergamon-Brassey, 1989), chap. 11. See also Young, *Compliance and Public Authority,* pp. 106–108, in which he discusses issues of interpretation in the context of deliberate attempts at evasion of obligation. We argue that alternative interpretations are frequently invoked in good faith. No doubt in practice there is often some of both. The question of the determinacy of legal rules has dominated twentieth-century American legal thought. Almost all lawyers now

acknowledge that there is considerable room for interpretation in even the most specific legal commands. See Morton J. Horwitz, *The Transformation of American Law: 1870–1960; The Crisis of Legal Orthodoxy* (New York: Oxford University Press, 1992).

39. See Duncan Kennedy, "Form and Substance in Private Law Adjudication," *Harvard Law Review,* 89 (June 1976): 1685; Ronald M. Dworkin, "The Model of Rules," *University of Chicago Law Review,* 35 (1967): 14; Louis Kaplow, "Rules versus Standards: An Economic Analysis," *Duke Law Journal,* 42, no. 3 (1992): 557–629.

40. NATO, Art. 3.

41. See David A. Koplow, "When Is an Amendment Not an Amendment? Modification of Arms Control Agreements without the Senate," *University of Chicago Law Review,* 59 (1993): 981, 985–1004, for a discussion of the problems and difficulties of the complexification of arms control treaties.

42. See Abram Chayes and Antonia Handler Chayes, "Compliance without Enforcement: State Behavior under Regulatory Treaties," *Negotiation Journal,* 7 (1991): 311. See also Louis B. Sohn, "Peaceful Settlement of Disputes in Ocean Conflicts: Does UNCLOS III Point the Way?" *Law and Contemporary Problems,* 46 (1983): 195–200. International adjudication and other methods of dispute resolution are discussed in Chapter 9.

43. *Report of the Advisory Panel on the Legality of a system for the Selective Adjustment of Quotas,* International Coffee Organization Doc. no. ICC-7-60(E) (1965); *Resolution 92,* International Coffee Organization Doc. no. ICC-7-Res.92(E) (1965); *Resolution 115: System for Selective Adjustment of Supply of Coffee,* International Coffee Organization Doc. no. ICC-8-Res.115(E)(1965).

44. See Oscar Schachter, "The Invisible College of International Lawyers," *Northwestern University Law Review,* 72 (1977): 217.

45. See Gloria Duffy, *Compliance and the Future of Arms Control: Report of a Project Sponsored by the Center for International Security and Arms Control* (Cambridge: Ballinger, 1988), p. 31–60.

46. See Antonia Handler Chayes and Abram Chayes, "From Law Enforcement to Dispute Settlement: A New Approach to Arms Control Verification and Compliance," *International Security,* 14 (1990): 147; Duffy, *Compliance and the Future of Arms Control,* p. 107, n. 49.

47. *Superior Oil Co. v. Mississippi,* 280 U.S. 390, 395 (1920).

48. Interim Agreement (SALT I), Art. V(3). See *Compliance with SALT I Agreements,* U.S. State Department Bureau of Public Affairs, July 1979, Special Report 55, p. 4. The issue was finally resolved by Art. XV(3) of SALT II, prohibiting the use over intercontinental ballistic missile launch silos of shelters that impede verification by national technical means.

49. Unilateral assertion is a traditional way of vindicating claimed "rights" in international law. In the spring of 1986, U.S. forces engaged in two such exercises, one off the Soviet Black Sea coast in the "exercise of the right of innocent passage"

(Richard Halloran, "2 U.S. Ships Enter Soviet Waters off Crimea to Gather Intelligence," *New York Times,* Mar. 19, 1986, p. A1, col. 5) and the other in the airspace over the Gulf of Sidra, which Libya considers its territorial waters and the United States does not. The Black Sea manouver was concluded with nothing more than some bumping between U.S. and Soviet ships, but in the Gulf of Sidra, U.S. aircraft sank two Libyan patrol vessels that had fired antiaircraft missiles. AP, "Soviets Officially Protest U.S. Ships 'Violation,' " *Chicago Tribune,* Mar. 19, 1986, sec. 1, at 9C; James Gerstenzang, "U.S. Destroys 2 Libya Vessels in New Strikes; 3 Lost in 2 Days," *Los Angeles Times,* Mar. 26, 1986, sec. I(CC), p. 1, col. 6; James Gerstenzang, "U.S. Moves Unopposed in the Gulf of Sidra; Libyan Forces Stay at Home," *Los Angeles Times,* March 27, 1986, sec. I(LF), p. 1, col. 2.

50. See *Consumers Union v. Kissinger,* 506 F2d. 136 (D.C. Circuit 1974).

51. Vienna Convention on the Law of Treaties, Art. 2(1)(a).

52. Kurt M. Campbell, Ashton B. Carter, Steven E. Miller, and Charles A. Zraket, "Soviet Nuclear Fission: Control of the Nuclear Arsenal in a Disintegrating Soviet Union," Center for Science and International Affairs Studies in International Security, no. 1, Harvard University (Nov. 1991), pp. 24, 25, 108.

53. Kenneth Hanf, "Domesticating International Commitments: Linking National and International Decision-Making," in Arild Underdal, ed., *The International Politics of Environmental Management* (Norwell, Mass.: Kluwer Academic Publishers, 1995).

54. *Report of the Secretariat on the Reporting of Data by the Parties in Accordance with Article 7 of the Montreal Protocol,* UNEP/OzL.Pro.3/5, pp. 6–12, 22–24, May 23, 1991, and *Addendum,* UNEP/OzL.Pro.3/5/Add.1, June 19, 1991.

55. For the establishment of the Ad Hoc Group of Experts, see *Report of the Second Meeting of the Parties to the Montreal Protocol on Substances That Deplete the Ozone Layer,* UNEP/OzL.Pro.2/3, June 29, 1990, Decision II/9, p. 15. At its first meeting in December of the same year, the Ad Hoc Group concluded that countries "lack knowledge and technical expertise necessary to provide or collect" the relevant data, and made a detailed series of recommendations for addressing the problem. *Report of the First Meeting of the Ad Hoc Group of Experts on the Reporting of Data,* UNEP/OzL.Pro/WG.2/1/4, December 7, 1990.

56. See, e.g., London Amendments to the Montreal Protocol.

57. FCCC, Art. 4(3).

58. IMF Agreement, Art. 14.

59. Montreal Protocol, Art. 5.

60. Abram Chayes, "Managing the Transition to a Global Warming Regime, or What to Do 'til the Treaty Comes," in *Greenhouse Warming: Negotiating a Global Regime* (Washington, D.C.: World Resources Institute, 1991), pp. 61–67.

61. Under Article 2 of START, the agreed reductions in strategic nuclear weapons are to take place over a seven-year period divided into three phases of three, two, and two years.

62. Abram Chayes and Antonia H. Chayes, "Adjustment and Compliance Processes in International Regulatory Regimes," in Jessica Mathews, ed., *Preserving the Global Environment,* (New York: W. W. Norton, 1991), pp. 280–308; Lawrence Susskind, *Environmental Diplomacy: Negotiating More Effective Global Agreements* (New York: Oxford University Press, 1994), pp. 30–37.

63. Vienna Convention for the Protection of the Ozone Layer, Art. 2(2).

64. Montreal Protocol, Art. 2(4).

65. London Amendments to the Montreal Protocol, Annex I, Art. 2A(5), 2B(3).

66. Copenhagen Amendments to the Montreal Protocol.

67. Additional protocols to LRTAP included the Protocol on Long-Term Financing of the Co-operative Programme for Monitoring and Evaluation of the Long-Range Transmission of Air Pollutants in Europe, and the Protocol concerning the Control of Emissions of Volatile Organic Compounds or Their Transboundary Fluxes. See also the Barcelona Convention, which was accompanied by the Protocol for the Prevention of Pollution of the Mediterranean Sea by Dumping from Ships and Aircraft, and the Protocol concerning Co-operation in Combating Pollution of the Mediterranean Sea by Oil and Other Harmful Substances in Cases of Emergency. The Protocol for the Protection of the Mediterranean Sea against Pollution from Land-based Sources followed in 1980; the land-based sources protocol contemplates that pollution will be eliminated in accordance with "standards and timetables" to be agreed to by the parties in the future. Art. 5(2). The Protocol on Specially Protected Areas was signed in Geneva in 1982.

68. ILO Constitution, Art. 405.

69. Helsinki Final Act, Art. 10.

70. See Young, *Compliance and Public Authority,* p. 109.

71. See Charles Lipson, "Why Are Some International Agreements Informal?" *International Organization,* 75 (1991): 4.

72. The 1977 Congress enacted a requirement for "adequate verification" of arms control agreements. This was described by Carter administration officials as a "practical standard" under which the United States would be able to identify significant attempted evasions in time to respond effectively. See Chayes and Chayes, "From Law Enforcement to Dispute Settlement," p. 148. It should be noted that when the Soviet Union in 1987 finally agreed to substantially unlimited on-site inspection, the United States drew back from its earlier insistence on that requirement, as it has in the chemical warfare negotiations.

73. Withdrawal from all U.S.-Soviet arms control agreements is permitted on short notice if "extraordinary events related to the subject matter of the treaty jeopardize the supreme interests" of the withdrawing party. See, e.g., ABM Treaty, Art. 15(2). The law of treaties also permits the suspension of a treaty in whole or in part if the other party has commited a material breach. See the Vienna convention on the Law of Treaties, Art. 60 (1),(2).

74. The closest approach to such an initiative was the mildly comic bureaucratic squabble in the closing years of the Reagan administration about whether the Kras-

noyarsk radar should be denominated a material breach of the ABM Treaty. See Paul Lewis, "Soviets Warn U.S. against Abandoning ABM Pact," *New York Times*, Sept. 2, 1988, sec. A, at 9, col. 1; Michael Lewis, "Minor Violations of Arms Pact Seen," *New York Times*, Dec. 3, 1988, sec. 1, at 5, col. 1.

75. See Joseph A. Yager, "The Republic of Korea," in Joseph A. Yager, ed., *Non-proliferation and U.S. Foreign Policy* (Washington, D.C.: Brookings Institution, 1980), p. 65, and Joseph A. Yager, "Taiwan," ibid., pp. 79–80.

76. David Sanger, "North Korea Assembly Backs Atom Pact," *New York Times*, Apr. 10, 1992, p. A3, col. 4; David Sanger, "North Korea Reveals More About Its Nuclear Sites," *New York Times*, May 7, 1992, p. A8, col. 3; The intitial U.S. response included behind-the-scenes diplomatic pressure and encouraging supportive statements on the issue by concerned states at IAEA meetings. See Leonard Spector, *Nuclear Ambitions: The Spread of Nuclear Weapons, 1989–1990* (Boulder, Colo.: Westview Press, 1990), pp. 127–130; Associated Press, "A Tense Year in Korea over Nuclear Standoff," *New York Times*, Aug. 14, 1994, p. 18, col. 1; Andrew Pollack, "Seoul Offers Help on Nuclear Power to North Korea," *New York Times*, Aug. 15, 1994, p. 1, col. 6.

77. Michael Gordon, "U.S.–North Korea Accord Has a 10-Year Timetable," *New York Times*, Oct. 21, 1994, p. A8(L), col. 5; "The U.S. and North Korea Reach Agreement on Nuclear Program," *U.S. Department of State Dispatch*, Oct. 31, 1994, p. 721; "U.S. and North Korea Recess Talks," *New York Times*, May 21, 1995, p. 3.

78. Countries that have not ratified the NPT include Argentina, Brazil, China, France, India, Israel, Pakistan, and South Africa. See Spector, *Nuclear Ambitions*, p. 430.

79. Reuters, "South Africa Signs a Treaty Allowing Nuclear Inspection," *New York Times*, July 9, 1991, p. A11, col. 6. South Africa signed a safeguards agreement with the IAEA on September 16, 1991. "Argentina and Brazil Sign Nuclear Accord," *The New York Times*, Dec. 14, 1991, p. A7, col. 5.

80. See Gary Becker, "Crime and Punishment: An Economic Approach," *Journal of Political Economy*, 76 (1968): 169; George J. Stigler, "The Optimum Enforcement of Laws," *Journal of Political Economy*, 78 (1970): 526. See also Young, *Compliance and Public Authority*, pp. 7–8, 111–127.

81. See Charles E. Lindblom, *Politics and Markets* (New York: Basic Books, 1977), pp. 254–255. At the domestic level, deciding whether to intensify enforcement of the treaty implicates a similar political process, as the continuous debates in the United States over GATT enforcement testify. Our work in progress includes a consideration of second-level enforcement.

82. See Peter M. Haas: "Protecting the Baltic and North Seas," in Peter M. Haas, Robert O. Keohane, and Mark A. Levy, eds., *Institutions for the Earth: Sources of Effective International Environmental Protection* (Cambridge, Mass.: MIT Press, 1993).

83. Steinar Andresen, "Science and Politics in the International Management of Whales," *Marine Policy*, 13 (2) (1989): 99; Patricia Birnie, *International Regulation of Whaling* (New York: Oceana, 1985).

84. 19 USC. 2411. See A. O. Sykes, "Constructive Unilateral Threats in International Commercial Relations: The Limited Case for Section 301," *Law and Policy in International Business*, 23 (1992): 263. Section 301, however, has been widely criticized as being itself a violation of GATT. See ibid., pp. 265–66, n.15, 16, 18. On the whaling episode, see Steinar Andresen, "Science and Politics in the International Management of Whales," p. 99; and see Chapter 4.

85. See Thomas O. Bayard and Kimberly A. Elliott, "'Aggressive Unilateralism' and Section 301: Market Opening or Market Closing," *The World Economy*, 15, (Nov. 1992): 685–706.

86. See Thomas C. Schelling, *Micromotives and Macrobehavior* (New York: Norton, 1978), pp. 91–110, for a discussion of critical-mass behavior models.

87. CITES, Art. 23.

88. See UPI, "Tokyo Agrees to Join Ivory Import Ban," *Boston Globe*, Oct. 21, 1989, p. 6, describing Japan's announcement of its intention not to enter a reservation on the last day of the conference, stating that it was "respecting the overwhelming sentiment of the international community." As to Hong Kong, see J. Perlez, "Ivory Ban Said to Force Factories Shut," *New York Times*, May 22, 1990, p. A14, col. 1. Great Britain entered a reservation for Hong Kong, which was not renewed after the initial six-month period. Five African ivory producing states with effective management programs entered reservations, but they agreed not to trade until at least the next meeting of the Conference of the Parties; see M. J. Glennon, "Has International Law Failed the Elephant?" *American Journal of International Law*, 84 (1990): 1, 17, and n. 150. At the 1992 meeting, they ended their opposition; see Bureau of National Affairs, "Five African Nations Abandon Effort to Resume Elephant Trade in CITES Talks," *BNA International Environmental Daily*, Mar. 12, 1992.

89. UPI, "Tokyo Agrees to Join Ivory Import Ban," *Boston Globe*, Oct. 21, 1989, p. 6.

90. Ostrom, *Governing the Commons*, p. 187.

91. Young, *International Governance*, p. 75.

92. Uruguay Round, Part II, Annex 2.

93. Free Trade Agreement between the USA and Canada, chap. 18–19, and NAFTA, chap. 19–20.

94. UNCLOS III, Part XV.

95. London Amendments to the Montreal Protocol, Annex III.

96. Montreal Protocol, Art. 10.

97. Intergovernmental Negotiating Committee for a Framework Convention on Climate Change, Doc. A/AC.237/67, July 8, 1994, par. 12.

98. Stephen D. Krasner, "Contested Sovereignty: The Myth of Westphalia," unpublished manuscript, 1994.

99. See Harold Hongju Koh, "Transnational Legal Process," *Nebraska Law Review* (Spring 1995).

100. Robert D. Putnam, *Making Democracy Work: Civic Traditions in Modern Italy* (Princeton, N.J.: Princeton University Press, 1993), p. 183.

Part I: Sanctions

1. Andreas F. Lowenfeld, "Remedies along with Rights: Institutional Reform in the New GATT," *The American Journal of International Law,* 88 (July 1994): 487; Robert E. Hudec, *The GATT Legal System and World Trade Diplomacy* (Salem, N.H.: Butterworth, 1990), pp. 198–200. Hudec notes, however, that such action has assumed a quasi-retaliatory significance in GATT practice.

2. GATT, Art. XXIII(2).

3. "Netherlands Measures of Suspension of Obligations to the United States," *Basic Instruments and Selected Documents,* 1st Supp., (1953): 32.

4. CITES, Art. 2.

5. CITES, Art. 10.

6. Montreal Protocol, Art. 4, par. 8. An effort by the United States and the Nordic countries to authorize true trade sanctions—i.e. restrictions on noncomplying parties—was unsuccessful. Richard E. Benedick, *Ozone Diplomacy: New Directions in Safeguarding the Planet* (Cambridge, Mass.: Harvard University Press, 1991), p. 183.

7. Recently, increasing attention has been given to the operation of informal, or "nonlegal," sanctions in this process, and it is now widely accepted that such informal pressures bear the major load in enforcing obligations arising within private economic and social relationships, with formal procedures playing only a backup role. See, e.g., Robert C. Ellickson, *Order without Law: How Neighbors Settle Disputes* (Cambridge, Mass.: Harvard University Press, 1991); David Charny, "Nonlegal Sanctions in Commercial Relationships," *Harvard Law Review,* 102 (1990): 375, 392–394. The seminal contribution is Stewart Macaulay, "Non Contractual Relations in Business," *American Sociological Review,* 28 (1963): 55.

8. Antonia Chayes and Abram Chayes, "From Law Enforcement to Dispute Resolution. A New Approach to Arms Control Verification and Compliance," *International Security,* 14 (Spring 1990): 140–164.

9. John Austin, "The Province of Jurisprudence Determined," in *Lectures on Jurisprudence* (London: John Murray 1861), p. 6.

10. See, e.g., Hedley Bull, *The Anarchical Society: A Study of Order in World Politics* (New York: Columbia University Press, 1977).

11. George W. Downs, David M. Rocke, and Peter M. Barsoom, "Is the 'No-Fault' Theory of Compliance Too Good to be True? The Role of Enforcement in Regulatory Regimes," paper presented at the Annual Meeting of the International Studies Association, Chicago, Feb. 22, 1995.

2. Treaty-Based Military and Economic Sanctions

1. See, e.g., "Address by President Harry S. Truman in San Francisco at the Closing Session of the United Nations Conference, June 26, 1945," in *Public Papers of the Presidents of the United States: Harry S. Truman: Containing the Public Messages, Speeches, and Statements of the President, April 12 to December 31, 1945* (Washington,

D.C.: USGPO, 1961), pp. 138–144; "Remarks by Dr. T. V. Soong, Minister for Foreign Affairs of the Republic of China, before the Plenary of the United Nations Conference on International Organization, Verbatim Minutes of the First Plenary Session," in *Documents of the United Nations Conference on International Organization,* San Francisco, 1945, vol. 1, (New York: United Nations Information Organizations, 1945), pp. 129–131; "Remarks by Dr. V. M. Molotov, People's Commissar for Foreign Affairs of the Union of Soviet Socialist Republics, before the Plenary of the United Nations Conference on International Organization, Verbatim Minutes of the First Plenary Session," in ibid., pp. 131–136.

2. Leland M. Goodrich, *The United Nations* (New York: Crowell Press, 1959), pp. 14–15.

3. See, e.g., "Statement of Joseph Paul-Boncour, Rapporteur, United Nations Conference on International Organization, Committee Three," Doc. 134, III/3/3, in *Documents of the United Nations Conference on International Organization, San Francisco, 1945,* p. 572: "The definite and important innovation of the Dumbarton Oaks proposals . . . is the obligation and preparation of coercive forces placed at the disposal of the Security Council to enforce its decisions." See also Doc. 881, III/3/3, pp. 508, 513.

4. UN Charter, Art. 42.

5. Inter-American Treaty of Reciprocal Assistance, Art. 6, 8, and 20. These provisions of the Rio Treaty are incorporated by reference in the Charter of the Organization of American States, Art. 18, 19. Actions taken under these provisions were presumably authorized by Article 53 of the UN Charter, permitting enforcement action by regional organizations with the authorization of the Security Council.

6. In four cases of limited retaliation—the Dominican Republic, a second round with Cuba, Libya, and Liberia—the United States channeled its response to lower-level provocations through international organizations. The decision to resort to multilateral rather than unilateral action does not seem to be based on any readily observable principle. We summarize them briefly here for the sake of completeness.

The Dominican Republic. On June 24, 1960, President Romulo Betancourt of Venezuela was injured in an assassination attempt. After an investigation, the OAS concluded that the attempt had been fomented by the Dominican dictator, Rafeal Trujillo, and voted to interrupt diplomatic relations with the Dominican Republic and impose partial economic sanctions, which were subsequently extended to cover petroleum products, trucks, and spare parts. Some months later Trujillo himself was assassinated, ending the Dominican campaign against Venezuela, which had been a personal vendetta. Soon thereafter, the OAS lifted the sanctions. See "Eighth Meeting of Consultation of Ministers of Foreign Affairs," Jan. 31, 1962, Res. VIII, Pan American Union, International Treaty of Reciprocal Assistance Applications, vol. 2, pp. 17–27; OEA/Ser. F/11.6, in ibid., *Department of State Bulletin,* 43 (1960): 358; OEA/Ser. G/II/ C-a-397 in Pan American Union, *International Treaty of Reciprocal Assistance, Applications,* vol. 2. For the U.S. role, see Jerome Slater, "The United States, the Organization of American States, and the Dominican Republic, 1961–1963," *International Organization,* 18 (Spring 1964): 273.

Cuba again. Although the United States' animus against Castro's Cuba ran long and deep, it was unable to get anything more than an arms embargo from the OAS until 1964, when an arms cache of Cuban origin was discovered in Venezuela. Again under U.S. and Venezuelan leadership, the OAS ordered the severance of diplomatic relations with Cuba and imposed mandatory sanctions covering all trade except food and medicine, presumably on the grounds that the Cuban action constituted a threat to the peace of the hemisphere. Some major Latin American countries were in dissent, and from the beginning compliance was by no means uniform. During the 1970s, Latin American countries began to resume diplomatic relations with Cuba. The sanctions were officially lifted in July 1975, although the United States, of course, maintained its unilateral embargo.

Libya. In 1991, three years after Pan Am flight 103 exploded over Lockerbie, Scotland, the United States and Great Britain officially charged two Libyan nationals with carrying out the attack and accused the Libyan government of being responsible for the bombing. When Colonel Qaddafi, the Libyan leader, denied the charges and refused to hand over the accused, the United States and the United Kingdom brought the matter to the UN Security Council. After issuing a warning, the council ordered a ban on air travel to and from Libya and an arms embargo, finding a threat to international peace and security in Libya's refusal to renounce terrorism by surrendering the accused. Cape Verde, China, India, Morocco, and Zimbabwe abstained. The sanctions had little impact, and although they were later tightened somewhat, talk of a ban on Libyan oil exports came to naught because of opposition from China and from European customers. See Andrew Rosenthal, "U.S. Accuses Libya as 2 Are Charged in Pan Am Bombing," *New York Times,* Nov. 15, 1991, p. A3; SC Res. 731, UN Doc. S/RES/731, Jan. 21, 1992; SC Res. 748. UN Doc. S/RES/748, Mar. 31, 1992. "Qaddafi Says He Won't Surrender Bomb Suspects," *New York Times,* Aug. 20, 1993, p. A8.

Liberia. The action against Liberia was even more marginal. The world had been content to leave the country's bloody civil and tribal war to the not-too-successful ministrations of the Economic Organization of West African States (ECOWAS), until the murder of five American nuns by rebel forces attacking Monrovia in October 1992. The Security Council, again at the initiative of the United States, imposed an arms embargo on all factions in the war. SC Res. 788, UN Doc. S/RES/788 (1992), Nov. 19, 1992. With that, the council returned to its other concerns.

7. Walter G. Hermes, *Truce Tent and Fighting Front,* United States Army in the Korean War (Washington, D.C.: Office of the Chief of Military History, United States Army, 1966), p. 8. This official history is relied on throughout the following discussion for the details of the military events.

8. Dean Acheson, "Crisis in America: An Examination of U.S. Policy," *Department of State Bulletin,* Jan. 23, 1950, pp. 111–118 (address before the National Press Club, Jan. 12, 1950).

9. SC Res. 82, UN SCOR, 5th year, 473rd mtg., p. 4, UN Doc. S/1501 (1950).

10. When the Soviet representative returned that summer, by prearrangement the General Assembly took over responsibility for the Korean operation. See "Uniting for

Peace Resolution," GA Res. 377A, 5 UN GAOR, Supp. 20 (A/1775), Nov. 3, 1950. See also L. H. Woolsey, "The 'Uniting for Peace Resolution' of the United Nations," *American Journal of International Law,* 45 (Jan. 1951): 129.

11. SC Res. 83, UN SCOR, 5th year, 474th mtg., p. 5, UN Doc. S/1511 (1950). Yugoslavia voted no; India and Egypt abstained; the Soviet delegate was still absent. The UN Temporary Commission on Korea, established in 1948 to facilitate reunification, was in South Korea when North Korea invaded, and was able to report definitively on the facts to the Security Council. See A. M. Rosenthal, "Red North Guilty—Security Council Acts Swiftly at U.S. Call to End Hostilities," *New York Times,* June 26, 1950, p. 1, col. 8.

12. SC Res. 84, UN SCOR, 5th year, 476th mtg., p. 5, UN Doc. S/1588 (1950).

13. Stephen E. Ambrose, *Eisenhower: Volume 1, 1890–1952* (New York: Simon and Schuster, 1983), p. 569.

14. See Abram Chayes, *The Cuban Missile Crisis: International Crises and the Role of Law* (Lantham, Md.: University Press of America, 1987). The literature on the Cuban missile crisis is voluminous and shows no signs of abating. The classic early works are Elie Abel, *The Missile Crisis* (Philadelphia: J. B. Lippincott, 1966); Graham Allison, *Essence of Decision: Explaining the Cuban Missile Crisis* (Boston: Little, Brown, 1971); and, of course, Robert F. Kennedy, *Thirteen Days: A Memoir of the Cuban Missile Crisis* (New York: W. W. Norton, 1971). Michael Beschloss's recent study provides important new information, including material that has become available from Soviet participants. Michael R. Beschloss, *The Crisis Years: Kennedy and Khrushchev 1960–1963* (New York: Edward Burlingame Books, 1991).

15. "Kennedy's Cuba Statement," *New York Times,* Sept. 5, 1962, p. 2, col. 5.

16. The MRBMs had a range of about 1,000 nautical miles, the IRBMs perhaps twice that. The president said they were "capable of striking most of the major cities of the Western Hemisphere, ranging as far north as Hudson Bay, Canada, and as far south as Lima, Peru." John F. Kennedy, "Radio and Television Report to the American People," Oct. 22, 1962, *Public Papers of the Presidents of the United States: Kennedy,* vol. 2 (Washington, D.C.: USGPO, 1963), p. 806. It appeared that the missiles were not yet operational, and it was not even clear whether the nuclear warheads were yet in Cuba. Kennedy, *Thirteen Days,* p. 35. In recent conversations, Soviet participants have asserted that twenty warheads had reached Cuba by early October, and twenty more were on the way. Beschloss, *The Crisis Years,* p. 495.

17. Chayes, *The Cuban Missile Crisis,* pp. 15–16.

18. OEA/Ser. G/II/C-a-463 (1962), pp. 31, 33; Pan American Union, *International Treaty of Reciprocal Assistance Applications,* vol. 2, pp. 111, 112; *Department of State Bulletin,* 47 (1962): 722, 723; and see, generally, Abram Chayes, Thomas Ehrlich, and Andreas F. Lowenfeld, *International Legal Process: Materials for an Introductory Course,* vol. 2 (Boston: Little, Brown, 1969), pp. 1069–1077.

19. Abram Chayes, "The Inter-American Security System and Cuban Crisis," in *Proceedings of the Third Hammarskjold Forum,* ed. Lyman M. Tondel, Jr. (Dobbs Ferry, N.Y.: Oceana Publications for the Association of the Bar of the City of New

York, 1964). (Statement of Abram Chayes, legal advisor to the State Department.)

20. See, e.g., Kennedy, *Thirteen Days,* pp. 108–109; Richard Reeves, *President Kennedy: Profile of Power* (New York: Simon and Schuster, 1993), pp. 419–420; Chayes, *The Cuban Missile Crisis.*

21. SC Res. 660, *International Legal Materials,* 29 (1990): 1323, 1325. The resolution stated that the Security Council was acting under Article 40, which provides that the council may take provisional measures before deciding on action to be taken under Articles 41 and 42. President Bush moved promptly to freeze Iraqi assets in the United States and impose a trade embargo. At the United States' urging, most European countries took similar action. Clyde H. Farnsworth, "Bush, in Freezing Assets, Bars $30 Billion to Hussein," *New York Times,* Aug. 3, 1990, p. 9A, col. 1; Alan Riding, "The Iraqi Invasion; West Europeans Join U.S. in Condemning Invasion," *New York Times,* Aug. 3, 1990, p. A10, col. 2.

22. SC Res. 661, *International Legal Materials,* 29 (1990): 1323, 1325.

23. R. W. Apple, Jr., "Bush Draws 'Line'; He Rules Out an Invasion of Kuwait—Troops Take Up Positions," *New York Times,* Aug. 9, 1990, p. A1, col. 6.

24. Ibid.

25. Michael R. Gordon, "After the War; Tensions Bedeviled Allies All the Way to Kuwait," *New York Times,* Mar. 24, 1991, sec. 1, p. 1, col. 1.

26. R. W. Apple, Jr., "Mideast Tensions; Message to Iraq: The Will and the Way," *New York Times,* Nov. 9, 1990, sec. 1, part 1, p. 18, col. 1.

27. Ibid.; Craig R. Whitney, "Mideast Tensions; British Warnings to Iraqis on War," *New York Times,* Nov. 7, 1990. p. A19, col. 1. The question of the use of force first came to the fore in mid-August when two Iraqi tankers were observed moving through the Gulf in defiance of the embargo. Secretary of State James Baker maintained that the United States was legally empowered to intercept the vessels as an act of collective self-defense in response to Kuwait's earlier request for assistance under Article 51. American ships fired across the bow of the tankers, but did not intercept or board them. Instead, the United States turned to the Security Council, which provided formal authorization to enforce the embargo. SC Res. 665, Aug. 25, 1990, *International Legal Materials,* 29 (1990): 1323, 1325.

28. SC Res. 678, Nov. 29, 1990, *International Legal Materials,* 29 (1990): 1560, 1565. Neither SC Res. 665, authorizing naval action to enforce the blockade, nor SC Res. 678, authorizing air and ground attacks on Iraq, specifically mentions the use of force. President Bush's tactics vis-à-vis Congress were similar to those pursued in the UN. After some weeks of debate about whether congressional authorization was required before the troops could be committed to battle, the president sought a joint resolution authorizing him "to use United States Armed Forces pursuant to United Nations Security Council Resolution 678 (1990) in order to achieve implementation of Security Council Resolutions 660 [et seq.]." Joint Res. no. 77, Jan. 14, 1991, 105 Stat. 3.

29. George Bush, "Address to the Nation on the Suspension of Allied Offensive Combat Operations in the Persian Gulf" (Feb. 27, 1991), *Weekly Compilation of*

Presidential Documents, Mar. 4, 1991 (Washington, D.C.: Office of the Federal Register, National Archives and Records Service), pp. 224–225; see also "Transcript of President Bush's Address on the Gulf War," *New York Times,* Feb. 28, 1991, p. 12A, col. 1. The postcombat phases of the Iraq case are discussed later in this chapter.

30. For example, the General Assembly passed a resolution sponsored by India on the repatriation of prisoners of war that the United States was ultimately forced to accept, despite its opposition. GA Res. 610, UN GAOR, 7th sess., 399th plenary mtg., p. 3 (1952), Dec. 3, 1952, reprinted in *Department of State Bulletin,* 27 (Dec. 8, 1972): 916–917. See Hermes, *United States Army in the Korean War,* pp. 402–403, 428.

31. See the exchange of letters between President Kennedy and Premier Khrushchev, Oct. 27–28, 1962, *Department of State Bulletin, 47 (1962):* 743–745; "Letter from President Kennedy to Premier Khrushchev, October 28, 1962," *Public Papers of the Presidents: Kennedy,* vol. 2, p. 814.

32. Michael Gordon and Gen. Bernard Trainor, *The Generals' War: The Inside Story of the Conflict in the Gulf* (Boston: Little, Brown, 1995), pp. 413–416.

33. See GA Res. 376, UN GAOR, 5th sess., Supp. no. 20, 294th plenary mtg., p. 9, UN Doc. A/1775, (1950).

34. Chayes, *The Cuban Missile Crisis,* pp. 67–68.

35. The question of whether these resolutions covered an invasion of Iraq to unseat Hussein was mooted when President Bush decided to suspend hostilities, and it was never resolved.

36. Thomas L. Friedman, "How U.S. Won Support to Use Mideast Forces; The Iraq Resolution—A U.S.-Soviet Collaboration," *New York Times,* Dec. 2, 1990, sec. 1, p. 1, col. 5.

37. Compare the difference beween the response of the OAS and that of the European allies of the United States, who were consulted individually, to the U.S. proposal for a quarantine during the Cuban missile crisis. See Chayes, *The Cuban Missile Crisis,* pp. 73–77.

38. J. L. Kunz, "Legality of the Security Council Resolutions of June 25 and 27, 1950," *American Journal of International Law,* 45 (Jan. 1951): 137–142.

39. Hermes, *United States Army in the Korean War,* p. 501.

40. Douglas Waller and John Barry, "The Day We Stopped the War," *Newsweek,* Jan. 20, 1992, p. 16. Iraqi losses were much higher of course. Military deaths were estimated at 70,000 to 100,000, and although civilian casualties during the war were between 2,000 and 3,000, the number of civilian deaths owing to civil unrest or war-related ailments in the aftermath was put at 100,000 to 120,000.

41. Robert J. Samuelson, "Don't Worry about the Cost," *Newsweek,* Feb. 4, 1991, p. 63.

42. Department of Defense, Office of Assistant to Secretary of Defense for Public Affairs, July 1994.

43. Lisa Martin, *Coercive Cooperation: Explaining Multilateral Economic Sanctions* (Princeton, N.J.: Princeton University Press, 1992), pp. 33–42.

44. See, e.g., George W. Shepherd, Jr., ed., *Effective Sanctions on South Africa: The*

Cutting Edge of Economic Intervention (New York: Greenwood Press, 1991); ILO Group of Independent Experts, *Financial Sanctions against South Africa,* (Geneva: ILO, 1991).

45. P.L. 99-440, 100 Stat 1086; Ronald Reagan, "Message to the House of Representatives Returning without Approval of a Bill concerning Apartheid in South Africa," (Sept. 26, 1986), *Public Papers of the Presidents of the United States,* (Washington, D.C.: USGPO, 1989), pp. 1278–1280.

46. The sanctions were terminated by SC Res. 460, UN SCOR, 34th year, 2181st mtg. (Dec. 21, 1979).

47. Article 2(7) of the Charter prohibits UN intervention "in matters which are essentially within the domestic jurisdiction of any state," but provides that "this principle shall not prejudice the application of enforcement measures under Chapter VII."

48. GA Res. 1761, UN GAOR, 17th sess., Supp. no. 17, 1165th plenary mtg., p. 9, UN Doc. A/5217, Nov. 6, 1962.

49. GA Res. 1755, UN GAOR, 17th sess., Supp. no. 17, 1152nd plenary mtg., p. 37, UN Doc. A/ 5217 (Oct. 12, 1962).

50. SC Res. 134, UN SCOR, 15th year, 856th mtg., p. 1, UN Doc. S/4300, Apr. 1, 1960. Also, in 1960, two African states challenged South African rule over southwest Africa in the International Court of Justice. The campaign for UN sanctions against South Africa interacted with the litigation. In 1966 the ICJ, after having provisionally accepted jurisdiction, reversed itself and decided, by a casting vote of the president, that the African parties had no standing to sue and dismissed the case. "South West Africa case (*Ethiopia v. South Africa; Liberia v South Africa*), Second Phase," *ICJ Reports* (1966): 6 (July 18). The General Assembly immediately terminated South Africa's mandate over the territory now called Namibia (GA Res. 2145, UN GAOR, 21st sess., Supp. 16, 1454th plen. mtg., p. 2, UN Doc. A/6316, Oct. 21, 1966), but the Security Council waited four years before concurring (SC Res. 276, UN SCOR, 25th year, 1529th mtg., p. 1, Jan. 30, 1970). The ICJ upheld the legality of these actions in an advisory opinion. "Legal Consequences for States of the Continued Presence of South Africa in Namibia (South West Africa) notwithstanding Security Council Resolution 276, (1970)," *ICJ Reports* (1971): 9 (Order no. 3 of Jan. 26).

51. UN SCOR, 15th year, 855th mtg., p. 4 (Apr. 1, 1960).

52. SC Res. 181, UN SCOR, 18th year, 1056th mtg., p. 7, UN Doc. S/5386 (1963).

53. The Security Council finally endorsed a voluntary arms embargo at the end of 1963, SC Res. 181, UN SCOR, 18th year, 1056th mtg., p. 7, UN Doc. S/5386 (1963), followed by SC Res. 182, 18th year, 1078th meeting, Dec. 4, 1963; a resolution "to strengthen the embargo of 1963" passed in 1970 with the United States abstaining, even though the resolution was not mandatory. SC Res. 282, U.N. SCOR, 25th year, 1549th mtg., p. 12 (July 23, 1970).

54. SC Res. 418, UN SCOR, 32nd year, 2046th mtg., p. 5 (1977). The inducing clause stated: "*Considering* that the policies and acts of the South African Government are fraught with danger to international peace and security."

55. SC Res. 569, UN SCOR, 40th year, 2602nd mtg., p. 8 (1985). In the United States, Congress enacted legislation, over President Reagan's veto, substantially implementing the French resolution. Public Law 99-440, 1000 Stat 1086. The European Community also adopted stringent sanctions in 1985 and 1986. EC General Decision Sept. 19, 1985, and EC General Decision Sept. 15, 1986; see Martin Holland, "The EC and South Africa: in search of policy for the 1990s," *International Affairs,* 64 (Summer 1988): 415. But as late as February 1987, the United States and the United Kingdom again vetoed a Security Council resolution that would have made this package of sanctions mandatory; France abstained. *Argentina, Congo, Ghana, United Arab Emirates and Zambia: draft resolution,* UN Doc. S/18705 (1987). See *United Nations Yearbook 1987,* pp. 134–135, UN Sales no. E.91.1.1.

56. In 1963, the United Kingdom vetoed a Security Council resolution "inviting" it not to transfer sovereignty to the Smith government. 18 UN SCOR, Supp. July–Sept. 1963, p. 164, UN Doc. S/5425/Rev. 1 (1963). The United States and France abstained. See *United Nations Yearbook 1963,* pp. 472–474, UN Sales no. 64.I.1.

57. By 1960 the Commonwealth had a majority of nonwhite members, among them five black African states. In 1961 the new African members of the British Commonwealth joined with the older ex-colonies, India, Pakistan, Ceylon, and Ghana, to reject South Africa's application for readmission after it became a republic. Central Office of Information, *Britain: An Official Handbook, 1963 Edition,* (London: Her Majesty's Stationery Office, 1963), p. 27.

58. SC Res. 216, UN SCOR, 20th year, 1258th mtg., p. 8 (Nov. 12, 1965). Almost all UN members complied.

59. SC Res. 217, UN SCOR, 20th year, 1265th mtg., p. 8 (Nov. 20, 1965). The inducing language of the resolution "*determines* that the situation . . . in Southern Rhodesia is extremely grave, . . . and that its continuance in time constitutes a threat to international peace and security."

60. See Chayes, Ehrlich, and Lowenfeld, *International Legal Process,* vol. 2, p. 1372. In the era of the civil rights movement in the United States, the Johnson administration, like the British government, was under internal political pressure to oppose the minority government in Rhodesia. It took an increasingly active role in the UN but continued to follow the British lead as to the pace and timing of UN action and resistance to the use of force.

61. SC Res. 232, UN SCOR, 21st year, 1340th mtg., p. 7 (Dec. 16, 1966). (Bulgaria, France, Mali, and the USSR abstained.) This was the first time in Security Council practice that it expressly invoked Chapter VII. The resolution barred imports from Rhodesia of a wide variety of commodities and the sale of arms, aircraft, and motor vehicles to Rhodesia.

62. SC Res. 253, UN SCOR, 23rd year, 1428th mtg., p. 5 (May 29, 1968), UN Doc. S/RES/253.

63. As in the Persian Gulf, the Security Council authorized the British to use force to intercept oil tankers bound for Beira, Mozambique, whence oil was pumped overland to Rhodesia. SC Res. 221, UN SCOR, 21st year, 1277th mtg., p. 5 (Apr. 9, 1966). The British, with the support of the United States and other western members,

resisted pressure from African and Soviet states for a resolution specifically invoking Chapter VII. At stake were both symbolic values and the possibility that such a resolution would be a prelude to a general authorization for the use of force. In 1970 Britain along with the United States, blocked a resolution to tighten the sanctions by extending them to Portugal and South Africa. *United Nations Yearbook 1970,* pp. 157–161, UN Sales no. E.72.I.1.

64. P.L. 92-156, 85 Stat. 423/7 1971, codified at 50 U.S.C. ;sm 98–98h (1972); see *Diggs v. Schultz,* 470 F.2d 461, 466 (D.C. Cir. 1972), cert. denied, 411 U.S. 931 (1973), where the court held, in accordance with the established rule, that although treaties are "the supreme law of the land" under Article VI of the Constitution, they rank no higher than statutes and thus can be overruled by a later act of Congress for domestic law purposes. Of course on the international plane, the United States was in violation of its legal obligations.

65. South Africa's destabilization policy was realized in part through the formation or control of puppet forces, of which Unita and the Mozambique National Resistance (NMR, or Renamo) are best known. Joe Hanlon, "On the Front Line Destabilisation, the SADCC states and sanctions," in Mark Orkin, ed., *Sanctions against Apartheid* (New York: St. Martin's Press, 1989), pp. 173–174; Helen Suzman, *In No Uncertain Terms* (New York: Alfred A. Knopf, 1993), pp. 210–211.

66. Preamble, Art. 1(3), Art. 55(c), Art. 56.

67. The European Convention for the Protection of Human Rights and Fundamental Freedoms was concluded earlier, but the Latin American one was even later. The Helsinki Final Act was not concluded until 1975. These developments and the repeated actions of the General Assembly and other UN organs (including the Security Council in these cases) led ultimately to the incoporation of fundamental human rights into general international law. No one can say exactly when this happened, but it was surely after the mid-1960s, when the Security Council began dealing with the African cases. The American Law Institute, *Restatement of the Law Third: The Foreign Relations Law of the United States,* (St. Paul, Minn.: American Law Institute Publishers, 1987), vol. 2, chap. 1, sections 701–703, p. 152.

68. Quoted in Chayes, Ehrlich, and Lowenfeld, *International Legal Process,* vol. 2, p. 1379–1380. No American in or out of politics was moved to write to the editor. The OAS committee used similar reasoning to justify its emphasis on internal Dominican electoral processes by citing "the existing relationship between the violation of human rights and the lack of effective exercise of representative democracy on the one hand, and the political tensions that affect the peace of the hemisphere on the other." Council of the OAS, *Second Report of the Subcommittee of the Special Committee to Carry Out the Mandate Received by the Council Pursuant to Resolution I of the Sixth Meeting of Consultation,* OAS Doc. CEW/CR V, 1961.

69. "Certain Expenses of the United Nations (Article 17, Paragraph 2, of the Charter) Advisory Opinion of 20 July 1962," *ICJ Reports* (1962): 151.

70. The same was true of Cambodia, Angola, and El Salvador; in none of those cases was Chapter VII invoked.

71. UN Chater, Art. 103.

72. SC Res. 713, Sept. 25, 1991, UN Doc. S/RES/713 (1991).

73. See, e.g., SC Res. 743, UN Doc. S/RES/743 (1992); SC Res. 757, UN Doc. S/RES/757 (1992); SC Res. 770, UN Doc. S/RES/770 (1992); SC Res. 787, UN Doc. S/RES/787 (1992). There are frequent references to cease-fire violations and to the importance of the delivery of humanitarian aid to the Security Council's efforts to restore peace and security to the area, but none to the transboundary impact of the continuing violence.

74. SC Res. 733, Jan. 23, 1992, UN Doc. S/RES/733 (1992).

75. SC Res 841, June 16, 1993, UN Doc. S/RES/841 (1993).

76. The following account draws on Sean Coté, "A Narrative of the Implementation of Section C of United Nations Security Council Resolution 687," unpublished paper, 1994.

77. SC Res 687, UN Doc. S/RES/687 (1991), Apr. 8, 1991, *International Legal Materials,* 30 (May 1991): 847–854. It also determined the Iraq-Kuwait boundary (rejecting all of Iraq's prewar claims) and imposed reparations (to be paid from a percentage of Iraq's petroleum sales). Cuba was the single negative vote; Ecuador and Yemen abstained. Although the resolution does not itself invoke Chapter VII, the legal theory is that it is carrying out earlier mandatory resolutions calling for the restoration of peace and security in the area.

78. "UN Role in the Persian Gulf and Iraqi Compliance with UN Resoutions," *Hearing before the Subcommittee on Europe and the Middle East and on Human Rights and International Organizations of the House Committee on Foreign Affairs,* 102nd Congress, 1st sess. (Oct. 21, 1991), p. 159 (testimony of Ambassador Thomas R. Pickering, former U.S. permanent respresentative to the United Nations, p. 2).

79. See statement by Maurizio Zifferero, head of the IAEA's UNSCOM team: "There is no longer any nuclear activity in Iraq." Associated Press, "UN Says Iraqi Atom Arms Industry Gone," *New York Times,* Sept. 4, 1992, p. A2.

80. Elaine Sciolino, "Kurds Will Die in Vast Numbers without Swift Aid, Agencies Say," *New York Times,* Apr. 10, 1991, p. A1, col. 4.

81. SC Res. 688, par. 1, 2, and 3, Apr. 5, 1991, *International Legal Materials,* 30 (May 1991): 859.

82. Patrick E. Tyler, "U.S. Scouting Refugee Sites Well Inside Iraq's Borders, Aiming to Lure Kurds Home," *New York Times,* Apr. 18, 1991, p. A1, col. 6; Neil A. Lewis, "Legal Scholars Debate Refugee Plan, Generally Backing U.S. Stand," *New York Times,* Apr. 19, 1991, p. A8, col. 1.

83. "Annex" (agreed to on Apr. 18, 1991), UN Doc. S/22663, May 31, 1991, *International Legal Materials,* 30 (May 1991): 862.

84. Patrick E. Tyler, "Kurd Reports Agreement on Autonomy," *New York Times,* June 24, 1991, p. 6, col. 4; Alan Cowell, "Iraqi Kurds Reject Autonomy Accord as Allied Plan Stirs Some Confidence," *New York Times,* June 30, 1991, p. 6, col. 1; Chris Hedges, "Kurdish Talks Frozen, Iraqis Advance Anew," *New York Times,* Nov. 26, 1991, p. A1, col. 2.

85. For an account of the administration of the sanctions, see David E. Reuther,

"Economic War and Compliance," paper prepared for the Fourth Freedom Conference on Economic Sanctions, University of Notre Dame, Notre Dame, Ind., Apr. 2–4, 1993.

86. See, e.g., *Note by President of the Security Council,* UN Doc. S/2335, Dec. 20, 1991, p. 1.

87. See Douglas Jehl, "U.S. Jet Patrolling Iraq Fires Missile at Artillery Site," *New York Times,* June 30, 1993, p. 3; Paul Lewis, "Iraq Agrees to Allow the UN to Monitor Weapons Industries," *New York Times,* July 20, 1993, p. 1, col. 2.

88. Alexander Shumilin, "Baghdad Looks for 'Weak Link' in Anti-Iraq Caolition," *Moscow News,* Apr. 1, 1994, p. 4; Konstantin Kapitonov, "How Iraq Is Circumventing UN Sanctions," *Moscow News,* June 10, 1994, p. 5; Alan Riding, "French Talk with Iraq Official, and Allies Are Angry," *New York Times,* Jan. 7, 1995, p. 6(L), col. 1.

89. *UN Chronicle,* vol. 30, no. 1 (Mar. 1993): 4.

90. See Conference on Yugoslavia, Arbitration Commission, Opinion no. 5, "On the Recognition of the Republic of Croatia by the European Community and Its Member States," *International Legal Materials,* 31 (1992): 1503. Slovenia moved in tandem with Croatia, also declaring its independence on June 25, 1991. See "On International Recognition of the Republic of Slovenia by the European Community and Its Member States," in ibid., p. 1512. But Slovenia borders on Western Europe, snuggled between Austria to the north and Italy to the west. It is small, ethnically homogenous, and has no common border with Serbia and no Serb population. Under these circumstances, its secession meant little to the Serbians. After a short and relatively bloodless clash with Slovene territorial defense units and police, the Yugoslav army unilaterally withdrew on July 18, leaving Slovenia to go its own way.

91. Liu, Hourong, "UN's Role in Solving Regional Conflicts Enhanced," *Beijing Review,* 35 (Jan. 27, 1992): 14.

92. SC Res. 713, 3009th mtg., UN Doc. S/RES/713 (1991).

93. SC Res. 743, 3055th mtg., UN Doc. S/RES/743 (1992). Full deployment was authorized on April 7 by SC Res. 749, 3066th mtg., UN Doc. S/RES/749 (1992). See also *Further Report of the Secretary-General Pursuant to Security Council Resolution 721* (1991), UN Doc. S/23592 (Feb. 19, 1992).

94. SC Res. 779, 3118th mtg., UN Doc. S/RES/779 (1992).

95. Stephen Kinzer, "Europe, Backing Germans, Accepts Yugoslav Breakup," *New York Times,* Jan. 16, 1992, p. A10, col. 3. The EC announced in December 1991 that it would recognize on January 15 any of the former Yugoslav republics that applied and that met previously promulgated conditions for recognition of new states concerning primarily the protection of human rights and minorities. European Community, "Declaration on Yugoslavia and on the Guidelines on Recognition of New States in Eastern Europe and in the Soviet Union (December 16, 1991)," *International Legal Materials,* 31 (1992): 1485. It established an Arbitral Commission of European high court judges to decide whether the conditions had been met. Although the tribunal found that neither Croatia nor Bosnia passed muster, the EC went ahead with recognition on schedule. Macedonia's recognition was deferred, although the

tribunal gave it a clean bill of health. The documentation is collected in Conference on Yugoslavia, Arbitration Commission, "Opinions on Questions Arising from the Dissolution of Yugoslavia" (Jan. 11 and July 4, 1992), in ibid, p. 1488.

96. David Binder, "U.S. Recognizes 3 Yugoslav Republics as Independent," *New York Times,* Apr. 8, 1992, p. A10; "3 Ex-Yugoslav Republics Are Accepted into UN," *New York Times,* May 23, 1992, p. 4.

97. SC Res. 757, 3082nd mtg., UN Doc S/RES/757 (May 30, 1992).

98. SC Res. 787, 3137th mtg., UN Doc. S/RES/787 (Nov. 16, 1992). The resolution also prohibits the transhipment of embargoed items across Yugoslav territory.

99. See Alan Cowell, "NATO and European Warships Blockade Yugoslavia," *New York Times,* Nov. 21, 1992, p. 3, col. 1. There were some intercepts but no serious fighting.

100. SC Res. 770, 3106th mtg., UN Doc. S/RES/770 (Aug. 13, 1992).

101. Richard Bernstein, "Unless Situation Improves, U.S. Should Quit Bosnia, Mediator Says," *New York Times,* July 14, 1993, p. A3, col. 1. As of mid-1993, UNPROFOR had 22,639 troops from thirty-two participating countries. Rosalyn Higgins, "The New United Nations and Former Yugoslavia," *International Affairs,* 69, no. 3 (July 1993): 472. Randall Ryan, "Constraints Test UN's Troops," *Boston Globe,* May 2, 1995, p. 1.

102. SC Res. 781, 3122nd mtg., UN Doc. S/RES/781 (Oct. 9, 1992).

103. SC Res. 816, 3191st mtg., UN Doc. S/RES/816 (Mar. 31, 1993).

104. See Robert S. Greenberger, "Security Council Votes to Enforce No-Fly Zone," *Wall Street Journal,* Apr. 1, 1993, p. A3. From April through July, NATO planes flew about 4,000 sorties, with 116 confirmed sightings of violators. Of 48 intercepts, 32 landed immediately, 19 evaded action, 1 left Bosnian airspace, and 5 disappeared. No offending aircraft was shot down. Chuck Sudetic, "Tough Calls: Enforcing a Flight Ban over Bosnia," *New York Times,* July 12, 1993, p. A8, col. 1.

105. Roger Cohen, "Sarajevo Standoff: Paralysis of Big-Power Diplomacy," *New York Times,* Sept. 7, 1994, p. A3, col. 1; Richard W. Stevenson, "Britain and France Criticize U.S. on Bosnia positions; U.S. Presses to Lift Arms Embargo on Bosnian Muslims," *New York Times,* Nov. 29, 1994, p. A16(L), col. 1; Elaine Sciolino, "House, Like Senate, Votes to Halt Bosnia Embargo," *New York Times,* Aug. 2, 1995, p. A6(L), col. 5.

106. For a persuasive presentation of the heterodox view that the economic embargo was ill-conceived and served only to exacerbate the situation, see Susan L. Woodward, "Economic Sanctions and the Disintegration of Yugoslavia, 1991–93: Questioning Political Assumptions," paper for the Fourth Freedom Conference on Economic Sanctions, University of Notre Dame, Notre Dame, Ind., Apr. 2–4, 1993.

107. Thomas G. Weiss, "Collective Spinelessness: UN Actions in the Former Yugoslavia," in Richard Ullman, ed., *The World and Yugoslavia's Wars: Implications for International Politics* (New York: Council on Foreign Relations, forthcoming).

108. "The United Nations and Somalia; The Squeezing of Sahnoun," *The Economist,* Nov. 7, 1992, p. 50.

109. Jane Perlez, "Deaths in Somalia Outpace Delivery of Food," *New York Times,* July 19, 1992, p. 1, col. 2.

110. SC Res. 733, Jan. 23, 1992, 3039th mtg., UN Doc. S/RES/733. The council was "aware" of the consequences of the situation in Somalia for the stability and peace of the region, and was "concerned that the continuation of this situation constitutes . . . a threat to international peace and security." But it was clear that the resort to Chapter VII was much less firmly anchored in transboundary ramifications than ever before.

111. SC Res. 751, Apr. 24, 1992, 3069th mtg., UN Doc. S/RES/751 (1992).

112. In response to UN secretary general Boutros-Ghali's angry comparison of the international concern about the "rich man's war" in Yugoslavia with the failure to take action in Somalia (see Trevor Rowe, "Aid to Somalia Stymied, UN Votes Relief, but Clan Blocks Effort," *Washington Post,* July 29, 1992, p. 1), the Security Council authorized an emergency airlift of humanitarian relief, but with little effect. SC Res. 767, July 27, 1992, UN Doc. S/RES/767 (1992).

113. "When the Coaxing Had to Stop," *The Economist,* Dec. 5, 1992, p. 16.

114. SC Res. 794, Dec. 3, 1992, 3145th mtg., UN Doc. S/RES/794 (1992).

115. SC Res. 814, Mar. 26, 1993, UN Doc. S/RES/814 (1993). Twenty-four countries contributed to the force. Donatella Lorch, "UN Moves Troops to Somali City and Vows Punishment for Attack," *New York Times,* June 8, 1993, p. A1, col. 1.

116. SC Res. 837, June 6, 1993, 3229th mtg. UN Doc. S/RES/837 (1993).

117. Douglas Jehl, "Somalia GI's: They're Bitter and Grousing," *New York Times,* Oct. 15, 1993, p. A13, col. 1.

118. Douglas Jehl, "The Somalia Mission: Overview; Clinton Doubling U.S. Force in Somalia, Vowing Troops Will Come Home in 6 months," *New York Times,* Oct. 8, 1993, p. A1, col. 6; Eric Schmitt, "The Somalia Mission: Clinton Reviews Policy in Somalia as Unease Grows," *New York Times,* Oct. 6, 1993, p. A1, col. 5.

119. Thomas Friedman, "The O.A.S. Agrees to Isolate chiefs of Haitian Junta," *New York Times,* Oct. 3, 1991, p. A1, col. 6; Thomas Friedman, "Regional Group Agrees to Increase Penalties on Haiti," *New York Times,* Oct. 9, 1991, p. A3, col. 1.

120. Barbara Crossette, "Haiti Dispute: Limits on U.S.; Other Concerns Appear to Block Strong Action," *New York Times,* May 19, 1992, p. A7, col. 1. See "European Economic Community—African, Caribbean, and Pacific Countries: Documents from Lomé Meeting," *International Legal Materials,* 14 (1975): 595; "European Economic Community—African, Caribbean, and Pacific Countries: Documents from Lomé II Meeting," *International Legal Materials,* 19 (Mar. 1980): 327.

121. See Secretary Baker, "Attack on Democracy in Haiti," *U.S. Department of State Dispatch,* 2, no. 40 (Oct. 7, 1991): 749 (address before the Organization of American States, Washington, D.C., Oct. 2, 1991).

122. Pamela Constable, "Dateline Haiti: Caribbean Stalemate," *Foreign Policy,* 89, (Winter 1992–93): 182. The OAS tried to beef up the sanctions in May 1992, primarily by "urg[ing] member states to deny port facilities to any vessel that does not abide by the embargo." "Restoration of Democracy in Haiti," Res. MRE/RES. 3/92,

May 17, 1992, *U.S. Department of State Dispatch,* 3, no. 26 (June 29, 1992): 525. See "Statement on Denying Use of United States Ports to Vessels Trading with Haiti, May 28, 1992," *Weekly Compilation of Presidential Documents,* 28, no. 22 (June 1, 1992): 941.

123. SC Res. 841, June 16, 1993, 3238th mtg., UN Doc. S/RES/841 (1993).

124. SC Res. 940, July 31, 1994, UN Doc. S/RES/940 (1994); Michael Wines, "As 3 Emissaries Claim Victory, Doubts Remain," *New York Times,* Sept. 20, 1994, p. A1(L), col. 5; Douglas Jehl, "Clinton Exults in Swift Success of U.S. Military Force in Haiti," *New York Times,* Oct. 7, 1994, p. A14(L), col. 1. James F. Dobbins, "Elections in Haiti: An Important Milestone," U.S. Department of State Dispatch, July 17, 1995, p. 567.

125. See Art. 18, 19. See also Inter-American Treaty of Reciprocal Assistance Art. 20. In the Haiti case, the OAS declined to use its mandatory powers to impose economic sanctions, and contented itself with "urging" an embargo.

126. See, e.g., Michael Taylor, "Cooperation and Rationality: Notes on the Collective Action Problem and Its Solution," in Karen Schweers Cook and Margaret Levi, eds., *The Limits of Rationality* (Chicago: University of Chicago Press, 1990), p. 225; Jon Elster, *The Cement of Society* (Cambridge: Cambridge University Press, 1989), pp. 40–41.

127. David M. Rowe, "The Domestic Political Economy of International Economic Sanctions," Center for International Affairs, Harvard University, Working Paper no. 93-1 (1993), p. 31.

128. Steven Greenhouse, "Washington Urges France to delay Rwanda Withdrawal," *New York Times,* Aug. 17, 1994, p. A12(L), col. l.

3. Membership Sanctions

1. Louis B. Sohn, "Expulsion or Forced Withdrawal from an International Organization," *Harvard Law Review,* 77 (1964): 1381, 1420.

2. Article 6 of the UN Charter states: "A Member of the United Nations which has persistently violated the Principles contained in the present Charter may be expelled from the Organization by the General Assembly upon the recommendation of the Security Council." The issue was controversial at the San Francisco Conference, and the records make it clear that Article 6 was intended to apply only "to Member States which were admittedly incorrigible and which violated the principles contained in the Charter in a grave or persistent manner." UN Conference on International Organization, *Documents,* vol. 7 (1945), pp. 330–331. No provision for withdrawal was included, but the conference adopted an interpretative declaration confirming the sovereign right of a member to withdraw in extraordinary circumstances. See Leland M. Goodrich and Edvard Hambro, *Charter of the United Nations: Commentary and Documents,* 2nd ed. (London: Stevens and Sonsa, Ltd., 1949). Only one state has done so: Indonesia withdrew in 1965.

3. The actions taken against South Africa, and more recently, Yugoslavia, have

been described as de facto suspensions. In 1974 South Africa was "suspended from participation in the General Assembly," and it did not send a delegation to the General Assembly until 1994, after the first free election. The case of Yugoslavia was treated as a problem of state succession. Both cases are discussed in this chapter.

4. See, e.g., IAEA, Art. XIX(B); IMF Agreement, Art. XXV sec. 2; International Coffee Agreement; WMO, Art. 31.

5. See David Mitrany, *The Functional Theory of Politics,* (New York: St. Martin's Press, 1976); Ernest B. Haas, *Beyond the Nation-State: Functionalism in International Organization* (Stanford, Calif.: Stanford University Press, 1964).

6. We do not consider here the International Monetary Fund's practice of refusing to advance additional credit to members that are seriously in arrears in repaying their drawings. Because the borrower is necessarily a member of the fund, this practice is treated in form as a suspension of one of the privileges of membership for a party that has failed to carry out its obligations, but in reality it is what any creditor does with a sufficiently delinquent debtor. It is a banking practice, not a membership sanction. This is discussed along with other IMF management techniques, in Chapter 10.

7. Yassin El Ayouty and William Zartman, eds., *The OAU after Twenty Years* (New York: Praeger, 1984); Richard F. Bissell, *Apartheid and International Organizations* (Boulder, Colo.: Westview Press, 1977), p. 15.

8. Calls for a voluntary economic cutoff had been made earlier. UN Doc. S/5386, UN SCOR, 18th year, 1056th mtg. of Security Council, Aug. 7, 1963, Suppl. for July, Aug., and Sept. 1963, p. 73; Security Council Res. 591, UN SCOR, 41st year, 2723rd mtg., Nov. 28, 1986.

9. UN SCOR, 29th year, 1808th mtg., Oct. 30, 1974, p. 17–18, and Suppl. for Oct.–Dec. 1974, pp. 34–35.

10. "International Labour Conference, Resolution 1, June 29, 1961," *ILO Official Bulletin,* 44, 45th sess. (1961): 16–17 (adopted by 163 votes to 0, with 89 abstentions).

11. International Labour Conference, 47th sess., 10th sitting, Geneva, June 12, 1963, *Record of Proceedings,* p. 135.

12. Ibid., pp. 135–141, 144, 145, 169, 170, 173; see also "ILO Parley Head Quits in Boycott," *New York Times,* June 16, 1963, p. 9, col. 3; "ILO Crisis Grows," *New York Times,* June 18, 1963, p. 27, col. 4.

13. International Labor Conference, "Report of the Director-General (Part II) to the International Labour Conference, 48th Session, 1964," *Record of Proceedings,* pp. 14–15; "Minutes of the 156th Session of the Governing Body, Geneva, June 28–29, 1963," *Record of Proceedings,* pp. 13–21.

14. *Minutes of the Governing Body, 159th Session, International Labour Office, June 11–13, 1964,* (Geneva: ILO, 1964), pp. 146–147. Despite South Africa's claim that these actions exempted it from the two-year notice requirement in the ILO withdrawal provision, the organization successfully insisted that South Africa pay regular member contributions for two years until the withdrawal took effect. *United Nations*

Yearbook 1965, (New York: United Nations Office of Public Information), p. 711; *United Nations Yearbook 1966,* p. 977.

15. *Report on the Activities of the International Telecommunication Union in 1964,* Section 6.1, (Geneva: ITU, 1965); "La conférence africaine se réunit mais ne peut poursuivre ses travaux," *Journal des Telecommunications,* vol. 31, no. 11 (Nov. 1964): 296.

16. *Report on the Activities of the International Telecommunication Union in 1965* (Geneva: ITU, 1966); George A. Codding and Anthony M.Rutkowski, *The International Telecommunication Union in a Changing World* (Dedham, Mass.: Artech House, 1982), pp. 41–61.

17. Bissell, *Apartheid and International Organizations,* p. 208; *Report on the Activities of the International Telecommunication Union in 1973,* Res. 31 (Geneva: ITU, 1974), p. 153; Codding and Rutkowski, *The International Telecommunication Union in a Changing World,* pp. 190–192.

18. *World Health Organization Official Records,* no. 127, 16th World Health Assembly, "Part I, Resolutions and Decisions," Annex 14, pp. 180–181.

19. *United Nations Yearbook 1963,* p. 615.

20. *World Health Organization Official Records,* no. 135, 17th World Health Assembly, Part I, Res. WHA17.50 p. 23 (1964); *World Health Organization Official Records,* no. 136, 17th World Health Assembly, Part II, 12th Plenary Meeting, pp. 201–202. Article 7 of the WHO constitution provides for suspension of voting rights by the World Health Assembly "in exceptional circumstances." WHO, *United Nations Treaty Series* vol. 14, pp. 185–285.

21. "Seventeenth World Health Assembly Meets in Geneva," *UN Review,* Apr. 1964, pp. 23–24

22. *World Health Organization Official Records,* no. 143, 18th World Health Assembly, Part I, "Resolutions and Decisions," Res. WHA18.48, p. 32 (1965).

23. *World Health Organization Official Records,* no. 157, 39th Sess. of Executive Board, Part I, "Resolutions," Annex 7, pp. 45–46 (1967).

24. *Report of the 12th Session of the Conference,* Nov. 16–Dec. 5, 1963, (Rome: FAO, 1964), p. 81.

25. Ibid., Res. no. 38/63, pp. 81–84.

26. *United Nations Yearbook 1963,* pp. 604–605.

27. UNESCO, *Report of the Director General,* 1955, p. 19; Doc. 42 EX/43, Paris, November 9, 1955, 42nd Sess. of the Executive Board; Doc. 42 EX/Decisions, Paris, Dec. 15, 1955, 42nd Sess. of the Executive Board; *Report of the Director General,* 1956, p. 15.

28. Resolution 9.12, *Records of the General Conference, 15th Session, Resolutions* (Paris: UNESCO, 1968), p. 87.

29. ESCOR, resumed 34th sess., 1239th mtg., Dec. 19, 1962, E/SR 1239, pp. 11, 17.

30. ECA Res. 84(V), Mar. 1, 1963, *ECOSOC Official Records,* 36th sess., Res. Supp. no. 10, p. 46. Action in accordance with this resolution resulted in the cancellation of or change of venue for a number of meetings scheduled for Africa, and played an important tactical role in the expulsion campaign of the ITU.

31. *Communication from the Ambassador of South Africa,* UN Doc. E/3820, July 19, 1963 ECOSOC, 36th sess. agenda item 12.

32. *ECOSOC Official Records,* July 2–Aug. 2, 1963, 36th sess., "Resolutions," Supp. no. 1, pp. 3–4.

33. H. G. Schermers, "Some Constitutional Notes on the 15th Congress of the Universal Postal Union," *International and Comparative Law Quarterly,* 14, (Apr. 1965): 632; "Summary of Activities: Fifteenth Universal Postal Congress," *International Organization,* 20, (1966): 834.

34. See, e.g., UPU Res. C2, "Expulsion of the South African Delegation from the XVIth Congress of UPU in Tokyo," *1969 UN Juridical Yearbook,* p. 119.

35. *Report on the Work of the Union 1979,* par. 1.1, (Berne: International Bureau of the Universal Postal Union, 1980).

36. Res. 1761 (XVII) of Nov. 6, 1962, *Official Records of the General Assembly, 17th Session,* Supp. no. 17 (A/5217), "Resolutions," agenda item 87, Doc. A/5166, p. 9.

37. *Minutes of the Plenary Meetings, 15th Session of the Assembly of the ICAO,* Doc. 8516 A15-P/5, Montreal June 22–July 16, 1965, pp. 137–142; see also "Conflict of UN Resolutions with Chicago Convention on Civil Aviation: Letter of ICAO to UN Dated March 30, 1966," UN Doc. A/6394, Apr. 1, 1966, reproduced in *International Legal Materials,* 5 (1966): 486.

38. ICAO Res. A18-4, GAOR, 26th sess., *Report of the Special Committee on Apartheid* (A/8422/Rev.1), Supp. no. 22, p. 52.

39. *United Nations Yearbook 1974,* p. 1011.

40. "Declaration concerning the Representation of South Africa," IAEA General Conference, Sept. 15, 1964, Doc. GC(VIII)/OR.84, Jan. 14, 1965.

41. Gary Clyde Hufbauer, Jeffrey J. Schott, and Kimberly Ann Elliott, *Economic Sanctions Reconsidered: Supplemental Case Histories,* 2nd ed. (Washington, D.C.: Institute for International Economics, 1990), pp. 405–406 (case 75-4, *U.S. v. South Africa*); IAEA General Conference, 23rd Regular Session, Dec. 5, 1979 (New Delhi), Doc. GC(XXIII)/OR.210, p. 2, and Doc. GC(XXIII)/OR.211, pp. 1–7; Michael T. Kaufman, "Nuclear Parley Bars South Africa," *New York Times,* Dec. 6, 1979, p. A14, col. 1.

42. *Annual Report of the WMO, 1975,* p. 88.

43. Bissell, *Apartheid and International Organizations,* p. 162; Kathleen Teltsch, "South Africa Is Suspended by UN Assembly," *New York Times,* Nov. 13, 1974, p. 1. The resolution is in *GAOR 29th Session, Plenary Meetings,* vol. 2, 2281st plenary mtg., pp. 839 ff.

44. O. A. Ozgur, *Apartheid: The United Nations and Peaceful Change in South Africa* (Dobbs Ferry, N.Y.: Transnational Publishers, 1982); *Financial Sanctions against South Africa: Report of a Study Concluded under Auspices of Group of Independent Experts* (Geneva: ILO, 1991).

45. Helen Suzman, *In No Uncertain Terms* (New York: Alfred A. Knopf, 1993), pp. 259–265; Stephen P. Davis, "Economic Pressure on South Africa: Does It Work?" in George W. Shepherd, Jr., ed., *Effective Sanctions in South Africa: The Cutting Edge of Economic Intervention* (New York: Greenwood Press, 1991), pp. 77–79.

46. UN SCOR, 461st mtg., Jan. 13, 1950, pp. 1–10. General Assembly Res. 609A(VI). The council approved the Credential Committee's report (accepting the credentials of the Republic of China). Similar action was taken in subsequent years.

47. At this time, the Soviet bloc in the UN, in addition to the USSR, included only Belorussia and the Ukrainian SSR (both of which had been admitted as original members at the insistence of the USSR to mitigate communist numerical inferiority in the organization), plus Poland and Czechoslovakia. Albania, Bulgaria, Hungary and Romania, having been wartime allies of Germany, were not admitted to membership until 1955. However, they joined some of the specialized agencies that did not require membership in the UN.

48. *United Nations Bulletin*, June 1, 1950, p. 504; ibid., June 15, 1950, p. 29.

49. The USSR also withdrew from the consultative conference on general nuclear disarmament in 1950, thereby suspending the six-power consultations. *United Nations Yearbook 1950*, pp. 415–416.

50. Ibid., pp. 415–416.

51. Ibid., pp. 10–11. See also Rupert Emerson and Inis L. Claude, Jr., "The Soviet Union and the United Nations: An Essay in Interpretation," *International Organization*, 6, (1952): 19–21.

52. "Members of the UN, the Specialized Agencies, IAEA, and GATT" (as of Dec. 1982), UN Secretariat ST/LIB/39, May 24, 1983.

53. Except for the WMO, which Poland did not join until 1950, Hungary until 1951, and Bulgaria until 1952.

54. Harold K. Jacobson, *The USSR and the UN's Economic and Social Activities* (Notre Dame, Ind.: University of Notre Dame Press, 1963), p. 10–11; Emerson and Claude, "The Soviet Union and the United Nations," p. 19.

55. For Czechoslovakia, these actions were taken in 1947, before the Soviet takeover in 1948, and one may speculate that for the other countries, also, the move antedated the imposition of strict Soviet control. All three countries had been members of the ILO before World War II, but they had to rejoin after it became a UN specialized agency. Bulgaria also joined the ILO in 1947, but Albania and Romania, which had been prewar members, did not rejoin until much later.

56. *World Health Organization Official Records, 2nd World Health Assembly*, pp. 17, 19, telegram dated Feb. 12, 1949, to the director general; "Russians Quitting UN Health Agency," *New York Times*, Feb. 17, 1949. The Soviets' charges sound eerily like the U.S. complaints about the specialized agencies two decades later, when it was in the minority. See also C. Osakwe, *The Participation of the Soviet Union in Universal International Organizations* (Leiden: Sijthoff, 1972), pp. 110, 117.

57. *United Nations Bulletin*, Apr. 1, 1949, p. 330; May 15, 1950, p. 446; Sept. 1, 1950, p. 224.

58. Ibid., June 1, 1950, p. 498; June 15, 1950, p. 529.

59. International Labour Conference, 33rd sess., Geneva, June 7, 1950, *Record of Proceedings*, pp. 6–9.

60. UNESCO General Conference, Extraordinary Session, Doc. 2 XC/6, Annex I, p. 3 (Paris, May 20, 1953).

61. FAO, Report of the Special Session of the Conference, Washington D.C., Nov. 3–11, 1950, p. 4; *FAO Bulletin,* July 1950, p. 9; *FAO Press Releases* I/R/350, Apr. 27, 1950, and I/R/379, Feb. 7, 1951.

62. Indeed, in one of the few successes for the Soviet policy, the Executive and Liaison Committee of the UPU seated the PRC representative, "in view of the strictly technical character of the UPU and the factual situation in China." *United Nations Bulletin,* June 1, 1950, p. 498. The UPU was one of the three agencies in which Soviet bloc states maintained membership throughout the period.

63. IMF, *Summary Proceedings: Annual Meeting 1954,* pp. 113–114, 137, 153–159.

64. *IMF Annual Report 1955,* p. 115.

65. Despite U.S. pressure, the United Kingdom and other important countries recognized the PRC. Nevertheless, many of them supported the United States in procedural moves in the UN. The United Kingdom recognized the PRC on January 6, 1950, in large part due to the situation of Hong Kong. The United Kingdom abstained on the Security Council vote taken January 13, 1950, stating that it was premature to discuss the matter before even a majority of the members of the Security Council had recognized the new government in China, but ultimately the United Kingdom voted against the United States on the (defeated) Indian draft resolution to seat the PRC government. See *United Nations Yearbook 1950,* pp. 425–429.

66. See *Hearings on Purchase of United Nations Bonds: Before the House Committee on Foreign Affairs,* 87th Congress, 2nd sess. (1962), pp. 366–367.

67. GA Res. 1731, UN Doc. A/5100 (1962), UN GAOR, vol. 16, Supp. 17, p 54 UN Charter Article 96 gives the assembly the power to request advisory opinions from the court, and Article 65 of the Statute of the International Court of Justice confers jurisdiction to entertain such requests. Other states in arrears also wanted the legal issue clarified but, unlike the USSR, professed themselves ready to pay if the court upheld the assessments. Abram Chayes, Thomas Ehrlich, and Andreas F. Lowenfeld, *International Legal Process: Materials for an Introductory Course,* vol. 1, (Boston: Little, Brown, 1968), p. 167.

68. "Certain Expenses of the United Nations," *ICJ Reports* (1962): 151.

69. *United Nations Yearbook 1964,* p. 29; "UN's Deadbeats," *New York Times,* June 16, 1963, p. 2E, col. 4. Ten members, including Hungary and Cuba, were more than two years in arrears just before the General Assembly convened in 1963, but they all paid up in time to avoid the issue.

70. See J. H. Spencer, "Africa at the UN: Some Observations," *International Organization,* 16 (1962): 378, noting that in the early 1960s, there was already a significant tendency for the Asian-African states to vote against the United States and with the Soviet Union on many cold war issues.

71. See Office of the Legal Advisor, U.S. Department of State, "Article 19 of the Charter of the United Nations: Memorandum of Law" (February 1964), pp. 8, 14,

17–25, reprinted in Chayes, Ehrlich, and Lowenfeld, *International Legal Process,* vol. 1 p. 219. Because, in the cases relied on, the delinquent state voluntarily refrained from voting until the arrearages had been paid, there were no clear-cut decisions on the point.

72. See the announcement of the secretary general at the beginning of the 19th session of the General Assembly, UN GAOR, vol. 19 (1964), p. 1286.

73. UN GAOR, vol. 19, 1329th Plenary Meeting, Feb. 16, 1965; ibid., 1330th Plenary Meeting, Feb. 18, 1965, pp. 1, 7. The debate is reprinted in Chayes, Ehrlich, and Lowenfeld, *International Legal Process,* vol. 1, pp. 229–242. Ambassador Stevenson's statement appears on p. 238.

74. Arthur J. Goldberg, "U.S. Finds UN Majority Unwilling to Enforce Article 19," *Department of State Bulletin,* 53 (1965): 454.

75. A special committee on peacekeeping expenditures was convened beginning in 1965 as part of the settlement of the whole affair. It produced draft principles that were never formally adopted but were followed for many years, including the one in the text. GA Res. 2006(XX), Feb. 18, 1965.

76. "Resolution of the Council of Delegates, April 26, 1961," *OAS Secretary General's Annual Report,* p. 12.

77. "Resolution VI, Eighth Meeting of Consultation of Ministers of Foreign Affairs," Jan. 31, 1962, OEA/Ser F/II.8, Doc. 68, pp. 17–19, Pan American Union, *Inter-American Treaty of Reciprocal Assistance, Applications,* vol. 2 (1964), pp. 75–76.

78. *Department of State Bulletin,* 46 (1962): 281.

79. See letter from the Cuban representative to the president of the Security Council, UN Doc. S/5086 (1962), UN SCOR, vol. 17, Supp. Jan.–Mar. 1962, pp. 88–90, 96; see also D. Larson, ed., *The Cuban Crisis of 1962, Selected Documents and Chronology* (Boston: Houghton Mifflin, 1963).

80. Although nearly every other Latin American country shares the view that political and economic change in Cuba is desirable, most have serious reservations about the U.S. policy of diplomatic and economic isolation and would prefer to effect change by integrating Cuba into the hemispheric community. See Peter Hakim, "The United States and Latin America: Good Neighbors Again?" *Current,* June 1992; "The Role of the OAS in the 1990s," *Hearing before the Subcommittees on Human Rights and International Organizations and Western Hemisphere Affairs of the House Committee on Foreign Affairs,* 101st Congress, 2nd sess., May 1, 1990, pp. 25–26.

81. SC Res. 777, Sept. 19, 1992, UN Doc. S/RES/777 (1992).

82. GA Res. 47/1, Sept. 22, 1992.

83. "Letter from Carl-August Fleischhauer, UN Under–Secretary General for Legal Affairs, to Mario Nobilio, Permanent Representative of the Republic of Croatia to the United Nations," UN Doc. A/47/485 (Sept. 29, 1992). See Yehuda Z. Blum, "UN Membership of the 'New' Yugoslavia: Continuity or Break?" *American Journal of International Law,* 86 (1992): 830; Vladimir-Djuro Degan, "Correspondents' Agora: UN Membership of the Former Yugoslavia," *American Journal of International Law,* 87 (1993): 240–251.

84. "CSCE Debates Balkan Crisis," *Facts on File,* July 23, 1992, p. 543, B3. The United States and the Russian Federation at the CSCE Council of Ministers meeting in Stockholm, issued a joint statement on December 14, 1992: "Russia and the United States hope that the people of Serbia will weigh the alternatives carefully. The choice is of returning to the community of nations or remaining in a pariah status, politically isolated and economically devastated because of the policies of the present regime. If the correct choice is made, Russia and the United States pledge to work with the Government of Serbia to restore its position in the world. If such a choice is followed by the fundamental change of policies for which Russia and the United States devoutly hope, the eventual relaxation and removal of the sanctions would be possible. Then Serbia, together with Montenegro, would be welcomed as a member of the UN, CSCE, and other institutions." *U.S. Department of State Dispatch,* 3, (Dec. 28, 1992): 914.

85. Jean E. Manas, "The Democracy Ideal and the Challege of Ethno-National Diversity: An Evaluation of the Council of Europe's Democracy Mission in Situations of Ethno-National Conflict," Carnegie Conflict Prevention Project, Working Paper no. 1, 1994.

86. Barbara Crossette, "UNESCO Woos Washington to No Avail," *New York Times,* Feb. 12, 1995, p. 8, col. 1. A thorough study of these three cases is found in Mark F. Imber, *The USA, ILO, UNESCO and IAEA: Politicization and Withdrawal in the Specialized Agencies* (New York: St. Martin's Press, 1989). This account relies primarily on Imber's work for its factual information.

87. Imber, *The USA, ILO, UNESCO and IAEA,* pp. 80–83. After the chairman announced that a motion to deny Israel's credentials had failed on a tie, the Malaysian delegate, who was recorded as not voting, asked to change his vote to support the motion. The legal counsel ruled erroneously that such a change, even after the announcement of the result of the vote, would be proper.

88. Other aspects of the whaling case are discussed in Chapter 4 and Chapter 11.

89. See Chapter 11.

90. *International Whaling Commission Report,* IWC Schedule, par. 10(e) (Feb. 1983).

91. In 1992 the IWC Scientific Committee estimated the number of minke whales at 760,000 in Antarctic waters and 114,000 in the North Atlantic. See "Whaling Panel Agrees to New Formula for Limited Catches," *New York Times,* July 4, 1992, p. 2, col. 1. However, the committee's estimates of whale populations have earned considerable skepticism.

92. See Chapter 4.

93. Keith Schneider, "Iceland Plans to Withdraw from International Whaling Agreement," *New York Times,* Dec. 28, 1991, p. 3, col. 1; Craig Whitney, "Norway Is Planning to Resume Whaling Despite World Ban," *New York Times,* June 30, 1992, p. A1, col. 3.

94. See Glenn Frankel, "Norway, Iceland Defy Ban, Will Resume Whale Hunts," *Washington Post,* June 30, 1992, p. A14.

95. Iceland's action was not the first withdrawal episode in the IWC. In 1958, when the organization was a virtual whaler's club, Norway and the Netherlands withdrew because the organization refused to make national allocations in the global quota it set on whale hunting. IWC, *Annual Report*, 1959, p. 6. Ultimately they returned, and the five principal Antarctic whaling countries reached an agreement outside the IWC on the division of the global quota.

96. Oran Young, et al., "Commentary: Subsistence, Sustainability, and Sea Mammals: Reconstructing the International Whaling Regime," *Ocean and Coastal Management*, 23 (1994): 117–127.

97. Robert O. Keohane, *After Hegemony: Cooperation and Discord in the World Political Economy* (Princeton, N.J.: Princeton University Press, 1984), pp. 89–93.

98. International Convention for the Regulation of Whaling, preamble.

99. Steinar Andresen, "Science and Politics in the International Management of Whales," *Marine Policy*, 13 (1989): 115–116.

4. Unilateral Sanctions

1. It is widely understood that in all social settings, from aboriginal villages to contemporary business deals, norms are enforced primarily by "nonlegal" sanctions rather than formal legal action. See, e.g., Stewart Macaulay, "Non-Contractual Relations in Business," *American Sociological Review*, 28 (1963): 55.

2. We call such measures unilateral sanctions, although the term is not wholly satisfactory, not least because such actions are often taken by a number of nations in concert. We mean to convey that the sanctions are not authorized by collective decison in accordance with agreed procedures. See Sidney Weintraub, *Economic Coercion and U.S. Foreign Policy: Implications of Case Studies of the Johnson Administration* (Boulder, Colo.: Westview Press, 1982), p. 4, for comment on the difficulty of defining the exact point on the spectrum at which pressure becomes "coercive." "A trade embargo or collective economic sanctions" are clearly so. In Chapter 10 we address the techniques of persuasion and shaming and shunning, corresponding to David Charny's categories of reputational and psychic sanctions and to what Robert Keohane calls "diffuse reciprocity." David Charny, "Nonlegal Sanctions in Commercial Relationships," *Harvard Law Review* 102 (1990): 375, 392–394; Robert Keohane, "Reciprocity in International Relations," in Robert O. Keohane, *International Institutions and State Power* (Boulder, Colo.: Westview Press, 1989), pp. 146–150.

3. Vienna Convention on the Law of Treaties, Art. 60(1).

4. When the issue was first put before the International Law Commission, however, the reporter could not find any examples of the exercise of the right of suspension for material breach. Herbert Briggs, the U.S. delegate, maintained that it "was based neither on state practice nor on the decisions of international tribunals, but on the theories of writers and on speculation." *1963 Yearbook of the International Law Commission*, vol. 1, (New York: United Nations, 1963), p. 112. But see "Opinion of the Legal Adviser," Aug. 12, 1963, in *Hearings on the Nuclear*

Test Ban Treaty before the Senate Committee on Foreign Relations, 88th Congress, 1st sess. (1963), pp. 37–40.

5. "The use of economic pressure in the conduct of foreign policy . . . is pervasive." Weintraub, *Economic Coercion and U.S. Foreign Policy,* p. 3.

6. Nondiscrimination is said to be the basic norm of the GATT. It is embodied in the requirement of most-favored nation treatment, Art. I, and national treatment, Art. III.

7. Generalized System of Preferences, United States Code, Title 19, Sec. 2461 (1988); see also Alan O. Sykes, "Constructive Unilateral Threats in International Commercial Relations: The Limited Case for Section 301," *Law and Policy in International Business,* 23, no. 2 (Spring 1992): 263–330, n. 123.

8. 19 USC. §§ 2411 et seq. Section 301 thus puts considerable power, at least over the tactics of U.S. trade policy, in private hands. Since 1984, the U.S. trade representative has also been authorized to initiate Section 301 actions on its own motion. The section provides that the president *must* retaliate if the ITC finds that the practice violates GATT obligations to the United States and *may* retaliate if the practice is found to be unfair or otherwise unduly burdensome to U.S. trade.

9. 19 USC. § 2420. Super 301 lapsed in 1990 but was reinstated at the height of the trade confrontation between the Clinton administration and Japan in the spring of 1994.

10. 16 USC. § 1821(e)(2) (Packwood-Magnuson); 22 USC. § 1978 (Pelly). As discussed later in this chapter, the Pelly Amendment sanction was threatened with some effect, but never actually imposed. "Message to the Congress Reporting on International Whaling Operations and Conservation Programs," Jan. 16, 1975, *Presidential Papers of President Gerald Ford, Book I* (Washington, D.C.: USGPO, 1977), p. 47. Congress then enacted the Packwood-Magnuson Amendment, because, in the words of the U.S. Supreme Court, it was "impatient with the Executive's delay in making certification decisions and refusal to impose sanctions." *Japan Whaling Association v. American Cetacean Society,* U.S. 221, 226, vol. 478 (1986). See also Gene S. Martin, Jr., and James W. Brennan, "Enforcing the International Convention for the Regulation of Whaling: The Pelly and Packwood-Magnuson Amendments," *Denver Journal of International Law and Policy,* 17, no. 2, (Winter 1989): 293–315.

11. Foreign Assistance Act of 1961, § 116, 22 USC. § 2151N (International Development and Food Assistaance Act); International Security Assistance and Arms Export Control Act of 1976, § 301, 90 Stat. 748 (1976), 22 USC. 2304; Foreign Assistance Act of 1961, P.L. 87-195, 75 Stat. 424, amended by P.L. 95-384, 92 Stat. 731, 22 USC. 2304. For an excellent general review of the legislative-executive interaction in the Carter administration, see Stephen B. Cohen, "Conditioning U.S. Security Assistance on Human Rights Practices," *American Journal of International Law,* 76, no. 2 (April 1982): 256–275. The campaign began in the early 1970s as a "sense of the Congress" provision, reflecting a post-Watergate resolve to shape a more principled foreign policy and a response to the resurgence of authoritarian governments in Latin America. Foreign Assistance Act of 1973, § 32 P.L. 93-189, 87 Stat. 714

(1973). The United States was not yet party to any of the many human rights conventions promulgated under the auspices of the United Nations and other international organizations, but in 1975, it signed the Helsinki Final Act, in which the parties undertook "to respect human rights and fundamental freedoms." This was supposed to be without binding legal effect. Helsinki Final Act, Art. VII.

12. "International Bank for Reconstruction and Development, P.L. 95-118, Legislative History," *U.S. Congressional and Administrative News*, (1977): 2742–2744.

13. Lisa Martin, *Coercive Cooperation: Explaining Multilateral Economic Sanctions* (Princeton, N.J.: Princeton University Press, 1992), p. 114.

14. P.L. 95-242, 92 Stat. 120-152 (1978), 22 USC. §§ 3201–3282, 42 USC. §§ 2011–2160(a). The legislative impetus was India's unexpected explosion of a "peaceful nuclear device" in 1974, severely shaking confidence in the NPT regime. The first steps were the Symington Amendment in 1976, Public Law 94-329, June 30, 1976, and the Glenn Amendment in 1977, Public Law 95-92, Aug. 4, 1977. Both, however, were subject to presidential waiver. See, generally, Jonathan B. Schwartz, "Controlling Nuclear Proliferation: Legal Strategies of the United States," *Law and Policy in International Business*, 20, no. 1 (1988): 1–61, for an extended discussion of the international agreements and domestic legislation governing nuclear commerce. Sanctions are discussed on pp. 51–61.

15. Atomic Energy Act § 129, 42 USC. § 2158; Foreign Assistance Act, §§ 669–670, 22 USC. §§ 2429–2429a; Export-Import Bank Act of 1945, § 2(b)(4), 12 USC. § 635(b)(4). Like the whaling sanctions, these were applicable whether or not the offending country was a party to the treaty.

16. In the one case in which the issue was raised, the export of nuclear materials to fulfill a contract to refuel India's Tarapur reactor, the House voted to override President Carter's waiver, but the Senate supported him by a vote of 48 to 46. For a full account of the episode, see Brian L. Schorr, "Testing Statutory Criteria for Foreign Policy: The Nuclear Non-Proliferation Act of 1978 and the Export of Nuclear Fuel to India," *New York University Journal of International Law and Politics*, 14, no. 2 (Winter 1982): 446–464.

17. *Immigration and Naturalization Service v. Chadha*, 462 U.S. 919 (1983). See Donald E. Clark, "Nuclear Nonproliferation Legislation after *Chadha*: Nonjusticiable Questions and the Loss of the Legislative Veto," *Syracuse Law Review*, 37, no. 3 (1986): 899–922.

18. Foreign Assistance Act of 1962, § 301(d)(3)(e), 76 Stat. 255, 260, 22 USC. § 2370, amending Foreign Assistance Act of 1961§ 620(d)(3) and adding Sec. 620(e). Congressional action followed the general expropriation of U.S. investments by the Castro government in Cuba and reflected an apprehension that other newly independent states with "Marxist" propensities would follow its example. Expropriation without "prompt adequate and effective compensation" is forbidden in a number of bilateral Friendship, Commerce, and Navigation Treaties to which the United States is a party, and is regarded by the United States, at least, as prohibited also by customary international law. See, e.g., "Treaty, with Exchanges of Notes, between the

United States of America and Ethiopia"; American Law Institute, *Restatement of the Law 3d, The Foreign Relations Law of the United States,* § 712 (1987). The amendment expressly prohibited presidential waiver and was enacted over the strong objection of the Kennedy administration. P.L. 87-565, Part III, § 301(d) Aug. 1, 1962. But in 1964, the amendment was itself amended to restore the normal presidential waiver authority. P.L. 88-633, Part III, § 301(d)(4), Oct. 7, 1964, 78 Stat. 1013, 22 USC. § 2370(e)(2).

19. Weintraub, *Economic Coercion and U.S. Foreign Policy,* p. 23. He would qualify that conclusion by recognizing that it is hard to measure "success," especially given the importance of "secondary" and "tertiary" objectives.

20. Published in two volumes (Washington, D.C.: Institute for International Economics, 1990). The authors warn that their data set "probably omits many uses of sanctions imposed between powers of the second and third rank" because of problems with documentation in English (p. 4).

21. Ibid., p. 10.

22. Ibid., pp. 93, 107.

23. Ibid., p. 107.

24. Ibid., pp. 2–3. However, the list contains a number of cases based on human rights violations, nonproliferation, and expropriation

25. But see, e.g., the cases listed as nos. 61-3 (the Berlin Wall), 79-1 (the Iranian hostage crisis); 38-1, 68-1, 76-3 (bilateral treaties of Friendship Commerce and Navigation); 78-1 (Non-Proliferation Treaty). In a significant number of the cases where for one reason or another there is no technical treaty violation, the conduct triggering sanctions is a breach of regime norms based on treaties and widely regarded as being of fundamental importance. Arguably these should be considered in a fair evaluation of the operation of sanctions in support of treaty regimes. Thus sixteen of the cases involve human rights violations, in eleven cases sanctions were imposed to induce nonparties to the NPT to follow the nonproliferation norms of that treaty, and four are responses to expropriations of property of Western nationals without compensation. All three of these categories are the targets of congressionally mandated sanctions

26. These figures are based on a compilation in Sykes, "Constructive Unilateral Threats in International Commercial Relations," pp. 263–330, and revised by adding cases filed since his article was published. Therefore our total of eighty-eight is slightly different from his and from the figure of eighty nine used by Thomas O. Bayard and Kimberly A. Elliott, "'Aggressive Unilateralism' and Section 301: Market Opening or Market Closing?" *The World Economy,* 15, no. 6 (Nov. 1992): 695. The case numbers appearing in subsequent notes are the docket numbers by which the cases are referenced in the Federal Register.

27. Sykes, "Constructive Unilateral Threats in International Commercial Relations," pp. 307–308. He found success in fifty-eight of eighty-three cases; the other five cases were still pending at the time of the study. Sykes does not give an overall success rate. We calculated the percentage in the text by adding successes in cases involving breaches of obligations under trade agreements (thirty-one), ibid., p. 310,

and successes in cases not involving breach (twenty-seven), ibid. p. 314. Our own count, based on a slight revision of the Sykes tables, shows that in 71 percent (sixty-two of eighty-eight cases), the government concerned withdrew the target restriction or made some accommodation with U.S. desires.

28. Bayard and Elliott, "'Aggressive Unilateralism' and Section 301," p. 697. Their numbers are thirty-six of sixty-seven cases. The authors modified their raw figure of eighty-nine investigations by eliminating pending cases or those too recently concluded to make a fair assessment of outcomes, and certain other cases. Ibid., p. 695, n. 14.

29. Ibid., pp. 695–696. In our review of the Sykes tabulation, we concluded that although in 71 percent of the cases (sixty-two out of eighty-eight), the state concerned made some accommodation with U.S. desires, in only 55 percent (fifty out of eighty-eight) did it withdraw the targeted restriction completely.

30. Ibid., p. 700. The record is better—73 percent—if cases involving the EC are excluded. And when GATT dispute panels were convened in alleged violations involving tariffs or quotas, i.e., where the GATT rules are clear, the success rate was much higher—77 percent. Ibid.

31. Sykes, "Constructive Unilateral Threats in International Commercial Relations," p. 312–313. (The one case to the contrary resulted in "lasting retaliation.") Bayard and Elliott agree: "But in almost half, the target country replaced the illegal trade barrier with another type of barrier or disagreed with the U.S. interpretation of what had been agreed." Bayard and Elliott, "'Aggressive Unilateralism' and Section 301," p. 700.

32. Robert Hudec, *Enforcing Internatonal Trade Law: The Evolution of the Modern GATT Legal System* (Salem, N.H.: Butterworth, 1993), pp. 245–249.

33. Bayard and Elliott, "'Aggressive Unilateralism' and Section 301," p. 691.

34. See Thomas Schelling, *The Strategy of Conflict* (Cambridge, Mass.: Harvard University Press, 1960), pp. 21–65, for the classic discussion of threats and promises.

35. The measures were not very serious. See "Message to the Congress Reporting on International Whaling Operations and Conservations Programs," Jan. 16, 1975, *Presidential Papers of President Gerald Ford, Book I,* (Washington, D.C. : USGPO, 1977), p. 47.

36. Martin and Brennan, "Enforcing the International Convention for the Regulation of Whaling," pp. 299–300.

37. *Facts on File,* Aug. 13, 1982, p. 586 E1; July 25, 1986, p. 541 A2

38. *Japan Whaling Association v. American Cetacean Society,* 478 U.S. 221 (1986).

39. Dean M. Wilkinson, "The Use of Domestic Measures to Enforce International Whaling Agreements: A Critical Perspective," *Denver Journal of International Law and Policy,* 17, no. 2 (Winter 1989): 281.

40. ICRW, Art. 12.

41. Letter from Acting Secretary of Commerce Donna Tuttle to the law firm of Arnold and Porter, cited in Martin and Brennan, "Enforcing the International Convention for the Regulation of Whaling," p. 314.

42. Wilkinson, "The Use of Domestic Measures to Enforce International Whaling Agreements," p. 288.

43. Steinar Andresen, "Science and Politics in the International Management of Whales," *Marine Policy,* 13 (Apr. 1989): pp. 111, 112. For a much less favorable appraisal, see Wilkinson, "The Use of Domestic Measures to Enforce International Whaling Agreements." However, the decision to threaten or invoke the sanctions had little to do with whether there was a violation of legal obligation. Of the fourteen cases, eleven involved countries that either were not parties to the ICRW or had legally opted out of the particular obligation.

44. The most significant application of sanctions (under a different section of the Marine Mammal Protection Act) was the ban on imports of Mexican tuna because the fishing methods killed an excessive number of dolphins, and it was imposed by the courts, not the executive branch. The Court of Appeals for the Ninth Circuit held that sanctions were mandatory. *Earth Island Institute v. Mosbacher,* 929 F.2d., 1449 (9th Cir. 1991). Mexico took the case to the GATT and won. GATT Doc DS21/R, Sept. 3, 1991). The standoff was settled by negotiations between the parties, but without adoption of the panel ruling. Bob Davis, "U.S., Mexico, Venezuela Set Accord Tuna," *Wall Street Journal,* Mar. 20, 1992, p. B10. The episode is not discussed in the text because no international treaty or regime was involved. The U.S. kill limitations are entirely unilateral.

45. *Japan Whaling Association v. American Cetacean Society,* 478 U.S. 221, 245 (1986).

46. Martin, *Coercive Cooperation,* p. 108.

47. Stephen B. Cohen, "Conditioning U.S. Security Assistance on Human Rights Practices," *American Journal of International Law,* 76, no. 2 (April 1982): p. 264.

48. Ibid., p. 270.

49. Sidney Weintraub, "Human Rights and Basic Needs in United States Foreign Aid Policy," in Paula R. Newberg, ed., *The Politics of Human Rights* (New York: New York University Press, 1980), p. 232.

50. Congress anticipated this and in the 1977 act called on the administration for "wide consultation" with the bank membership to generate support for human rights linkage. P.L. 95-118, § 703(b), 91 Stat. 1069, Oct. 3, 1977, 22 USC. § 262d, 262e. Lisa Martin argues that the administration went through the motions but made no real effort to organize joint action in the councils of the multilateral institutions.

51. Martin, *Coercive Cooperation,* p. 118; see also pp. 115–119.

52. Lawrence Scheinman, *The International Atomic Energy Agency and World Nuclear Order* (Washington, D.C.: Resources for the Future, 1987), pp. 184–185.

53. See *Hearings before the Subcommittees on Asian and Pacific Affairs and on International Economic Policy and Trade of the House Committee on Foreign Affairs,*

Pakistan's Illegal Nuclear Procurement in the United States, 100th Congress, 1st sess., July 22, 1987.

54. International Security and Development Cooperation Act of 1985, § 902, P.L. 99-83, 99 Stat. 268, 22 USC. § 2375(e).

55. Weintraub, *Economic Coercion and U.S. Foreign Policy,* p. 10.

56. The "Super-301" cases provide some anecdotal evidence in support of deterrence. Countries seemed to expend considerable effort to avoid being placed on the list.

57. Hufbauer, Schott, and Elliott, *Economic Sanctions Reconsidered,* p. 102 (italics in original).

58. Ibid., p. 76.

59. Ibid.; see also Martin, *Coercive Cooperation,* p. 12.

60. Case no. 301-11. According to Bayard and Elliott, the episode involved less than $50 million in trade. Bayard and Elliott, "'Aggressive Unilateralism' and Section 301," p. 687. The issue was settled by an agreement in 1986 providing for mutual tariff concessions.

61. Hufbauer, Schott, and Elliott, *Economic Sanctions Reconsidered,* p. 79.

62. Keohane, "Reciprocity in International Relations," pp. 132–157.

63. Robert Axelrod, *The Evolution of Cooperation* (New York: Basic Books, 1984), p. 185.

64. Richard Perle, "Responding to Soviet Violations Policy (RSVP) Study," memorandum to the President and the Secretary of Defense, December 1985.

65. See Abram Chayes and Antonia Handler Chayes, "Living under a Treaty Regime: Compliance, Interpretation and Adaption," in Antonia Handler Chayes and Paul Doty, eds. *Defending Deterrence: Managing the ABM Treaty Regime into the 21st Century* (MacLean, Va.: Pergamon-Brassey, 1989), pp. 197–216; Gloria Duffy, *Compliance and the Future of Arms Control,* report of project sponsored by the Center for International Security and Arms Control, Stanford University, and Global Outlook, 1988.

66. Ibid., pp. 31–60.

67. Although the United States did not adopt a tit-for-tat policy, it was not prepared to remain passive either. The issues were pressed in many forums and at the highest diplomatic and political levels. Ultimately, corrective Soviet action on both Krasnoyarsk and the problem of telemetry encryption became a U.S. condition for concluding the START I treaty.

68. Testimony of State Department Legal Advisor Abraham S. Sofaer before the Senate Foreign Relations Committee, *ABM Treaty Interpretation Dispute: Hearing before the Subcommittee on Arms Control, International Security and Science of the House Committee on Foreign Affairs,* 99th Congress, 1st sess., 4, 13 (1985). Intense academic and political criticism developed immediately. See, e.g., Abram Chayes and Antonia Handler Chayes, "Testing and Development of 'Exotic' Systems under the ABM Treaty: The Great Reinterpretation Caper," *Harvard Law Review* 99, no. 8 (June 1986): 1956. Senator Sam Nunn held extensive hearings and issued a definitive

report challenging both the administration's substantive interpretation and the "Sofaer doctrine" on the significance of executive branch representations to the Senate. Senator Sam Nunn, "Interpretation of the ABM Treaty—Part IV: An Examination of Judge Sofaer's Analysis of the Negotiating Record," *Congressional Record*, daily ed., May 20, 1987, pp. S6809–6831.

69. John Rhinelander and Sherri Wasserman Goodman, "The Legal Environment," in Chayes and Doty, eds., *Defending Deterrence*, p. 43; Section 225 of the National Defense Authorization Act for Fiscal Years 1988 and 1989, Report 100-446, 100th Congress, 1st Sess., 1987; Section 223 of the National Defense Authorization Act for Fiscal Year 1989, Report 100-989, 100th Congress, 2nd sess., 1988.

70. See Robert E. Hudec, *The GATT Legal System and World Trade Diplomacy*, 2nd ed. (Salem, N.H.: Butterworth, 1990), pp. 5–9.

71. Burton Bollay, "U.S. Target of Criticisms at GATT," *New York Times*, June 6, 1989, p. D1, col. 6. See also "For the Round to Be a Success, the Community Says, Section 301 Will Have to Go; EC Sees Return to Multilateral Solutions," *International Trade Reporter*, 7 (May 20, 1990): 615. See also Sykes, "Constructive Unilateral Threats in International Commercial Relations," p. 265, n. 15, 16.

72. See, e.g., Jagdish Bhagwati and H. Patrick, eds., *Aggressive Unilateralism: America's 301 Trade Policy and the World Trading System* (Ann Arbor: University of Michigan Press, 1990); Sykes, "Constructive Unilateral Threats in International Commercial Relations," p. 266, n. 18. Sykes himself is cautiously favorable.

73. See, e.g., "Dunkel Calls for Political Courage, not Rhetoric in Uruguay Round," *BNA International Trade Daily*, Aug. 21, 1991. Prominent cases of delays in implementing GATT panel rulings that favored the United States include cases concerning Canada's import restrictions on ice cream and yogurt (see Hudec, *Enforcing Internatonal Trade Law*, pp. 575–576) and Korea's restriction on beef imports (ibid., pp. 554–556). The United States has not been innocent on this score, however. A well-known U.S. delaying action was its refusal to implement the GATT panel finding that U.S. tax legislation authorizing domestic international sales corporations (DISCs) was inconsistent with GATT. The panel decision was first delivered in 1976, and the issue was finally settled in 1984. Robert E. Hudec, "Reforming GATT Adjudication Procedures: The Lessons of the DISC Case," *Minnesota Law Review*, 72, no. 6 (June 1988): 1443–1509. The Uruguay Round dispute settlement understanding will make the adoption of panel reports automatic and will in other ways eliminate the possibilities for delay and strategic behavior by respondents. See Chapter 9.

74. The deadline is not as rigid as it seems. The EC Citrus Preferences Case, 301-11, the only one in which the EC ultimately counterretaliated, took more than ten years, and a number of cases initiated in the 1980s are still open.

75. Moreover, under Section 301, the United States imposes sanctions on the target country only, in violation of GATT's basic principle of most-favored-nation treatment, which requires that trade restrictions as well as benefits must be applied equally to all trading partners.

76. Sykes, "Constructive Unilateral Threats in International Commercial Rela-

tions," pp. 291–307, examines the issues in detail, concluding that there is a case for "threat strategies" in certain limited circumstances, even in the absence of the violation of an agreement. His analysis does not take into account the multilateral impacts discussed in the text.

77. Of the cases in the Sykes sample, twenty-seven of the thirty-four "nonbreach" cases fall into two categories closely related to GATT. Most of them seek to impose GATT-like principles on areas of trade not yet covered at the time, such as information or services. The remainder seek to impose GATT rules on states like China, that, although nonmembers, are seeking admission to the club. Again it could be said that successful application of sanctions would further liberalize the trade regime. In each of these categories, however, the issues—membership or the application of GATT rules to new fields of trade—were under negotiation within GATT. Resorting to unilateral sanctions could readily be seen to be an attempt to preempt these negotiations and impose a result dictated by the United States.

78. See Hudec, *Enforcing International Trade Law*, pp. 228, 230.

79. Urugay Round, Dispute Settlement Understanding, MTN/FA, II-A2 (Dec. 15, 1993). The new WTO dispute settlement procedures are discussed at greater length in Chapter 9.

80. The phrase is taken from Bhagwati and Patrick, eds., *Aggressive Unilateralism: America's 301 Trade Policy*.

81. Andrew Pollack, "They Eat Whales, Don't They?" *New York Times*, May 3, 1993, p. A4(L); "Norway to Hunt Whales," *New York Times*, Apr. 14, 1993, p. A7(L); George Bush, "Letter to Congressional Leaders Reporting on Whaling Activities of Norway," *Weekly Compilation of Presidential Documents*, Dec. 28, 1992, p. 2381–2382. President Clinton dismissed the possibility of imposing sanctions against Norway for its decision to revive commercial whaling, while pressing for a negotiated settlement of the issue. *Weekly Compilation of Presidential Documents*, May 23, 1994, p. 1100.

82. J. J. Holst, foreign minister of Norway, Norweigian Information Service, *Norinform Weekly Edition*, no. 26 (Aug. 31, 1993): 1.

83. Hufbauer, Schott, and Elliott, *Economic Sanctions Reconsidered*, p. 111.

84. See, e.g. Keohane, "Reciprocity in International Relations," pp. 132–157. Keohane defines "specific reciprocity" as "exchanges of roughly equal value in which the actions of each party are contingent on the prior actions of others in such a way that good is returned for good and bad for bad" (p. 136).

85. The conclusion is based on two computer tournaments in which experts in game theory were invited to submit programmed solutions to an iterated prisoners' dilemma game. The "tit-for-tat" approach did the best of the fifteen programs submitted in the first round, and of the sixty-three programs in the second round. Axelrod, *The Evolution of Cooperation*, pp. 27–54. Discussion of other aspects of the prisoners' dilemma will be found in Chapter 6.

86. But as both Axelrod and Keohane are quick to recognize, the result may also degenerate into an unending series of defections as each side returns bad for bad. See Axelrod, *Evolution of Cooperation*, p. 138; Keohane, "Reciprocity in International

Relations," pp. 138–139. See also Rian Malan, *My Traitor's Heart* (New York: Atlantic Monthly Press, 1990), depicting the relationships between blacks and Boers in South Africa as just such an inescapable round of negative reciprocity.

87. Axelrod conducted one experimental run with a low (1%) misperception rate. "As expected, these misunderstandings resulted in a good deal more defection between the players. A surprise was that TIT FOR TAT was still the best decision rule." Axelrod, *Evolution of Cooperation,* pp. 182–183.

88. However, Section 301 is not limited to GATT violations; it encompasses other practices deemed by the United States to be unfair. Ex ante, the foreign country cannot tell what the USTR will consider cooperation and what defection, which introduces a certain lack of clarity into the system. The significance of these deficiencies in observability is confirmed by the Bayard and Elliott finding of 76 percent success (as compared with 54 percent overall) in cases targeting "traditional border measures—tariffs and import and export quotas on goods—[that are] more transparent, objectives [that] are easier to define and . . . more likely to be clearly GATT illegal." Bayard and Elliott, "'Aggressive Unilateralism' and Section 301," p. 694.

89. 22 USC. § 2370(e)(1).

90. Foreign Assistance and Related Programs Appropriations Act of 1970, § 502D

91. Hufbauer, Schott, and Elliott, *Economic Sanctions Reconsidered,* p. 111.

92. Robert Axelrod, *Evolution of Cooperation,* p. 174.

93. Ibid., p. 188. "The importance of the next encounter between the same two individuals must be great enough to make defection an unprofitable strategy when the other player is provocable." Ibid., p. 174.

94. Ibid., p. 183.

95. Bhagwati and Patrick, eds., *Aggressive Unilateralism,* pp. 22, 150. Hudec, *Enforcing Internatonal Trade Law,* p. 112, n. 13, says the EC has retaliated only twice against the United States.

96. GATT, *United States—Restrictions on Imports of Tuna,* Report of the Panel, Doc. DS21/R, Sept. 3, 1991.

97. The difference is not confined to treaty-related issues. Consider the congressional mandate of sanctions against South Africa, over Reagan's veto, and against Iraq, vetoed by Bush. Ronald Reagan, "Message to the House of Representatives Returning without Approval a Bill Concerning Apartheid in South Africa," Sept. 26, 1986, *Public Papers of the Presidents of the United States* (Washington, D.C.: USGPO, 1986), pp. 1278–1280; Michael Wines, "Bush Weighs a Veto of Sanctions for the Spread of Chemical Arms," *New York Times,* Nov. 1, 1990, p. A12, col. 5.

98. GATT Doc. L/5607 (March 2, 1984), reported in *Basic Instruments and Selected Documents,* 31st Supp., pp. 67–74; see also Hudec, *Enforcing Internatonal Trade Law,* pp. 512–513; "Military and Paramilitary Activities in and against Nicaragua Nicaragua v. United States of America, Merits," *ICJ Reports* (1991): p. 554.

99. Martin, *Coercive Cooperation,* p. 244.

100. See John Galting, "On the Effect of International Economic Sanctions, with Examples from the Case of Rhodesia," *World Politics,* 19 (Apr. 1967): 385.

101. Hufbauer, Schott, and Eliot, *Economic Sanctions Reconsidered,* p. 97 (italics in original).

102. Bayard and Elliott, "'Aggressive Unilateralism' and Section 301," p. 688 and table 2. It is significant that the EC is the only entity to counterretaliate against a Section 301 action. It is also the only party other than the United States to have enacted a similar authority, and then not until its trade parity with the United States was well established.

103. Ibid., p. 703; see also p. 698.

104. Bayard and Elliott say that in Section 301 cases, the USTR is much more aggressive against Japan than against the EC. Ibid., pp 703. Invoking the GATT against the EC doesn't seem to work either. "Cases in which GATT panels were convened, other than those involving the EC, were successful 73 percent of the time (vs. 55 percent overall). Six of nine panel cases involving the EC ultimately were judged to be failures; in all but one case . . . the EC changed the offending practice but exploited ambiguities in GATT and bilateral agreements to continue to protect its agricultural producers and processors." Ibid., p. 700.

5. Norms

1. See Friedrich V. Kratochwil, *Rules, Norms and Decisions: On the Conditions of Practical and Legal Reasoning in International Affairs,* (Cambridge: Cambridge University Press, 1989), p. 10; Edna Ullman-Margalit, *The Emergence of Norms* (Oxford: Clarendon Press, 1977), p. 12; Margaret Jane Radin, "Risk-of-Error Rules and Non-Ideal Justification," *Nomos,* 28 (1986): 45, n. 3.

2. Not surprisingly, debate about the definition and interaction of rules, principles, and standards in the legal literature is endless. See, e.g., Ronald Dworkin, *Taking Rights Seriously* (Cambridge, Mass.: Harvard University Press, 1977), pp. 22–28; Duncan Kennedy, "Form and Substance in Private Law Adjudication," *Harvard Law Review,* 89 (1976): 1685; Frederick Schauer, *Playing by the Rules: A Philosophical Examination of Rule-Based Decision-Making in Law and in Life* (Oxford: Clarendon Press, 1991), pp. 12–15.

3. *Head Money* cases, 112 U.S. 580 (1984). *United States v. Palestine Liberation Organization,* 695 F.Supp 1456 (S.D.N.Y. 1988), shows that it is not always easy to be clear enough.

4. See Morton J. Horwitz, *The Transformation of American Law, 1870–1960* (New York: Oxford University Press, 1992), pp. 123–128.

5. *Filartiga v. Pena-Irala,* 630 F.2d 876 (2d Cir. 1980); *North Sea Continental Shelf* case, *ICJ Reports 1969,* pp. 3, 44.

6. Stephen D. Krasner, "Structural Causes and Regime Consequences: Regimes as Intervening Variables," in Stephen D. Krasner, ed., *International Regimes* (Ithaca, N.Y.: Cornell University Press, 1983), p. 2. Krasner provides short distinguishing definitions of "principles," "norms" and "rules," but not much seems to turn on

these differences. See also Jock A. Finlayson and Mark W. Sacher, "The GATT and the Regulation of Trade Barriers: Regime Dynamics and Function," in ibid., pp. 275–277.

7. Some are contingent, in the sense that if the actor wants to achieve some result, he or she must conform to the norms that prescribe the approved procedures. These "secondary" or "enabling" rules define procedures by which actors can establish or change legal relationships. See H. L. A. Hart, *The Concept of Law* (Oxford: Clarendon Press, 1961), pp. 27–28.

8. Norms also differ from rules of games, in which the rules define the activity. Moral precepts and codes of etiquette, while they are also prescriptions for action in situations of choice that carry a sense of obligation to obey, are distinguished in other ways from norms that are the components of regimes.

9. Talcott Parsons, "Power and the Social System," in Steven Lukes, ed., *Power* (New York: New York University Press, 1986), p. 121.

10. See Jon Elster, *The Cement of Society* (Cambridge: Cambridge University Press, 1989), p. 15; see also, e.g., Kratochwil, *Rules, Norms, and Decisions*, pp. 152–153.

11. See Gary J. Miller, "Managerial Dilemmas: Political Leadership in Hierarchies," in Karen Schweers Cook and Margaret Levi, eds., *The Limits of Rationality* (Chicago: University of Chicago Press, 1990), pp. 337–341. See also Kratochwil, *Rules, Norms, and Decisions*, p. 104.

12. See, e.g., Ullman Margalit, *The Emergence of Norms*, p. 89.

13. Thomas C. Schelling, *The Strategy of Conflict*, 2nd ed. (Cambridge, Mass.: Harvard University Press, 1980), pp. 106–107.

14. Vienna Convention on the Law of Treaties, Art. 2(1)(a). "Treaties," as defined in Art. 2, sec. 2 of the U.S. Constitution, are a relatively small subset of the broad class of agreements giving rise to international obligation—those that are submitted to the Senate for advice and consent to ratification. In recent years, this practice has been employed in only a small fraction of U.S. international agreements. See Barry E. Carter and Phillip R. Trimble, *International Law* (Boston: Little, Brown, 1991), pp. 79, 169–172

15. Stanley Hoffman, *Duties beyond Borders: On the Limits and Possibilities of Ethical International Politics* (Syracuse, N.Y.: Syracuse University Press, 1981), p. 62.

16. Ronald Dworkin, *Law's Empire* (Cambridge, Mass.: Belknap Press of Harvard University Press, 1986), pp. 62–67, 88, 91.

17. Ibid., p. 413.

18. See, generally, Guido Calabresi, *A Common Law for the Age of Statutes* (Cambridge, Mass.: Harvard University Press, 1982), e.g., p. 21.

19. Richard H. Fallon, "Reflections on Dworkin and the Two Faces of Law," *Notre Dame Law Review*, 67 (1992): 553, 556.

20. Kratochwil, *Rules, Norms, and Decisions*, p. 124: "Moral facts expressed in rules of conduct are valid not because of threatened deprivations, but because of their duty-imposing character, which is in turn a precondition for the legitimacy of phys-

ical sanctions." See also ibid., pp. 128–129; Jon Elster, "When Rationality Fails," in Cook and Levi, eds., *The Limits of Rationality,* pp. 19–51, 45.

21. Alexander Wendt, "Anarchy Is What States Make of It: The Social Construction of Power Politics," *International Organization,* 46 (1992): 391, 399; Elster, *The Cement of Society,* pp. 97–107; Fallon, "Reflections on Dworkin and the Two Faces of Law," p. 557 ("Law is . . . grounded in shared standards of conduct and socially enforced pressure to conform").

22. Fallon, "Reflections on Dworkin and the Two Faces of Law," p. 565.

23. Hoffman, *Duties beyond Borders,* p. 16. Hoffman notes that he has only "a limited amount of sympathy" for this argument.

24. Ibid., p. xii.

25. Max Weber, "Politics as a Vocation," (1921) in Hans H. Gerth and C. Wright Mills, eds. *From Max Weber: Essays in Sociology* (New York: Oxford University Press 1946), p. 127. See also Hoffman, *Duties beyond Borders,* p. 28; Arthur L. Stinchcombe, "Reason and Rationality," in Cook and Levi, eds., *The Limits of Rationality,* pp. 302–306.

26. Hoffman, *Duties beyond Borders,* p. 29.

27. Oliver Hart, "An Economist's Perspective on the Theory of the Firm," in Oliver E. Williamson, ed., *Organization Theory: From Chester Barnard to the Present and Beyond* (New York: Oxford University Press 1990), p. 156; Terry M. Moe, "The Politics of Structural Choice: Toward a Theory of Public Bureaucracy," in ibid., p. 133. See also Robert C. Clark, "Why So Many Lawyers? Are They Good or Bad?" *Fordham Law Review,* 61 (Nov. 1992): 285–287. For a comprehensive statement of the law of fiduciary duties, see Austin Wakeman Scott and William Franklin Fratcher, *The Law of Trusts,* 4th ed. (Boston: Little, Brown, 1987).

28. Kratochwil, *Rules, Norms, and Decisions,* pp. 10–11: "As in the public-choice literature, the term 'actor' refers in my discussion variously to individuals and collectivities, and often inferences are made from individual to collective-actor behavior without explicit attention being paid to the problems that occur on various levels of analysis. While neither I nor anyone else can deny significant differences between individual choices and those filtered through group or organizational channels, the simplifying assumption here is that the initial metaphor is heuristically fruitful and that it leads us to the discovery of important new insights." See also Alexander Wendt, "Anarchy Is What States Make of It," p. 397, n. 21; Thomas M. Franck, *The Power of Legitimacy among Nations* (New York: Oxford University Press, 1990), pp. 4–5.

29. See Kratochwil, *Rules, Norms, and Decisions,* pp. 99–102. The following discussion draws generally on Kratochwil, chap. 4 and 5

30. Philip E. Tetlock, Linda Skitka, and Richard Boettger, "Social and Cognitive Strategies for Coping with Accountability: Conformity, Complexity and Bolstering," *Journal of Personality and Social Psychology,* 57, no. 4 (1989): p. 632. See also Paul A. Anderson, "Justifications and Precedents as Constraints in Foreign Policy Decision-Making," *American Journal of Political Science,* 25, no. 4 (Nov. 1981): 740: "'Politics'

to a very large extent consists of making statements justifying past and future deci-sions, and of criticizing justifying actions made by others" (citing Kjell Goldmann, *International Norms and the War between States* [Stockholm: Laromedelsforlagen, 1971], p. 22).

31. See, e.g., Franck, *The Power of Legitimacy among Nations,* p. 61: "The perfor-mance of states in the international community is constantly subject to qualitative evaluation of other states, institutions and processes."

32. Hans Morgenthau, *Politics among Nations* (New York: Alfred A. Knopf, 1978), p. 282.

33. See Oscar Schachter, "The Invisible College of International Lawyers," *North-western University Law Review,* 72 (1977): 217; Franck, *The Power of Legitimacy among Nations,* pp. 55–56.

34. See discussion in Chapter 4. A general analysis of the effect of legalism in administering the ABM Treaty is found in Harold Muller, "The Internalization of Principles, Norms and Rules by Governments: The Case of Security Regimes," paper prepared for the conference, The Study of Regimes in International Relations, Tüb-ingen, Germany, July 14–18, 1991, pp. 14–25.

35. Kratochwil, *Rules, Norms, and Decisions,* p. 214, and see generally chap. 10. Frank I. Michelman, "Law's Republic," *The Yale Law Journal,* 97 (July 1988): 1537: "All that I, or anyone, can offer is an argument, not a demonstration, about the constitution's meaning."

36. Kratochwil, *Rules, Norms, and Decisions,* p. 9.

37. Hoffman, *Duties beyond Borders,* p. 43.

38. Kratochwil, *Rules, Norms, and Decisions,* pp. 38–39; Schelling, *The Strategy of Conflict,* pp. 106–107.

39. Roger Fisher and William Ury, *Getting to Yes* (Boston: Houghton Mifflin, 1981), chap. 5.

40. The classic lament is found in Herbert Wechsler, "Toward Neutral Principles of Constitutional Law," *Harvard Law Review,* 73 (1959): 1.

41. Frank I. Michelman, "Justification (and Justifiability) of Law in a Contradic-tory World ," in *Justification, Nomos,* 28 (1986): 73 (italics in original).

42. UN Charter, Art. 1(2) and Art. 2(4). See also Art. 2(7) prohibiting interven-tion in matters that are essentially within the domestic jurisdiction of any state. The tension is recurrent in post–World War II legal instruments. See, e.g., Helsinki Final Act, Art. IV and Art. VIII.

43. GATT, Art. XXIV.

44. Hoffman, *Duties beyond Borders,* p. 21.

45. The extreme is Wittgenstein's claim that "no course of action could be deter-mined by a rule, because every course of action can be made out to accord with the rule." Ludwig Wittgenstein, *Philosophical Investigations,* trans. G. E. Anscombe (New York: Macmillan, 1953), p. 81, par. 201.

46. Margaret Jane Radin, "Risk-of-Error Rules and Non-Ideal Justification," in Kratochwil, *Rules, Norms and Decisions,* pp. 38–39.

47. Franck, *The Power of Legitimacy among Nations,* p. 73.

48. LTBT, Art. I(1)(b). It is said that in the Russian text the word "debris" is rendered as "fallout," in itself raising a considerable interpretative problem.

49. Abram Chayes, Thomas Ehrlich, and Andreas F. Lowenfeld, *International Legal Process: Materials for an Introductory Course,* vol. 2 (Boston: Little, Brown, 1969), pp. 1024–1043. Years later, when President Reagan included Soviet venting incidents in his reports to Congress of noncompliance with arms control agreements, nobody took it seriously. The practice had modified the norm.

50. GATT, Art. III.

51. See the GATT panel decision in *Mexico, Canada and EC v. United States: Taxes on Petroleum and Certain Imported Substances [Superfund taxes],* Doc. L/6175 (June 5, 1987), *Basic Instruments and Selected Documents,* 34th Supp. (1988), pp. 136–166.

52. See IMF, Art. IV sec. 1.

53. Interim Agreement (SALT I), Art. V(3); U.S. State Department Bureau of Public Affairs, July 1979, Special Report 55, *Compliance with SALT I Agreements,* p. 4.

54. ICRW, Art. VIII(1).

55. Fallon, "Reflections on Dworkin and the Two Faces of Law," p. 554.

56. Kratochwil, *Rules, Norms, and Decisions,* p. 97.

57. Dworkin, *Law's Empire,* p. 413.

58. Michelman, "Law's Republic," p. 1528–1529. "The legal form of plurality is indeterminacy—the susceptibility of the received body of normative material to a plurality of interpretive distillations, pointing toward differing resolutions of pending cases and, through them, toward differing normative futures."

59. Kratochwil, *Rules, Norms, and Decisions,* p. 102: "In international relations, where authoritative determinations analogous to umpires' rulings are the exception, the parties themselves must constantly interpret each others' moves and renegotiate the reality in which they operate."

60. Radin, "Risk-of-Error Rules and Non-Ideal Justification," p. 36.

61. Wendt, "Anarchy Is What States Make of It," p. 417.

62. Robert O. Keohane and Joseph S. Nye, *Power and Interdependence: World Politics in Transition* (Boston: Little, Brown, 1977), p. 9 (quoting Alex Inkeles, "The Emerging Social Structure of the World," *World Politics,* 27 [July 1975]: 479).

63. See *The Paquete Habana,* 175 U.S. 677, 699 (1900): "The Empire of Japan (the last State admitted into the rank of civilized nations)."

64. Clark, "Why So Many Lawyers?"

65. Robert O. Keohane, "U.S. Compliance with Commitments: Reciprocity and Institutional Enmeshment," paper prepared for Program on International Political Economy and Security seminar, University of Chicago, Oct. 24, 1991.

66. David Kennedy, "The Move to Institutions," *Cardozo Law Review,* 8 (1987): 841–988.

67. We adopt Oran Young's terminology distinguishing between "institutions" as networks of norms, rules, and practices and "organizations" as a subset of institutions having physical embodiment, personnel, a seat, and so forth. See Oran R.

Young, *International Cooperation: Building Regimes for Natural Resources and the Environment* (Ithaca, N.Y.: Cornell University Press), p. 32. By these lights, the family is an institution. So is the market. The stock exchange is an organization. This is not to say that the rules, procedures, division of powers, etc., of an organization are all laid out in its charter or in acts formally taken pursuant to it. On the contrary, the organization is the center of a complex web of informal norms, rules, and practices that have a good deal to do with how the formal prescriptions are carried out, and sometimes evaded. The functioning of the organization cannot be understood without reference to these informal elements.

68. The nuclear arms control regime between the United States and the Soviet Union included several treaties—some ratified and some not—a fairly continuous negotiating process extending for more than three decades, and national verification procedures. This arrangement subsisted with only the rudimentary organizational structure of the Standing Consultative Commission, which had no permanent staff or headquarters. Some of the strongest and most effective international organizations, although constituted by treaty, do not have responsibility for administering a regulatory treaty, for example NATO and the World Bank. Other organizations have administrative responsibility for several treaties, for example, the Antarctic Treaty Consultative Parties. And some regimes comprise more than one organization. Thus the IAEA has major compliance responsibilities under the NPT, but the Treaty of Tlatlelco, establishing a Latin American nuclear free zone, has its own organizational structure and a secretariat located in Mexico City.

69. Talcott Parsons, "Power and the Social System," in Steven Lukes, ed., *Power* (New York: New York University Press, 1986), p. 119.

70. See, e.g., "Arrangement Concerning the International Registration of Marks, Apr. 14, 1891," 18 Martens 2d 842 (creating Madrid Union for the international Registration of Marks and establishing an International bureau for that purpose); see also Universal Postal Union's International Bureau and International Telecommunication Union's Administrative Council.

71. For example, responsibility for administering developed country financial contributions to compliance under a number of environmental treaties is given to a complex arrangement involving the Global Environmental Facility of the World Bank, the UN Environment Program, and the UN Development Program. For the negotiations leading up to a similar result in the Montreal Protocol, which set the precedent, see Richard Elliot Benedick, *Ozone Diplomacy: New Directions in Safeguarding the Planet* (Cambridge, Mass.: Harvard University Press, 1991), pp. 183–188.

72. By "formal organization" we mean one that is established by a formal, legally binding constitutive instrument. Many important international organizations do not fit this definition. Examples are the Nuclear Suppliers Group (NSG), the Conference on Security and Co-operation in Europe (although it has promulgated many "nonbinding organizational acts"), the Coordinating Committee on Multilateral Report Controls (COCOM), and the Group of Seven. Like "hard" and "soft" international law, there are hard and soft international organizations. These organizations have

many of the characteristics of formal organizations, often including a set of regular procedures by which the organization takes action and some kind of agreed instrument outlining functions and powers. The central elements of the analysis in this chapter applies to soft organizations as well.

73. Abram Chayes, *The Cuban Missile Crisis: International Crises and the Role of Law* (Lanham, Md.: University Press of America, 1987), p. 104.

74. Discussions of norms in the international relations or rational choice literature often proceed in terms of an implicit model of simple prohibitions—"thou shalt nots"—of which the speed limit is a paradigmatic example. If norms are designed to regulate conduct, they do so by telling actors what they can and cannot do. The phenomenon of institutions highlights a different category of "facilitative" or "enabling" norms. See Hart, *The Concept of Law*, pp. 27–28.

75. Alexander Wendt, "The Agent Structure Problem in International Relations Theory," *International Organization*, 41, no. 3 (Summer 1987): 359: "Social structures have an inherently discursive dimension in the sense that they are inseparable from the reasons and self-understandings that agents bring to their actions."

76. Franck, *The Power of Legitimacy among Nations*, p. 26.

77. Ibid., p. 152: "Each action is judged by all states in terms of its projected effect if all were to act similarly."

78. See Russell Hardin, "The Social Evolution of Cooperation," in Cook and Levi, eds., *The Limits of Rationality*, pp. 362–363.

79. See E. P. Thompson, *Whigs and Hunters: The Origin of the Black Act* (London: Allen Lane, 1975), at, e.g., p. 269.

80. See F. V. Meyer, *International Trade Policy* (New York: St. Martin's Press, 1978), p. 142; Charles Lipson, "The Transformation of Trade: The Source and Effects of Regime Change," in Krasner, ed., *International Regimes*, pp. 254–257; and Robert Hudec, *Enforcing Internatonal Trade Law: The Evolution of the Modern GATT Legal System* (Salem, N.H.: Butterworth, 1993), pp. 95–98, evaluating the twelve-year GATT litigation over U.S. tax legislation providing for Domestic International Sales Corporations (DISC).

81. Thomas Hobbes, *Leviathan*, ed. Michael Oakeshott (New York: Collier Books, 1962), p. 132.

82. Vienna Convention on the Law of Treaties, Art. 52. An extended attack on the binding character of "unequal treaties" concluded between colonial powers and protectorates and other states in subordinate positions failed to achieve acceptance. Duress against the representative of a state, however, is grounds for avoidance. Ibid., Art. 51

83. Here also, formal treaty law fails fully to reflect reality. A violation of internal law in the process by which a state consents to a treaty does not invalidate the action on the international plane. "Vienna Convention on the Law of Treaties," Art. 46.

84. One of the reasons cease-fire agreements are often so fragile is that they are of necessity concluded hastily, between military leaders or officials who do not have the opportunity to develop broader political assent.

85. See, e.g., David Koplow, "When Is an Amendment Not an Amendment? Modification of Arms Control Agreements without the Senate," *University of Chicago Law Review,* 59 (1992): 981, 1009–1023, discussing provisions in recent arms control agreements for modifications without the necessity of formal amendment; and ibid., pp. 1023–1031, discussing practice in other fields. An early and important example of such rule-making authority is the "Convention on International Aviation," Art. 52, 54(1).

86. Cf. Jurgen Habermass, "Discourse Ethics: Notes on a Program of Philosophical Justification," in Selya Benhabib and Fred Dallmayr, eds., *The Communicative Ethics Controversy* (Cambridge, Mass.: MIT Press, 1990), p. 85.

87. For the importance of consensus arrangements in ensuring that all major interests are taken into account at the stage of regime formation, see Oran R. Young, *International Governance: Protecting the Environment in a Stateless Society* (Ithaca, N.Y.: Cornell University Press, 1994), pp. 99–100.

88. See, e.g., CITES, Art. XV(3); Montreal Protocol, Art. 11.3(a) and (b).

89. GATT, Art. XXV(3), (4). The new WTO Charter carries this voting formula forward for most actions, but requires a three-fourths majority for interpretations and waivers (WTO Charter, Art. IX). Adoption of a dispute panel report is by negative consensus (Art. XVI).

90. The original model is, we believe, in the UNCLOS voting procedures, Art. 312. See, e.g. Basel Convention on Hazardous Wastes, Art. 17(3) (amendment procedure); WTO Agreement, Art. IX(1)

91. See Susan S. Lieberman, "1992 CITES Amendments Strengthen Protection for Wildlife and Plants," *Endangered Species Technical Bulletin,* 18, no. 1 (1993). See also *Adams v. Vance,* 570 F.2d 950 (1977), a suit brought by Inuit Indians of Alaska to compel the U.S. secretary of state to exercise U.S. opt-out rights against an IWC decision to impose a moratorium on subsistence hunting of the bowhead whale. The decision quotes extensively from an affidavit by the Honorable Patsy Mink, assistant secretary of state for oceans and international environmental and scientific affairs, who said that if the United States were to opt out after its consistent record of pressuring other countries not to object to IWC quota decisions, "this government's credibility and leadership in international whale conservation woud be severely compromised. Foreign governments would regard this U.S. objection . . . as evidence of U.S. hypocrisy on whale conservation." Ibid., p. 956, n. 13.

92. Other organizations with two well-defined classes of parties in interest protect minority rights by providing for concurrent majorities. Thus commodity agreements have required concurrent votes by consumers and producers to exercise granted powers. International Coffee Agreement, Art. 14. UN Economic and Social Council, Res. 30(IV), Mar. 28, 1947, adopted in GATT, Ad. Art. XX, establishes the requirement of "two house" voting for all commodity agreeements. The arrangements for administering the fund under the Montreal Protocol provide for decisions by a two-thirds majority including simple majorities of the donor and donee countries respectively. London Amendments to the Montreal Protocol, Art. 10(9).

93. There are subtle differences between consensus and unanimity, of course. The consensus procedure allows a state to accept an action in silence (perhaps offering an explanation of its position after the decision) rather than requiring it to stand up and be counted in favor of it. Perhaps this accounts for the difficulty experienced in breaking the consensus.

94. See 19 UN GAOR 1286 (1964) (announcement of consensus voting scheme by UN Secretary General); 19 UN GAOR 1329–1330 (1965) (speech by Albanian representative).

95. Modern U.S. constitutional law, of course, has been marked by a flowering of Equal Protection Clause jurisprudence, the heart of which is the prohibition of invidious discrimination. Frank Michelman sets out the requirement more carefully in the context of judicial decision: "Decision according to law involves generalization over cases, a course of reasoning in which the instant case is assimilated to an at least somewhat general class of cases to which the categorically framed norm can then be applied with prescriptive force." Michelman, "Justification (and Justifiability) of Law in a Contradictory World," p. 73.

96. The issue is illustrated in the debate over the voting rules for the Executive Committee of the multilateral ozone fund. Developing countries opposed the interim voting formula that required separate majorities of developed and developing country representatives with favorable votes accounting for two-thirds of global CFC consumers, a formula that gave veto power to a few developed countries. In the London Amendments, the formula was changed to require a two-thirds majority of the representatives, with separate majorities of the developing and developed country groups. See Benedick, *Ozone Diplomacy*, p. 185. To date, all decisions in the committee have been taken by consensus. But the voting rules for the Global Environmental Facility, which administers funds under the Climate Change Convention, reverted to a form of weighted voting requiring a majority of 60 percent of the thirty-two members of the Council, amounting to a 60 percent majority of the total contributions to the fund. The effect is to give the industrialized countries a veto. "Instrument for the Establishment of the Restructured Global Environment Facility." GEF Council meeting, Washington, D.C., July 12–13, 1994. Doc. GEF/C.1/1.

97. See, e.g., Tyrone Ferguson, *The Third World and Decision Making in the International Monetary Fund: The Quest for Full and Effective Participation* (London: Pinter, 1988).

98. See, e.g., Arpad Prangler, "The Fourth Review Conference of the Non-Proliferation Treaty," *A Periodic Review of the United Nations,* 14, no. 1 (1991): 125–154. See Janne Nolan, *Trappings of Power: Ballistic Missiles in the Third World* (Washington, D.C.: Brookings Institution, 1991), p. 60; "U.S. Stops Nuclear Testing; Test Ban Group Praises Initiative," U.S. Newswire, Oct. 1, 1992; "The Politics of Testing," *National Journal,* 24 (Oct. 3, 1992): 2264.

99. Antarctic Treaty.

100. Convention on the Conservation of Antarctic Marine Living Resources.

101. See Willy Ostreng, "The Conflict and Alignment Pattern of Antarctic Politics: Is a New Order Needed?" in Arnfinn Jorgensen-Dahl and Willy Ostreng, eds., *The Antarctic Treaty System in World Politics* (New York: St. Martin's Press, 1991), pp. 433–450; Mohamed Haron, "The Ability of the Antarctic Treaty System to Adapt to External Challenges," in ibid, pp. 299–308.

102. See Hart, *The Concept of Law*, pp. 181–189; H. L. A. Hart, "Positivism and the Separation of Law and Morals," *Harvard Law Review*, 71 (1958): 593; Lon L. Fuller, "Positivism and Fidelity to Law—A Reply to Professor Hart," *Harvard Law Review*, 71 (1958): 630.

103. Hart, *The Concept of Law*, pp. 201–207.

104. Franck, *The Power of Legitimacy among Nations*, p. 24, defines legitimacy as "*a property of a rule or rule-making institution which itself exerts a pull towards compliance on those addressed normatively because those addressed believe that the rule or institution has come into being and opereates in accordance with generally accepted principles of right process.*" (italics in original).

105. See Lon L. Fuller, "The Morality of Law," *Villanova Law Review*, 10 (1965): 655; see also Young, *International Governance*, pp. 62, 73–74, 109–110.

106. Oran R. Young, "The Politics of International Regime Formation: Managing Natural Resources and the Environment," *International Organization*, 43, no. 3 (Summer 1989): 368–369. For a sophisticated discussion of the problem of equity in treaty negotiation, see Edward A. Parson and Richard J. Zeckhauser, "Equal Measures or Fair Burdens: Negotiating Environmental Treaties in an Unequal World," in Henry Lee, ed., *Shaping National Responses to Climate Change* (Washington, D.C.: Island Press, 1995).

6. Transparency, Norms, and Strategic Interaction

1. The seminal work is George J. Stigler, "The Economics of Information," *Journal of Political Economy*, 69, no. 3 (1961): 213–225. See also, e.g., Elinor Ostrom, *Governing the Commons: The Evolution of Institutions for Collective Action* (Cambridge: Cambridge University Press, 1990), pp. 96–97, 193–199; Robert O. Keohane, "The Demand for International Regimes," in Stephen D. Krasner, ed., *International Regimes* (Ithaca, N.Y.: Cornell University Press, 1983), pp. 161–167; James D. A. Boyle, "A Theory of Law and Information: Copyright, Spleens, Blackmail and Insider Trading," *California Law Review*, 80 (Dec. 1992), especially 1443–1457, "The Economics of Information."

2. The collective action problem as classically defined by Mancur Olson is that the private incentives of individuals dictate that their aggregate contributions to the production of collective goods will be insufficient to provide an optimal supply of the goods. See Mancur Olson, Jr., *The Logic of Collective Action: Public Goods and the Theory of Groups* (Cambridge, Mass.: Harvard University Press, 1965), chap. 1. In a sense, the treaty itself can be thought of as defining an agreed solution to a collective action problem that must be continuously maintained.

3. See, generally, Kenneth W. Abbott, "'Trust but Verify': The Production of

Information in Arms Control Treaties and Other International Agreements," *Cornell International Law Journal,* 26, (1993): 26–38.

4. Edna Ullman-Margalit, *The Emergence of Norms* (Oxford: Clarendon Press, 1977), p. 78.

5. John Gerard Ruggie, "Multilateralism: The Anatomy of an Institution," *International Organizations,* 46, no. 3 (Summer 1992): 582 (the solution of coordination problems "is neither complex nor particularly demanding"). See also Ullman-Margalit, *The Emergence of Norms,* p. 15.

6. Arthur A. Stein, "Coordination and Collaboration Regimes in an Anarchic World," in Krasner, ed., *International Regimes,* pp. 130–131.

7. WHO, Art. 64. See Robert O. Keohane, "The Demand for International Regimes," in Krasner, ed., *International Regimes,* pp. 161–167.

8. "Agreement concerning Interim Arrangements Relating to Polymetallic Nodules of the Deep Sea Bed, 1982," Schedule, TIAS 10562; "Provisional Understanding Regarding Deep Seabed Matters," Art. 3, 1984, UKTS 24 (1985).

9. Ullman-Margalit, *The Emergence of Norms,* chap. 3.

10. Professor Henry Hart used to tell his law school students that the white line down the center of the road was among the most important of legal inventions.

11. Thomas C. Schelling, *The Strategy of Conflict* (Cambridge, Mass.: Harvard University Press, 1960), pp. 57–58.

12. ICAO, p. 295. See Thomas Buergenthal, *Lawmaking in the International Civil Aviation Organization* (Syracuse, N.Y.: Syracuse University Press, 1969). Safety and equipment rules for ocean transport do not achieve the same almost unbroken compliance, because the system is technologically and operationally much more forgiving than air traffic.

13. "Treaty concerning the Establishment of a General Postal Union" (1874).

14. ITU, Dec. 9, 1932, 49 Stat. 2391.

15. Steven A. Holmes, "Cuba Cutting Direct Phone Service from U.S.," *New York Times,* July 4, 1993, p. 13, col. 1.

16. The system was established by the 1963 Space Radiocommunication Conference. See David M. Leive, *International Telecommunications and International Law: the Regulation of the Radio Spectrum* (Leyden: A. W. Sijthoff, 1970), pp. 209–214.

17. ITU, Art. 48.

18. Not everyone is happy with the first come, first served rule, and developing countries have argued for a set-aside of orbital slots so that they will not be preempted by the early arrival of the more technologically advanced states. See the "Bogatá Declaration," 1976, reprinted in *Journal of Space Law,* 6 (1979): 193. Eight equatorial countries asserted sovereignty over superjacent arcs of the geostationary orbit. The issue is a perennial subject of debate in the UN Committee on the Peaceful Uses of Outer Space, and in 1989 the ITU agreed to reserve at least one orbital slot for any national system providing domestic services. See Milton Smith, "The Space WARC Concludes," *American Journal of International Law,* 83 (1989): 596.

19. LRTAP, Protocol on Long-Term Financing of the Cooperative Programme for

Monitoring and Evaluation of Long-Range Transmission of Air Pollutants in Europe (1978); see Marc A. Levy, "European Acid Rain: The Power of Tote-Board Diplomacy," in Marc A. Levy, Robert Keohane, and Peter Haas, *Institutions for the Earth*, p. 80; OECD, "Recommendation on Principles Governing Transfrontier Pollution, Title E, Principle of Information and Consultation, November 21, 1974," OECD Doc. C(74)224, reprinted in *International Legal Materials*, 14 (1975): 242, 246.

20. Levy, "European Acid Rain," pp. 91–94, 174, table 3.6. Within the next five years, many members had exceeded the target. Levy argues that the protocols to LRTAP performed regulatory functions not in the sense of imposing a constraint on state action, but as part of a consensus-building process, "indicating both what behavior was considered legitimate and which countries had accepted such a standard as a guide to national policy . . . Who was responsible and who was not." Ibid., p. 77.

21. Ibid., pp. 87–88.

22. See Ostrom, *Governing the Commons*, p. 34, on the importance of improving scientific understanding to remove uncertainty effects that inhibit cooperative action

23. Two protocols were also signed—the Protocol for the Prevention of Pollution of the Mediterranean Sea by Dumping from Ships and Aircraft, and the Protocol Concerning Co-operation in Combating Pollution of the Mediterranean Sea by Oil and Other Harmful Substances in Cases of Emergency—but these simply recapitulated the Convention on the Prevention of Marine Pollution by the Dumping of Wastes and Other Matter, and the International Convention Relating to Intervention on the High Seas in Cases of Oil Pollution Casualties, universal treaties that were already in force.

24. Barcelona Convention, Art. 10 and 11.

25. Peter M. Haas, *Saving the Mediterranean: The Politics of International Environmental Cooperation* (New York: Columbia University Press, 1990), p. 100.

26. Ibid.

27. Ibid, p. 101.

28. Ibid, pp. 129–132.

29. Haas, Keohane, and Levy, "Conclusion," in *Institutions for the Earth*.

30. *The Memorandum of Understanding on Port State Control* (The Hague: Netherlands Government Printing Office, 1989) (information pamphlet).

31. Ronald Bruce Mitchell, *Intentional Oil Pollution at Sea: Environmental Policy and Treaty Compliance* (Cambridge, Mass.: MIT Press, 1994), p. 136.

32. NPT, Art. I and IV.

33. Non–nuclear weapon states party to the NPT, currently in the neighborhood of 125 states, have agreed to place *all* their nuclear activity under safeguards. NPT, Art. 3. Under the arrangements described, nuclear importers not parties to the NPT submit to inspection only with respect to the imported materials or facilities. India is not a party to the NPT, and the material for its nuclear test in 1974 came from an indigenously constructed heavy water reactor.

34. See, e.g., "Monitoring Procedures in Venezuela Restructuring Agreements,"

New York, Feb. 26, 1986, reproduced in *International Legal Materials,* 25 (Mar. 1986): 477.

35. UN GA Res. 46/36L, Dec. 9, 1991, UN Doc. A/RES/43/36, *International Legal Materials,* 31 (1992): 469.

36. See Edward J. Laurance, Siemon T. Wezeman, and Herbert Wulf, *Arms Watch: SIPRI Report on the First Year of the UN Register of Conventional Arms* (London: Oxford University Press, 1993); Ian Anthony, "Assessing the UN Register of Conventional Arms," *Survival,* 35, no. 4 (Winter 1993–94): 113–129. Antonia H. Chayes and Abram Chayes, "The UN Register: Transparency and Cooperative Security," in Malcolm Chalmers, Owen Green, Edward J. Laurance, and Herbert Wulf, eds., *Developing the UN Register of Conventional Arms* (West Yorkshire, England: University of Bradford, 1994), pp. 197–224.

37. Michael Taylor, *Community, Anarchy and Liberty* (Cambridge: Cambridge University Press, 1982), pp. 48–50.

38. Carlisle Ford Runge, "Institutions and the Free Rider: The Assurance Problem in Collective Action," *The Journal of Politics,* 46 (1984): 160. Runge builds on Amartya Sen's original formulation of the assurance problem in "Isolation, Assurance and the Social Rate of Discount," *Quarterly Journal of Economics,* 81 (1967): 112–124.

39. Runge, "Institutions and the Free Rider," particularly pp. 161–162.

40. Treaty on the Prohibition of the Emplacement of Nuclear Weapons and Other Weapons of Mass Destruction on the Seabed and the Ocean Floor.

41. Treaty of Principles Governing the Activities of States in the Exploration and Use of Outer Space, Including the Moon and Other Celestial Bodies, Art. 4.

42. Antarctic Treaty, Art. I, V.

43. Daniel O. Graham, "Arms Control and National Security," *USA Today* (magazine), Jan. 1985, p. 14.

44. Montreal Protocol, Art. 3(c), as amended by London Amendments, Annex II, Art. 1(O), and the Copenhagen Amendments, Annex III, Art. 1(H).

45. Richard Benedick, *Ozone Diplomacy: New Directions in Safeguarding the Planet* (Cambridge, Mass.: Harvard University Press, 1991), pp. 25–26.

46. Ibid., pp. 100–101, 150–52.

47. Elinor Ostrom notes that analysis of the prisoners' dilemma has stressed the importance of the unenforceability of agreements to cooperate, but in the original model, the prisoners are forced to act independently when they are placed in separate cells. "Acting independently in this situation is the result of coercion, not its absence." Ostrom, *Governing the Commons,* p. 39. Sen also emphasizes the "isolation paradox" in the prisoners' dilemma situation. See Sen, "Isolation, Assurance and the Social Rate of Discount," pp. 112–115. See also Carlisle Ford Runge, "Common Property Externalities: Isolation, Assurance, and Resource Depletion in a Traditional Grazing Context," *American Journal of Agricultural Economics,* 75 (Nov. 1981): 597–598.

48. Ullman-Margalit, *The Emergence of Norms,* p. 21.

49. Sen, "Isolation, Assurance and the Social Rate of Discount"; Runge, "Institutions and the Free Rider"; Ostrom, *Governing the Commons,* pp. 1–28; Michael

Taylor, "Cooperation and Rationality: Notes on the Collective Action Problem and Its Solutions," in Karen Schweers Cook and Margaret Levi, eds., *The Limits of Rationality* (Chicago: University of Chicago Press, 1990), p. 222.

50. See Lawrence Freedman, *The Evolution of Nuclear Strategy* (New York: St. Martin's Press, 1981), pp. 182–189; Arthur A. Stein, "Coordination and Collaboration Regimes in an Anarchic World," in Krasner, ed., *International Regimes*, pp. 128–129.

51. It is arguable whether either side could actually have done anything to alter the basic strategic balance at the levels of armament that had been achieved by the 1970s. Antonia Handler Chayes and Abram Chayes, "From Law Enforcement to Dispute Resolution: A New Approach to Arms Control Verification and Compliance," *International Security*, 14, no.4 (Spring 1990): 151. Policy makers were not inclined to argue, however.

52. LTBT.

53. Interim Agreement (SALT I).

54. ABM Treaty. The treaty allowed each side two ground-based ABM sites, later reduced to one.

55. Chayes and Chayes, "From Law Enforcement to Dispute Resolution," pp. 154–155. The effect was to push putative verification requirements to increasingly unattainable levels. Both the "Comprehensive Test Ban Treaty" and SALT II were victims of unrealistic verification requirement.

56. Helsinki Final Act, *Document on Confidence-Building Measures and Certain Aspects of Security and Disarmament,* I, Department of State Publication 8826, General Foreign Policy Series 298 (Aug. 1975).

57. Jonathan Dean, *Watershed in Europe: Dismantling the East-West Military Confrontation* (Lexington, Mass.: Lexington Books, 1987), p. 113.

58. "Document of the Stockholm Conference" (SC 9), in John Borawski, *From the Atlantic to the Urals: Negotiating Arms Control at the Stockholm Conference* (Washington, D.C.: Pergamon-Brassey, 1988), Appendix B, pp. 221–245.

59. Ibid., Appendix B, par. (66). A country need not accept more than three inspections a year all told, nor more than one from any single country. Ibid., par. (67), (68).

60. Borawski, *From the Atlantic to the Urals*, p. 111. See also Timothy E. Wirth, "Confidence- and Security-Building Measures," in Robert E. Blackwill and F. Stephen Larrabee, eds., *Conventional Arms Control and East West Security* (Durham, N.C.: Duke University Press, 1989), p. 342; Adam-Daniel Rotfeld, "CSBMs in Europe: A Future-Oriented Concept," in ibid., p. 329.

61. For example, the dispatching of Russian troops to Chechnya was inconsistent with CFE requirements. Reuters, "Chechnya War Requires Treaty Lapse," *New York Times*, Apr. 17, 1995, p. A2, col. 3.

62. Garrett Hardin, "The Tragedy of the Commons," *Science*, 162 (1968): 1244.

63. Carlisle Ford Runge, "Common Property Externalities, Isolation, Assurance, and Resource Depletion in a Traditional Grazing Context," *American Journal of*

Agricultural Economics, 75 (Nov. 1981): 595–596; Carl J. Dahlman, *The Open Field System and Beyond: A Property Rights Analysis of an Economic Institution* (Cambridge: Cambridge University Press, 1980).

64. Ostrom, *Governing the Commons*, p. 187

65. Ibid, p. 186

66. Robert Axelrod, *The Evolution of Cooperation* (New York: Basic Books, 1984).

67. Ibid., p. 54.

68. Ostrom, *Governing the Commons*, pp. 96–97. See also Keohane, "The Demand for International Regimes," pp. 148–149.

69. Ostrom, *Governing the Commons*, pp. 97, 187

70. Mancur Olson, *The Logic of Collective Action: Public Goods and the Theory of Groups*, 2nd ed. (Cambridge, Mass.: Harvard University Press, 1971), chap. 1 and 2. See also Michael Taylor, *Community, Anarchy and Liberty* (Cambridge: Cambridge University Press, 1982), pp. 51–52. The question is whether the international community is small or large, for these purposes. The primary actors in the system number fewer than two hundred, and a much smaller number are significant participants in most international cooperative ventures. The group of professional diplomats who operate the system is larger, but not unmanageable, and those dealing with particular problems often work in smaller subgroups that have close professional and personal relations across national boundaries.

71. Ostrom, *Governing the Commons*, p. 126. The agreement governing the West Basin dates from 1953 and the Central Basin from 1965. "The level of infractions has been insignificant during that time." Ibid., p. 125.

72. Ibid., p. 126.

73. Court action has been taken against new pumpers who have tried to take water without first purchasing the rights. Ibid.

74. Notionally, the behavior required by the treaty can be regarded as that which the parties decided was necessary to produce the desired collective goods.

75. FCCC, Art. 4(1) and (2).

76. Taylor, "Cooperation and Rationality," pp. 229–230. Taylor describes this phenomenon as "a Chicken nesting in a Prisoners' Dilemma supergame."

77. Olson, *The Logic of Collective Action*, pp. 33–36; Jon Elster, *The Cement of Society: A Sudy of Social Order* (Cambridge: Cambridge University Press, 1989), chap. 2.

78. Freedman, *The Evolution of Nuclear Strategy*, p. 395; Robert Jervis, *The Illogic of American Nuclear Strategy* (Ithaca, N.Y.: Cornell University Press, 1984) chap. 3, 4.

79. Oran R. Young, "The Effectiveness of International Institutions: Hard Cases and Critical Variables," in James N. Rosenau and Ernst-Otto Czempiel, eds. *Governance without Government: Order and Change in World Politics* (Cambridge: Cambridge University Press, 1992), pp. 176–177.

80. Antonia H. Chayes and Paul Doty, *Defending Deterrence: Managing the ABM Treaty Regime into the 21st Century* (Washington, D.C.: Pergamon-Brassey, 1989), p. 3; see also Ashton B. Carter, "Underlying Military Objectives," ibid., p. 18.

7. Reporting and Data Collection

1. Louis Kaplow and Steven Shavell, "Optimal Law-Enforcement with Self-Reporting of Behavior," Harvard Law School Program in Law and Economics, Discussion Paper no. 95 (Aug. 1991), p. 1: "[A] commonly observed feature of law enforcement is . . . self-reporting of behavior—reporting by parties of their own harm-producing actions to an enforcement authority."

2. Kaplow and Shavell say that lawbreakers report "because they fear more severe treatment if they do not." Ibid., p. 1. If this is in fact the motivation, it may have a parallel on the international side, where, under the pervasive norm of good faith, fair reporting will operate as an excuse or at least a palliative for nonperformance in all but the most egregious cases.

3. David Hearst and Paul Brown, "Soviet Union Illegally Killed Great Whales," *The Guardian,* Feb. 12, 1994, p. 3.

4. MARPOL, Art. X(2), XII.

5. GAO Report, *International Environment: International Agreements Are not Well Monitored,* GAO RCED-92-43 (Jan. 1992), pp. 26–27. The study actually examined eight agreements, but one of them, the Basel Convention, had not yet come into force, so there was no experience to measure. Ronald Mitchell shows a 49 percent reporting rate for all OILPOL and MARPOL parties in 1990. See Ronald B. Mitchell, *Intentional Oil Pollution at Sea: Environmental Policy and Treaty Compliance* (Cambridge, Mass.: MIT Press, 1994), p. 132, table 4-2. See also Paul Stephen Dempsey, "Compliance and Enforcement in International Law: Oil Pollution of the Marine Environment by Ocean Vessels," *Northwestern Journal of International Law and Business,* 6 (1984): 485.

6. Gerard Peet, *Operational Discharges from Ships: An Evaluation of the Application of the Discharge Provisions of the MARPOL Convention by Its Contracting Parties* (Amsterdam: AIDEnvironment, 1992), pp. 5–6; Gerard Peet, "The MARPOL Convention: Implementation and Effectiveness," *International Journal of Estuarine and Coastal Law,* 7 (1992): 283.

7. Mitchell, *Intentional Oil Pollution at Sea* p. 134. It is not insignificant that the overall reporting percentage increased from 23 percent to 41 percent from 1984 to 1985, and among developed countries from 43 percent to 65 percent.

8. Ibid.

9. ILO Constitution, Art. 19(5)(c) and (6)(c), and Art. 22; Art. 19(5)(e) and (6)(d); Art. 19(7)(b)(iv) and (v), amended as of Oct. 9, 1946.

10. Ernest B. Haas, *Beyond the Nation-State: Functionalism and International Organization* (Stanford, Calif.: Stanford University Press, 1964), pp. 265–267; see also International Labor Conference, *Record of Proceedings* (1962), p. iii

11. International Labor Conference, *Record of Proceedings* (1980), 37/4–10. Nations supported the proposal for different reasons: Kuwait believed blacklisting for reporting failures was used for political propaganda (37/6, par. 24); France found it to be unfair to underdeveloped countries (37/5, par. 20). But there was agreement

that reporting failures were serious. Compromises were made for cases of special difficulties and for cases of progress (37/4, par. 15; 37/7, par. 30; 37/7, par. 30.)

12. Montreal Protocol, Art. 2, 5(1).

13. United Nations Environment Program, (UNEP), *Report of the Second Meeting of the Parties to the Montreal Protocol on Substances That Deplete the Ozone Layer,* Decision II/9, Doc. no. UNEP/OzL.Pro2/3 (June 29, 1990), p. 15.

14. UNEP, *Report of the First Meeting of the Ad Hoc Group of Experts on the Reporting of Data,* UN Doc. no. UNEP/OzL.Pro/WG.2/1/4 (Dec. 7, 1990).

15. London Amendments to the Montreal Protocol, Art. 10(1).

16. UNEP, *Report of the First Meeting of the Ad Hoc Group of Experts on the Reporting of Data,* pp. 6–7.

17. Fourth Meeting of the Parties to the Montreal Protocol on Substances That Deplete the Ozone Layer, Report of the Secretariat, *The Reporting of Data by the Parties to the Montreal Protocol on Substances That Deplete the Ozone Layer,* UN Doc. UNEP/OzL.Pro.4/6, Aug. 26, 1992.

18. The experience is reviewed in Edward A. Parson and Owen Grenne, "Implementation Measures to Protect Stratospheric Ozone," *Environment* (Mar. 1995).

19. The International Monetary Fund recognized the problem from the outset. The members' obligation to provide information is qualified by the statement that "the Fund shall take into consideration the varying ability of members to furnish the data requested." IMF Agreement, Art. VIII, sec. 5(b).

20. GAO, *International Environment,* p. 25.

21. As noted, the various studies of MARPOL reporting are not easy to reconcile. Mitchell cites figures indicating that nineteen out of forty-nine developing-country parties to OILPOL/MARPOL reported in 1990, for an overall percentage of 38 percent. The reporting rate for developed countries was 68 percent. Mitchell, *Intentional Oil Pollution at Sea,* p. 132, table 4-2.

22. GAO, *International Environment,* pp. 26–27.

23. International Maritime Organization, "Convention on the Prevention of Marine Pollution by Dumping Wastes and Other Matter," *Reporting on Activities Related to Waste Disposal and Incineration at Sea,* Doc. no. LC.2/Circ.318, June 2, 1993, p. 1.

24. Ibid., p. 3.

25. None of the treaties reported on by the GAO had secretariats in excess of 20 members, including clerical and administrative personnel, and most were in single digits. GAO, *International Environment,* p. 31, table 2.2.

26. See Jon Wolfsthal, "CIA Says North Korea Nearing Bomb; Inspections Pact Signed," *Arms Control Today,* 22, no. 2 (Mar. 1992): 26. The problem is more complex than it appears from the text. The reporting requirement is in the safeguards agreement, not in the text of the NPT, so technically it does not come into play until the party has signed that agreement. The IAEA takes the position that all NPT parties should sign safeguards agreements, but a number have yet to do so. If a party has no nuclear program, the IAEA does not regard it as in violation of its obligations. North

Korea adhered to the NPT in 1985 but did not sign a safeguards agreement until February 1992, and it did not file its declaration until some months later. Steven R. Weisman, "North Korea Signs Accord on Atom-Plant Inspections," *New York Times,* Jan. 31, 1992, p. A1.

27. Report of the Secretary General, *Status of International Human Rights Instruments and the General Situation of Overdue Reports,* UN Doc. HRI/MC/1992/3 (Sept. 25, 1992).

28. "Human Rights Questions: Implementation of Human Rights Instruments," *Report of the Fourth Meeting of Persons Chairing the Human Rights Treaty Bodies,* UN Doc. A/47/628, Nov. 10, 1992, p. 19. Apparently some human rights bodies already follow this practice.

29. SALT II, Art. XVII(3) and Agreed Statement

30. Strobe Talbott, *Endgame: The Inside Story of SALT II* (New York: Harper and Row, 1979), p. 98.

31. INF, Art. IX.

32. Talbott, *Endgame,* p. 97.

33. See "Report on Soviet Noncompliance with Arms Control Agreements," White House Office of the Press Secretary, Mar. 30, 1992, pp. 2–10. See also R. Jeffrey Smith, "Bush Backs Arms Treaty Compromise," *Washington Post,* Apr. 12, 1991, p. A16.

34. UN SC Res. 687, Apr. 3, 1991, UN Doc. S/RES/687 (1991). The resolution, according to its terms, did not go into effect until it was "accepted" by Iraq (par. 33). Compliance with the weapons dismantling and destruction provisions of the resolution also had to be verified. The process is discussed in Chapter 8.

35. As of Sept. 1993, Iraq still had not disclosed the names of scientific and technical personnel or European suppliers for its nuclear project, but these are not expressly called for in the cease-fire resolution. As of November 1993, Iraqi authorities had responded to five procurement-related questions specified by the IAEA; the IAEA noted that "a preliminary assessment indicates that, while the procurement issues (e.g. the source of suppliers and the dealers) have been reasonably covered, the extent of foreign advice concerning the centifuge uranium enrichment program has been grossly understated." UN Doc. S/26685, p. 7.

36. It also seems likely that North Korea's declaration was more voluminous and complete than it would otherwise have been because it expected to be subject to such scrutiny. Nayan Chanda, "Bomb and Bombast," *Far Eastern Economic Review,* Feb. 10, 1994, p. 16.

37. Haas, *Beyond the Nation-State,* pp. 254–255.

38. P. H. Kooijmans, *The Role of Non-Governmental Organizations in the Promotion and Protection of Human Rights* (Leiden: Stichting Nscm-Boekerij, 1990), pp. 16–17. For the 1988 session of the UN Commission on Human Rights, 119 NGOs registered themselves, and "practically all of them collect, process and publish data on human rights violations." Ibid.

39. Social Science Research Council Project on National Implementation and

Compliance with Environmental Accords, *Conference Proceedings,* June 18, 1993, remarks of John Gavitt, CITES enforcement officer.

40. Ibid., remarks of Rene Coenan, IMO technical officer.

41. Ibid., remarks of Vivian Shendon, Dupont Corp., and Laura Campbell, deputy coordinator, Ozone Secretariat.

42. Ibid., remarks of Iwona Rummel Bulska, Basel Convention coordinator.

43. See, e.g., UNEP, *Report of the Secretariat on the Reporting of Data by the Parties in Accordance with Article 7 of the Montreal Protocol,* UN Doc. no. UNEP/OzL.Pro.3/5 (May 23, 1991), pp. 33–34.

44. See Alexandre Kiss, "The Protection of the Rhine against Pollution," *Natural Resources Journal,* 25 (1985): 613, 627.

45. UN Doc. no. UNEP/WG, 2/5 annex (Feb. 1975). Haas, *Saving the Mediterranean,* pp. 96–107

46. Ibid, p. 285.

47. Hearst and Brown, "Soviet Union Illegally Killed Great Whales," p. 3.

48. IMF Agreement, Art. VIII(5).

49. See, e.g., International Coffee Agreement, Sept. 16, 1982, Art. 53; "International Natural Rubber Agreement" (1979), Cmnd. 8929, Art. 45; Wheat Trade Convention, Art. 3.

50. See, e.g., Barcelona Convention, Art. 20; Vienna Convention for the Protection of the Ozone Layer, Art. IV and Annex II; FCCC, Art. 5, 9, 12. See also J. H. Ausubel and D. G. Victor, "Verification of International Environmental Agreements," *Annual Review of Energy and the Environment,* 17 (1992): 17–18.

51. See Marc A. Levy, "European Acid Rain: The Power of Tote-Board Diplomacy," in Peter M. Haas, Robert O. Keohane, and Marc A. Levy, *Institutions for the Earth: Source of Effective International Environmental Protection,* (Cambridge, Mass.: MIT Press, 1993), pp. 78–81; Abram Chayes, "Managing the Transition to a Global Warming Regime, or What to Do 'til the Treaty Comes," *Greenhouse Warming: Negotiating a Global Regime* (Washington, D.C.: World Resources Institute, 1991), pp. 65–66.

52. International Slavery Convention, Art. 7.

53. See, e.g., ILO Constitution, Art. 19(5)(c) and (6)(c), 19(5)(e), (6)(d), 19(7)(b)(iv) and (v), and 22; International Covenant on Civil and Political Rights, Art. 40 ("reports on the measures they have adopted which give effect to the rights recognized herein"); International Covenant on Economic, Social and Cultural Rights, Art. 16, 17; CITES, Art. VIII(7)(requiring periodic reports on implementation measures); ICRW, Protocol, Art. XI(4) (requiring reports of relevant laws and infractions) MARPOL goes further and asks for a report of the enforcement effort in the form of penalties actually imposed for infringement of the treaty: Art. 11(f) and Protocol of 1978. Similar requirements were included in the predecessor agreement, OILPOL, Art. X(2), XII.

54. Montreal Protocol, Art. 7(2).

55. CWC, Art. IV(7)(b) and V(9)(b).

56. International Covenant on Civil and Political Rights, Art. 40.

57. See, e.g., Montreal Protocol, Art. 7(1).

58. CWC, Art. III(1)(a)(existing weapons), Art. III(1)(b) (old or abandoned weapons), Art. III(1)(c) (chemical weapons production facilities). Reports are also required on riot-control agents, which are not prohibited by the convention except for use in warfare (ibid., Art. III[1][e]) and laboratories and test sites (Art. III[1][d]).

59. CWC, Annex 2, Part V(A).

60. "Lake Lanoux Arbitration *(France v. Spain),* Arbitral Tribunal, November 16, 1957," *International Law Reports,* 24 (Lauterpacht ed., 1957): 101.

61. Declaration of the United Nations Conference on the Human Environment, June 16, 1972, Recommendation 3. See Louis B. Sohn, "The Stockholm Declaration on the Human Environment," *Harvard International Law Journal,* 14 (1973): 423. But see also OECD, "Recommendation on Principles Governing Transfrontier Pollution, Title E, Principle of Information and Consultation, November 21, 1974," OECD Doc. C(74)224, reprinted in *International Legal Materials,* 14, (1975). 242, 246.

62. Rio Declaration, Principle 19, A/Conf.151/5/Rev. 1, June 13, 1992.

63. See, e.g., Nordic Environmental Protection Convention (1974); Convention on the Protection of the Rhine against Chemical Pollution (1976); UNCLOS III, Part XII (1982); Convention on Early Notification of a Nuclear Accident (1986) See, generally, Elizabeth P. Barratt-Brown, "Building a Monitoring and Compliance Regime under the Montreal Protocol," *Yale Journal of International Law,* 16 (1991): 519; Scott A. Hajost et al., "An Overview of Enforcement and Compliance Mechanisms in International Environmental Agreements," *Proceedings of the International Enforcement Workshop* May 8–10, 1990.

64. Basel Convention, Art. 6 and Annex V (Mar. 12, 1989).

65. UNEP, Ad Hoc Working Group of Experts for the Exchange of Information on Trade and Management of Potentially Harmful Chemicals (in Particular Pesticides) in International Trade, *Report of the Working Group on the Work of Its Third Session,* UN Doc. UNEP/WG.155/6 (Feb. 1987) (London Guidelines).

66. CITES, Art. III and IV.

67. Mark C. Trexler, "The Convention on International Trade in Endangered Species of Wild Fauna and Flora: Political or Conservation Success?" (Ph.D. diss., University of California, Berkeley, 1990), pp. 54–56; SSRC Project on National Implementation and Compliance with Environmental Accords, *Conference Proceedings,* June 18, 1993, remarks of Piers Blaikies.

68. GAO, *International Environment,* p. 28.

69. See Abram Chayes, Thomas Ehrlich, and Andreas F. Lowenfeld, *International Legal Process: Materials for an Introductory Course,* vol. 1 (Boston: Little, Brown, 1968), pp. 617–621. Ultimately the certificate was supplemented by a requirement that stamps, which were distributed to each member in proportion to its quota, be affixed to each shipment to control *ex quota* exports. Ibid.

70. GATT, Art. XIX, XXIV (7).

71. RAND Corp. study N-2536-USDP, Dec. 1986. The study indicates that members were evading the requirement by reporting late or even after the deal had been concluded, which was regarded as testimony to the effectiveness of the notification system. As a result, the guidelines were modified in 1992 requiring notification thirty working days in advance of the bid closing date.

72. SALT II, Art. XVI; START I, Notifications Protocol, Parts VI–VII, Senate Treaty Doc. 102-20 (1991).

73. Agreement on Notification of Launches of Intercontinental Ballistic Missiles and Submarine-Launched Ballistic Missiles, Art. I.

74. "Document of the Stockholm Conference on Confidence- and Security-Building Measures and Disarmament in Europe," par. (29)–(54), *Arms Control and Disarmament Agreements* (Washington, D.C.: U.S. Arms Control and Disarmament Agency, 1990), pp. 325–330.

75. See SALT II, Art. IV(9), prohibiting testing of more than one new type of ICBM. Article IV prohibited changes in diameter of existing missiles of more than 15 percent, or a change of depth of more than 32 percent; Interim Agreement (SALT I). The START agreement bans types of ICBMs not specifically limited in the treaty, all new heavy ICBMs, missiles with more than ten reentry vehicles, and launchers for new ICBM types that can be used with others. START I, Art. V.

76. Mitchell, *Intentional Oil Pollution at Sea,* p. 191.

77. See, e.g., *Sale of Children, Report Submitted by Mr. Vitit Munjarborn, Special Rapporteur of the Commission on Human Rights, in Accordance with Commission Resolution 1992/76,* E/CN.4/1993/67; *Report on the Situation of Human Rights in Haiti, Submitted by Dr. Marco Julio Bruni Celii, Special Rapporteur of the Commission on Human Rights, in Accordance with Commission Resolution 1992/77,* E/CN.4/1993/47; *Report on the Situation of Human Rights in Nyanmar, prepared by Mr. Yozo Kota, Special Rapporteur of the Commission on Human Rights, in Accordance with Commission Resolution 1992/58,* E/CN.4/1993/37.

78. See Social Science Research Council Project on National Implementation and Compliance with Environmental Accords, *Conference Proceedings,* June 18, 1993, remarks of Jacques Bernay, CITES deputy secretary general; Rene Coenan, IMO technical officer (London Convention); Vivian Shendon, Dupont Corp.; and Professor James Finerman (ozone).

79. See M. J. Peterson, "International Fisheries Management," in Haas, Keohane, and Levy, *Institutions for the Earth,* p. 267; Peter M. Haas, "Protecting the Baltic and North Seas," in ibid, pp. 148, 150.

80. Ausubel and Victor, "Verification of International Environmental Agreements," pp. 17, 20.

81. Ibid., pp. 13, 21; J. Eric Smith, "The Role of Special Purpose and Nongovernmental Organizations in the Environmental Crisis," in David A. Kay and Eugene B. Skolnikoff, eds., *World Eco-Crisis: International Organizations in Response* (Madison, Wis.: University of Wisconsin Press, 1972), pp. 135–159.

82. Mitchell, *Intentional Oil Pollution at Sea,* p. 175.

83. UN GA Res. 43/53, Dec. 6, 1988, A/RES/43/53 (1988).

84. FCCC, Art. 21(2).

85. Mitchell, *Intentional Oil Pollution at Sea,* p. 143.

86. FCCC, Art. 12; ibid., Art. 4.

8. Verification and Monitoring

1. See Sidney Graybeal and Patricia McFate, "Introduction: The Role of Verification," in Sidney Graybeal, George Lindsey, James MacIntosh, and Patricia McFate, eds., *Verification to the Year 2000* (Ottawa: The Arms Control and Disarmament Division, External Affairs and International Trade, 1991), p. 3.

2. For a sampling of the literature see, e.g., ibid.; Michael Krepon and Mary Umberger, eds., *Verification and Compliance: A Problem Solving Approach* (Cambridge, Mass.: Ballinger Publishing, 1988).

3. See, e.g., J. H. Ausubel and D. G. Victor, "Verification of International Environmental Agreements," *Annual Review of Energy and the Environment,* 17 (1992): 1; Wolfgang Fischer, *The Verification of International Conventions to Protect the Environment and Common Resources* (Jülich: Forschungszentrum Julich GmbH, 1990).

4. The complexities and difficulties of verifying this type of agreement are illustrated by the breakdown of the Angola peace accords. See *Report of the Secretary General on the UN Angola Verification Mission* (UNAVEM II), S/22627 (1991), S/23671 (1992), and S/24556 (1992).

5. "The United States should satisfy itself that a comfortable buffer of conspicuous and time-consuming tests and manufacturing, site preparation, construction, satellite launching, and other deployment activity stands between a breakout decision by Soviet leaders and achievement of a militarily threatening Soviet ABM." Ashton Carter, "Underlying Military Objectives," in Antonia Chayes and Paul Doty, eds., *Defending Deterrence* (Washington, D.C.: Pergamon-Brassey, 1989), p. 18

6. ABM Treaty, Art. III, V.

7. George Bunn and Wolfgang K. H. Panofsky, "Arms Control Compliance and the Law," Working Paper of the Center for International Security and Arms Control, Stanford, Calif., 1988, p. 7; U.S. Senate Foreign Relations Committee, *Hearings on the SALT II Treaty,* 96th Cong., 1st sess. (1979), part 2, p. 241.

8. U.S. Senate Foreign Relations Committee, *Hearings on the INF Treaty,* 100th Cong., 2nd sess. (1988), p. 41. See Bunn and Panofsky, "Arms Control Compliance and the Law," pp. 7–8. But see also Patricia B. McFate, "The Shape of Things to Come: New Concepts in Arms Control Verification," in Steven Mataija and J. Marshall Beier, eds., *Multilateral Verification and the Post-Gulf Environment: Learning From the UNSCOM Experience* (Toronto: Center for International and Strategic Studies, York University, 1992), pp. 68–69.

9. "Statement by the United States Representative (Baruch) to the United Nations Atomic Energy Commission, June 14, 1946," in *Documents on Disarmament 1945–1959,* vol. 1 (Washington, D.C.: U.S. Department of State, 1960), p. 7.

10. Michael Krepon, "The Politics of Treaty Verification and Compliance," in Kosta Tsipis, David Hafemeister, and Penny Janeway, eds., *Arms Control Verification: The Technologies That Make It Possible* (Washington, D.C.: Pergamon-Brassey, 1986), pp. 20–32; Roger Clark and John Baruch, "Verification of a Comprehensive Test Ban," in Frank Barnaby, ed., *A Handbook of Verification Procedures* (Basingstoke: Macmillan, 1990), p. 159; Gordon Thompson, "Verification of a Cut-Off in the Production of Fissile Material," in ibid., pp. 278–279. See also Glenn T. Seaborg, *Kennedy, Khrushchev and the Bomb* (Berkeley: University of California Press, 1981), pp. 178–191. In fact, President Kennedy had authorized a move to six inspections, but Arthur Dean, the U.S. negotiator never made the offer and Khrushchev's sincerity was never tested.

11. For example, in SALT I the unit of account was the launcher—as opposed to the missile itself—precisely because launchers were easier to count. Strobe Talbott, *Deadly Gambits* (New York: Alfred A. Knopf, 1984), pp. 212, 238.

12. See, e.g., *Testimony of Secretary of Defense Harold Brown before the Senate Committee on Armed Services, Hearings on S. 2571 (Defense Authorization)*, 95th Cong., 2nd sess. (1978), part 1, p. 616.

13. ABM Treaty, Art. XIII; Antonia Handler Chayes and Abram Chayes, "From Law Enforcement to Dispute Settlement: A New Approach to Arms Control Verification and Compliance," *International Security*, 14, no. 4 (Spring 1990): 159.

14. ABM Treaty Art. XII(2) and (3); SALT I, Art. V(2) and (3).

15. Strobe Talbott, *Endgame: The Inside Story of SALT II* (New York: Harper and Row, 1979), p. 98.

16. For example, SALT I required advance notification of launches and "functionally related observable differences" to distinguish heavy bombers from air-launch cruise missile launchers. SALT I, Art. XV (2) and (3), XVI (1), and II (3), "Fourth Agreed Statement." Counting rules made assumptions about warhead numbers based on testing, and about bomb or ALCM numbers by averaging. See Michael Krepon, "Counting Rules," in Krepon and Umberger, eds., *Verification and Compliance*, pp. 124–140.

17. Sidney Graybeal and Patricia McFate, "Recent and Current Trends in Bilateral Verification," in Graybeal, et al., eds., *Verification to the Year 2000*. See also, e.g., General Advisory Committee on Arms Control and Disarmament, *A Quarter Century of Soviet Compliance: Practices under Arms Control Commitments, 1958–1983* (Washington, D.C.: USGPO, 1984).

18. See Chayes and Chayes, "From Law Enforcement to Dispute Settlement," p. 149; Stephen J. Flanagan, "Safeguarding Arms Control," in Krepon and Umberger, eds., *Verification and Compliance*, pp. 224–225.

19. Amendment 1516 passed by fifty-six votes to thirty-five. It stated, "The Congress recognizes the principle of United States–Soviet equality reflected in the antiballistic missile treaty and urges and requests that [future negotiations] would not limit the United States to levels of intercontinental strategic forces inferior to the limits

provided for the Soviet Union." *Congressional Record,* vol. 118, pp. 30623 et seq., 92nd Cong. 2nd sess. (1972).

20. See, e.g., General Advisory Committee on Arms Control and Disarmament, *A Quarter Century of Soviet Compliance,* on the high degree of verification that was desired by the Reagan administration. William E. Burrows, *Deep Black: Space Espionage and National Security* (New York: Random House, 1987); p. 339; Lloyd Jensen, *Negotiating Nuclear Arms Control,* (Columbia: University of South Carolina Press, 1988), p. 41.

21. For example, the Senate held up ratification of the Conventional Forces in Europe agreement in the spring of 1991 when the Soviet Union redefined three mechanized infantry divisions with almost one thousand new tanks as "coastal defense units" and claimed that they were "naval forces" outside of the scope of the treaty. Strong diplomatic pressure from all the other parties to the treaty, including states from the former Soviet bloc, forced the Soviets to drop this line of argument. See R. Jeffrey Smith, "Bush Backs Arms Treaty Compromise," *Washington Post,* Apr. 12, 1991, p. A16.

22. Ashton B. Carter, William J. Perry, and John D. Steinbruner, "A New Concept of Cooperative Security," Brookings Occasional Paper (Washington, D.C.: Brookings Institution, 1992), p. 1.

23. INF, Art. XI. See also, Protocol regarding Inspections Relating to the Treaty between the United States of America and the Union of Soviet Socialist Republics on the Elimination of Their Intermediate-Range and Shorter-Range Missiles.

24. CFE, Art. VIII and Art. XIV, Protocol on Inspections; START I, July 31, 1991, Protocol on Inspections and Continuous Monitoring Activities.

25. CWC, Annex on Implementation and Verification; START II, Art. XI(14) and Protocol on Inspections, Art. XVI.

26. "Proposal for the Third Review Conference of the Biological Weapons Convention," *Report of the Federation of American Scientists Working Group on Biological and Toxin Weapons Verification,* Oct. 1990.

27. INF, Part IV(A), pp. 88–104, and Part V (closeout provisions).

28. INF, Art. XI(6)(portal monitoring provisions); START II, Art. XI(14), Protocol on Inspections, Art. XVI (portal monitoring provision); CFE, Art. VIII; Art. XIV (portal monitoring provision).

29. INF, Art. XI(5)(short notice inspection provision); CWC, Part X (short-notice inspection provisions); START I, Art. XI (short-notice inspection provision); CFE, Art. VIII and Art. XIV, Protocol on Inspection (short-notice inspection provision).

30. Amy Woolf, "Cooperative Measures in START Verification," Congressional Research Service Report 91-492F, 1991, p. 4; Patricia B. McFate, "The Shape of Things to Come," p. 70.

31. Treaty on Open Skies, Misc 13 (1992), Cm 2067. David A. Koplow, "When Is an Amendment Not an Amendment? Modification of Arms Control Agreements without the Senate," *University of Chicago Law Review,* 59 (1992): 985–1009.

32. Giuseppe Schiavone, *International Organizations: A Dictionary and Directory* (London: Macmillan, 1992), pp. 130–133.

33. NPT, Art. III.7.

34. IAEA Doc. INFCIRC 153, May 1971, reprinted in *International Legal Materials,* 10 (1971): 855. See Ben Sanders, "IAEA Safeguards: A Short Historical Background," in David Fischer, Ben Sanders, Lawrence Scheinman, and George Bunn, eds., *A New Nuclear Triad: The Non-Proliferation of Nuclear Weapons, International Verification and the International Atomic Energy Agency* (Southhampton: Mountbatten Centre for International Studies, 1992), pp. 2–4.

35. Frank von Hippel and Barbara G. Levi, "Controlling Nuclear Weapons at the Source: Verification of a Cutoff in the Production of Plutonium and Highly Enriched Uranium for Nuclear Weapons," in Tsipis, Hafemeister, and Janeway, eds., *Arms Control Verification,* p. 357.

36. David Kay, "The IAEA: How Can It Be Strengthened?" unpublished paper, p. 7. Kay observes that IAEA inspectors visited the site of Iraq's Al Tuwaitha Nuclear Research Center every six months and never inquired about the uses of the other seventy buildings on the same site.

37. Lawrence Scheinman, "Nuclear Safeguards and Non-Proliferation in a Changing World Order," *Security Dialogue,* 23 (Dec. 1992): 41; Lawrence Scheinman, "Lessons from Post-War Iraq for the International Full-Scope Safeguards Regime," *Arms Control Today,* 23 (Apr. 1993): 4.

38. Elaine Sciolino, "U.S. Says Iraqis' Uranium Is Still Enough for One Bomb," *New York Times,* May 1, 1991, p. A14. In addition, the inventory failed to list other known and suspected nuclear weapons development laboratories and high-speed centrifuges.

39. Paul Lewis, "UN Aides Say Iraq May Be Concealing Nuclear Material," *New York Times,* June 15, 1991, pp. A1, 4.

40. UN Doc. S/23165 (Security Council, 1991), p. 5

41. John R. Walker, "The UNSCOM Experience: Orientation," in Mataija and Beier, eds., *Multilateral Verification and the Post-Gulf Environment,* p. 89; John Simpson, "The Iraqi Nuclear Programme and the Future of the IAEA Safeguards System," in J. B. Poole and R. Guthrie, eds., *Verification Report 1992: Yearbook on Arms Control and Environmental Agreements* (London: Vertic, 1992), p. 252.

42. David Sanger, "North Korea Spurns Nuclear Agency Demand," *New York Times,* Feb. 14, 1993, p. A1; Kay, "The IAEA: How Can It Be Strengthened?"

43. "U.S. and North Korea Recess Talks," *New York Times,* May 21, 1995, p. 3.

44. See *Strengthening the Effectiveness and Improving the Efficiency of the Safeguards Program: A Report by the General Director,* IAEA Doc. no. GOV/2784, Feb. 21, 1995; Gamini Seneviratne, "New IAEA Safeguards System to Be Applied in Two Phases," *Nuclear Fuel,* 20 (July 31, 1995): 10.

45. CWC, Art. IX.

46. "An ACT Interview with Amb. Stephen J. Ledogar: The End of the Negotiations," *Arms Control Today,* 22, no. 8 (Oct. 1992): 8–9.

47. CWC, Annex on Implementation and Verification, Part X, C, par. 38, 41, and Art. IX (20). Michael Krepon, "Verifying the Chemical Weapons Convention," *Arms Control Today*, 22, no. 8 (Oct. 1992): 22; see also Charles C. Flowerree, "The Chemical Weapons Convention: A Milestone in International Security," in ibid., p. 3, and James F. Leonard, "Rolling Back Chemical Proliferation," in ibid., p. 13.

48. By contrast, the CFE verification procedure has evolved into what has been termed "coordinated bilateral" verification. Alan Crawford, "Interrelationship of Verification Methods: Working Group Summary," in Mataija and Beier, eds., *Multilateral Verification and the Post-Gulf Environment*, p. 132. While actual inspections are initiated and performed by individual states, smaller NATO states have set up multinational teams of inspectors. NATO shares technologies, training, inspections, and data to avoid duplication and to maximize the sites and types of inspections a host country has to accept. Mark Lowenthal, "The CFE Treaty: Verification and Compliance Issues," Congressional Research Service Issue Brief 91009 (1991), p. 9.

49. See Fischer, *The Verification of International Conventions*, p. 20.

50. *GAO Report: International Agreements Are not Well Monitored*, GAO RCED-92-43 (Jan. 1992), pp. 23–28.

51. See, e.g., *Report of the Secretariat of the Montreal Protocol on the Reporting of Data*, Nov. 14, 1990, UNEP/OzL.Pro. See also Chapter 7 of this volume.

52. OILPOL, Art. III(c)(i).

53. See, generally, Ronald Mitchell, *Intentional Oil Pollution at Sea: Environmental Policy and Treaty Compliance* (Cambridge, Mass.: MIT Press, 1994), chap. 4, for a history of the amendments and the negotiations leading to them.

54. Copenhagen Amendments to the Montreal Protocol.

55. Marc A. Levy, "European Acid Rain: The Power of Tote-Board Diplomacy," in Peter M. Haas, Robert O. Keohane, and Marc A. Levy, eds., *Institutions for the Earth* (Cambridge, Mass.: MIT Press, 1993).

56. Lawrence E. Susskind and Jeffrey Cruikshank, *Breaking the Impasse: Consensual Approaches to Resolving Public Disputes* (New York: Basic Books, 1987), pp. 113–117.

57. UNEP/WG, 2/5 annex, (Feb. 1975). The Mediterranean Action Plan, Med-Plan, designed by the United Nations Environment Programme, was adopted in conjunction with the Barcelona Convention for the Protection of the Mediterranean Sea Against Pollution (Feb. 1976), a framework agreement to protect the Mediterranean and to seek to control specific pollutants in the future. See also Peter Haas, *Saving the Mediterranean* (New York: Columbia University Press, 1990), pp. 97–100.

58. Peter Sand, "Regional Approaches to Transboundary Air Pollution," in John Helm, ed., *Energy Production, Consumption and Consequences* (Washington, D.C.: National Academy Press, 1990), p. 259.

59. Ronald Mitchell, "Intentional Oil Pollution of the Oceans," in Haas, Keohane, and Levy, eds., *Institutions for the Earth*, pp. 206–221.

60. ICRW, Protocol, Dec. 2, 1956. The protocol did not go into effect until 1959. The IOS itself was adopted first on a regional basis in 1967 and was fully imple-

mented in only 1977. See Patricia Birnie, *The International Regulation of Whaling* (New York: Oceana Publications, 1985), pp. 703–704.

61. Birnie, *International Regulation of Whaling,* p. 471.

62. Antarctic Treaty, Art. I, V.

63. Philip Quigg, *A Pole Apart: The Emerging Issue of Antarctica,* (New York: New Press, 1983), p. 147; Nicola Donlon, "Prospects for the Verification of the Environmental Protection Protocol to the Antarctic Treaty," in Poole and Guthrie, eds., *Verification Report 1992,* p. 261, 262. See also Jeffrey Myhre, *The Antarctic Treaty System: Politics, Law and Diplomacy* (Boulder, Colo.: Westview Press, 1986), pp. 36–37.

64. Protocol on Environmental Protection to the Antarctic Treaty, Art. VI, VIII, XIII.

65. *Summary Report: The Operation of the Ramsar Bureau's Monitoring Procedure 1988–1989,* (Gland, Switzerland: Ramsar, 1990); interview with Ronald Mitchell.

66. *Report of the Fourth Meeting of the Parties to the Montreal Protocol on Substances That Deplete the Ozone Layer,* Annex IV, par. (d), UNEP/OzL.Pro.4/15, November 25, 1992.

67. UNEP/WG, 2/5 annex (Feb. 1975). See Haas, *Saving the Mediterranean,* 112–113, 115.

68. Barcelona Convention, Annex I(A)(8). See Peter M. Haas, *Saving the Mediterranean,* p. 109.

69. FCCC, Art. 4(3).

70. FCCC, Conference of the Parties, 1st sess., Berlin, June 6, 1995, the Berlin Mandate, Doc. no. FCCC/CP/1995/7/Add. 1, p.4

71. Montreal Protocol, Art. 5(1).

72. FCCC, Art. 4(1) and (2). In the Convention on Biological Diversity, major undertakings are qualified by the phrase "as far as possible and appropriate."

73. See, e.g., Task Force on the Comprehensive Approach to Climate Change, *A Comprehensive Approach to Addressing Potential Climate Change* (Washington, D.C., 1991), chap. 8, "Market-Based Incentives."

74. Fischer, *The Verification of International Conventions to Protect the Environment and Common Resources,* p. 30.

75. Julian Robinson, Jeanne Guillemin, and Matthew Meselson, "Yellow Rain: The Story Collapses," *Foreign Policy* (Fall 1987): 117. This issue was raised in the noncompliance reports of the mid-1980s; see, e.g., United States Arms Control and Disarmament Agency, *Soviet Noncompliance,* unclassified report, Feb. 1, 1986, p. 14. But see also "Analysis of the President's Report on Soviet Noncompliance with Arms Control Agreements: An Arms Control Association Staff Analysis," in *Arms Control Today,* Apr. 17, 1987, p. 11A (asserting that there was no evidence that the Soviets had used toxins as alleged); Philip J. Hilts, "U.S. and Russian Researchers Tie Anthrax Deaths to Soviets," *New York Times,* Mar. 15, 1993, p. A6.

76. Speech by Ronald F. Lehman II, director of the U.S. Arms Control and Disarmament Agency, to the World Affairs Council, Riverside, Calif., Mar. 1, 1991, p. 4.

77. See e.g., Robert M. Cook-Deegan, *Winds of Death: Iraq's Use of Poison Gas against Its Kurdish Population: Report of a Medical Mission to Turkish Kurdistan* (Somerville, Mass.: Physicians for Human Rights, 1989). See also reports of the UN secretary general on investigations of UN experts: S/15834 (1983), S/16433 (1984), and S/17911 (1986) citing evidence of use; S/18852 (1987) documenting the first civilian casualties; S/19823 (1988) documenting the first mass attack; and S/20063 (1988) documenting Iraqi soldiers afflicted. In none of these reports was blame assessed on a particular party.

78. Montreal Protocol, Art. 1(6).

79. *Montreal Protocol Report of the First Meeting of the Parties,* Helsinki, UNEP, May 6, 1989.

80. *Report of the First Meeting of the Ad Hoc Group of Experts on the Reporting of Data,* MPDoc no. UNEP/OzL.Pro/WG.2/1/4 (Dec. 7, 1990). Once this verification capacity is achieved, it may also enhance the government's ability to comply with the substantive obligations of the treaty. See Richard E. Benedick, *Ozone Diplomacy* (Cambridge, Mass.: Harvard University Press, 1991), pp. 157, 186–187 (discussing country-specific studies).

81. "Intermediate Range Nuclear Forces Treaty Implementation," in *Report to the Chairman, Committee on Governmental Affairs,* U.S. Senate, Appendix 4, GAO/NSIAD-91-262.

82. Office of Public Information, On-Site Inspection Agency, U.S. Department of Defense, Sept. 1994.

83. Congressional Budget Office, *U.S. Costs of Verification and Compliance under Pending Arms Treaties: Summary,* pp. xi, 41, 61; "Arms Control Funding Summary," chart prepared by OSD/Acquisition and received by authors. These are OSIA-specific costs and are additional to national intelligence costs.

84. International Atomic Energy Agency, *The Agency's Programme and Budget for 1995 and 1996* (Vienna: IAEA, 1994), p. 3.

85. Office of the Assistant Secretary for Public Affairs, U.S. Department of Defense, July 1994.

86. Conversation with Justin Smith, Chemical Weapons Convention, Sept. 1994.

87. Jonathan Dean, *Watershed in Europe: Dismantling the East-West Military Confrontation* (Lexington, Mass.: Lexington Books, 1987).

88. See Joseph P. Harahan, *On-Site Inspections under the INF Treaty: A History of the On-Site Inspection Agency and INF Treaty Implementation, 1988–1991* (Washington, D.C.: USGPO, 1993).

89. Linda Netsch, "Fostering Compliance: The On-Site Inspection Experience," unpublished paper, 1992.

90. See, e.g., UN Group of Qualified Government Experts, *Verification and the United Nations* (New York: United Nations, 1990); J. B. Poole ed., *Verification Report 1991: Yearbook on Arms Control and Environmental Agreements* (London: Vertic, 1992), p. 229.

91. Interview with Dr. Hans Blix, Vienna, Jan. 22, 1992.

92. Brenda Fowler, "Atom Agency Seeks Stronger Safeguards System," *New York Times,* Dec. 7, 1991, p. A3.

93. James MacIntosh, "Likely Evolution of the Trends in Multilateral Verification over the Next 10 Years," in Graybeal et al., eds., *Verification to the Year 2000,* pp. 32–34; See John Simpson, "The Iraqi Nuclear Programme and the Future of the IAEA Safeguards System," in Poole and Guthrie, eds., *Verification Report 1992,* p. 253: "Many in Washington favor an arrangement in which a permanent version of the UN Security Council Special Commission acts as the NPT trouble-shooting body, by-passing the IAEA Special Inspection procedures and the small unit set up in its Secretariat in 1991 to receive such informaton. The core issue is: which group should be given access to United States' intelligence information on clandestine weapon programs."

94. This figure is derived from the following unclassified verification research budgets for fiscal year 1993: Department of Energy, $220 milion; Defense Nuclear Agency, $67.5 million; Defense Atomic Research Projects Agency, $26.5 million; and Arms Control and Disarmament Agency, significantly less than $1 million. Obtained directly from the budget or financial offices of the respective agencies, Aug. 11, 13, and 18, 1993.

95. Janne Nolan, ed., *Global Engagement: Cooperation and Security in the 21st Century* (Washington, D.C.: Brookings Institution, 1994).

96. See Josef Klinger and Jiri Malek, "Seismic Methods for Verification," in Jurgen Altmann et al., eds., *Verification at Vienna: Monitoring of Reductions of Conventional Armed Forces* (Philadelphia: Gordon and Breach Science Publishers, 1992), pp. 188–195; Patricia M. Lewis, "Technological Aids for On-Site Inspection and Monitoring," in John Grin and Henry Van der Graaf, eds., *Unconventional Approaches to Conventional Arms Control Verification: An Exploratory Assessment* (New York: St. Martin's Press, 1990), pp. 226–234.

97. Lewis, "Technological Aids for On-Site Inspection and Monitoring," pp. 203–222.

98. Alex DeVolpi, "Tags and Seals for Arms Control Verification," in Altmann et al., eds., *Verification at Vienna,* pp. 242–254.

99. John Simpson, "The Iraqi Nuclear Programme and the Future of the IAEA Safeguards System," in Poole and Guthrie, *Verification Report 1992,* p. 252; Scheinman, "Lessons from Post-War Iraq for the International Full-Scope Safeguards Regime," p. 4.

100. CWC, Annex II, Part VI. Parties are prohibited from transferring Schedule I chemicals to nonparties, and, after three years from entry into force, trade in potentially dangerous precursor and dual-use chemicals categorized as Schedule II chemicals also prohibited. During that first three-year period, end-use certificates for the transfer of Schedule II chemicals are required (Part VII C). Transfer of Schedule III chemicals requires end-use certificates permanently (Part VIII C).

101. Inteview with Jon Jennekens, deputy director general for safeguards, IAEA, Vienna, Jan. 23 and 24, 1992.

102. Interview with Dr. Hans Blix, Vienna, Jan. 22, 1992; interview with Ambassador Rolf Ekeus, Vienna, Mar. 30, 1992.

103. Under Nunn-Lugar, $900 million had been committed as of late 1993, and $300 million obligated by mid-1994. But as with the internationally promised $24 billion, actual expenditures have proceeded at a glacial pace. (Telephone interview with Laura Holgate, Office of the Assistant Secretary of Defense for International Security Affairs, Sept. 1994).

104. According to the Department of Defense, Office of Public Affairs, a revolving fund has been pledged for HEU purchases at the market price, Sept. 1994.

105. London Amendments to the Montreal Protocol, Art. 10.

106. FCCC, Art. 4(3); Convention on Biological Diversity, Art. 20(2).

9. Instruments of Active Management

1. Of the treaties reviewed, nearly one-third include some provision for interpretive or implementation advice within the secretariat's domain.

2. Personal correspondence and conversations. Susan Strange, "IMF: Money Managers," in Robert Cox and Harold Jacobson et al., eds., *The Anatomy of Influence: Decision Making in International Organizations* (New Haven, Conn.: Yale University Press, 1974), p. 269.

3. UN Conference on Environment and Development, *Agenda 21* (New York: UN, 1993), chap. 37.

4. Peter M. Haas, *Saving the Mediterranean: The Politics of International Environmental Cooperation* (New York: Columbia University Press, 1990), pp. 79–81.

5. London Amendments to the Montreal Protocol.

6. *Draft Report of the Third Meeting of the Executive Committee of the Interim Multilateral Fund for the Implementation of the Montreal Protocol,* Annex III, Art. 11(2)(e), (f) and (g), UN Doc. UNEP/OzL.Pro/ExCom/3/18, May 6, 1991, p. 29. The contents of the country programs include: a statement of the strategy of implementation of the protocol, indicating the respective roles of government and supporting multilateral and bilateral agencies; an action plan encompassing investment and technical assistance projects, preinvestment studies, and any additional policy analysis required; and timetable for each activity, and for an action plan review.

7. Project proposals that had been submitted before the adoption of the programmatic requirement were grandfathered.

8. Mr. Mateos, chairman of Executive Committee of the Interim Multilateral Fund for Implementation of the Montreal Protocol, paraphrased in *Report of the Fourth Meeting of the Parties to the Montreal Protocol on Substances that Deplete the Ozone Layer,* UN Doc. UNEP/OzL.Pro.4/15, pp. 6–7.

9. See Edward A. Parson and Owen Grenne, "Implementation of Measures to Protect Stratospheric Ozone," *Environment* (Mar. 1995).

10. FCCC, Art. 11; Biodiversity Convention, Art. 20–21.

11. FCCC, Art. 4(7); Biodiversity Convention, Art. 20(4).

12. GEF Instrument of Governance, *Instrument for the Establishment of the Restructured Global Environment Facility*, GEF Council Meeting, Washington, D.C., July 12–13, 1994, Doc. GEF/C.1/2.

13. *Report of the Intergovernmental Negotiating Committee for a Framework Convention on Climate Change on the Work of Its 11th Session, Held at New York, 6–17 February, 1995*, Doc. A/AC.237/91/add.1, Mar. 8, 1995, p. 45.

14. Of the treaties reviewed in our study, just over half have some dispute resolution provision. The Treaty Information Project at the University of Washington has 44,000 treaties in its database, covering the period 1900–1983; a quantitative study of these treaties by Curtis Reithel found only one-fourth had express provisions for dispute resolution. He found that dispute clauses have increased in relative terms over time, and that international organizations were "among the most progressive forces in making for general acceptance of a precedent for pacific settlement and inclusion of dispute clause provisions as part of normal treaty activity." Curtis George Reithel, "Dispute Settlement in Treaties: A Quantitative Analysis" (Ph.D. diss., University of Washington, 1972), p. 169.

15. More than 90 percent of cases actually filed in court are settled without trial, and the majority of disputes do not even reach the stage of formal filing. Herbert Kritzer "Adjudication to Settlement: Shading in the Gray," *Judicature*, 70 (1986): 161.

16. See, e.g., GATT, Art. XXII and XXIII(1).

17. See, e.g., "Treaty between United States of America and Italy" (1928, entered into force January 20, 1931), 46 Stat 2890, Treaty Series no. 831.

18. UN Charter, Art. 92.

19. *International Court of Justice, Yearbook: 1991–1992*, no. 46 The Hague: ICJ, 1992), pp. 73–111. The Act of Bogatá, designed originally as the instrument for settling legal disputes between members of the OAS, provided for universal submission of such disputes to the ICJ. It was invoked for the first time in 1986 by Nicaragua in its suit against Honduras, and has since subsided into obscurity. *Border and Transborder Armed Actions (Nicaragua v. Honduras), Jurisdiction and Admissibility, ICJ Reports 1988*, p. 69.

20. Statute of the International Court of Justice, Art. 36(1).

21. *International Court of Justice, Yearbook: 1991–1992*, pp. 111–28. Treaties before 1945 referring to the PCIJ are automatically taken to apply to the ICJ.

22. Vienna Convention on Diplomatic Relations, Optional Protocol.

23. *United States Diplomatic and Consular Staff in Teheran (United States v. Iran), ICJ Reports 1980*, p. 3.

24. *Military and Paramilitary Activities in and against Nicaragua (Nicaragua v. United States), ICJ Reports 1986*, p. 14; U.S.-Nicaragua FCN Treaty, Art. XXIV. The United States is party to more than twenty such FCN treaties, most concluded since World War II. They establish the basis for international commerce, investment, and tourism. They all provide for binding adjudication in the ICJ to settle disputes arising under the treaty. David Scheffer, "Non-Judicial State

Remedies and the Jurisdiction of the International Court of Justice," *Stanford Journal of International Law,* 27 (1990): 83. Yet in only two cases in the forty-five year history of the ICJ has one of these provisions been invoked: the *Nicaragua* case, in which the United States unsuccessfully opposed jurisdiction, and the *ELSI* case, which was submitted to the court by special agreement of the parties. *Electtronica Sicula S.p.A. (ELSI) (United States v. Italy), ICJ Reports 1989,* p. 15. For a list of U.S. treaties containing compromissory clauses for submission of disputes to the ICJ, see F. Morrison, "Treaties as a Source of Jurisdiction, Especially in U.S. Practice," in Lori Damrosch, ed., *The International Court of Justice at the Crossroads* (Dobbs Ferry, N.Y.: Transnational Publisher, 1987), pp. 58–81.

25. See, e.g., "Nomination of the Netherlands Workers' Delegate to the Third Session of the International Labor Conference, Advisory Opinion No. 1 (July 31, 1922)," in Manley O. Hudson, ed., *World Court Reports,* vol. 1, (Washington, D.C.: Carnegie Endowment for International Peace, 1934), p. 113; "Competence of the International Labor Organization with Respect to Agricultural Labor, Advisory Opinion No. 2 (August 12, 1922)," in ibid., p. 122.

26. See e.g., "German Settlers in Poland, Advisory Opinion No. 6 (September 10, 1923)," in ibid., p. 207; "Exchange of Greek and Turkish Populations, Advisory Opinion No. 10, (Febuary 21, 1925)," ibid., p. 421.

27. J. F. MacMahon and Michael Akehurst, "Settlement of Disputes in Special Fields," in Sir Humphrey Waldock, ed., *International Disputes: The Legal Aspects* (London: Europa Publications, 1972), pp. 211, 217. The "special tribunal" referred to in the text was authorized by Article 37 of the ILO Constitution "for the expeditious determination of any dispute or question relating to the interpretation of a Convention" promulgated by the ILO. Articles 26–34 establish a procedure for handling complaints by members that another member is not observing such a convention.

28. Ibid., p. 221.

29. Ibid., pp. 224–25. Many of the bilateral air transport agreements have arbitration provisions, but only a handful of cases have been submitted under them. See, e.g., "Air Services Agreement between the United States and the United Kingdom," Feb. 11, 1946, 60 Stat 1499 (1946).

30. MacMahon and Akehurst, "Settlement of Disputes in Special Fields," p. 229.

31. Ibid., p. 232. Article 56 of the IMCO Convention provides that "legal questions" that cannot otherwise be settled shall be referred to the International Court of Justice for an advisory opinion. The one case was *Constitution of the Maritime Safety Committee of the Inter-Governmental Maritime Consultative Organization, Advisory Opinion, ICJ Reports 1960,* p. 150. The court determined that, under the convention, Liberia and Panama were entitled to be elected to the Safety Committee because of the tonnage registered under their flags.

32. MacMahon and Akehurst, "Settlement of Disputes in Special Fields," p. 232.

33. Ibid., p. 233.

34. UPU, Art. 32.

35. MacMahon and Akehurst, "Settlement of Disputes in Special Fields," p. 230. From 1972 to 1990, only one case was submitted to arbitration. *Report on the Work of the Union* (Bern: International Bureau of the Universal Postal Union, 1981), p. 96 (for the years 1965–1974, 1976–1983, 1985–1990, paragraphs on Inquiries, Opinions [On Matters in Dispute and Others] and Arbitration).

36. The only situation in which the court has come close to developing a systematic body of law under a particular treaty is with respect to the status of Namibia (then South-West Africa) under the mandate granted to South Africa by the League of Nations and the UN trusteeship system, which has been before the ICJ on a number of occasions. *International Status of South-West Africa, Advisory Opinion, ICJ Reports 1950*, p. 128. Thereafter two more advisory opinions upheld special voting rights provisions and approved an oral hearing procedure adopted by the General Assembly for dealing with reports and petitions on South-West Africa. *South-West Africa: Voting Procedure, Advisory Opinion, ICJ Reports 1955*, p. 67; *Admissibility of Hearings of Petitioners by the Committee on South West Africa, Advisory Opinion, ICJ Reports 1956*, p. 23. In *South West Africa (Ethiopia v. South Africa; Liberia v. South Africa), Second Phase, ICJ Reports 1966*, p. 6, the court dismissed a case challenging what was in effect the annexation of the territory by South Africa as contrary to its obligations under the mandate, on the ground that Ethiopia and Liberia, the complainants, lacked standing to bring suit. Finally, after the General Assembly terminated the mandate and the Security Council called on South Africa to withdraw from the territory, the court in an advisory opinion found that the continued presence of South Africa in the territory was illegal. South Africa rejected the ruling, however, and it had little effect at the time. *Legal Consequences for States of the Continued Presence of South Africa in Namibia (South West Africa), ICJ Reports 1971*, p. 16. See Henry Richardson, "Constitutive Questions in the Negotations for Namibian Independence," *American Journal of International Law*, 78 (1984): 76.

37. The *Corfu Channel* case did not involve a treaty: *Corfu Channel (United Kingdom v. Albania), ICJ Reports 1949*, p. 4; nor did the suits over French nuclear testing in the Pacific: *Nuclear Tests (Australia v. France; New Zealand v. France), ICJ Reports 1974*, p. 253.

38. *United States Diplomatic and Consular Staff in Tehran (United States v. Iran), ICJ Reports 1980*, p. 3; *Military and Paramilitary Activities in and against Nicaragua (Nicaragua. v. United States), ICJ Reports 1986*, p. 4. There were also a number of cold war cases in which the United States and the United Kingdom sought unsuccessfully to sue the Soviet Union or Eastern European states in connection with aerial incidents, although none of the respondents had accepted the court's jurisdiction. See, e.g., *Aerial Incident of 10 March 1953 (United States v. Czechoslavakia), ICJ Reports 1956*, p. 6 (order of March 14).

39. *Aerial Incident of 3 July 1988 (Iran v. United States), ICJ Reports 1991*, p. 187;

Questions of Interpretation and Application of the 1971 Montreal Convention Arising from the Aerial Incident at Lockerbie (Libyan Arab Jamahiriya v. United Kingdom), Request for the Indication of Provisional Measures, ICJ Reports 1992, p. 3; *Application Instituting Proceedings against Yugoslavia (Serbia and Montenegro) for Violating the Convention on the Prevention and Punishment of the Crime of Genocide (Bosnia and Herzegovina v. Yugoslavia [Serbia and Montenegro]), Application Filed March 20, 1993,* ICJ Communiqué no. 93/4 (Mar. 22, 1993).

40. Report of the Secretary General, General Assembly, 47th Sess. A/47/277 S/24111, June 17, 1992.

41. Learned Hand, *Three Lectures on Legal Topics* (New York: Association of the Bar of the City of New York, 1926), p. 105.

42. See Abram Chayes, "A Common Lawyer Looks at International Law," *Harvard Law Review,* 78 (1965): 1396.

43. See Abram Chayes, "The Role of the Judge in Public Law Litigation," *Harvard Law Review,* 89 (1976): 1281.

44. See Lon L. Fuller, "The Forms and Limits of Adjudication," *Harvard Law Review,* 92 (1978): 353; Donald L. Horowitz, *The Courts and Social Policy* (Washington, D.C.: Brookings Institution, 1977), pp. 255–298.

45. Keith Highet, "Winning and Losing: The Commitment of the United States to the International Court—What Was It, What Is It, and Where Has It Gone?" *Transnational Law and Contemporary Problems,* 1 (1991): 157, 198. In fact, U.S. constitutional tradition requires separate Senate approval of any agreement to submit to binding arbitration.

46. Border disputes, presenting sharply bipolar and quintessentially legal issues, and where the parties were prepared for a dispositive settlement, have sometimes been adjudicated successfully. See, e.g., *Temple of Preah Vihear (Cambodia v. Thailand),* ICJ Reports 1962, p. 6; *Land, Island, and Maritime Frontier Dispute (El Salvador/Honduras: Nicaragua Intervening),* ICJ Reports 1992, p. 351. Similarly, the court has been a mechanism for the settlement of maritime boundary disputes. See, e.g., *North Sea Continental Shelf Cases (Federal Republic of Germany v. Denmark; Federal Republic of Germany v. Netherlands),* ICJ Reports 1969, p. 3; *Case concerning the Continental Shelf (Tunisia/Libyan Arab Jamahiriya),* ICJ Reports 1984, p. 18; *Case concerning Delimitation of the Maritime Boundary in the Gulf of Maine Area,* ICJ Reports 1984, p. 246; *Case concerning the Continental Shelf (Libyan Arab Jamahiriya/Malta),* ICJ Reports 1985, p. 13.

47. *Compliance with SALT I Agreements, Bureau of Public Affairs,* Special Report no. 55 (Washington, D.C.: U.S. Department of State, July 1979).

48. Antonia Handler Chayes and Abram Chayes, "From Law Enforcement to Dispute Resolution: A New Approach to Arms Control Verification and Compliance," *International Security,* 14 (1990): 152–154.

49. INF, Art. XIII.

50. CWC, Art. XIV(2). The IAEA is the product of an earlier era and refers disputes or questions concerning the interpretation of its statute to the ICJ. IAEA,

Art. XVII. As in the CWC, the Board of Governors is empowered to refer serious instances of noncompliance to the Security Council.

51. CWC, Art. IX(2).

52. CWC, Art. IX (8)–(22) For an evaluation of the effectiveness of this inspection system, see Michael Krepon, "Verifying the Chemical Weapons Convention," *Arms Control Today*, 22, no. 8 (Oct. 1992): 19–24. See also, Brad Roberts, ed., *The Chemical Weapons Convention: Implementation Issues*, Significant Issues Series, vol. 14, no. 13 (Washington, D.C.: Center for Strategic and International Studies, 1992).

53. For disputes arising in the course of inspections, there is a four-tier approach to settlement: first, inspectors are to negotiate with the inspected state; if they cannot agree, the dispute is referred to the director of the Technical Secretariat, who then negotiates with the state; if the dispute continues to be intractable, it is referred to the Executive Council, which makes a recommendation to the Conference of the Parties; in turn, the Conference can refer the matter to the Security Council. CWC, Art. IX, XII.

54. CWC, Art. XII.

55. ICAO, Art. 84.

56. Thomas Buergenthal, *Law-Making in the International Civil Aviation Organization* (Syracuse, N.Y.: Syracuse University Press, 1969), p. 195.

57. MacMahon and Akehurst, "Settlement of Disputes in Special Fields," p. 224.

58. Buergenthal, *Law-Making in the International Civil Aviation Organization*, pp. 162–166.

59. Ibid., pp. 195–197. Owen Fiss makes the same point in criticizing the domestic alternative dispute resolution movement. See Owen M. Fiss, "Against Settlement," *Yale Law Journal*, 93 (1984): 1073.

60. An appeal from the decision of the Executive Directors would go to the Board of Governors. IMF Agreement, Art. XVIII(b). In 1969, this article was amended to provide for a special Committee on Interpretation: First Amendment to Articles of Agreement of the International Monetary Fund, Art. XVIII.

61. Ibid., Art. V (emphasis added). See Gardner, *Sterling Dollar Diplomacy*, p. 113.

62. Pursuant to Decison no. 71-2, Sept. 26, 1946, in IMF, *Selected Decisions of the Executive Directors and Selected Documents*, 3rd issue (1965), p. 54.

63. Decision no. 284-4, Mar. 10, 1948, in ibid., p. 19.

64. Decision no. 102-(52-11), Feb. 13, 1952, in ibid., p. 21. The only repayment obligation in the Articles of Agreement was limited to years in which the drawer's monetary reserves had increased. IMF Agreement, Art. 5, sec. 7.

65. As we discuss in Chapter 10, these strictures sound more draconian than they are in practice.

66. Decision No. 155-(52/57), Oct. 1, 1952, in IMF, *Selected Decisions of the Executive Directors and Selected Documents*, 3rd issue (1965), p. 24.

67. IMF Agreement, Art. V; "Proposed Second Amendment to the IMF Agreement," *International Legal Materials*, 15 (1976): 546, 550–555.

68. See Decision no. 5392-(77/63), Apr. 29, 1977, *Selected Decisions and Docu-*

ments of the IMF, vol. 10 (1983), p. 10. See also Chapter 10 for a fuller discussion of this process.

69. International Coffee Agreement, (1962), Art. 61(1). All of the successor agreements have substantially the same dispute settlement provisions.

70. Ibid., Art. 61(2). The panel is to be composed of two persons nominated by the importing members, two persons nominated by the exporting members, and a chairman selected unanimously by the four nominated panelists.

71. Ibid., Art. 35(1).

72. *Report of the Advisory Panel on the Legality of a System for the Selective Adjustment of Quotas,* International Coffee Organization Doc. no. ICC-7-60(E) (1965).

73. *Resolution 92,* International Coffee Organization Doc. no. ICC-7-Res. 92(E) (1965).

74. International Coffee Organization, Doc. no. ICC-8-Res. 115(E) (1965).

75. Under the ABM Treaty, Art. XIII, the Commission is "to consider questions concerning compliance with the obligations assumed and related situations which may be considered ambiguous."

76. ABM Treaty, Unilateral Statement B. See also Sidney Graybeal and Patricia McFate, "Assessing Verification and Compliance," and Abram Chayes and Antonia Handler Chayes, "Living Under a Treaty Regime," in Antonia Handler Chayes and Paul Doty, eds., *Defending Deterrence: Managing the ABM Treaty into the 21st Century* (Washington, DC: Pergamon-Brassey, 1989), pp. 179, 186; 207, respectively.

77. Ibid.; See also Gloria Duffy et al., *Compliance and the Future of Arms Control* (Stanford, Calif.: Stanford University Press, 1988), pp. 35–37.

78. INF, Art. XIII, sec. 1(b).

79. David A. Koplow, "When Is an Amendment Not an Amendment? Modification of Arms Control Agreements without the Senate," *University of Chicago Law Review,* 59 (1992): 1008–1009.

80. INF Inspection Protocol, Art. XI, sec. 4, Elimination Protocol, Art. V, sec. 2.

81. See Koplow, "When Is an Amendment Not an Amendment?" p. 1012.

82. Memorandum of Agreement regarding the Implementation of the Verification Provisions of the Treaty between the United States of America and the Union of Soviet Socialist Republics on the Elimination of Their Intermediate Range and Shorter-Range Missiles, cited in Koplow, "When Is an Amendment Not an Amendment?" p. 1013.

83. See ibid., p. 1015.

84. START I, "Protocol on Inspections and Continuous Monitoring Activities," Art. XVIII, sec. 4. According to David Koplow, the language appears in substantially verbatim form in at least seven of the related treaty documents. Koplow, "When Is an Amendment not an Amendment?" pp. 1020–1021, n. 211. Koplow's main interest, as his title suggests, is the impact of these provisions on the constitutional distribution of treaty-making powers between the president and the Senate.

85. PNE Treaty, Verification Protocol; TTBT, Verification Protocol.

86. CFE, Art. XVI, sec. 5.

87. See John H. Jackson, "World Trade Rules and Environmental Policies: Congruence or Conflict?" *Washington and Lee Law Review,* 49 (1992): 1227. The article contains a previously unpublished memorandum by Professor Jackson on GATT intepretative powers. Ibid., pp. 1269–1275.

88. Uruguay Round, Art. IX(2). The article cautions that this authority shall not be used "in a manner that would undermine the amendment provisions."

89. Jackson, "World Trade Rules and Environmental Policies," pp. 1272–1273.

90. MacMahon and Akehurst, "Settlement of Disputes in Special Fields," p. 217.

91. Ibid., p. 212.

92. Ibid., pp. 212–213.

93. UPU, Art. 113.

94. *Report on the Work of the Union* (Bern: International Bureau of the Universal Postal Union) for the years 1965–1974, 1976–1983, 1985–1990, paragraphs on "Inquiries," "Opinions (On Matters in Dispute and Others)," and "Arbitration."

95. MacMahon and Akehurst, "Settlement of Disputes in Special Fields," p. 221.

96. Ibid., p. 229.

97. Ibid., p. 233.

98. Ibid., p. 232.

99. The general comments, known as GCs, are collected in UN Doc. HRI/GEN/1, Sept. 4, 1992, pp. 1–34.

100. IAEA Doc. INFCIRC/153, May 1971, reprinted in *International Legal Materials,* 1 (1971): 855.

101. Louis B. Sohn, "Peaceful Settlement of Disputes in Ocean Conflicts: Does UNCLOS III Point the Way?" *Law and Contemporary Problems,* 46 (1983): 195.

102. Ibid., p. 196.

103. UNCLOS III, Annex VII.

104. Convention on the Law of the Sea, Art. 297; Sohn, "Peaceful Settlement of Disputes in Ocean Conflicts," pp. 197–198.

105. Sohn, "Peaceful Settlement of Disputes in Ocean Conflicts," p. 198; James K. Sebenius, *Negotiating the Law of the Sea* (Cambridge, Mass.: Harvard University Press, 1984), p. 128.

106. Sohn, "Peaceful Settlement of Disputes in Ocean Conflicts," pp. 198–199. The chamber has jurisdiction over disputes among states, and between states and the International Seabed Authority and the Enterprise, the operational management bodies for seabed mining. Contractual disputes between the Enterprise and private concerns are to be handled by commercial arbitration.

107. Ronald Reagan, "Proclamation 5030—Exclusive Economic Zone of the United States of America," issued Mar. 10, 1983, *Public Papers of the Presidents of the United States* (Washington, D.C.: USGPO, 1984) p. 380. There is some evidence that Professor Sohn's "impasse" prevails, at least on issues involving naval navigation in South American waters.

108. Robert E. Hudec, *Enforcing International Trade Law: The Evolution of the Modern GATT Legal System* (Salem, N.H.: Butterworth Legal Publishers, 1993). The

appendix lists, summarizes, classifies, and analyzes all 207 complaints. It is invaluable. The following account is based on pp. 11–14.

109. Ibid.

110. Ibid.

111. Ibid.

112. Robert E. Hudec, "GATT or GABB? The Future Design of the General Agreement on Tariffs and Trade," *Yale Law Journal*, 80 (1971): 1299.

113. See Hudec, *Enforcing International Trade Law.*

114. Only two highly politicized decisions remained unimplemented as long as five years after submission. The first concerned discriminatory provincial taxes in Canada on sales of South African gold coins. But although Canada blocked adoption of the panel report by the council, Ontario removed the taxes within a month of the panel ruling. See Hudec, *Enforcing International Trade Law.* The second was a ruling against the United States on the embargo of sugar exports from Nicaragua. Although the council adopted the report with the United States not voting, the United States refused to comply with the ruling until the end of the civil war in Nicaragua. Ibid., pp. 512–513, 518–520.

115. Uruguay Round, Understanding on Rules and Procedures Governing the Settlement of Disputes, Art. 20.

116. The terms of the 1992 agreement are found in "Understanding on Rules and Procedures Governing the Settlement of Disputes under Articles XXII and XXIII of the General Agreement on Tariffs and Trade," in GATT Secretariat, *Draft Final Act Embodying the Results of the Uruguay Round of Multilateral Trade Negotiations, Dec. 20, 1991,* S.1–S.23, GATT Doc. MTN.TNC.W/FA, S.1–S.23 (1991). The provisions are discussed in Miquel Montaña Mora, "A GATT with Teeth: Law Wins over Politics in the Resolution of International Trade Disputes," *Columbia Journal of Transnational Law,* 31 (1993): 141–159.

117. Montaña I. Mora, "A GATT with Teeth," p. 159.

118. Free Trade Agreement between the United States of America and Canada, chapter 19.

119. North American Free Trade Agreement. See David S. Huntington, "Settling Disputes under the North American Free Trade Agreement," *Harvard International Law Journal,* 34 (1993): 407.

120. Harold S. Russell, *The Helsinki Declaration: Brobdingnag or Lilliput? American Journal of International Law,* 70 (1976): 242. For a brief description of the CSCE and its principles, activities, and membership, see "Fact Sheet: Conference on Security and Cooperation in Europe (CSCE)," *U.S. Department of State Dispatch,* vol. 3, no. 52, p. 915(2), Dec. 28, 1992.

121. "Charter of Paris for a New Europe, Guidelines for the Future" (Paris, Nov. 21, 1990); "Security," par. 6 (London: H.M.S.O., 1991).

122. "Draft by the Delegation of Switzerland of a Convention on a European System for the Peaceful Settlement of Disputes," CSCE/II/B/I. The Swiss draft follows the pattern of the 1948 Act of Bogatá, the stillborn dispute settlement convention of

the OAS. A general description of the early efforts at realizing a dispute settlement system for the CSCE through the experts' meeting in Valletta, Malta, is provided by Michael Froman, "Trouble in Paradise or Brave New World: Making Malta Manageable," May 1, 1991, unpublished paper on file with the authors.

123. "Draft by the Delegation of Switzerland of a Convention on a European System for the Peaceful Settlement of Disputes," CSCE/II/B/I. By the 1989 CSCE meeting in Vienna, the scope and detail of potential dispute settlement mechanisms had been scaled down somewhat, and a new Meeting of Experts was authorized for Valletta, to consider "mandatory involvement of a third party" as the first step in the settlement of a limited category of disputes. "Concluding Document of the Vienna Meeting 1986 of the Participating States of the Conference on Security and Co-operation in Europe, Held on the Basis of the Provisions of the Final Act Relating to the Follow-up to the Conference, November 4, 1986–January 17, 1989," *International Legal Materials,* 28, (1989): 527. "Annex I, the Agenda of the Valletta Meeting of Experts on Peaceful Settlement of Disputes," is at p. 549.

124. "A Personal View of International Dispute Resolution: The CSCE Meeting of Experts on Peaceful Settlement of Disputes," address by Michael Young, then deputy legal advisor, U.S. Department of State, Apr. 30, 1991, to Harvard University Ford Foundation and Pew Charitable Trust Fellows. The Americans were influenced as well by some striking successes in the international arena with a variety of third-party interventions, most recently the complex settlement in Namibia. Less overt may have been the reluctance to embrace any binding processes, and particularly the use of the ICJ in matters that the Americans regarded as political after U.S. withdrawal of its submission to ICJ jurisdiction during the *Nicaragua* case.

125. Conference on Security and Co-operation in Europe, "Summary of Conclusions of the Berlin Meeting of the Council, Including Arrangements for Consultation in Emergency Situations and Peaceful Settlement of Disputes: Summary of Conclusions, June 21, 1991," reprinted in *International Legal Materials,* 30, (1991): 1348, 1350. In addition, the ministers designated the Conflict Prevention Centre as the nominating institution for the CSCE Dispute Settlement Mechanism as described in Section V of the Valletta Provisions for Peaceful Settlement of Disputes. Ibid., p. 1355. The Conflict Prevention Centre was formed in 1991 after a 1986 decision of the CSCE ministers.

126. In the draft report of February 6, 1991, the negotiators left the name of the dispute settlement body in brackets as the "CSCE Dispute Settlement [Unit][Entity][Committee][Team][Group][Body]" before finally dubbing it the "Dispute Settlement Mechanism."

127. Conference on Security and Co-operation in Europe, "Report of the CSCE Meeting of Experts on Peaceful Settlement of Disputes, Sections VII, VIII and XI," *International Legal Materials,* 30 (1991): 382, 393–394. The process can be triggered only by a party to the dispute. The United Kingdom's proposal that noninvolved CSCE members as well as disputants could request the mechanism did not prevail,

although any member may still bring a dispute to the attention of the Committee of Senior Officials of the CSCE.

128. See Conference on Security and Co-operation in Europe, "Decision on Peaceful Settlement of Disputes including the Convention on Conciliation and Arbitration within the CSCE (December 15, 1992)," *International Legal Materials,* 32 (1993): 551.

129. See ibid., Annex 4, pp. 551, 570.

130. See K. J. Holsti, "A 'Zone of Civility' in European Relations? The CSCE and Conflict Resolution," Appendix C, in Michael Bryant, *The CSCE and Future Security in Europe,* Canadian Institute for International Peace and Security, Working Paper no. 40, Mar. 1992.

131. Vienna Convention for the Protection of the Ozone Layer, Art. 11(5).

132. London Amendments to the Montreal Protocol, Annex III.

133. FCCC, Art. 13.

134. Ibid., Art. 14(5)

135. Biodiversity Convention, Art. 27.

136. See, e.g., Oran O. Young, *International Governance: Protecting the Environment in a Stateless Society* (Ithaca, N.Y.: Cornell University Press, 1994), pp. 76–77.

137. Vienna Convention on the Law of Treaties, Art. 39–41.

138. London Amendments to the Montreal Protocol, Annex II, Art. 1(k)–(m); Copenhagen Amendments to the Montreal Protocol, Annexes I, II, and III G.

139. ICAO, Art. 54(1).

140. See ITU, Art. 11, 58.

141. See International Coffee Agreement, Art. 18, 28–45.

142. INF, Art. XI, sec. 4. See, generally, David A. Koplow, "When Is an Amendment Not an Amendment?: Modification of Arms Control Agreements without the Senate," *University of Chicago Law Review,* 59 (1992): 981.

143. U.S. Senate Committee on Armed Services, *NATO Defense and the INF Treaty: Hearings and Meetings before the Senate Committee on Armed Services, United States Senate,* Senate Hearing no. 100-493, pt. 4, 100th Cong., 2nd sess., 1988, p. 410–411, 460–461.

144. See, e.g., Basel Convention, Annexes I and II, Art. 18(3), (2) and 17(2), (3), (4).

145. Montreal Protocol, Art. 2(10)(a)(ii).

146. CWC, Art. XV (4), (5).

10. Policy Review and Assessment

1. Robert Keohane, *After Hegemony, Cooperation and Discord in the World Political Economy* (Princeton, N.J.: Princeton University Press, 1984), p. 88; see Oran O. Young, *International Governance: Protecting the Environment Politics in a Stateless Society* (Ithaca, N.Y.: Cornell University Press, 1994), pp. 1–3.

2. CITES, "Italy: Recommendations of the Standing Committee," *Notification to the Parties,* no. 675, June 30, 1992. Alberta Sbragia and Philip Hildbrand, "The European Community: The Paradox of Weakness," in Harold Jacobson and Edith Brown Weiss, eds., *National Compliance with International Environmental Accords* (Social Science Research Council, forthcoming). After Italy changed its CITES enforcement legislation, the Standing Committee withdrew its recommendation. "Italy: Suspension of the Recommendations of the Standing Committee," *Notification to the Parties,* no. 722, Feb. 19, 1993.

3. See Ernst B. Haas, *Beyond the Nation-State: Functionalism and International Organization* (Stanford, Calif.: Stanford University Press, 1964), p. 254 n. 18.

4. Ibid., p. 257; see also Walter Galenson, *The International Labor Organization: An American View* (Madison: University of Wisconsin Press, 1981), pp. 204–205. Only about one-third of the infractions, the more serious cases, are listed in the *Committee of Experts Report.* The remainder are referred directly to the country concerned with a request for information on corrective actions. Ibid., p. 326 n. 21.

5. Haas, *Beyond the Nation-State,* p. 257.

6. The ILO is unique among international organizations in its tripartite system of representation, where official government delegates are flanked by (supposedly) independent representatives of employers and workers. See also Haas, *Beyond the Nation-State,* p. 251.

7. Haas, *Beyond the Nation-State,* p. 267 ("special paragraph"); International Labor Conference, *Record of Proceedings,* 60th sess. (1975), p. 675 ("direct contacts").

8. Poland was listed in a special paragraph in 1982. See International Labor Conference, *Record of Proceedings,* 68th sess., (1982), sec. 31, p. 11. From 1983 to 1986 Poland avoided blacklisting for nonimplementation by not appearing at the Conference Committee discussions. Refusal to appear and respond to an adverse report is itself an automatic blacklist offense—in some ways the most condemnatory of listings—but it permitted Poland to avoid the embarrassment of a public defense of its actions. Altogether, the total number of special paragraphs and blacklistings in the 1980s came to more than eighty, but the large majority were for reporting failures. See International Labor Conference, *Record of Proceedings,* 72d sess., (1986), sec. 31, p. 19, par. 106; ibid., 71st sess. (1985), sec. 30, p. 14, par. 100; ibid., 70th sess., (1984), sec. 35, p. 15, par. 95; ibid., 69th sess., (1983), sec. 31, p. 17, par. 98.

9. Direct contacts were instituted in 1968 "in an effort to eliminate certain types of divergencies . . . with a view to eliminating misunderstandings and avoiding a deadlock." International Labor Conference, *Record of Proceedings,* 60th sess. (1975), p. 675.

10. The figures are as of Dec. 31, 1991. See International Labor Conference, 79th sess., (1992), *Lists of Ratifications by Convention and by Country,* pp. xi (total number of conventions), 227 (U.S. ratifications).

11. Galenson, *The International Labor Organization,* p. 206; Haas, *Beyond the Nation-State,* p. 268.

12. See Benjamin J. Cohen, "Balance of Payments Financing: Evolution of a Regime," in Stephen D. Krasner, ed., *International Regimes* (Ithaca, N.Y.: Cornell University Press 1983), pp. 315, 332.

13. In recent years the fund has established a number of special facilities on somewhat less stringent terms to deal with special problems, like the oil price increases of the 1970s, or to finance some kinds of structural economic adjustment programs. For these purposes it has not confined itself to the pooled contributions of the members but has resorted to borrowing and other sources of funds. See Peter B. Kenen, "The Use of IMF Credit," in Catherine Gwin and Richard E. Feinberg, eds., *The International Monetary Fund in a Multipolar World: Pulling Together,* (New Brunswick, N.J.: Transaction Books, 1989), pp. 69, 73–76.

14. The "postwar transitional period" stretched out for a long time. Most European governments did not accept the convertibility obligations of the IMF Agreement until the late 1950s, and Japan did not until 1964. Some eighty developing countries continue to maintain some exchange restrictions and are thus technically in the "transitional period." In deference to these realities, the 1976 amendments to the IMF Agreement change the title of Article XIV from "Transitional Period" to "Transitional Arrangements," and eliminated the "postwar" reference. See IMF Agreement, Second Amendment, Art. XIV.

15. Ibid., Art. IV, sec. 3.

16. Ibid.

17. Ibid., Art. IV, sec. 1.

18. See International Monetary Fund, *Selected Decisions and Selected Documents of the International Monetary Fund,* vol. 17 (New York, 1992), pp. 7–25. Voting in these organs is weighted in proportion to the size of the member's quota, with various critical decisions requiring super majorities. Action is usually by consensus, without a formal vote. See, e.g., R. S. Eckaus, "How the IMF Lives with Its Conditionality," *Policy Sciences,* 19 (1986): 237, 243.

19. See, e.g., "A Conversation with Mr. de Larosière," *Finance and Development,* 19 (June 1982): 4–6; "The IMF's Role in a Changing World: A Conversation with William B. Dale, Deputy Managing Director of the Fund," *Finance and Development,* 21 (Mar. 1984): 2–3. See also William C. Hood, "Surveillance over Exchange Rates," *Finance and Development,* 19 (Mar. 1992): 9–12; G. G. Johnson, "Enhancing the Effectiveness of Surveillance," *Finance and Development,* 22 (Dec. 1985): 2 6; Eduard Brau, "The Consultation Process of the Fund," *Finance and Development,* 18 (Dec. 1981): 13–16.

20. Until the mid-1970s, IMF lending went to developing and developed countries alike. See Jacques J. Polak, "Strengthening the Role of the IMF in the International Monetary System," in Gwin and Feinberg, eds., *The International Monetary Fund in a Multipolar World,* pp. 45, 47–51. In recent years, as an element of major debt rescheduling in developing countries, a procedure known as "enhanced surveillance" has emerged. See "Chairman's Summing Up of the Discussion of the Role of the Fund in Assisting Members with Commercial Banks and Official Creditors," Executive Board

Meeting 85/132, Sept. 4, 1985, in IMF, *Selected Decisions and Selected Documents,* vol. 17, p. 51. See also "Monitoring Procedures in Venezuelan Restructuring Agreement," excerpts reprinted in *International Legal Materials,* 25 (1986): 477. The fund conducts a study and develops an economic policy package as in ordinary surveillance activities, but here the bite is sharper. The process is nominally voluntary, but public creditors and commercial banks insist on an IMF seal of approval before they will participate in rescheduling or provide new resources. See Peter B. Kenen, *Financing, Adjustment, and the International Monetary Fund,* Studies in International Economics (Washington, D.C.: Brookings Institution, 1986), pp. 52–53.

21. The World Bank and the IMF collaborate closely, with regular joint participation in missions and exchanges of views of financial and technical-assistance programs. World Bank, *The World Bank Annual Report 1991* (Washington, D.C., 1991), p. 44. Guidelines for collaboration between the World Bank and the IMF have been in place since 1986. The most recent review was in March 1989. See ibid, pp. 99–100.

22. Nicole Ball, *Pressing for Peace: Can Aid Induce Reform?* ODC Policy Essay no. 6 (Washington, D.C., 1992); p. 51 ibid., p. 76 n. 21 (1991 examples). See also Nicole Ball, "Levers for Plowshares: Using Aid to Encourage Military Reform," *Arms Control Today,* 22 (Nov. 1992): 12 n. 3, citing Paul Blustein, "World Bank, IMF to Press Defense Cuts," *Washington Post,* Oct. 18, 1991. At the same time, the World Bank initiated a coordinated campaign to take military expenditures into account in decisions on structural adjustment lending. See Nicole Ball, *Pressing for Peace,* p. 51. See also Barber B. Conable, Jr., "Growth—Not Guns," *Washington Post,* Dec. 24, 1991, cited in Ball, "Levers for Plowshares," pp. 11, 17, n. 1.

23. Board of Governors, 1991 Annual Meeting, Bangkok, Thailand, IMF Press Release no. 64, Oct. 17, 1991, quoted in Ball, *Pressing for Peace,* p. 32. The following account relies on Nicole Ball's analysis.

24. Ibid., p. 51, quoting Barber B. Conable, Jr., speaking at the joint World Bank–IMF annual meeting, Sept. 25, 1989.

25. Ibid., p. 52. David Fisk, UK environment negotiator, has said the most important function of a treaty is to give him leverage in the domestic political process. Interview with David Fisk, Bellagio, Italy, Jan. 28, 1992.

26. See Kenen, *Financing, Adjustment,* p. 52: "Governments are not monolithic, and those officials who must deal with balance of payments problems do not always win their bureaucratic battles. In fact, they are handicapped because they are concerned with the external side of economic policy and do not have strong political constituencies. The Fund can help them during the policymaking process by giving them justification for proposing painful measures and by raising their resistance to pressures for compromise." Robert E. Hudec, *Enforcing International Trade Law: The Evolution of the Modern GATT Legal System* (Salem, N.H.: Butterworth Legal Publishers, 1993), p. 358: "International institutions always have allies within the domestic political framework . . . The way that international institutions exert influence on domestic politics, therefore, is by strengthening the hand of the domestic allies they already have."

27. Ball, *Pressing for Peace,* p. 55 (naming the World Bank as the pioneer in this form of pressure.)

28. Ibid., pp. 56 (Pakistan, with the World Bank also cooperating), 57 (India).

29. See Ball, "Levers for Plowshares," pp. 11, 12.

30. Under a standby arrangement, a member is assured of access to a specified amount of fund resources for a fixed period of time without consideration of the member's economic situation beyond that spelled out in the initial agreement. Most standby arrangements include "phasing," which provides for a specified amount of finance to be available at specified intervals during the standby period. At each interval, a member's access to finance is made dependent on compliance with performance criteria specified in the member's stabilization program. If the policy objectives of the program are not being observed, the criteria operate automatically to suspend (or "interrupt") the member's access to fund finance. See Cohen, "Balance-of-Payments Financing," pp. 315, 322.

31. See Kendall W. Stiles, "IMF Conditionality: Coercion or Compromise?" *World Development,* 18 (1990): 959, Kendall W. Stiles, "Bargaining with Bureaucrats: Debt Negotiations in the International Monetary Fund," *International Journal of Public Administration,* 9 (1987): 1; Andrew Crockett, "Issues in the Use of the Fund's Resources," *Finance and Development,* 19 (June 1982): 10, 11. Cf., as to World Bank structural adjustment lending, Paul Moseley, *Conditionality as Bargaining Process: Structural Adjustment Lending, 1980–86,* Essays in International Finance no. 168 (Princeton, N.J.: Department of Economics, International Finance Section, Princeton University, Oct. 1987).

32. Eckaus, "How the IMF Lives with Its Conditionality," pp. 237, 243. The author argues that the IMF staff has considerable autonomy in this process, since "it is only after an agreement has been reached between the country and the staff, with the Managing Director's approval, that the Managing Director brings the agreement to the Executive Board for its approval." He says that the Executive Board has never rejected an agreement proposed by the managing director and no member has ever appealed to the Executive Board against a negative decision by the managing director. Ibid., pp. 243, 251 n. 16. For a detailed account of this negotiating process in the context of Mexico's debt rescheduling in 1982, see Joseph Kraft, *The Mexican Rescue* (New York: Group of Thirty, 1984).

33. See Andrew Crockett, "Issues in the Use of Fund Resources," *Finance and Development,* 19 (June 1982): 10, 13–14.

34. See United Kingdom letter of intent in Abram Chayes, Thomas Ehrlich and Andreas Lowenfeld, *International Legal Process,* vol. 2 (Boston: Little, Brown, 1968), pp. 776–779. See also Eckaus, "How the IMF Lives with Its Conditionality," pp. 237, 239, 251 n. 18.

35. Henry S. Bienen and Mark Gersovitz, "Economic Stabilization, Conditionality, and Political Stability," *International Organization,* 39 (1985): 729, 736–737: "The IMF identifies monetary expansion, caused by deficits in the government budget, as the basic mechanism that generates balance-of-payments deficits. Given

this analysis, the IMF prescribes a decrease in monetary expansion to be achieved through narrowing the government's budget deficit. Expenditures must be reduced relative to revenues by decreasing subsidies, public-enterprise deficits, public employment, public-sector wages, and government expenditures on investment." See also, e.g., Eckaus, "How the IMF Lives with its Conditionality," pp. 237, 241.

36. Jeffrey D. Sachs, "Strengthening IMF Programs in Highly Indebted Countries," in Gwin and Feinberg, eds., *The International Monetary Fund in a Multipolar World*, pp. 101, 107 (citations omitted).

37. Kenen, "The Use of IMF Credit," pp. 69, 75.

38. See Stiles, "Bargaining with Bureaucrats," p. 1. See also C. David Finch, "Let the IMF Be the IMF," *International Economy*, 2, no. 1 (Jan./Feb. 1988): 129. The members of the G-7, whose voting power dominates the fund, would never submit themselves to this discipline, whatever the intrinsic merits of the medicine. C. David Finch, "Conditional Finance for Industrial Countries," in Gwin and Feinberg, eds., *The International Monetary Fund in a Multipolar World*, p. 91.

39. See Scott R. Sidell, *The IMF and Third-World Political Instability: Is There a Connection?* p. 6 (Basingstoke: Macmillan, 1988).

40. See, e.g., Stiles, "IMF Conditionality: Coercion or Compromise," pp. 959, 963–965; cf. Moseley, *Conditionality as Bargaining Process.*

41. Bienen and Gersovitz, "Economic Stabilization, Conditionality, and Political Stability," p. 729, 745.

42. "The IMF: Facing New Challenges: An Interview with Michel Camdessus, Managing Director of the International Monetary Fund," *Finance and Development*, 25 (June 1988): 2, 5.

43. Bienen and Gersovitz, "Economic Stabilization, Conditionality, and Political Stability," p. 747.

44. Ibid., p. 732.

45. See "Background Briefing by Senior Treasury Official, Department of the Treasury, Re: The Upcoming IMF–World Bank Meeting," Federal News Service, May 3, 1990: "It is not a credible solution to simply dismiss countries from the Fund entirely and leave them with absolutely no alternatives to improve their situations."

46. Kenen, *Financing, Adjustment.*

47. Jorge Marshall, José Luis Mardones, and Isabel Marshall, "IMF Conditionality: The Experiences of Argentina, Brazil and Chile," in John Williamson, ed., *IMF Conditionality* (Washington, D.C.: Institute for International Economics, 1983), pp. 275, 299–300.

48. Ibid., pp. 299–300.

49. Ibid., p. 300.

50. "Why Bankers Need Not Fear for Brazil," *The Economist*, Apr. 20, 1985, p. 85.

51. Sachs, "Strengthening IMF Programs in Highly Indebted Countries," p. 107.

52. Kenen, *Financing, Adjustment*, p. 47.

53. The extreme reluctance to use coercive measures is illustrated by the IMF practice with respect to arrearages. Here the fund is involved not just as a regulator

charged with the promoting adherence to monetary norms, but as a lender dealing with a defaulting debtor. Like any other financial institution, the fund's failure to enforce repayment could threaten its own credibility and access to funds. The stated policy is that the fund will not consider requests for use of its resources "as long as the member concerned has overdue payments to the Fund." See International Monetary Fund, Executive Board Meeting EBM/84/54, pp. 37–38, *Selected Decisions and Selected Documents,* vol. 17, p. 165. The bar takes effect three months after the payment has become overdue. Under increasing pressure from the major contributors, led by the United States, the fund has established a carefully graduated set of measures to be taken against a member remaining in arrears, culminating in suspension of voting rights after eighteen months. "Procedures for Dealing with Members with Overdue Financial Obligations to the Fund," Executive Board Meetings 89/100 and 89/101, July 27, 1989, *Selected Decisions and Selected Documents,* vol. 17, pp. 167, 170. Between 1985 and 1991, ten states were declared ineligible to use the fund's resources on account of nonpayment of arrears. International Monetary Fund, *IMF Annual Report* (New York, 1991), p. 67. None have been suspended, and only three have been the subject of a "declaration of non-cooperation," the second of the graduated steps. Some of these countries are among the poorest in the world, and there is widespread, if tacit, recognition that it is unrealistic to expect them to repay their obligations in full. So the fund has helped to organize loans from bilateral aid donors and private banks to permit members to pay off the arrears and regain access to the fund's resources. "Excerpts from the Chairman's Summing Up at the Conclusion of the Discussion of Overdue Financial Obligations to the Fund Executive Board Meeting, 85/170," Nov. 25, 1987, *Selected Decisions and Selected Documents of the IMF,* vol. 17 (1992), pp. 165, 166. The first new drawing from the IMF is used to pay off these interim loans. *The Economist* remarked: "With the help of semantic nicety, what the Fund is trying to do with its problem loans is to reschedule them in all but name." "The IMF in Africa: When a Loan Is not a Loan," *The Economist,* Nov. 17, 1990, p. 109.

54. OECD Agreement. Successor to the Marshall Plan's Organization for European Economic Cooperation (OEEC), where many review techniques were first developed.

55. See "Code of Liberalisation of Current Invisible Operations (Mar. 1992)," adopted Dec. 12, 1961, Council Act [OECD/C(61)95], and "Code of Liberalisation of Capital Movements" (Mar. 1992), adopted Dec. 12, 1961, Council Act [OECD/C(61)96], both much amended since. The OECD normally acts by recommendation, but it is authorized to take binding decisions by unanimous vote. OECD Agreement, Art. 5. Originally a party could not reinstate a reservation once it had withdrawn it, which resulted in a very cautious approach to withdrawals. In 1964 the Capital Movements code was amended to establish a "B list" as to which a party could make and remove reservations at will.

56. See OECD Committee on Capital Movements and Invisible Transactions, *Turkey: First Examination of Reservations to the Code of Liberalisation of Capital*

Movements (Note by the Secretariat), DAFFE/INV/90.3, Feb. 22, 1990, par. 24; OEDC, Committee on Capital Movements and Invisible Transactions, *Turkey: Examination of Reservations to the Code of Liberalisation of Capital Movements (Note by the Secretariat)*, Addendum 2 to DAFFE/INV/90.3, Mar. 27, 1990, 14–15; OEDC Council, *Turkey: First Examination of Position Under the Code of Liberalisation of Capital Movements (Report by the Committee on Capital Movements and Invisible Transactions)*, July 23, 1990, par. 4.

57. See ibid.

58. And this despite increasingly strict obligations; see OECD, *Liberalisation of Capital Movements and Financial Service in the OECD Area* (Paris, 1990), especially diagram 1.

59. OECD Press Communiqué, "Environment Committee Meeting at Ministerial Level: An Environmental Strategy for the 1990s," Paris, Jan. 31, 1991, SG/PRESS(91)9, p. 8. The following account is based primarily on personal interviews with OECD officials conducted in January 1994.

60. See C/M/139 (meeting of Mar. 26, 1980) and C/M/169 (meeting of July 12, 1983), cited in Hudec, *Enforcing International Trade Law*, p. 194 n. 20.

61. A trade policy review mechanism was adopted in April 1989. See "Decisions of Apr. 12, 1989, (L/6490), Functioning of the GATT System," in GATT, *Basic Instruments and Selected Documents*, 36th Supp. (Geneva, July 1990), p. 403.

62. See "Country Reviews Launched," *GATT Focus*, no. 68 (Feb. 1990): 13.

63. See "Trade Liberalization and Fiscal Discipline Transform Mexican Economy," GATT Press Release no. 1571 (GATT/1571), Apr. 8, 1993; *GATT Focus*, no. 99 (May–June 1993): 5, 6; *GATT Focus*, no. 100 (July 1993): 9.

64. WTO Agreement, TPRM.

65. Summaries of these two reports are released by the GATT just prior to their consideration by the GATT council. See, e.g., "GATT Trade Policy Review—Canada," GATT Press Release no. 1484 (GATT/1484), July 16, 1990 (including report by the GATT Secretariat—Summary Observations, pp. 2/3–11, and Canada's report, pp. 12/13–16).

66. WTO Agreement, par. A (i), (ii).

67. See "Council Examines trade régimes of Uruguay and Korea," *GATT Focus*, no. 92 (Aug. 1992): 1, 2: "Internally, the public sector deficit was to be eliminated by 1993" (regarding Uruguay, in Uruguay's reply); ibid., pp. 1, 4: "Tariffs on textiles, chemicals and electrical machinery would be reduced by 8 percent by 1994." (regarding Korea, in Korea's reply); "Trade Policies of Norway, Switzerland and Nigeria Reviewed," *GATT Focus*, no. 84 (Sept. 1991): 2, 3: "Norway has committed itself to dismantling all trade distorting support [to the fish and fish products sector] by January 1993"); ibid., p. 4: "The Nordic position in the Uruguay round regarding textiles and clothing was to bring trade in these products under the general rules of GATT not later than 31 December 1999" (regarding Norway, in Norway's reply); "Council Reviews Trade Policies of the EC, Hungary and Indo-

nesia," *GATT Focus,* no. 81 (May–June 1991): 2, 8: "The move towards full currency convertibility was to be completed by 1994" (regarding Hungary, in Hungary's reply).

68. WTO Agreement, TPRM, par. C (i), (vi), (vii).

69. See, e.g., "Council Examines Trade of Bangladesh and Canada," *GATT Focus,* no. 91 (July 1992): 7, "Concerns" (regarding Canada), and 5, "Praises and Concerns" (regarding Bangladesh); "Council Reviews Trade Regimes of Thailand and Chile," *Gatt Focus,* no. 83 (Aug. 1991): 5, "Some Questions" (regarding Chile); "Trade Policies of Norway, Switzerland and Nigeria Reviewed," *GATT Focus,* no. 84 (Sept. 1991): 5, "Clarification" (regarding Switzerland).

70. See, e.g., Uruguay Round, Agreement on Agriculture, Art. 17–18, Agreement on Sanitary and Phytosanitary Measures, Art. 38, Agreement on Safeguards, Art. 36.

71. LRTAP, Art. 8(g).

72. Ibid., Art. 6. A virtually identical requirement appears in the 1988 nitrogen oxide protocol, Art. 7.

73. Marc A. Levy, "European Acid Rain: The Power of Tote-Board Diplomacy," in Peter M. Haas, Robert O. Keohane, and Marc A. Levy, eds., *Institutions for the Earth: Sources of Effective International Environmental Protection* (Cambridge, Mass.: MIT Press, 1993), pp. 75, 91.

74. Ibid., pp. 75, 90–91.

75. FCCC, Art. 12.

76. Ibid., Art. 4 (2)

77. Ibid., Art. 3(1)

78. Ibid., Art. 12(2). The provisions applicable to developed countries were foreshadowed in Abram Chayes, "Managing the Transition to a Global Warming Regime, or What to Do 'til the Treaty Comes," in *Greenhouse Warming: Negotiating a Global Regime* (Washington, D.C.: World Resources Institute, 1991), p. 64: "The parties would be required to submit a detailed report annually (a) on their emissions of specified greenhouse gases and (b) on the policies and programs they were carrying out in fulfillment of their obligations under the treaty. A country report would include specific emissions targets and commitments with respect to contemplated administrative or legislative actions."

79. FCCC, Art. 12(5).

80. See Owen Greene, "International Environmental Regimes: Verification and Implementation Review," *Environmental Politics,* 2, no. 4 (Winter 1993): 165: "Many govenments have tended to resist or neglect the development of effective implementation review processes associated with environmental agreements. It is easy in general to understand why states and other powerful actors can often share an interest in limiting the effectiveness of international institutions."

81. FCCC, Art. 7(2)(e). Contrast this with the injunction to "review reports submitted by its subsidiary bodies and provide guidance to them." Ibid., Art. 7(2)(j).

82. FCCC, Conference of the Parties, 1st Sess., Berlin, June 6, 1995, the Berlin Mandate, Doc. no. ICCC/CP/1995/7/Add. 1, p. 4.

83. CWC, Art. III(1)(a)(v), Annex on Implementation and Verification, Part IV (A)(6).

84. Ibid., Art. IV(7)(a).

85. Ibid., Art. V(9)(a).

11. Nongovernmental Organizations

1. The international struggle against slavery was recognized in 1815 at the Congress of Vienna, when eight European states solemnly declared "that it was fit that this detestable traffic should be swept from the face of the earth." C. K. Wesbster, ed., *British Diplomacy 1813–1815* (London: Bell and Sons, 1921), p. 395.

2. Elizabeth V. Perkins, "Comparative Pressure Group Politics and International Relations: The Case of Non-Governmental Organizations at the United Nations" (Ph.D. diss., Texas Tech University, 1977), pp. 10–11.

3. See John Carey, *UN Protection of Civil and Political Rights* (Syracuse, N.Y.: Syracuse University Press, 1970), p. 131; Lyman White, "Non-Governmental Organizations and Their Relations with the United Nations," in Clyde Eagleton and Richard N. Swift, eds., *Annual Review of United Nations Affairs, 1951* (New York: New York University Press, 1952), pp. 165, 171. In addition, they were responsible for Article 71, which requires the UN Economic and Social Council (ECOSOC) to "make suitable arrangements for consultation with non-governmental organizations which are concerned with matters within its competence." Under these arrangements, the purposes of consultation were not only to provide "expert information and advice" but also "to enable organizations which represent important segments of public opinion to express their views." Thus, from the beginning, the UN recognized an important political dimension in the work of the NGOs. NGOs recognized by ECOSOC are accorded quasi-official status, with the right to attend the meetings of ECOSOC and its subsidiary bodies, to submit written comments and even to make oral interventions on matters of interest. Perkins, "Comparative Pressure Group Politics," pp. 10–11.

4. *Master List of Human Rights Organizations* (Cambridge, Mass.: Human Rights Internet, 1994).

5. Alexander Kiss and Dinah Shelton, *International Environmental Law,* (New York: Transnational Publishers, 1991), p. 38.

6. Peter Haas, Marc Levy, and Edward Parson, "Earth Summit: How Should We Judge UNCED's Success?" *Environment,* 34 (1992): 28–31.

7. Nearly twenty-nine thousand are listed in the *Yearbook of International Organizations 1993/1994: Volume 1, Organization Descriptions and Cross-References,* 30th ed. (K. G. Saur: London: 1993), p. 1698.

8. Ibid., p. 1761.

9. Perkins defines NGOs simply as "private non-profit voluntary associations," noting that they vary widely in subject matter, purpose, organization and size. Perkins, "Comparative Pressure Group Politics," p. 6.

10. UN Charter, Art. 1(3).

11. See Clement Nwankwo, "The Civil Liberties Organization and the Struggle for Human Rights and Democracy in Nigeria," in Larry Diamond, ed., *The Democratic Revolution: Struggles for Freedom and Pluralism in the Developing World* (New York: Freedom House, 1992).

12. Anselm Chidi Odinkalu and Osaze Lanre Ehonwa, *Behind the Wall: A Report on Prison Conditions in Nigeria and the Nigerian Prison System* (Surulere, Lagos: Civil Liberties Organization, 1991), p. 227.

13. Ibid.

14. The almost indiscriminate reliance on "hard" and "soft" law sources is characteristic of activity in the field of international human rights.

15. Olisa Agbakoba, "Some Operational Strategies of a Human Rights NGO at the National Level," referenced in letter from Anselm Chidi Odinkalu, CLO staff attorney, to Melissa Crow, Jan. 18, 1993.

16. ECOSOC Res. 153(XLVIII) May 27, 1970, Subcommission on Prevention of Discrimination and Protection of Minorities Res. 1(XXIV) Aug. 13, 1971.

17. Within weeks of the coup, Amnesty International secretary general Martin Ennals had a meeting at the UN with the Chilean foreign minister, who invited Amnesty International to visit Chile to investigate conditions. The delegation, under the leadership of Professor Frank Newman of the University of California, Berkeley, Boalt Hall Law School, interviewed a number of officials, leading lawyers, diplomats, and human rights workers, although they did not see any member of the junta. The first Amnesty International report, issued in late 1973, was based not only on the findings of evidence developed by the delegation but also on other information submitted by lawyers, organizations, and families of prisoners. In January the Chilean government publicly rejected the report. Amnesty International, *Chile: An Amnesty International Report* (London: Amnesty Internatonal Publications, 1974). The International Commission of Jurists, an NGO made up of prominent international law scholars and practitioners, monitors human rights problems worldwide, particularly when judicial conduct is involved. It is not to be confused with the International Court of Justice.

18. ECOSOR 56, Supp. 5, sec. B., 1974, p. 56.

19. Perkins, "Comparative Pressure Group Politics," p. 221.

20. Doc. E/CN.4/1160, pp. 53–54; Res. 8 (XXVII).

21. Perkins, "Comparative Pressure Group Politics," p. 231; *Report of the Ad Hoc Working Group Established under Resolution 8 (XXXI) of the Commission on Human Rights to Inquire into the Present Situation of Human Rights in Chile,* Feb. 4, 1976, Doc. E/CN.4/1188.

22. Perkins, "Comparative Pressure Group Politics," p. 231.

23. UN Doc. A/RES/3448 (XXX).

24. The Chilean government issued a public statement rejecting the report in its entirety without commenting on its substance; the president of the Supreme Court publicly attacked Amnesty International in his opening address on Jan. 19, 1974. Amnesty International, *Chile*, p. 8; "Chile," *Latin American Newsletters*, Jan. 25, 1974, p. 32.

25. Perkins, "Comparative Pressure Group Politics," pp. 218–235; U.S. House Committee on Foreign Affairs, *International Protection of Human Rights, 1973: Hearings before the Subcommittee on International Organizations and Movements of the House Committee on Foreign Affairs*, 93rd Cong., 1st sess. (1973), p. 550.

26. *Chile: Human Rights and the Plebescite* (Washington, D.C.: An Americas Watch Report, 1988); U.S. House Committee on Foreign Affairs, *International Protection of Human Rights, 1973: Hearings before the Subcommittee on International Organizations and Movements*, p. 550, et seq.; Amnesty International, *Chile*.

27. The Universal Declaration is not a treaty and was specifically stated to be aspirational when it was first promulgated in 1948. Bess Furman, "Human Rights Pact Hailed in Capital; Mrs Roosevelt Explains Plans for UN Covenant," *New York Times*, Mar. 5, 1948, p. 10. With the passage of time, however, it has been largely assimilated into general international law, and its provisions are regarded as legally binding. Although the USSR abstained, it was important in the domestic Soviet context that it had not opposed.

28. Human Rights Committee, "Statement of Purposes (1970)," reprinted in George Saunders, ed., *Samizdat: The Voices of the Soviet Opposition* (New York: Monad Press, distributed by Pathfinder Press, 1974), p. 39.

29. Andrei Sakharov, *Memoirs*, trans. Richard Lourie (London: Hutchinson, 1990), p. 320. Note: it may be difficult in retrospect to separate Sakharov's independent actions from his actions as the leader of the Human Rights Committee.

30. Orlov as quoted in Joshua Rubenstein, *Soviet Dissidents: Their Struggle for Human Rights* (1980), pp. 249–250.

31. Ludmilla Alexeyeva, *Soviet Dissent: Contemporary Movements for National, Religious, and Human Rights*, trans. Carol Pearce and John Glad (Boston: Beacon Press, 1987), p. 336.

32. Michael Rinzler, "Battling Authoritarianism through Treaty: Soviet Dissent and International Human Rights Regimes," *Harvard International Law Journal*, 35 (Spring 1994): 461–498.

33. Paul Goldberg, *The Final Act: The Dramatic, Revealing Story of the Moscow Helsinki Watch Group* (New York: William Morrow, 1988), p. 90.

34. Andrew Moravcsik, "Lessons from the European Human Rights Regime," in *Advancing Democracy and Human Rights in the Americas* (Washington, D.C.: Inter-American Dialogue, 1994), pp. 35–58.

35. Testimony of Ludmilla Alexeyeva, in Allan Wynn, ed., *The Fifth International Sakharov Hearings*, Proceedings, April 1985 (Andre Deutsch, 1986), p. 35.

36. Rubenstein, *Soviet Dissidents*, p. 220.

37. Max M. Kampelman, *Entering New Worlds: The Memoirs of a Private Man in Public Life* (New York: HarperCollins Publishers, 1991), p. 275.

38. Thomas Buergenthal, ed., *Human Rights, International Law and the Helsinki Accord* (Montclair, N.J.: Allanheld, Osmun, 1977); Goldberg, *The Final Act;* Ludmilla Alexayeva, "The Fate of the Helsinki Groups and Participants in the Helsinki Movement in the USSR," in Wynn, ed., *The Fifth International Sakharov Hearings,* pp. 33–35.

39. Andrew Moravcsik, "Explaining International Human Rights Regimes: Liberal Theory and Western Europe," *European Journal of International Relations,* 1, no. 2 (1995): 174.

40. David A. Sanger, "Nuclear Material Dumped Off Japan," *New York Times,* Oct. 19, 1993, p. A1.

41. Ibid. A Greenpeace vessel tracked the Russian tanker, filmed the dumping operations, and then made the films available to international news organizations, including Japanese television networks. Craig R. Whitney, "Russia Halts Nuclear Waste Dumping in Sea," *New York Times,* Oct. 22, 1993, p. A9.

42. Whitney, "Russia Halts Nuclear Waste Dumping in Sea."

43. David E. Pitt, "Nations Back Ban on Atomic Dumping," *New York Times,* November 13, 1993, p. 7.

44. James Cameron and Ross Ramsay, "Participation by Non-Governmental Organizations in the World Trade Organization," Global Environmental and Trade Study, Study no. 1.

45. See Ronald B. Mitchell, *Intentional Oil Pollution at Sea* (Cambridge, Mass.: MIT Press, 1994), pp. 130–135.

46. Mitchell, *Intentional Oil Pollution at Sea,* p. 134; Gerard Peet, *Operational Discharges from Ships: An Evaluation of the Application of the Discharge Provisions of the MARPOL Convention by its Contracting Parties* (Amsterdam: AIDEnvironment, 1992).

47. Mitchell, *Intentional Oil Pollution at Sea,* pp. 132–136.

48. See, e.g., World Meteorological Organization, *Report of the International Conference on the Assessment of the Role of Carbon Dioxide and of other Greenhouse Gases in Climate Variations and Associated Impacts,* Villach, Austria, Oct. 9–15, 1985, WMO-No. 661, World Climate Programme; J. Pernetta and P. Hughes, *Implications of Expected Climate Changes in the South Pacific Region: An Overview,* UNEP Regional Seas Reports and Studies no. 128 (Nairobi: UNEP, 1990); South Pacific Regional Environment Programme (SPREP), *Report of the SPC/UNEP/ASPEI Intergovernmental Meeting on Climatic Change and Sea Level Rise in the South Pacific,* South Pacific Commission, Noumean (1989).

49. *Ministerial Declaration regarding Climate Change of the Caribbean,* Caribbean Environment Ministers, Jamaica, 1990.

50. Michael Wilford, "Law: Sea-Level Rise and Insurance," *Environment,* 35 (May 1993): 2.

51. "Small Island Nations Face Big Issues at Barbados Conference," *UN Chronicle,* June 1994, p. 66; Ian Williams, "Letter from Barbados," *New Statesman and Society,* May 13, 1994, p. 11.

52. Quoted in Sidney Holt, "Whale Mining and Whale Saving," *Marine Policy,* 9 (July 1985): 199. Holt himself says: "The whale was about to become the *symbol* for organizations concerned with environmental protection: 'saving the whale' is for millions of people a crucial test of their political ability to halt environmental destruction." Ibid., p. 12. Steinar Andresen suggests some of the reasons that whales (and elephants) have become avatars: "Their sheer size, rarity and the fact that they are believed to be quite intelligent all matter. Also 'the apparent simplicity of the issue,' and the fact that some of the smaller marine mammals are rather 'cute' (compared to less fortunate creatures, for instance fish) have facilitated mobilization of the public and made them excellent fund raisers." Steinar Andresen, "Science and Politics in the International Management of Whales," *Marine Policy,* 13 (April 1989): 108.

53. Certain whale species are protected as endangered under CITES as well as by the quotas set by the IWC.

54. Holt, "Whale Mining and Whale Saving," p. 192. Holt is a leading cetaceologist who has acted as scientific advisor to the Food and Agriculture Organization and to the Seychelles delegation to the IWC, one of the leading proponents of the moratorium.

55. 22 USC. § 1978 (Pelly Amendment, 1971); 16 USC. § 1821(E)(2) (Packwood-Magnuson Amendment, 1979). The Packwood-Magnuson Amendment was introduced at the suggestion of Defenders of Wildlife. R. Michael M'Gonigle, "The 'Economizing' of Ecology: Why Big, Rare Whales Still Die," *Ecology Law Quarterly,* 9 (1980): 201. The Marine Mammal Protection Act of 1972 had already outlawed all imports of whale products. 16 USC. § 1361–1421. In addition to legislative lobbying, the NGOs resorted to the courts in an effort, ultimately unsuccessful, to force the imposition of sanctions against Japan. See *Japan Whaling Association v. American Cetacean Society,* 478 US 221 (1986). See also James M. Zimmerman, "Baldridge/ Murazumi Agreement: The Supreme Court Gives Credence to an Aberration in American Cetacean Society III," *Boston College Environmental Law Review,* 14 (1987): 257.

56. The moratorium contemplated a phase-in period and therefore did not actually go into effect until 1986.

57. "To Japan with Love," *Greenpeace Examiner,* Spring 1982, p. 20.

58. Vincent, "Money Changes Everything," *Greenpeace Examiner,* Apr.–June 1985, p. 19.

59. "Direct Action in Japan," *Greenpeace,* Mar.–Apr. 1988, p. 22.

60. "Whales to Go," *Greenpeace,* Jan.–Feb. 1991, p. 20.

61. See "Boycott Update," *Greenpeace Examiner,* Winter 1980, p. 3; "Iceland's Whalers Feel the Heat," *Greenpeace Examiner,* Jan.–Feb. 1989, p. 18. The victory proved short-lived, however, for when the IWC renewed the moratorium in 1992,

Iceland left the organization and announced its intention to resume whaling. See Chapter 4.

62. "Economic Sanctions Needed to Halt Norwegian Whaling, Environmentalists Say," *BNA Environmental Daily*, Nov. 19, 1992, p. 13. In Japan, Norway, and Iceland, NGOs have responded with a defense of the whalers' way of life. Colin Nickerson, "A Call to Save the Whale Meat," *Boston Globe*, Feb. 4, 1993, p. 2.

63. Hutchison, "Between the Harpoon and the Whaler," *Greenpeace Examiner*, Summer 1981, pp. 14–15; Plowden, "Peru Pressed to Retract Her IWC Objection," *Greenpeace Examiner*, Winter 1983, p. 12.

64. Long, "Campaign in Spain: Direct Action to Save the Whales, Direct Action to Save Our Ship," *Greenpeace Examiner*, Winter 1980, p. 18. The *Rainbow Warrior* was finally arrested by the Spanish navy and taken into port.

65. "Assault on the Whales: How Long Can They Endure So Wide a Chase?" *Greenpeace Examiner*, Jan.–Mar. 1985, p. 14; Busby, "Whaling at the Crossroads," *Greenpeace Examiner*, Oct.–Dec. 1986, p. 117.

66. Daniel Francis, *A History of World Whaling* (New York: Viking, 1990), pp. 235–237; Richard Ellis, *Men and Whales* (New York: Alfred A. Knopf, 1991), p. 451.

67. During the whole period of the 1970s and 1980s, whaling unsanctioned by IWC commercial schedules continued, either by states not party to the treaty or those who had opted out of the particular decision, or under the guise of scientific research. Greenpeace estimated that by 1990, 13,650 whales had been killed in these ways. Greenpeace, "Outlaw Whalers," *1990 Report*, p. 1. But Ronald Mitchell concludes that member states are significantly constrained by IWC regulation and that even nonparties "are not able to continue indefinitely flaunting the international regulations agreed to by the other major nations of the world." Ronald B. Mitchell, "Membership, Compliance and Non-compliance in the International Convention for the Regulation of Whaling, 1946–Present," paper presented at the 17th Annual Whaling Symposium, Sharon, Mass., Oct. 1992, pp. 17–21.

68. Andresen, "Science and Politics in the International Management of Whales," p. 109.

69. Ibid., pp. 108–109.

70. See International Union for the Conservation of Nature, "Position Statement on Whaling—1973," *IUCN Bulletin*, 4 (1973): 29; "IUCN's Statement to the International Whaling Commission," *IUCN Bulletin*, 8 (1977): 39; IUCN/World Wildlife Fund, "IUCN/WWF Statement on Whaling 1982," *IUCN Bulletin*, 13 (1982): 51; World Wildlife Fund, *WWF Yearbook, 1980–81*, p. 352. Still, M'Gonigle places a greater emphasis on the role of NGOs in applying political pressure, directly and through the media, and in calling attention to instances of noncompliance. M'Gonigle, "The Economizing of Ecology," pp. 195–202.

71. Navid, "Commission on Environmental Policy, Law and Administration (CEPLA) Investigates," *IUCN Bulletin*, 10 (1979): 89. Greenpeace placed before the IWC Infractions Committee detailed evidence that Chile had been operating an

illegal catcher-factory ship, complete with the names of the ship's crew and cargo manifests showing that the meat was shipped to Japan. Five days later, the Chilean IWC representative announced that Chile would terminate all whaling. Frizell, "One Step Closer," *Greenpeace Examiner,* Summer 1981, p. 8. Greenpeace also presented evidence against Spain for quota violations. Ibid. A Greenpeace exposé of Japan's pirate whaling trade with Taiwan, which was not a member of the IWC, led to the shutdown of the Taiwanese industry and in addition, according to Greenpeace, was a "major embarrassment to the Japanese government, which had claimed Japan no longer dealt with pirate whalers." "Taiwan Stops Whaling," *Greenpeace Examiner,* Winter 1980, p. 4.

72. Bruce J. Stedman, "The International Whaling Commission and the Negotiation for a Global Moratorium on Whaling," in L. Susskind, E. Siskind, and J. W. Breslin, eds., *Nine Case Studies in International Environmental Negotiation* (Cambridge, Mass.: MIT-Harvard Public Disputes Program, May 1990).

73. Patricia Birnie, "The Role of Developing Countries in Nudging the International Whaling Commission from Regulating Whaling to Encouraging Nonconsumptive Uses of Whales," *Ecology Law Quarterly,* 12 (1985): 961–962. J. Gulland, "The End of Whaling?" *New Scientist,* Oct. 29, 1988, p. 45; Jeremy Cherfas, *The Hunting of the Whales* (London: Bodley Head, 1988), p. 118.

74. Leslie Spencer, "The Not So Peaceful World of Greenpeace," *Forbes,* Nov. 11, 1991, p. 174.

75. Birnie, "The Role of Developing Countries in Nudging the International Whaling Commission," p. 937–975.

76. Andresen, "Science and Politics in the International Management of Whales," p. 109.

77. IWC Schedule, Feb. 1983, par. 10(e). See Ronald B. Mitchell, *Membership, Compliance and Non-compliance in the International Convention for the Regulation of Whaling,* p. 7: "These zero quotas were passed in large measure because environmental groups succeeded in convincing nations that had little material interest in whaling to join the IWC and vote for zero quotas."

78. Chris Frizell, "Victory! IWC Votes Whaling Phaseout," *Greenpeace Examiner,* Summer 1982, p. 6.

79. Jane Perlez, "Kenya, in Gesture, Burns Ivory Tusks," *New York Times,* July 19, 1989, p. A5, col. 1.

80. Greg Neale, "Elephant Jamboree Nobody Will Forget," *Sunday Telegraph,* Oct. 15, 1989, p. 16.

81. CITES, Art. II(1), (2). "Specimens" are defined as any recognizable part of a listed plant or animal or derivative thereof. Ibid., Art. I(b).

82. Ibid., Art. III(3)(c), prohibits the import of Appendix I specimens unless a management authority of the importing state is satisfied that "the specimen is not to be used for *primarily* commercial purposes." (emphasis added).

83. Ibid., Art. IV(2).

84. Ibid., Art. XV. See Chapter 10 of this volume.

85. Simon Lyster, *International Wildlife Law* (Cambridge: Grotius Publications, 1985), p. 268.

86. See Michael J. Glennon, "Has International Law Failed the Elephant?" *American Journal of International Law,* 84 (1990): 12.

87. *U.S. Fish and Wildlife Service Report, 1982–83.* (Washington, D.C.: Department of the Interior, Fish and Wildlife Service). During this period, the NGOs, the WWF in particular, supported the regulatory program by conducting training for African wildlife officers and financing research on ivory marking to distinguish legal from illegal ivory. Lyster, *International Wildlife Law,* p. 272; World Wildlife Fund, *WWF Yearbook 1980–81.*

88. Each exporting country was to enact legislation or regulations making exports above quota illegal, and thus noncertifiable under Appendix II procedures.

89. Ian Douglas-Hamilton, "Report," *Swara* (journal published by the East African Wildlife Society). His study showed a decline of 78 percent from 1973 in unprotected areas, and an overall drop of 51 percent. Ian Douglas-Hamilton, "Slaughter of Elephants Escalates," *Boston Globe,* Mar. 28, 1988, p. 33, col. 2.

90. Douglas-Hamilton, "Slaughter of Elephants Escalates."

91. Ibid.

92. Raymond Bonner, "Crying Wolf over Elephants: How the International Wildlife Community Got Stampeded into Banning Ivory," *New York Times Magazine,* Feb. 7, 1993, p. 16; Raymond Bonner, *At the Hand of Man: Peril and Hope for Africa's Wildlife* (New York: Knopf, 1993).

93. Ibid., p. 16.

94. William K. Stevens, "Huge Conservation Effort Aims to Save Vanishing Architect of the Savanna," *New York Times,* Feb. 28, 1989, p. C1.

95. Philip Shabecoff, "Seeing Disaster, Groups Ask Ban on Ivory Imports," *New York Times,* June 2, 1989, p. A9. The two organizations feared that the anticipated negotiation of an international agreement to end the ivory trade would set off an "orgy" of killing of the remaining elephant population.

96. *New York Times,* June 9, 1989, p. A24, quoted in Michael J. Glennon, "Has International Law Failed the Elephant?" *American Journal of International Law,* 84 (1990): 16. Even Japan and Hong Kong, the major importers, announced significant restrictions on ivory trade.

97. Jane Perlez, "Kenya, in Gesture, Burns Ivory Tusks," *New York Times,* July 19, 1989, p. A5, col. 1.

98. Bonner, "Crying Wolf over Elephants," p. 18.

99. Glennon, "Has International Law Failed the Elephant?" p. 16.

100. Ibid.

101. Bonner, "Crying Wolf over Elephants," p. 18.

102. Ibid., pp. 19–20.

103. Ibid., p. 20. Compare letter from David McTaggert of Greenpeace International to Greenpeace supporters: "Greenpeace was raised on saving whales."

104. Ibid., p. 20.

105. World Wildlife Fund, *Traffic USA*, Mar. 1990.

106. "Tokyo Agrees to Join Ivory Imports Ban," *Boston Globe*, Oct. 21, 1989, p. 6, col. 3.

107. Phillip van Niekerk, "Dispute on Ivory Clouds Elephant's Future," *Boston Globe*, July 10, 1989, p. 1, col. 1.

108. "Tokyo Agrees to Join Ivory Imports Ban," *Boston Globe*, Oct. 21, 1989, p. 6, col. 3

109. See Susan S. Lieberman, "1992 Amendments Strengthen Protection for Endangered and Threatened Wildlife and Plants," *Endangered Species Technical Bulletin*, 17, no. 1 (1993): 4.

110. Jane Perlez, "Ivory Trading Ban Said to Force Factories to Shut," *New York Times*, May 22, 1990, p. A14; "US Ivory Market Collapses after Import Ban," *New York Times*, June 5, 1990, p. C2. A new cycle seemed to be beginning in late 1993, when a full-page ad ran in the *New York Times* headlined, "Save the Tiger. Boycott Taiwan." *New York Times*, Oct. 31, 1993, sec. 4, p. 18. Some time earlier, accounts appeared of China's banning trade in rhino and tiger parts, and of the seizure in India (on evidence supplied by the Indian NGO Traffic India) of half a ton of tiger bone worth $650,000, destined for China. Sheryl WuDunn, "Beijing Bans Trade in Rhino and Tiger Parts," *New York Times*, June 6, 1993, p. 19, col. 1; "Bones of Some 20 Tigers Seized by Police in India," *New York Times*, Sept. 7, 1993, p. A11, col. 1.

111. Moravcsik, "Lessons from the European Human Rights Regime," pp. 35–58.

112. Alan Riding, "China Wins Fight on Rights Groups: Conference in Vienna Ejects Nongovernment Monitors from Key Committee," *New York Times*, June 17, 1993, at A15.

12. Revitalizing International Organizations

1. Peter Haas, Robert O. Keohane, and Marc S. Levy, eds., *Institutions for the Earth Sources of Effective International Environmental Protection* (Cambridge, Mass.: MIT Press, 1993), p. 409.

2. "Faceless international bureaucrats" is taken from a Public Citizen advertisement, *Washington Post*, Dec. 14, 1992, p. A20. Alexander M. Bickel, *The Least Dangerous Branch: The Supreme Court at the Bar of Politics* (New York: Bobbs-Merrill, 1962); see also *The Federalist Papers*, no. 78 (New York: New American Library, 1961), p. 490 (Hamilton).

3. The *Yearbook of International Organizations 1993/1994*, vol. 1 (New Providence, R.I.: K. G. Saur, 1994), lists more than five thousand intergovernmental organizations, including universal and regional memberships and ranging in focus from cybernetics to social problems to resources, see pp. 1698–1699, 1752–1754.

4. Abram Chayes, *The Cuban Missile Crisis: International Crises and the Role of Law* (Lanham, Md.: University Press of America, 1987), pp. 70–71.

5. In a country like the United States, with a strong tradition of legislative

participation in foreign affairs, one or more legislative committees will also have or be assigned jurisdiction over matters concerning the treaty.

6. See Oran O. Young, *International Governance: Protecting the Environment in a Stateless Society* (Ithaca, N.Y.: Cornell University Press, 1994), chap. 4–5.

7. Robert Keohane, *After Hegemony: Cooperation and Discord in the World Political Economy* (Princeton, N.J.: Princeton University Press, 1984), p. 97.

8. Lisa Martin, "Credibility, Costs, and Institutions: Cooperation on Economic Sanctions," *World Politics,* 45, no. 3 (Apr. 1993): 418.

9. See Michael Taylor, *Community, Anarchy and Liberty* (Cambridge: Cambridge University Press, 1982), pp. 28–29. See also the description of "even-up" strategies in Robert C. Ellickson, *Order without Law: How Neighbors Settle Disputes* (Cambridge, Mass.: Harvard University Press, 1991), pp. 225–229.

10. Personal conversation with the authors. See also Richard E. Benedick, *Ozone Diplomacy* (Cambridge, Mass.: Harvard University Press, 1991), pp. 158–161.

11. Oran R. Young, "The Effectiveness of International Institutions: Hard Cases and Critical Variables," in James Rosenau and Ernst-Otto Czempiel, eds., *Governance without Government: Order and Change in World Politics* (New York: Cambridge University Press, 1992), p. 177.

12. See e.g., Graham T. Allison, *The Essence of Decision: Explaining the Cuban Missile Crisis,* (Boston: Little, Brown, 1971), pp. 164–181, esp. p. 167.

13. Indeed, in 1993, the World Bank created an elaborate internal review mechanism—an Inspection Panel to act as an ombudsman to ensure that the organization complies with its own procedures in the environmental field and more generally. See IBRD Res. No. 93-10, Sept. 22, 1993. See also Ibrahim Shihata, *The World Bank Inspection Panel* (New York: Oxford University Press, 1994).

14. Abram Chayes, "An Inquiry into the Workings of Arms Control Agreements," *Harvard Law Review,* 85 (Mar. 1972): 905, 919–945.

15. See Harold Jacobsen and Edith Brown Weiss, eds., *National Compliance with International Environmental Accords* (Social Science Research Council, forthcoming).

16. Kenneth Hanf, "Domesticating International Commitments: Linking National and International Decison-Making," in Arild Underdal, ed., *The International Politics of Environmental Management* (Norwood, Mass.: Kluwer Academic Publishers, 1995).

17. Richard E. Neustadt, *Presidential Power and the Modern Presidents: The Politics of Leadership from Roosevelt to Reagan* (New York: The Free Press, 1990), p. 130–131; Allison, *The Essence of Decision,* p. 168; Graham T. Allison, *Remaking Foreign Policy: The Organizational Connection* (New York: Basic Books, 1976).

18. The classic work is Kenneth J. Arrow: *Social Choice and Individual Values* (New York: Wiley and Sons, 1951), pp. 80–81.

19. See Peter M. Haas, "Banning Chlorofluorocarbons: Epistemic Community Efforts to Protect Atmospheric Ozone," in Peter M. Haas, ed., *Knowledge, Power, and International Policy Coordination, International Organization,* 46, no. 1 (special issue,

Winter 1992): 201. See p. 211 for Tolba's decisive intervention to clarify scientific uncertainty at a crucial point in the negotiations by organizing, on his own authority, a multinational meeting of atmospheric scientists. See also Richard Elliot Benedick, *Ozone Diplomacy: New Directions in Safeguarding the Planet* (Cambridge, Mass.: Harvard University Press, 1991), pp. 6–7, 71–77, 155–186; Oran Young, "Political Leadership and Regime Formation: On the Development of Institutions in International Society," *International Organizations*, 45, no. 3 (Summer 1991): 293.

20. IAEA press release (February 26, 1992), PR 92/12.

21. Ronald B. Mitchell, *Intentional Oil Pollution at Sea: Environmental Policy and Treaty Compliance* (Cambridge, Mass.: MIT Press, 1994), pp. 140, 146.

22. London Amendments to the Montreal Protocol, Art. 10. The funds are to be administered by the World Bank, under a complicated arrangement in which UNEP and the UN Development Program have advisory roles. Final decisions are reserved to a committee of the parties, with equal representation from developed and developing countries. Ibid., Annex IV, Appendix IV, Terms of Reference for Interim Multilateral Fund.

23. FCCC, Art. 4(3); Convention on Biological Diversity, Art. 20(2).

24. FCCC, Art. 4(7). See also Convention on Biological Diversity, Art. 20(4).

25. Jason L. Finkle and Barbara B. Crane, "The World Health Organization and the Population Issue: Organizational Values in the United Nations," *Population and Development Review*, 2, no. 3 (Sept.–Dec. 1976): 368.

26. World Health Assembly Res. 19.43 (May 1966), quoted in Finkle and Crane, "The World Health Organization and the Population Issue," p. 375.

27. Ibid., pp. 381–384.

28. Ibid., p. 376.

29. Robert O. Keohane and Joseph S. Nye, "Transgovernmental Relations and International Organizations," *World Politics*, vol. 27, no. 1 (Oct. 1974): 45–46.

30. Stanley Fish, *Doing What Comes Naturally: Change, Rhetoric, and the Practice of Theory in Literary and Legal Studies* (Durham, N.C.: Duke University Press, 1989), pp. 141–142. See also Gerald Postema, "Protestant Interpretation and Social Practices," *Law and Philosophy*, 6 (1987): 283; Ronald Dworkin, *Law's Empire* (Cambridge, Mass.: Harvard University Press, 1986), pp. 46–55.

31. Robert E. Hudec, *Enforcing International Trade Law: The Evolution of the Modern GATT Legal System*, (Salem, N.H.: Butterworth Legal Publishers, 1993), p. 11.

32. Personal correspondence and conversations. Susan Strange, "IMF: Monetary Managers," in Robert Cox and Harold K. Jacobson, eds., *The Anatomy of Influence: Decision Making in International Organizations* (New Haven, Conn.: Yale University Press, 1974), p. 267.

33. Finkle and Crane, "The World Health Organization and the Population Issue," p. 378; see also p. 384.

34. Ibid., pp. 384–385.

35. Keohane and Nye, "Transgovernmental Relations and International Organizations," p. 51.

36. Peter M. Haas, *Saving the Mediterranean: The Politics of International Environmental Cooperation* (New York: Columbia University Press, 1990), pp. 104–107, 217.

37. Ibid., pp. 216–218.

38. Peter M. Haas, "Do Regimes Matter? Epistemic Communities and Mediterranean Pollution Control," *International Organization*, 43, no. 2 (Summer 1989): 388.

39. Peter M. Haas, "Introduction: Epistemic Communities and International Policy Coordination," in Haas ed., *Knowledge, Power, and International Policy Coordination*, pp. 2, 3. The fullest examination of the theory to date is to be found in this special issue of *International Organizations*. The first formulations seemed rather narrowly confined to groups in the natural sciences, but the concept has been extended to communities of economists, central bankers, and strategic analysts. Indeed the members are not necessarily practitioners of a single academic discipline; rather, they are defined by a set of shared normative and principled beliefs, shared notions about causal linkages, shared criteria of validity, and a common policy enterprise.

40. Ibid., pp. 1–35, 27. See also Emanuel Adler and Peter M. Haas, "Conclusion: Epistemic Communities, World Order, and the Creation of a Reflective Research Program," in Haas, ed., "Knowledge, Power, and International Policy Coordination," *International Organization*, 46, no. 1 (Winter 1992): 385–387 ("epistemic communities" as engines of institutional learning).

41. Epistemic communities are distinguished from ordinary interest groups and bureaucracies along four dimensions: shared principles, causal beliefs, validity tests, and policy orientation. While the members of interest groups may have shared principles and interests, they do not have a common knowledge base or causal beliefs. Bureaucrats, however, may have none of these attributes in common with their colleagues. Haas, "Introduction: Epistemic Communities," pp. 18–20.

42. Ibid., p. 17.

43. Adler and Haas, "Conclusion: Epistemic Communities," p. 374.

44. Ibid., pp. 381, 382.

45. G. John Ikenberry, "A World Economy Restored: Expert Consensus and the Anglo-American Postwar Settlement," in Haas, ed., *Knowledge, Power, and International Policy Coordination*, p. 304.

46. Adler and Haas, "Conclusion: Epistemic Communities," p. 375.

47. "Reform Proposals Circulate during the 46th Assembly," *UN Chronicle*, 29 (Mar. 1992): 9–11; Boutros Boutros-Ghali, "The Dues of Peace," *New Perspectives Quarterly*, 9 (Fall 1992): pp. 58–60; "Foundation Experts Outline Ways to Finance a More Effective UN," *UN Chronicle*, 30, (June 1993): 73; Frank Prial, "Low on Cash, UN Tightens Belt," *New York Times*, Aug. 29, 1993, p. 12(1), col. 5.

48. See Eugene Skolnikoff, *The International Imperatives of Technology: Technological Development and the International Political System* (Berkeley: Institute of International Studies, University of California, 1972).

49. The UN Commission for Trade and Development (established in 1964) and

UNDP (established in 1965) resemble more closely the older UN specialized agencies, but they are regarded as developing-country organizations, counterbalancing the dominance of the West in the earlier entities.

50. Benedick, *Ozone Diplomacy*, p. 185–186. Andrew Jordan, "Paying the Incremental Costs of Global Environmental Protection: The Evolving Role of GEF," *Environment*, 36 (July–Aug. 1994): 13–18; David Fairman, "Report of the Independent Evaluation of the Global Environment Facility Pilot Phase," *Environment*, 36 (July–Aug. 1994): 25–30. It is anticipated that the GEF will become the administrator for resources transferred under the Climate Change and Biodiversity Conventions.

51. UNEP, *1992 Annual Report of the Executive Director: Twenty Years after Stockholm*, (Nairobi, 1993); pp. 137–140; *Draft Decision on Agenda Item V(d)(iv)*, FCCC Conference of the Parties, 1st sess., Doc. FCCC/CP/1995/L.4, Apr. 4, 1995.

52. Haas, Keohane, and Levy, eds., *Institutions for the Earth*, pp. 421–423.

53. Ibid., p. 422.

54. See Weiss and Jacobson, *National Compliance with International Environmental Accords.*

55. See Joel D. Aberbach, Robert D. Putnam, and Bert A. Rockman, *Bureaucrats and Politicians in Western Democracies* (Cambridge, Mass.: Harvard University Press, 1981), p. 46, comparing and contrasting the roles of bureaucrats and politicians in the context of policy-making.

56. Stanley Hoffman, *Duties beyond Borders* (Syracuse, N.Y.: Syracuse University Press, 1981), p. 213.

Index